THE GUNFIGHTERS

ALSO BY BRYAN BURROUGH

Forget the Alamo:
The Rise and Fall of an American Myth
(with Chris Tomlinson and Jason Stanford)

Days of Rage:
America's Radical Underground, the FBI,
and the Forgotten Age of Revolutionary Violence

The Big Rich:
The Rise and Fall of the Greatest Texas Oil Fortunes

Public Enemies:
America's Greatest Crime Wave and the Birth of the FBI, 1933–34

Barbarians at the Gate:
The Fall of RJR Nabisco
(with John Helyar)

Dragonfly:
NASA and the Crisis Aboard Mir

Vendetta:
American Express and the Smearing of Edmond Safra

THE GUNFIGHTERS

How Texas Made
the West Wild

BRYAN BURROUGH

PENGUIN PRESS   NEW YORK   2025

PENGUIN PRESS
An imprint of Penguin Random House LLC
1745 Broadway, New York, NY 10019
penguinrandomhouse.com

Image credits appear on pages 413–14.

Maps by Jeffrey L. Ward

Book design by Daniel Lagin

LIBRARY OF CONGRESS CATALOGING-IN-PUBLICATION DATA
Names: Burrough, Bryan, 1961– author.
Title: The gunfighters : how Texas made the West wild / Bryan Burrough.
Other titles: How Texas made the West wild
Description: New York : Penguin Press, 2025. |
Includes bibliographical references and index.
Identifiers: LCCN 2024054199 (print) | LCCN 2024054200 (ebook) |
ISBN 9781984878908 (hardcover) | ISBN 9781984878915 (ebook)
Subjects: LCSH: Frontier and pioneer life—West (U.S.) |
Gunfighters—Texas—Biography. | Gunfights—West (U.S.)—History. |
Honor—Texas—History—19th century. |
Violence—West (U.S.)—History—19th century.
Classification: LCC F591 .B919 2025 (print) | LCC F591 (ebook) |
DDC 976.4/05—dc23/eng/20250226
LC record available at https://lccn.loc.gov/2024054199
LC ebook record available at https://lccn.loc.gov/2024054200

Printed in the United States of America
1st Printing

The authorized representative in the EU for product safety and compliance is
Penguin Random House Ireland, Morrison Chambers, 32 Nassau Street,
Dublin D02 YH68, Ireland, https://eu-contact.penguin.ie.

For Amy

CONTENTS

Prologue   I

1. **The Thing About Texas**   13

2. **The First Gunfighters**   31

3. **The Cauldron:**
   Texas, 1865 to 1871   51

4. **The Killing Machine:**
   John Wesley Hardin's Texas, 1868 to 1874   69

5. **Gunfighters of the Cattle Kingdom:**
   Kansas, 1871   89

6. **"Get Your Guns, You Texas
   Sons of Bitches, and Fight":**
   The Rise of Wyatt Earp and Ben Thompson, 1871 to 1876   111

7. **Legends in the Making:**
   Dodge City, 1876 to 1883   131

8. **"You Have Lived Long Enough":**
   Bat Masterson, Luke Short, and Beyond   151

9. **The Trouble with Jesse James:**
   The Midwest (Sigh), 1869 to 1882   169

10. **The Taming of Texas:**
    Texas, 1874 to 1884   187

11. **The Texas Invasion of New Mexico:**
New Mexico, 1872 to 1878   209

12. **The Rise of Billy the Kid:**
New Mexico, 1879 to 1880   227

13. **The Hunts for Billy the Kid:**
New Mexico, 1880 to 1884   245

14. **Tombstone:**
Arizona, 1878 to 1881   261

15. **The Fight Is Made:**
Tombstone, 1881 to 1882   285

16. **The Deadliest Feud:**
Arizona, 1883 to 1892   305

17. **The Assassins:**
Range Wars, Tom Horn, and "Deacon" Jim Miller   323

18. **Death Alley:**
Oklahoma, 1891 to 1896   339

19. **The Outlaw Trail:**
Butch Cassidy in the Gloaming   357

Epilogue: *From Headlines to History*   375

Acknowledgments   383

Notes   385

Bibliography   395

Illustration Credits   413

Index   415

TEXAS REBELS AND FEUDS ★ *1865–1876*

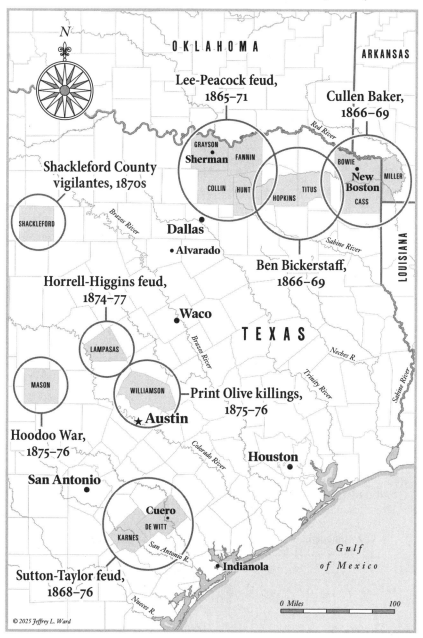

N

OKLAHOMA

ARKANSAS

Lee-Peacock feud,
1865–71

Cullen Baker,
1866–69

GRAYSON

Sherman FANNIN

BOWIE

Shackleford County
vigilantes, 1870s

COLLIN HUNT

HOPKINS

TITUS

New
Boston

MILLER

CASS

SHACKLEFORD

Brazos River

Dallas

• Alvarado

Sabine River

LOUISIANA

Ben Bickerstaff,
1866–69

Horrell-Higgins feud,
1874–77

Waco

TEXAS

Neches R.

Brazos River

Trinity River

LAMPASAS

MASON

WILLIAMSON

Print Olive killings,
1875–76

Sabine River

★ Austin

Hoodoo War,
1875–76

Colorado River

Houston

San Antonio

Cuero

DE WITT

Gulf
of Mexico

KARNES

San Antonio R.

Sutton-Taylor feud,
1868–76

• Indianola

Nueces R.

0 Miles   100

© 2025 Jeffrey L. Ward

JOHN WESLEY HARDIN'S TEXAS ★ 1853–1874

N

OKLAHOMA

ARKANSAS

Red River

TEXAS

Dallas

Sabine River

LOUISIANA

1 Bonham/Born 1853

8 Longview/Arrested, 1871

4 Navarro County/Fled here, 1868

5 Towash/Killed a gambler, 1870

Brazos River

Trinity River

9 Near Fairfield/Killed a man escaping from state police, 1871

18 Comanche/Killed a deputy, 1874

Waco

6 Horn Hill/Killed a man at a circus, 1870

7 Kosse/Killed a pimp, 1870

13 Hemphill/Shot a state policeman, 1872

10 Near Belton/Claims to have killed three bounty hunters, 1871

14 Trinity/Shot by a gambler, 1872

Brazos River

2 Sumpter/Boyhood home

3 Killing of Maje Holshousen, 1868

Colorado River

Austin

11 Gonzales/Found refuge with cousins, 1871–74

Houston

15 Escaped from jail, 1872

San Antonio

12 Smiley/Killed a state policeman, 1871

17 Albuquerque/Killed Jack Helm, 1873

16 Cuero/Killed a deputy, 1873

San Antonio River

Nueces River

• Indianola

Gulf of Mexico

0 Miles 100

© 2025 Jeffrey L. Ward

KANSAS COW TOWNS ★ 1870–1882

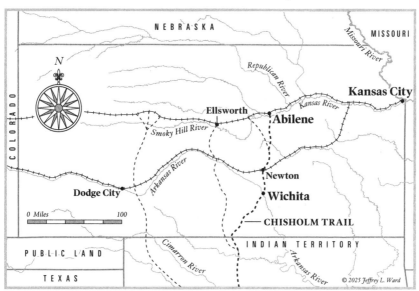

NEBRASKA

MISSOURI

Missouri River

Republican River

COLORADO

N

Kansas City

Kansas River

Ellsworth

Abilene

Smoky Hill River

Arkansas River

Newton

Dodge City

Wichita

0 Miles   100

—— CHISHOLM TRAIL

INDIAN TERRITORY

Cimarron River

PUBLIC LAND

Arkansas River

TEXAS

© 2025 Jeffrey L. Ward

NEW MEXICO ★ 1874–1884

UTAH TERR.

COLORADO

N

COLFAX COUNTY

Clay Allison gunfights,
1874–75

• Cimarron

Santa Fe
•

East Las Vegas/
Multiple gunfights,
1879–80

• Albuquerque

ARIZONA TERRITORY

NEW MEXICO TERRITORY

Rio Grande

Fort Sumner/
Billy the Kid's base,
1880–81

Reserve/
• Elfego Baca siege, 1884

Lincoln/Center of
Lincoln County War,
1878–81
• Ruidosa R.

Pecos River

Roswell/
John Chisum
headquarters

•
Silver City/
Billy the Kid's
boyhood home

LINCOLN COUNTY

• Mesilla

• El Paso

Rio Grande

TEXAS

MEXICO

0 Miles   100

© 2025 Jeffrey L. Ward

WYATT EARP'S ARIZONA ★ *1879–1882*

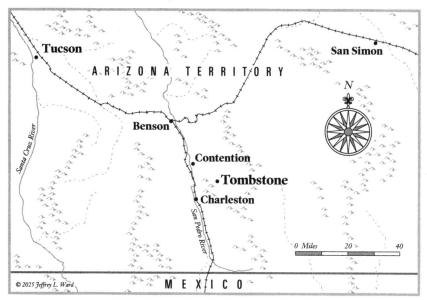

OK CORRAL GUNFIGHT, TOMBSTONE ★ *October 26, 1881*

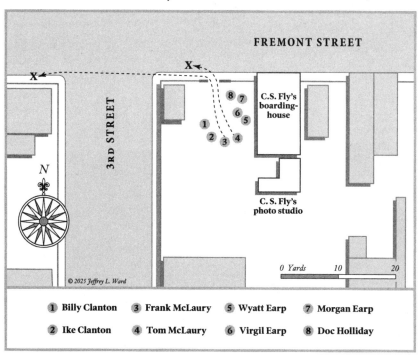

1 Billy Clanton   3 Frank McLaury   5 Wyatt Earp   7 Morgan Earp

2 Ike Clanton   4 Tom McLaury   6 Virgil Earp   8 Doc Holliday

THE PLEASANT VALLEY WAR ★ *1882–1892*

N

Flagstaff •

Little Colorado River
• Holbrook

Verde River

Mogollon Rim

• Springerville

FORT APACHE
RESERVATION

T O N T O   B A S I N
Pleasant Valley

Phoenix •

Globe •

Gila River

ARIZONA TERRITORY

Tucson •

0 Miles   20   40   60

© 2025 *Jeffrey L. Ward*

BUTCH CASSIDY'S WEST ★ *1866–1900*

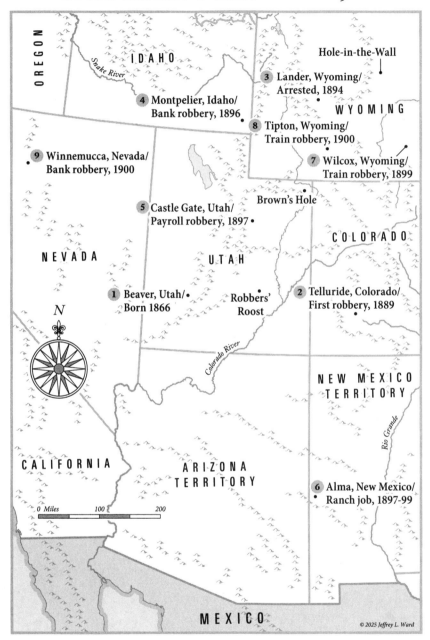

OREGON

Snake River

IDAHO

Hole-in-the-Wall

3 Lander, Wyoming/
Arrested, 1894

4 Montpelier, Idaho/
Bank robbery, 1896

WYOMING

8 Tipton, Wyoming/
Train robbery, 1900

9 Winnemucca, Nevada/
Bank robbery, 1900

7 Wilcox, Wyoming/
Train robbery, 1899

5 Castle Gate, Utah/
Payroll robbery, 1897 •

Brown's Hole

COLORADO

NEVADA

UTAH

N

1 Beaver, Utah/
Born 1866

Robbers'
Roost

2 Telluride, Colorado/
First robbery, 1889

Colorado River

NEW MEXICO
TERRITORY

Rio Grande

CALIFORNIA

ARIZONA
TERRITORY

6 Alma, New Mexico/
• Ranch job, 1897-99

0 Miles   100   200

MEXICO

© 2025 Jeffrey L. Ward

Prologue

I was raised in a little town . . . called Abilene, Kansas. We had
as our marshal for a long time a man named Wild Bill Hickok. . . .
Now that town had a code, and I was raised as a boy to prize that
code. It was: meet anyone face to face with whom you disagree. . . .
If you met him face to face and took the same risks he did, you
could get away with almost anything, as long as the bullet was in
the front.

—PRESIDENT DWIGHT D. EISENHOWER, 1953

Just before six o'clock on a Friday afternoon, July 21, 1865, three
months after Robert E. Lee surrendered at Appomattox, two men
stepped into the square in Springfield, Missouri, a scraggly village of
twelve hundred toward the state's southwest corner. Alongside loomed
the Greene County Courthouse and its pillared Greek Revival facade.
Across from it ran a line of storefronts, where a crowd was gathering.
Rumors of what was about to happen had been spreading all day.

The man on the north side of the square was Davis Tutt, an iras-
cible twenty-eight- or twenty-nine-year-old Confederate soldier turned
gambler. In a photograph, Tutt has cat eyes and a goatee. That day, by
one account, he wore a long leather duster. By all accounts, he was

carrying a pistol and also, fatefully, a gold pocket watch, a Waltham model.

The man facing him on the south side of the square was James Butler "Wild Bill" Hickok, a twenty-eight-year-old Union scout turned gambler. Hickok had weary eyes and a nose so long it almost reached his upper lip; one wag had nicknamed him "Duck Bill." He wore his hair long and greasy. That day, by most accounts, Hickok had a Colt Navy revolver in his hand. By all accounts, he wanted his watch back.

Apparently—because stories explaining this are all over the map—Hickok had warned Tutt not to cross the square with his watch, which Tutt had snatched up to settle a gambling debt.* From a distance estimated at seventy-five yards, Hickok yelled, "Dave, here I am."

He then slid his pistol back into its holster.

"Don't you come across here with that watch," he added.

Everyone, it appears, understood what had to happen. Some versions say the two men turned and stood sideways, cutting their eyes toward the other for a long moment or two. Others say Tutt took a step forward. However it began, they pulled their pistols simultaneously. Tutt shot from the hip. Hickok thrust forward his left forearm, carefully laid his Colt across it, and fired at the same time.

Gun smoke rose, then dispersed in the breeze. All around, the townspeople stared. Suddenly a red stain could be seen spreading across Tutt's chest. "Boys, I'm killed!" he shouted.

Tutt staggered forward onto the courthouse steps, then lurched back into the street, where he fell dead, shot through the heart. As he

---

*The backstory of all this, as is common in so many Old West gunfights, remains murky to this day. The two men had apparently been friends. Hickok may or may not have fathered a child by Tutt's sister. They may or may not have quarreled over a woman. Whatever the background, all accounts agree they bickered over the size of a gambling debt during a game of cards at the Lyon House Hotel earlier that week. Tutt, it's said, claimed the debt was thirty-five dollars. Hickok insisted it was twenty-five. Tutt snatched up Hickok's watch to settle the difference.

did, Hickok, unblemished, wheeled around to confront a group of Tutt's pals loitering to one side. "Aren't you satisfied, gentlemen?" he asked coolly. "Put up your shootin' irons, or there'll be more dead men here." The men slowly backed away.[1]

The Hickok–Tutt face-off, the first Wild West–style gunfight to gain national attention after the Civil War, is often called the first gunfight of the Old West. It wasn't, not by a long shot, but it did herald the onset of a host of strange new phenomena in the western half of the country that soon enthralled the nation. Seven months later, in February 1866, came America's first peacetime bank robbery, in Liberty, Missouri, pulled off by former Confederate guerrillas who may have included a teenager named Jesse James. A year after that came the first train robbery, outside Seymour, Indiana, staged by a band of toughs called the Reno Gang. That summer the first of the great postwar cattle drives rumbled up from Texas into Missouri.

From these disparate events arose a series of new American myths and archetypes, few as enduring as the Old West gunfighter. This book is a history of what's been called the Gunfighter Era, the years between Hickok's shoot-out in 1865 and 1901, when the last of the great western outlaws, Butch Cassidy and Harry Longabaugh, the Sundance Kid, walked onto a Brooklyn wharf and boarded a steamship to South America. During this period, for the first time, men such as Hickok and Wyatt Earp and Billy the Kid rose to fame on the strength of their prowess killing other Americans, usually with revolvers. Which, if you think about it, is more than a little strange. Men shot each other on the streets of Boston and Baltimore every evening and were dismissed as thugs and criminals; no one remembers them today, and rightly so.

But the shootings out west fascinated then, and fascinate now, in large part because they became an element of the creation myth a young nation craved, a dream that promised that in America any man could survive and even thrive alone on skills he could learn himself.

The frontier, free of eastern civilization's smothering rules and laws, its strangling political machines and disapproving pulpits, emerged as the ideal venue for the worship of this new American individualism.

"The story of the West," a California professor named Thomas K. Whipple wrote in 1943, "is our Trojan War, our Volsunga Saga, our Arthurian cycle or Song of Roland."[2] Florid comparisons to be sure, yet they strike a chord. And at the heart of this American myth stands the hero every legend requires, maybe the purest expression of solitary fortitude, the supreme individualist, the American Achilles, the American Thor, the American Lancelot: a man alone with that great equalizer, a gun.

The gunfighter.

The men behind the myth, the Hickoks and Earps, would become legends. For decades they crowded to the center of American popular culture, on the page and on the screen. Today, with gun violence a polarizing political issue, their legacy is more challenging. There are those who believe telling their stories amounts to glorifying the kind of violence so many have come to abhor.

Love them or hate them, they are undeniably a part of our shared history, our culture, of what America is today. Which raises the question: What exactly was a gunfighter? As it's used here, the term simply refers to anyone in the Old West who took part in one or more notable exchanges of gunfire among civilians—not involving Native Americans or the military. He could come from any walk of life but was often an officer of the law, such as Pat Garrett or Heck Thomas; an outlaw, like Sam Bass or Joaquin Murrieta; a gambler, like Luke Short or Ben Thompson; a feudist, like the Texans Print Olive and Jack Helm; a cattleman, such as Clay Allison; or that rarest of species, a gun for hire, à la Tom Horn or the Texas assassin Jim Miller.

And what exactly is a "notable" gunfight, or as I call it, a "marquee" gunfight? It's one that, for whatever reason—outlandish or unusual circumstances, the notoriety of a participant, or a compelling backstory—seemed important enough to remember. They're the ones that made the newspapers and the history books.*

Though they fought in the nineteenth century, the fame of men like Earp and Hickok mushroomed during the twentieth, thanks to modern media, especially Hollywood films. In fact, though firearms have been part of American culture's DNA since Jamestown, the very concept of the "gunfighter" is largely a twentieth-century construct; for the longest time, in other words, the gunfighter wasn't really a thing. Men who shot each other were written about, certainly, but in the 1800s their fame consistently trailed that of cowboys and "Indian fighters"; when he appeared in a Wild West show, Hickok was a flop. He fared little better on the page. As the historian John Boessenecker observes, "heroes of nineteenth-century western fiction, particularly dime novels, were rarely gunfighters, but instead were soldiers, scouts, mountain men, cowboys, and detectives."[3]

Gunfighters, like most Old West figures, were all but forgotten for decades, a lapse that ended with a magazine writer's pointed question in 1925—"Who remembers Billy the Kid?"—that ignited an explosion of Western biographies and memoirs in the 1920s and beyond, books that reintroduced Billy and Hickok and Earp and others to a new generation. The bestselling ones were pretty much dreck, daisies of fact sprinkled across a field of myth and lore, especially those pumped out

---

*And yes, it is true that many didn't. Those gunfights that didn't make a newspaper or book at some point, and one suspects there must be many, are mostly lost to history. There are entire theaters of frontier violence where killings appear to have been commonplace, yet almost certainly were, as they say in modern parlance, underreported. A case in point is the Texas–Mexico border, where lore attributes hundreds of killings to obscure gunmen. Candidly, there's not much an author can do to remedy that. This book isn't intended to be a survey of all Old West gunfights, just the ones we remember most clearly.

by the era's most prominent author of Westerns, a newspaperman named Walter Noble Burns. Hollywood, though, smelled an audience.

The gunfighter's popularity was seeded here. The word itself had first surfaced in a newspaper or two in 1874; it was one of several terms in use by the 1880s. Most papers preferred "gun-man," later "gunman." The New Mexico gunfighter Clay Allison used "shootist." In a 1907 article, the onetime Dodge City sheriff Bat Masterson floated the term "man-killers." Early writers didn't spend much time debating categories, but to the extent they did, they sorted the violence-prone into groups: Outlaws. Mountain men. Gamblers. Cowboys. Lawmen. Feudists. Detectives.

The book that popularized the idea that all these men were essentially the same—that they were all "gunfighters"—didn't appear until 1934. The groaningly titled *Triggernometry: A Gallery of Gunfighters* was written by an El Paso author named Eugene Cunningham. In its foreword, the writer Eugene Manlove Rhodes traces how the term "gunfighter" finally caught on during the 1920s. A new word seemed necessary after newspapers began using "gunman" to describe urban gangsters, which, as Rhodes put it, brought the "implication of coward, of baby-killer," not at all the way many felt Earp and Hickok should be remembered.[4] Thus writers latched on to the less judgmental alternative, gunfighter.

In the seventeen profiles that make up *Triggernometry*, Cunningham didn't especially care what a man did for a living, or which side of the law he walked on. What he cared about was skill with a revolver; the book's subtitle promised "technical notes on leather slapping as a fine art." Cunningham's genius was to take a single skill shared by most all Western archetypes—cowboys, mountain men, etc.—and roll it into a new category. His subjects were typically brave and true, of course, but they also boasted something that felt new: technical expertise. Above all, Cunningham prized a man's speed using a pistol; he may have coined the term "quick-draw artist."*

Triggernometry didn't draw much attention. Its notion of the gunfighter as a kind of bygone artisan of death might be forgotten but for a Hollywood screenwriter named André De Toth, hired by Twentieth Century–Fox to craft a "prestige" Western on the order of John Ford's *Stagecoach*. In the resulting film, 1950's *The Gunfighter*, De Toth drew on Cunningham's ideas to create a protagonist whose sole identity was his history of (reluctantly) killing other men.

This was something fresh, a Western antihero who didn't fight Injuns, sing sappy songs, or ride with comely women in the moonlight. He just consistently found himself, you know, in situations where he was obliged to shoot someone. Which happens. The movie starred Gregory Peck as "Jimmy Ringo"—very much to be confused with Johnny Ringo of Tombstone fame—a celebrated gunfighter whose story is told via flashback during a day in which he ends up facing off against a trio of gunmen who seek to claim his legend. All the tropes of hundreds of later cinematic gunfighters are here: Ringo's stolid mien, his loneliness, his honor and troubled past, the woman he left behind.

The Gunfighter and its explication of one man's fateful choices struck a nerve in an America beginning to retreat from New Deal–era ideas of collectivism toward older, more conservative notions of individual accountability. It spawned myriad imitators in the 1950s alone, from highbrow fare such as *High Noon* and *Shane* to trifles like *The Last of the Fast Guns*. But its deepest impact was on the new medium of

---

*This is actually a position worth challenging because the necessity of the fast draw had been persuasively dismissed by both Earp and Hickok, who told writers during their lives that a hurried first shot inevitably missed its mark. It was accuracy that mattered, as Hickok showed Davis Tutt.

television, whose fifties-era programming was dominated by Western dramas. A head-spinning ninety-two Western-themed series aired during the decade; by my tally, thirty-eight featured a gunfighter (and yes, I counted the animated *Quick Draw McGraw*).

A television gunfighter was typically a good-hearted sheriff defending his town, as in *Gunsmoke*, or, just as often, a wandering sort who drifted the West righting wrongs, as in *Have Gun—Will Travel* or *Cheyenne*—both structures ideal for episodic weekly programming, though the latter, needless to say, with little parallel in history. Hickok, Earp, Bat Masterson, and even Johnny Ringo got their own shows. In the process, an American archetype was born. The gunfighter has been a stalwart of American entertainment ever since.

Most over the age of twelve understood that much of what they saw in television Westerns was hooey. Every shoot-out seemed to be a fast-draw contest, the kind *Triggernometry* dwelled upon. In reality, that sort of thing was exceedingly rare; there are maybe a dozen I can cite in these pages. This kind of questioning led in the 1960s and '70s to a series of books that attempted to sort fact from fiction. It's a measure of how tenuous the gunfighter concept remained that one of the first was titled *The Gunfighter: Man or Myth?*[5]

In these new works, authors such as Joseph Rosa, Robert M. Utley, and Robert DeArment, along with a handful of venturesome professors like Roger McGrath and Richard Maxwell Brown, introduced rigor to the field of Old West history by mining period documents, newspapers, and memoirs. Their research produced portraits of gunfighters that hewed much closer to reality, along with discoveries large and small.

At the time he took his first law enforcement job in Kansas, we now know, Wyatt Earp was a federal fugitive—an escaped prisoner, no less. He and his brothers had been so deeply involved in prostitution that one author refers to them as "The Fighting Pimps." Jesse James is now viewed as less a midwestern Robin Hood than a quasi-political Reconstruction figure, the last crusading Confederate. One of the most infamous Texas gunfighters, meanwhile, "Wild" Bill Longley, has been unmasked as an impostor. I could go on. There's even a catty little theory that, despite Paul Newman's idyllic bicycle rides with Katharine Ross, the Butch Cassidy of history was probably gay.

Today, despite such insights, the gunfighter's day as an American icon is clearly passing. With due respect to Taylor Sheridan and his television Westerns, most narrative entertainments once set in the Old West now take place in outer space. In the 1970s, when I was growing up, men like Hickok and Bat Masterson remained household names. Nowadays, as those weaned on early television pass, Jesse James and Billy the Kid still get a nod of recognition, and Hollywood has elevated Wyatt Earp and Butch Cassidy to sainthoods they probably don't deserve. But the likes of Hickok and Masterson tend to draw blank stares, while their lesser-known peers, from Bill Doolin and Dallas Stoudenmire to King Fisher and Mysterious Dave Mather, are all but forgotten.

Reading their stories today, one is struck by the arbitrary nature of fame. Was Billy the Kid truly any more significant a figure than Cullen Baker, who terrorized Northeast Texas for years, or Jim Miller, who some consider the deadliest Old West gunman of all? A gunfighter's fame endures, in almost every case, in direct proportion to his engagement with the written word, because he either talked to a journalist or two, as Hickok did; wrote an autobiography, John Wesley Hardin's route; fired off letters to governors and newspapers à la Jesse James and Billy the Kid; or became involved in a shoot-out so spectacular it drew national attention, as happened to Wyatt Earp. Those gunmen who were every bit as deadly, yet who fought their battles in obscurity— ever hear of Pink Higgins or Ed Tewksbury? No, you haven't—ended up relegated to the dustbin of history.

Three things to note before getting started. This book is a survey, meaning its primary sources—other than newspapers.com—are the hundreds of books that sag atop my office shelves. I am deeply indebted to the many talented writers who labored to produce them; for those who wish to explore certain storylines in more depth, I've included reading recommendations in the chapter footnotes.

Also: Some readers may be tempted to draw lines between gun violence on the frontier and gun violence today, which is fine. I do think there are stories and lessons here that shed light on the origins of our modern problems, but by and large, I am more interested in the culture and behaviors that gave rise to gun violence on the nineteenth-century frontier than extending the story to explain how it led to today's political and policy challenges. There is probably a great book that examines the story of gunfighters through the lens of Columbine and Parkland and Uvalde, but this really isn't it.

And last: Previous books have tended to treat Old West violence as essentially random, as unrelated bursts of gunplay. And of course, that's true. The flutter of Jesse James's hummingbird wings didn't cause a storm of bullets in Dodge City. But the more I learned about frontier gunfights, the more curious I became about their causes. As I delved deeper, I began to sense certain commonalities in behavior.

It started with something Hickok mentioned in passing as he prepared to meet Davis Tutt that Friday afternoon in 1865. A friend asked why he was doing it. Hickok explained about the watch, then added: "You don't want me to give up my honor, do you?"

"No, Bill," the man replied. "You must keep your honor."[6]

Hickok, in other words, didn't face off with Tutt over a watch. He did it because he felt his honor had been challenged. This rang a bell. I'd read similar comments in frontier literature before. That Missouri gunfight, in fact, felt very much like a duel, something generations of American men had used to settle matters of honor.

In time I developed a theory, one I'll test gently here, about the role of honor on the nineteenth-century frontier, and about how one state, Texas—which produced far more gunfights and far more gunfighters than any other—disproportionately influenced its parameters. Because killing to defend one's honor? Duels? Feuds?

It all feels a little, well, Southern.

CHAPTER ONE

The Thing About Texas

Sometimes I strike an unprotected town
Paint it red.
Choke the sheriff, turn the marshal upside down
On his head.
Call for drinks for all the party
And if chinned by any smarty
Pay in lead.

—EXCERPT FROM "THE WILD COWHAND,"
A POEM PUBLISHED IN THE *FORT WORTH*
DAILY GAZETTE, CIRCA 1886[1]

The Old West was a kaleidoscope of personal violence. From Texas to Montana, everyone from the U.S. cavalry to buffalo hunters to homesteaders fought Native American tribes. From California to Nebraska, outlaws preyed on trains and lonely stagecoaches. On the Mexican border, ranchers and lawmen fought bandits. The frontier was home to a plethora of lethal, Appalachian-style family and political feuds. And almost everywhere, cattlemen fought dirty little wars with cattle rustlers, settlers, and sheepherders.

All these conflicts involved guns, but what concerns us here are the civilian gunfights of note, the ones cited repeatedly in the Western canon, those that form the core of the gunfighter legends. They're the confrontations that made figures such as Wyatt Earp and Wild Bill Hickok and Billy the Kid famous and helped make the West "wild." These incidents, it must be said, amount to the tiniest fraction of violence in the Old West. They don't include the massacres of Latinos along the Mexican border, or of Chinese immigrants in California, or thousands of other gun deaths. They're simply the ones we most remember, the ones that passed into legend.

Here's the thing. If you study these marquee gunfights at any length, something jumps out at you about the participants. In Kansas, in Wyoming, in New Mexico, in Arizona, all across the frontier, a startling number of these deadly encounters involved a single kind of person:

A Texan.

It's true. Texas cowboys, cattlemen, and outlaws took part in, and often initiated, the notable gunfights of Earp's Tombstone and Dodge City, the manic shoot-outs of Billy the Kid's New Mexico, the showdowns of Hickok's Abilene, and the cattle wars of Wyoming. And that's to say nothing of the gun battles in Texas itself, which saw more than any other state. Take away Texans—Texas cowboys, Texas outlaws, and Texas lawmen—and the American Gunfighter Era shrinks to insignificance.

One Texas historian, Bill O'Neal, has made a fair attempt at a statistical analysis. O'Neal identified 589 major gunfights on the postwar frontier—nearly 30 percent, 160, occurred in Texas.[2] "No other Western commonwealth was the arena of even half as many shootings," O'Neal noted in a 2011 article. Moreover, he found, "more gunfighters were born in Texas than in any other state or territory, and more died in Texas than in any other state . . . 10 of the deadliest 15 spent most of their careers in Texas."[3]

The link between Texans and gunfighter violence is not some modern notion. That the Texan was a rootin' tootin' rowdy with a smoking six-shooter is so much a part of the Lone Star mythos it's a cliché. So it's eye-opening to discover how much truth there is to it. The association of Texans and lethal gunfights was established as early as the 1870s. You can find editorials published in New York that decried Texas-born gun violence in 1878.

"The name of Texas became the synonym for savagery," the writer Emerson Hough, who lived on the frontier, noted in 1907. "So many bad men of Texas have attained reputation far wider than their state that it became a proverb upon the frontier that any man born on Texas soil would shoot, just as any horse born there would 'buck.'"[4]

What interests me is less the *number* of gunfights Texans took part in than their impact, their role in shaping the way the Old West has been remembered. I don't want to overstate this. Texans, after all, had no monopoly on gun violence. They didn't ride with Jesse James at Northfield, or Joaquin Murrieta in the Gold Rush, or the Daltons at Coffeyville. They weren't at Bodie or Virginia City or any of the mining camps where gun violence was prevalent. Yet even a cursory review of Western literature suggests their impact was wide and deep. What I'm positing is that from Arizona to Wyoming to Kansas, Texans and the business they introduced and dominated on the frontier, open-range cattle ranching, had an influence on the Gunfighter Era that is far more pervasive than we remember today.

Skeptical? Maybe look at it this way: It's clear from articles at the time that Texans got blamed for an awful lot of gunfighter-style violence. So the question becomes: Was that blame justified? Was there something different about the behavior of Texans? Or was this all a matter of skewed perception? In the end, here's what I say:

You bet your ass Texans were different.

———

OF THE FIFTY STATES, TEXAS IS THE ONLY ONE TO DEFEAT A FOREIGN power at war, the only one to emerge as an independent nation as a result. During much of the nineteenth century, it was the only state with not one but two violent frontiers—the Mexican border, where Texans fought bandits and the incursions of an embittered Mexican army, and the Native American frontier, the site of hundreds of desperate battles and atrocities involving the Comanche and their allies, which cut the state in half on a diagonal into the 1870s.

What emerged was a highly martial culture, its people deeply attuned to violence and expert at it.* It's no surprise it was Texans who first popularized the newfangled revolvers that ushered in the Gunfighter Era. But there's another issue here, one a facility with firearms doesn't explain, and this goes to motivation, the why of it: Why were Texans involved in so many gunfights? Why shoot someone in the first place? And why did people on the frontier, Texans especially, seem to do it so very often?

Scholars have debated frontier violence for decades.† Most suggest

---

*And yes, while it's not the focus of this book, elements of this culture persist to this day. I could supply any number of examples, but here are two favorites: (1) The unofficial slogan of Texas Tech University in Lubbock is "Guns up," a salutation that comes with a hand gesture, extending the thumb and index finger in the universal sign of a pistol. As wonderful as my Tech friends are, I have a hard time imagining this being acceptable anyplace but Texas. (2) I have often heard people speak of how many Texas children develop a fascination with guns. I hadn't realized how true this was until my wife told me how her oldest son, at the age of two and a half, tore his toast into the shape of a pistol and ran around the kitchen "shooting" her while yelling "Bang! Bang!" Can you guess where he ended up attending college?

†You may wonder: Was the Old West really as violent as it appears on television and in film? Fascinating question. In the 1960s, when academics began to challenge many long-held beliefs about history, it became fashionable to say such portrayals were vastly overblown. Over the years, a series of books have drawn praise for debunking the idea that the frontier was wild at all. In *The Wild, Wild West*, the journalist Peter Lyon explored what he called "the Wild Western garbage heap" in what his publisher termed "a hilarious dissection of much of

it was the inevitable product of any frontier society, and that's true as far as it goes. Wide-open, unsettled land typically means less law enforcement. It also tends to attract young, unsettled men, who are inclined to alleviate the boredom of underdeveloped space with alcohol, all factors cited to explain violence in the Old West. But too much booze and too few sheriffs doesn't in itself explain why people shoot each other; if it did, pool parties and ZZ Top concerts would be frequent sites of mayhem. There has to be a perceived *reason*, even a stupid one, for someone to resort to deadly force.

Could there be a distinct reason so many men shot each other in the Old West? Was there something unique about the place, the time, the people? Men like Doc Holliday and Johnny Ringo, after all, didn't emerge from just anywhere—not the frontiers of Canada or Australia or the Trans-Appalachian frontier of the early 1800s. They rose in a

---

the nonsense" of western history. A professor named David Hamilton Murdoch called his book *The American West: The Invention of a Myth.*

The serious academic debate erupted in 1968 after an upstate New York professor named Robert R. Dykstra crunched the numbers on murders in Dodge City and other Kansas cow towns and claimed their reputations for violence were wildly overstated, that the narrative of a violent frontier was in fact a myth. Buoyed by generous reviews and like-minded skeptics, Dykstra was still at it forty years later when a new generation of historians began applying Big Data techniques and quantitative analysis to examine the numbers. The most important work was done by a trio of academics led by Randolph Roth at Ohio State, whose work, including the acclaimed 2009 book *American Homicide*, reached a surprising conclusion: the Old West really was as violent as we once thought.

I'll spare you the academic arcana. But long story short, Roth and company pored over every available bit of data to compile homicide rates based on the number of people murdered as a percentage of 100,000 people. A rate of 9 per 100,000 is considered high, 35 extremely high. The murder rate on the postwar western frontier, Roth discovered, averaged out to be around 60, which, having grown up aware of Dykstra's contentions, frankly stunned me. A UCLA professor named Roger McGrath studied the notorious California mining town of Bodie between 1877 and 1883 and judged it a startling 116. Roth and company found homicide rates in the five main Kansas cow towns, ranging from 53 in Wichita to 317 in Abilene, averaged out to a whopping 155. "By any measure," Roth and company noted in a 2011 paper, "these towns were extremely homicidal." Today the debate seems pretty much over, and we can say with a high degree of certainty that while, no, gunfighters didn't face off in the streets of Dodge City or Abilene every Saturday at four, the Old West was in fact extraordinarily violent.

specific place, in a specific window of time, in a fateful intersection of new technology, commerce, and culture.

Culture is the underexplored variable here. At base, a gunfight was a product of certain human behaviors—mostly the whens and whys of personal violence—that were shaped by unwritten societal codes; that is, the way a society dictates how people resolve their conflicts. In modern society, depending on the severity of the dispute, Americans are expected to turn to the lawsuit, the police, or, increasingly, the internet. In the Old West, not so much.

So, what was it about Texans in the 1800s? I have a theory. First, that the Old West developed elements of a distinct code around violence, an evolution of older American norms. Second, that crucial components of these norms emanated from a region of America whose influence on western customs has been shortchanged:

The South. That's right, the South.

Make no mistake, antebellum Texas was every inch a Southern state, its dominant business slave-picked cotton, deeply hostile to people of color, fully half its early colonists from just two states, Alabama and Tennessee. And yet, while new scholarship has demonstrated the profound influence Southern customs had on the West's political development, less discussed is the impact Southern mores may have had on people on the ground, on how people on the frontier lived, including how they handled their disputes.*

To understand Southern codes of behavior and how they influenced violence in the Old West, it helps to suss out the gunfighter's origins. Finding literary antecedents, by the way—and the gunfighter lives as much in literature as history—is easy. A staple of tales told around the world, he is the New World version of the wandering man

---

*The notion that Southern views shaped the West's political development is explored in Heather Cox Richardson's fascinating 2020 book, *How the South Won the Civil War.*

of violence, the medieval swordsman, the Cossack, the samurai. In America, where those who pursue settled lives have long been fascinated by those who don't, he belongs to the second or third generation of "frontiersmen," heroes of narratives inspired by John Smith, Daniel Boone, Davy Crockett, and Kit Carson. He is Natty Bumppo's swaggering nephew, only with a six-shooter and an attitude. The gunfighter's emergence as a hero in so many American stories is an extension of the tales we've told for eons.

The forerunners of history's gunfighters, though, of Ben Thompson and Harvey Logan and Pat Garrett, can seem harder to identify. There were no broadly famous American gunmen or even lawmen before their time.* Some might argue for any number of outlaws who worked the Mississippi and Ohio River frontiers between 1790 and 1830; men such as the river pirate Samuel Mason and the murderous Harpe brothers come to mind. None, however, were known for their prowess with firearms. Daniel Boone and Davy Crockett were renowned frontiersmen, but they faced off against more Native Americans and bears than citizens.

The gunfighter's true antecedent, I'd argue, is the duelist, a figure born in medieval Europe who found keen popularity in the antebellum South. The duel was deeply ingrained in European societies, especially in Britain and Ireland, the source of so many immigrants to America. It arrived with the earliest British settlers; a duel with swords was reported in Massachusetts the year after the Pilgrims landed. Duels remained rare, however, until the Revolutionary War when, according to one history, a dueling fad sprang up "rather suddenly."[5]

Historians identify two likely causes: the number of Americans exposed to British and French officers preoccupied with honor and prone

---

*Yes, if you wanted to stretch a bit—like, a lot—you could reach back to Europe and tick off any number of infamous British highwaymen. Or pirates. Or ruffians through the ages. What I'm looking for here is the gunfighter's American precursor, not his ancestor.

to defending it via duel; and the schism between Tories and Patriots, which produced a generation of men who could be terribly sensitive to any questioning of their loyalties. By the time foreign forces left in 1782, William Oliver Stevens has written, "the code of honor they had brought to America had taken firm root during the eight years of war. It was now recognized as an American institution."[6]

There's a tendency to dismiss antebellum duels as the pastime of a lunatic fringe. In fact, from the late 1700s until the 1840s, dueling was a staple of American and especially Southern life. Many cities actually had unofficial "dueling grounds." In St. Louis duelists repaired to a sandbar in the Mississippi River known as Bloody Island: the future senator Thomas Hart Benton killed a rival there in 1817. Outside Washington, men faced off at the Bladensburg Dueling Grounds in Maryland. Maybe the busiest venue was in New Orleans, beneath a canopy of gnarled oaks at the foot of Esplanade Avenue in today's City Park. At the height of the dueling craze between 1834 and 1844, a local paper noted, "scarcely a day passed without duels being fought at the Oaks." Ten separate duels were fought there on a single Sunday in 1839.*[7]

A list of noted duelists would include Andrew Jackson, the only president so involved; Senator Henry Clay; and Sam Houston, who as a young Tennessee congressman aimed a tad low and shot a rival in the, um, groin. In 1842 Abraham Lincoln, then a legislator in Illinois, reluctantly accepted a challenge from an opponent and, upon learning he was a skilled marksman, chose to fight with broadswords; bloodshed was avoided only when seconds talked the men out of it. It's said the fifth president, James Monroe, once sought to duel the second, the prickly John Adams, until talked out of it by the fourth, James Madison. The most famous duel was between Aaron Burr and Alexander

---

*Duels in New Orleans were typically fought with swords and were thus notably less lethal.

Hamilton in Weehawken, New Jersey, in 1804. There was an uproar when Burr killed Hamilton. After that, duels all but vanished from the North.

Below the Mason-Dixon Line, though, they remained not only accepted but embraced, even exalted. But then the antebellum South was a legendarily violent place. Everyone commented on it, travelers, memoirists, Tocqueville. Their journals are replete with arguments devolving into fistfights and shootings in the blink of an eye; an Englishman found the South as "barbarous as a jungle inhabited by wild beasts." Wrote another: "The darkest side of the southerner is his quarrelsomeness, and recklessness of human life."[8] The numbers are shocking; the homicide rate in Florida's cotton districts during the 1830s was fifty times that of the Northeast.[9]

Some historians blame slavery, some the heat, some the fact that many Southerners descended from the Scots and Irish, both renowned for their honor codes, violence, and clannishness—and their dueling. Others note that until the rise of cotton, Southern commerce was dominated by livestock trades, by the raising and selling of cattle, pigs, and horses. Through the ages such "herding societies" have tended to be off-the-charts violent, the better to deal with those who steal things with four legs. (The same, as we'll see, could be said of Texas cattlemen.)

Whatever else it was, then, much of the violence was a clear product of the South's obsession with honor. Honor was its social currency, the yardstick by which men were measured. Any insult, any slight, anything that might diminish a man's honor demanded a response, often a violent one, whether a punch in the face, a challenge to a duel, or, if families got involved, a full-blown feud. Some blame the lack of other measurements of status, university degrees and financial statements being in short supply in the years before the Civil War.*

---

*The financial angle is a compelling one. Many planters borrowed heavily, yet their most

The best explanation may be the simplest. Because enslaved Black people did almost all the planters' actual work, the South developed something new in America, a ruling class whose lives were defined by idleness and leisure pursuits. Glancing about for role models, the planting classes came to revere, and emulate, European-style aristocracy, for whom honor was sacrosanct. Quite simply, it was the way aristocrats—and Southerners—kept score. Those who aspired to join the upper class, meaning practically everyone else, were obliged to follow suit to have any hope of advancement. In time, certainly by the early 1800s, the primacy of honor permeated every facet of Southern society.*

When we talk about a Southern honor code, we mean the broadly understood rules that defined how a man in the antebellum South was expected to act. While everyone defines it a bit differently, the code in general required a man to be honest, courteous, brave, and prepared to use violence, even deadly violence, to defend his honor. From this sprang a host of behaviors that made the South distinct, including emphasis on lavish entertainment and oratory, and the routine personal violence, the duels and feuds, the rejection of meager legal remedies for vigilantism, and the zeal for gambling, dancing, and hunting.

Much of the South remained a frontier society in the years before the Civil War, and in the absence of functioning law enforcement,

---

valuable assets—land and enslaved Black people—were, if not illiquid, not quickly salable. Access to credit, to ready cash, thus became paramount. Southern credit markets remained opaque into the late 1800s, meaning lenders handed out money largely on a man's reputation. Honor, this argument goes, thus became synonymous with creditworthiness. Which is a fine explanation for why it mattered to the upper classes, if less so for everyone else. Hickok's desire to retrieve his watch from Davis Tutt, I'm guessing, had little to do with Southern credit markets.

*Not that most outsiders admitted this for a long time. For decades academics were leery of even acknowledging the Southern honor code's existence, much less studying it: How could a culture that enslaved generations of Black people, the reasoning went, have any semblance of honor? Then, in 1982, a University of Florida professor named Bertram Wyatt-Brown published the game-changing *Southern Honor: Ethics and Behavior in the Old South*, a six-hundred-page opus demonstrating how notions of honor shaped almost every component of antebellum society. Wyatt-Brown is the bible on the subject, a very heavy read, but definitive.

Southerners turned to the honor code to regulate society. Thus was born its deep tradition of extralegal violence. If a man was accused of theft or murder, his fellow citizens might shoot, burn, whip, or hang him in public; lynching, infamously, was a mainstay of Southern society for two centuries, generally targeting Black people. In 1835, in St. Louis, a Black man accused of murder was chained to a tree and burned alive while a thousand people watched and cheered.

Would that such incidents were rare. They were not. If mob justice like this is maintained with any regularity, it becomes vigilantism, a key component of the gunfighter ethos. In America, vigilantism was born in the South; scholars trace the first such movements to upstate South Carolina in the 1760s. Even a defensible phenomenon in theory often becomes appalling in practice. When people hew to their best selves, vigilantes can enforce laws against violent crime. When they don't, and they usually don't, you get the Ku Klux Klan.

Feuds, which typically occurred when an entire family's honor was besmirched, were also rife, and could be sparked by just about anything: a woman scorned, a paterfamilias insulted. Many were political. While Appalachian rivalries such as the Hatfields and McCoys are more famous, the feud between the Tutt and Everett families in Arkansas during the 1840s was nearly as deadly, so too the Turk–Jones feud in Missouri during the same period. Both conflicts started with fistfights during election campaigns and spiraled out of control.

In the nineteenth century, all these honor-sensitive behaviors—the duels, the feuds, the vigilantism—faded from northern life.* But they lived on in the West, where they provided the conflicts that so

---

*Not totally, of course. There was a serious feud or two in Vermont, of all places, as late as the 1860s. Vigilantes, meanwhile, remained active in the Missouri and Ohio River valleys into the 1870s, though historians point out that most of those involved had recently emigrated from the South. In time, people in the North, I've seen one or two authorities write, replaced the worship of honor with the worship of virtue.

often produced gunfighters of note. The nastiest feuds of U.S. history took place in the Old West. Some of the worst happened in Texas, and even when they didn't, featured Texas gunmen. Western vigilantes, often led by cattlemen "protecting" their herds, likely killed far more people than outlaws ever did. One historian identifies a "lynching belt" spanning cattle country from Texas to Montana; between 1882 and 1903, its per capita lynching rate surpassed the South's.*[10]

It's the mano a mano purity of the duel that resonates, though, the duel that speaks to the American preoccupation with individualism, the duel that morphed into the frontier gunfight. There were obvious differences, it's true. The formal duel was typically, and by design, a much more mannered affair, a kind of gunfight by appointment, complete with written rules. Though more than a few duels disintegrated into manic shoot-outs, we remember the gunfight as a wilder thing, a duel with its hair on fire.

The differences were evolutionary, as much about changes in geography and culture as advances in weaponry. Duels were common in the Southern upper classes from at least 1800, especially in the cities, Charleston and New Orleans being centers of dueling culture. Officially, they were controversial; clergymen were forever calling for their abolition. Laws were passed here and there, and ignored. Many, including women, argued that duels were necessary "as a check on general murder," as one history puts it.[11] In a duel, after all, the violence between men could be controlled, or at least contained.

They were often prompted by the wrong word—literally, a trigger

---

*There is an argument here that such behavior would happen on any frontier, that commonalities between Old West and Southern behaviors simply sprang from the fact that the South was long a frontier too. I doubt that. What swayed me was the clear difference in extrajudicial violence between the early Southern frontiers and those in the North. With some exceptions, such as a wild 1840 shoot-out in Iowa known as the Bellevue War, early Iowa, Wisconsin, and Minnesota just didn't see anything approaching the levels of violence Texas and its neighbors did. Nor do I see evidence they suffered even a fraction of the honor-based behaviors Southern frontiers did.

word. In her book *Gentlemen's Blood*, Barbara Holland lists common ones such as "liar," "poltroon," "coward," "puppy," "fornicator," "madman," and "bastard." Burr killed Hamilton over "despicable." Hamilton's son Philip was killed over "damned rascals." In the hurly-burly political world of the early 1800s, Holland notes, there were duels prompted by allegations of treason, incest, and, my personal favorite, devil worship. The ultimate insult, though, was to beat a rival with a cane or—wait for it—pull his nose, which suggested that the nose-pulled was both a liar and a social inferior. In 1798 a merchant named James Jones did both to a New York judge named Brockholst Livingston. In the resulting duel, Jones was killed. Livingston went on to serve on the Supreme Court.

Rules for the formal duel were outlined in an 1838 pamphlet by, of all people, the governor of South Carolina, who leaned heavily on a 1777 code issued in Ireland known as the code duello. In the event of an insult, the South Carolina code held, the insulted gentleman was to send a letter requesting a retraction. If refused, or ignored, he could issue a challenge to duel, either by private letter or in a public notice posted at a tavern, on a street corner, or in a newspaper, where it typically appeared under the headline A CARD. Once the duel was agreed to—and to decline such a challenge was social and political suicide—the place and time were to be mutually agreed upon, as were the weapons, usually smoothbore pistols.

Each duelist brought a friend, his "second," who was to remain impassive and, where possible, attempt to broker a peaceful resolution. If such efforts failed, the duelists stood facing each other; sometimes they faced away and walked ten or twenty paces. At some point one of the seconds would give "the signal," typically shouting "Fire!" If either duelist shot before that, his opponent's second was permitted to shoot at him. If both duelists missed, and they often did, they could try again if they wanted. Or not.

Those were the written rules, at least. In practice, the only thing all duels had in common was that no one followed the written rules. There's one in the literature where two men faced off at five feet, one of them claiming he was nearsighted. When they faced each other, their guns actually overlapped. Both died instantly.

Among men of lower classes, contests tended to be less structured. Hand-to-hand fights could veer toward the gruesome. Men circled each other, arms extended, waiting for an opening. Kicking in the crotch was acceptable, as was the biting off of ears and noses, and the breaking of arms and legs. Some matches ended when one gent managed to press his thumb so far into his opposite's eyeball it popped out. Both Virginia and Kentucky passed laws against eye gouging.[12] Such tactics were said to be a specialty of Georgians, who were renowned for growing their fingernails long and sharp. The combat-prone in Tennessee might clip on metal "Devil's claws," a swipe of which, we're told, "would take off half a man's face."[13]

The nature of duels began to change as the South's population moved west, especially after the 1810s. The frontier South was a rougher place than Charleston or New Orleans. Migrants were often society's have-nots—second sons, loafers, drifters, debtors, "the restless, the reckless, the disgraced," as one history puts it.[14] Perhaps unsurprisingly, frontiersmen had less use for the duel's formalities. It's possible to spy glimpses of the duelist-to-gunfighter evolution here, in early Mississippi, Louisiana, Arkansas, Tennessee, and Missouri, where public life could be coarse, the wearing of guns more common, and the honor code maybe a tad more intense among those eager to regain a station in life they had lost. Perhaps as a result, the duels were less concerned with nose pulling and public notices and mannered seconds than in flat-out killing.

"The farther one traveled toward the western fringe of the Southern States," William Oliver Stevens wrote in a 1940 history of dueling, "the more artillery a man needed to stuff into his pockets and belt. . . . In general there was throughout this section a state of lawlessness amounting to savagery, where every man was his own officer of the law, judge and executioner, and where any personal affront, real or fancied was a crime. No individual could stand alone against the overwhelming public sentiment in favor of the code."[15]

The most notorious Southern duelist was a fiery Mississippian named Alexander Keith McClung, known as "The Black Knight of the South." It's safe to say McClung had issues. Raised in Kentucky, a nephew of the Supreme Court justice John Marshall, he joined the navy at seventeen and was thrown out for wounding a man in a duel. Back home, he killed a cousin in a duel. Shunned, he moved to Vicksburg, a hive of frontier duels, where he emerged as a flamboyant, cape-wearing lawyer and editor known for fits of rage. In his most famous duel, in 1834, he shot another lawyer in the mouth from over a hundred feet, an informal distance record. After service in the Mexican War and a diplomatic stint in Bolivia—more duels there, it appears—McClung committed suicide in 1855. Had he lived a few years longer and moved a few states west, he'd have been known as a gunfighter.

Another who embodied the migration of the violent, honor-sensitive Southerner to the frontier, Jim Bowie, might be viewed as a transitional figure, a kind of proto-gunfighter. An obscure slave trader deeply engaged in land frauds in his native Louisiana, Bowie rocketed to fame in 1827 after a riotous duel known as the Sandbar Fight, for its location on a Mississippi River islet. The duel itself ended with a handshake after the participants fired and missed. But a brawl broke out afterward, during which Bowie, on hand as a second, was shot and stabbed repeatedly, yet managed to impale his assailant with a massive short-sword-like knife that came to be called, yes, the bowie knife.

The incident somehow reached the eastern newspapers. Overnight Bowie and his monstrous knife entered folklore. The knife became a staple of gory, duel-like confrontations throughout both the frontier South and the Old West. Bowie later followed the trail of the debt-ridden and distressed into Mexican Texas, where, following a series of gun battles with Native American tribes, he ended up a leader of the settlers' revolt and famously died at the Alamo.

Maybe the best example of the transition from duels to gunfights is Hickok's showdown with Davis Tutt in 1865. The historian Dick Steward places this contest squarely in Missouri's deep dueling tradition. Somewhat as gentlemen nailed up notices calling out their opponents, Hickok had clearly done something similar, spreading word of the looming confrontation. What resulted was, in almost every way, a classic Southern duel, only with revolvers, a gunfight by appointment. "No western figure better epitomized the transition from duelist to gunslinger than . . . 'Wild Bill' Hickok," Steward writes. The fight marks the "transition from the punctilio of the code duello to a new and far more lethal form of personalized combat."[16]

This is not to suggest duels were common in the Old West. They weren't. In fact, outside Gold Rush California, they were all but unknown; even then, westerners had little use for formalities. What you did see a lot of, though, was an exchange of words or the throwing of a punch followed by what sounds like a throwaway line but is actually the invitation to a kind of duel, commonly involving the word "outside," as in "Let's take this outside" or "I'll see you outside."

The duelist's legacy in the Old West was less about the physical structure of an armed confrontation than the reasons underlying it. Thousands of Southerners flowed west in the 1800s, and with them went their honor codes. What went too was a notion by then imbued in generations of Southerners, and codified to an extent by the dueling craze, that extrajudicial violence was a permissible, even accept-able, way to resolve disputes. On the way west, this mindset evolved into something new, something explosive, thanks in large part to that ultimate frontier Southerner, the one who first melded the passions of the Old South to the six-shooter: the Texan.

CHAPTER TWO

The First Gunfighters

Almost from the beginning, the rest of America sensed it. There was something bigger about the Texan, something louder, more assertive, more violent. A lot of this was Civilized America's penchant for saying such things about almost any frontiersman. They had been saying much the same about Kentuckians for years when the Texans, thanks to victory in their long-shot rebellion against Mexico, suddenly roared onto the national stage in the 1830s. The legend makers greeted them with open arms. "Who knows what embryo heroes this Texian war may not bring forth?" a Boston paper wondered.[1]

At first, the fascination wasn't directed so much at any individual Texan—most Americans, and certainly most eastern writers, had never met one—but at the collective Texan, the one who fought and died at the Alamo and defeated Santa Anna at San Jacinto. Writers who toured Texas in those early years tended to reinforce creaky frontier tropes—everything was bigger and badder and scarier and deadlier—and Texans mostly loved it, proudly embracing these aborning myths. There was, after all, more than a little truth to them. One memoirist asked a dinner table lined with fourteen Texans how many had killed a man; eight raised their hands.

In his 1952 *The Typical Texan: Biography of an American Myth*, Joseph Leach identifies a trio of Texans the press soon decided were representative: Davy Crockett, the fallen Tennessee congressman and early-frontier icon, among the most famous men in America when he died at the Alamo; Sam Houston, the hero of San Jacinto; and William "Big-Foot" Wallace, an early Texas Ranger who during an eastern tour delighted reporters by offering up the cornpone anecdotes they craved, going on about tarantulas so big they killed cows, and monster snakes, and the Texas lady who got "seventeen proposals before breakfast."[2]

For every Texas fan, though, there was a critic, especially among abolitionists who feared its entry into the Union would tip the precarious national balance. Through the 1840s, the New York papers regularly savaged Texas as, in the words of Horace Greeley, a "den of thieves" and a "rendezvous for rascals for all the continent," a lawless land with, as the New York *Dispatch* put it, an "utterly appalling" number of murders and assassinations.[3]

If such carping was overblown, it's certainly true that Texas was a violent place, its borders especially. After the revolution, it pretty much stayed at war, first against Mexican raiders, then against Native American tribes, for forty years. Comanche riders could strike deep into its heartland, ranging as far as the Gulf Coast in one storied 1840 raid. Murder, rape, and the kidnapping of women and children remained common on the frontier into the 1870s. Even if eastern papers overstated things, combat was, of necessity, in the Texan's DNA.

It took only a few years, in fact, for reality to catch up with the national imagination, but it did, and spectacularly. What paved the way, what forever changed the nature of personal violence in Texas, and in the Old West, and for that matter in much of the world, was a sudden leap in technology, an invention that arrived with little fanfare in 1836, a few months after the fall of the Alamo. It was a new kind of hand-gun, the revolver, and Texans were not only the first to seriously use it, they actually headed back east to perfect it.

To appreciate how revolutionary this was, a little Gun History 101 is in order. The earliest firearms, bamboo or metal tubes that shot projectiles launched by the ignition of gunpowder, appeared in China around 1250. Versions spread to the Arab world and then to Europe by the 1300s. By the 1700s single-shot muskets were in wide use and helped Americans conquer the Appalachian frontier. There was just one problem. Muskets had to be reloaded by hand, which took a professional at least twenty seconds and an amateur longer. In twenty seconds, a Comanche warrior could fire five or six arrows. An opponent wielding a bowie knife or spear could run you through.*

Until the 1800s, the common way to fire more often was to use a gun with multiple barrels, typically rotated to make each shot. Thus *bang*, then manually rotate the barrel, then *bang*, then reload both cylinders. Many like this were built; most were hard to use and prone to malfunction. The most popular, the pepperbox pistol, allowed a shooter to fire via three barrels; it appeared around 1790 and was widely used in America after 1830. In 1818 an American inventor living in London named Elisha Collier patented the first true revolver. At the time, most guns fired when the hammer struck a piece of flint, creating a spark in a tiny metal pan holding gunpowder, igniting it; you had to add powder to fire again. But cocking Collier's revolver dispensed a pinch of powder into the pan, a process that could be repeated five times, allowing for repeat firing. Though the gun's five barrels still had to be rotated manually, it was a major step forward, if still primitive. As a commercial venture, it went nowhere.

---

*So yes, while Americans could and did have fights with pistols before the advent of the revolver, as in dueling, it could be a frightfully slow means of combat and, thus, a good way to get yourself killed.

Which is where things stood when a seventeen-year-old merchant seaman named Samuel Colt dreamed up a new kind of revolver during a voyage to India in 1831. In the great tradition of American inventors, Colt was a nobody from nowhere, a New England textile maker's son who as a boy became obsessed with blowing stuff up, including, famously, an intricate operation using a long electric wire to detonate explosives beneath a river raft during a Fourth of July celebration. (The raft survived, but the underwater explosion impressively drenched onlookers.) When his schoolmasters frowned on Colt's buoyant firing of a purloined cannon at another Fourth, he was sent to sea.

There, he thought a lot about guns. He had heard soldiers muse about one that might fire five or six times without rotating cylinders or reloading—Colt called it "the impossible gun"—and he sketched out the design of a revolver whose hammer, when cocked, rotated the cylinder. This was the idea that changed everything.

Back at his father's factory, Colt built prototypes of a revolving rifle and handgun. Over the next few years, he worked with a gunsmith to perfect the design, and in 1835 sailed to London, where patents were easier to obtain, and secured his first. A year later he obtained a U.S. patent and, backed by a group of New Jersey venture capitalists, began making and trying to sell his new guns.

By the end of 1837, Colt's factory had produced a thousand revolving guns—and sold precisely none. The guns worked, but Colt's marketing, for whatever reason, didn't. He had managed to wangle a demonstration for President Jackson, and following Jackson's endorsement, sold some of his five-shot pistols to the army, which tried them during Florida's Second Seminole War, to decent if unspectacular reviews. The pistols were fine for five shots, but after that, they basically had to be disassembled to reload. The world yawned. By 1843 Colt was bankrupt. His factory closed.

It was then that the Texans rode to his rescue. Before going under, Colt had sold 108 pistols to the embryonic Texas navy. It barely used them. But as fate would have it, when the navy was phased out in 1843, its revolvers were passed on to a scrappy little outfit few Americans had ever heard of: the Texas Rangers. Originally a militia raised to fight Native Americans, the Rangers had existed in one form or another since 1823 but hadn't become an official arm of government until the revolt against Mexico, when a contingent of fifty-six Rangers was employed as scouts. In 1838, beset by heavy Comanche raids, the new nation of Texas formed another ten companies, which expelled the Cherokee from East Texas and patrolled the Comanche frontier.

The Rangers were a ragtag lot in those first years, many of them bearded, with long greasy hair, dressed in their own clothes, riding their own horses, and firing their own guns. From 1840, a cool young captain named John C. "Jack" Hays professionalized them, leading the men through riding and shooting drills and weeding out slackers. Under Hays, the Rangers learned to travel fast and light, often at night, typically in groups of ten or twenty who hunted for their meals and slept on the ground. Their baptism under fire came in 1840 at the Battle of Plum Creek, near present-day Lockhart, when a force of six hundred Comanche returning from that famous Gulf Coast raid encircled the Texas army. A Ranger contingent begged to lead a charge and did, routing the Native American warriors in a running battle of ten miles or more.

The odd victory aside, Hays was keenly aware that his men were at a disadvantage against the Comanche, expert riders whom one writer has termed the "best light cavalry in history."[4] The Rangers carried a standard frontier rifle of the period, a version of the Kentucky flintlock muzzleloader. It was accurate to two hundred yards, but of little use at close quarters, where the Comanche were most lethal. Pistols of the day were no better, single-shot flintlocks, inaccurate and prone to misfire. Hays was desperate for something deadlier.

Jack Hays's discovery of the Texas navy's discarded five-shot Colt revolvers was the moment frontier gunmanship changed forever. The turning point came on June 9, 1844, when Hays and fourteen of his men, looking for Comanche raiders in the Hill Country northwest of San Antonio, found some. A private named Noah Cheery was high atop a tree they were about to fell when he suddenly yelped, "Jerusalem, captain, yonder comes a thousand Indians!" It was more like a hundred, and they swiftly withdrew into a thicket, where they taunted the Rangers into attacking them. Hays was badly outnumbered, but eyeing his new Colt revolvers, he decided to engage anyway, mounting up, circling around to the base of a hill behind the Comanche, and charging.

It was unlike any charge in human history to that moment. When the Rangers fired their muskets, they didn't dismount and reload, as they always had. Instead, they rode hard into the raiders, pulling and firing their revolvers left and right. It quickly devolved into the nastiest kind of hand-to-hand fighting. The Comanche never had a chance. Twenty-three of them died at what came to be known as the Battle of Walker's Creek. One Ranger was killed. "Never," wrote one historian, "was a band of Indians more surprised than at this charge." As a dumbstruck Comanche chief put it afterward, "I will never again fight Jack Hays, who has a shot for every finger on the hand."[5]

Hays and the Comanche may have grasped the impact of Sam Colt's devastating new technology, but until the swashbuckling Rangers and their deadly new approach to close combat burst into the national consciousness during the Mexican War in 1846, no one else did, not even Colt himself, who was off designing underwater explosives and newfangled gun cartridges. Colt's unlikely champion turned out to be a soft-spoken twenty-nine-year-old Ranger named Samuel H.

Walker, who had nearly died at Walker's Creek when pinned to the ground with a lance.

In the Mexican War's opening weeks, when Walker and a group of Rangers were among the first to join Zachary Taylor's army fighting the Mexicans in South Texas, he led a series of daring raids and night missions, charging through enemy lines in the darkness. In one skirmish, after a cannonball felled his horse, a Mexican lancer charged him. Walker pulled his Colt, shot the lancer dead, then leaped atop his foe's horse to rejoin the fray. The press caught wind of his exploits and made Walker the war's first hero, probably the most celebrated since Andrew Jackson won the Battle of New Orleans in 1815. Overnight, he became the subject of battle paintings and poetry.

In late 1846, Walker headed east to raise money and arms for a new regiment. In New Orleans and Washington, he was mobbed by cheering throngs. At some point he received a letter from Sam Colt asking his opinion of the revolvers. "With improvements," Walker replied, "I think they can be rendered the most perfect weapon in the World for light mounted troops." This exchange, Colt's biographer writes, "initiated one of the most remarkable relationships in the history of American manufacturing."[6] In the ensuing months, Colt and the young Ranger worked closely on an improved revolver, made of stronger English-forged steel, far easier to reload, and with sharper sights.

What they ended up with was a fifteen-inch, four-and-a-half-pound behemoth ("It would take a Texan to shoot it," Colt fretted) now with six cylinders, the famed Colt Walker, the first six-shooter, father of a line of six-shot revolvers that would come to define violence in the Old West. This time Colt had no problem with sales. Even before the gun entered production, Walker prevailed upon the army to order it. His fame made everything an event. The press hailed the new Colt as a game-changing weapon.

Orders flooded in. Walker, alas, did not live to witness the gun's impact. Returning to Mexico, he was killed in battle.* But the innovations he urged, and the Rangers' embrace of the new revolvers, put Texans at the forefront of the firearms world for years to come. "Every culture or subculture has had its distinctive arm: the Macedonians their 18-foot phalanx pike, the Romans their Spanish short-sword," writes T. R. Fehrenbach. "In the 1840s the name of Texas became indelibly linked with the Colt's revolver."[7]

The Colt Walker, like the cotton gin and Fulton's steamboat, changed America in ways no one had imagined. In a matter of months, the new guns triggered the first spasms of the Gunfighter Era. Perhaps surprisingly, as pivotal as Texans had proven to be to the six-shooter's story—and would be again—it didn't happen in Texas.

It happened instead on a chaotic frontier opening half a continent away. Barely ninety days after Walker's death, in January 1848, a man stepping beside a sawmill in the foothills of the Sierra Nevada spied something sparkle in the river below. It was gold. It was California.

FOR ALMOST AS LONG AS WRITERS HAVE CHRONICLED THE OLD WEST, Hickok's showdown with Davis Tutt in 1865 was seen as the first Western-style gunfight of significance, suggesting the Gunfighter Era was exclusively a postwar phenomenon. Nothing, it turns out, could be further from the truth, though the facts took a century to reemerge, thanks largely to two researchers, William B. Secrest and John Boessenecker. A commercial artist, Secrest began exploring the careers of obscure Gold Rush–era gunmen during the 1950s. Boessenecker, a San Francisco attorney, joined him in 1984. Their work, born of years

---

*If you want to know more about Colt and Walker, the book to read is *Revolver: Sam Colt and the Six-Shooter That Changed America*, by Jim Rasenberger.

poring over nineteenth-century newspapers, clearly establishes early California as the first theater of the gunfighter age, a kind of manic prologue.*

Though little remembered today, California in the 1850s was the first place where civilians turned the new Colts on each other with regularity. It spawned a slew of western firsts—the first headline OUT-LAWS AND VIGILANTES, the first steely sheriffs, the first six-shooter confrontations—and some of its wildest gunfights, including probably the deadliest, eleven bandits killed by a single man on a lonely mountain trail.[†]

The discovery of gold drew a torrent of people from across the globe, transforming California from a sleepy Mexican colony of twenty thousand people into a riotous American state of a quarter million in four short years. Tented encampments perched on hillsides spread across the mining regions on the western edges of the Sierra Nevada in North Central California. An American military administration, its only legal representatives a few judges, ran things until statehood in September 1850, and even then it took several years for a rudimentary law enforcement structure to gel.

It's difficult to overstate the anarchy gold brought. In terms of violence, Gold Rush California had every kind of crazy. Much of it bore a racial component, as late-arriving Americans forcibly ejected Mexican, Chilean, and Chinese miners from their claims. Race riots and gang warfare, especially among Chinese tongs, were common. Outlaw gangs roamed everywhere. Overwhelmed by crime, San Francisco and an infant Los Angeles were ruled by vigilante committees for

---

*The best of the resulting books is probably Boessenecker's 1999 *Gold Dust & Gunsmoke: Tales of Gold Rush Outlaws, Gunfighters, Lawmen, and Vigilantes.* I have consulted it liberally.

†One could reasonably include the 1850s-era strife in "Bleeding Kansas" here as well, though much of that violence was paramilitary in nature and is thus largely excluded from the gunfighter canon.

years. The Bay Area one alone lynched more than eighty men. Many killings, as in much of the early West, never resulted in an arrest, much less a trial. If the fight was viewed as a fair one, especially if the dead man drew first, the killer usually walked away a free man.*

Thousands of young men left their homes for the first time in these years to work on this hypermasculine frontier, unmoored from the stabilizing influences of churches, wives, and mothers, where rot-gut alcohol, fisticuffs, and all manner of gambling pursuits defined idle time. "Our amusements here on Sunday are drinking, swearing, fighting and gambling, more than I ever saw in my life before," one forty-niner wrote his brother back in Wisconsin. "I eschew all but fighting. I have had two or three fights since I came here. Can't help it. Must defend myself. I do it up in short order either with a knife or a club."[8]

Knives were fine for a Sunday brawl, but on a frontier where any gold a man found might have to be defended against thieves, just about everyone wore a pistol. Pepperbox models were common, but Colt, capitalizing on the success of the Walker Colt, began producing smaller, easier-to-use guns that poured into California, notably a new "pocket pistol" with a three-inch barrel, the .44-caliber Dragoon Army revolver, and especially the .36-caliber Navy pistol. A settler recalled this period as one "when the strong, with revolver and bowie knife, were law."[9]

Gold Rush California had more than a little Southern flavor. Any number of Southerners assumed prominent positions, including the Texas Revolution hero Ben McCulloch and the Texas Ranger Jack Hays, who became sheriffs. During the 1850s, at a time when duels were declining in the South, more were fought in California than any U.S. state or territory. Southerners, who made up maybe 40 percent of the population, initiated almost all of them.

---

*This was an outgrowth of the legal doctrine known as "no duty to retreat," which, roughly speaking, holds that deadly force is justifiable in self-defense, an idea imported from English common law and codified by the U.S. Supreme Court in 1921.

Two of the better-known Gold Rush gunfighters were Southern gamblers. Georgia-born Henry J. Talbot, known as Cherokee Bob for his Native American ancestry, emerged as a distinctive figure in the mining camps: long black hair, beaver-trimmed coat and gloves, pistol, bowie knife. In 1854, after knifing two men in an argument, he was sent to the new San Quentin prison. After two bloody escape attempts, he was pardoned in 1860 and left the state, leaving a trail of perforated opponents across the Mountain West. He knifed a constable, then wounded a deputy in a saloon fight in Carson City, Nevada; fled to Washington, where he killed two soldiers in a brawl; then fled again, to Florence, in what's now Idaho. On January 5, 1863, after being ejected from a party, he and a pal named Poker Bill Willoughby accosted two dance hall managers in the street. All four men drew pistols and fired. Willoughby and Cherokee Bob fell dead.

A contemporary, "Longhair Sam" Brown, an Alabamian who came west via Texas, was a brute, a big, bluff braggart with flowing red hair. Arriving in 1850, Brown killed five men, most during arguments over cards, before serving time for manslaughter. Moving on to Virginia City, Nevada, he killed four more, including one shot over billiards, one lying in a stupor, and another stabbed for a barroom jostling. Legend attributes to Brown all sorts of wild-eyed behavior, to wit, riding into town shouting, "I wanna eat a man for breakfast!" In 1861 he finally threatened the wrong one, a German named Henry Van Sickle who, after mounting up and chasing Brown for miles, cornered him, leveled his shotgun, and as he squeezed the trigger, uttered in a thick accent the immortal words, "Sam, now I kills you."[10]

Far and away, though, most of those who achieved renown with a gun in early California were outlaws and the men who chased them.*

---

*Early California gunfighters, honorable mention: Tiburcio Vásquez was an especially persistent bandit who, between stays at San Quentin (and four bloody attempted prison breaks), compiled a dizzying record of cattle thefts, burglaries, and robberies, including the sacking

Really, the Gold Rush had bandits the way the Okefenokee Swamp has mosquitoes. During the 1850s they roamed up and down the state seemingly at will, robbing miners in the north and rustling cattle in the south. Only one would achieve anything like long-lasting fame, the Old West's most infamous Latino outlaw, Joaquin Murrieta, a hard-riding bandit chief who's periodically been dismissed as a legend despite the fact that his severed head was displayed after his demise. Lore holds that he was spurred to a life of crime when American miners drove him off his claim, raped his wife, and lynched his brother, which is one amazing origin story if unsupported by any known facts. The truth appears more prosaic.

Whatever Murrieta's motivations, and given the treatment of Mexicans at the time, revenge could certainly have been one, modern scholarship indicates he rode quietly for a year or two with his brother-in-law's outlaw band before suddenly hitting the headlines in 1852, one of several members of the gang implicated in the Los Angeles murder of General Joshua Bean, a brother of Judge Roy Bean, who later achieved fame in Texas as the so-called Law West of the Pecos.

It was the turning point in Murrieta's career, the moment when, once a vigilance committee strung up his brother-in-law and two close friends, he headed north to raise a gang of his own. A smallish, fair-complected Sonoran with shoulder-length brown hair, a wispy beard, and a dark unibrow, Murrieta was twenty-three when he fled to the mining region after Bean's death. There, in early 1853, he rode into history leading what one author terms "the bloodiest crime spree of the Gold Rush."[11] It might have been the bloodiest in Old West history.

---

of the town of Kingston, not to mention myriad gunfights, between 1855 and his hanging in 1875. A tall Tennessean named Thomas J. Hodges, aka Tom Bell, escaped from prison in 1855 and assembled a huge, multiracial gang that pulled off a series of spectacular stagecoach and packtrain robberies, prompting one of the state's largest manhunts; a posse hanged him in 1856. Ben K. Thorn, a lawman in Calaveras County, engaged in multiple shoot-outs over a nearly fifty-year career.

Over two months, Murrieta's gang rampaged across the goldfields, murdering as many as forty Chinese and Anglo miners in dozens of robberies. It left behind a region in deep shock. In the ensuing uproar, people beseeched the government to do something. In May the legislature finally did, allotting money for a temporary ranger service led by a strapping six-foot-two onetime army scout, Harry Love, who hired twenty-one men, mostly veterans who had seen fighting in Texas and Mexico, including one who claimed to have met Murrieta.

Love and his rangers rode across Central California interrogating various Mexicans for six weeks before capturing another of Murrieta's brothers-in-law, who told of several mountain hideouts the bandit used. Love found one and then, at daybreak on July 25, 1853, headed down a winding canyon onto the floor of the San Joaquin Valley. Out on the plain, they could see smoke from a campfire. As the rangers rode up, the encampment suddenly erupted in activity, people running everywhere. The rangers charged in, guns drawn. Caught by surprise, the men, mostly Mexicans, stopped and put their hands up.

One, a slender sort with a unibrow, stepped forward, unarmed.

"Talk to me," he said. "I am the leader of this band."

"This is Joaquin, boys!" the rider who knew him yelled. "We have got him at last!"

At that, one or more of the Mexicans threw off their serapes and opened fire. Murrieta ran for a horse, jumped atop it, and leaped down a fifteen-foot embankment. Several rangers rode up and opened fire. Two bullets struck Murrieta's horse, which crumpled. Rolling free, Murrieta ran down a rocky arroyo. He made it maybe thirty yards before three bullets struck him in the back. He fell. "Don't shoot any more, I'm dead," he said in Spanish when the men ran up. And he was.

To claim a reward, Love had Murrieta's head cut off. It was jammed into a jar and preserved with spirits, creating one of the Old West's signature trophies.* Almost from the beginning, though, doubters questioned whether it was Murrieta's. The doubts grew after the 1854 publication of an imaginative booklet that portrayed him as a victim of scorching Anglo oppression, a narrative that gained popularity over the years in the face of genuine Anglo oppression. It's a good story, maybe even true, but there are few facts to support it. Yet somewhat like the myths that surround the Battle of the Alamo, so many people wanted to believe it that the legend came to overshadow, and nearly blotted out, history.

For all this, Murrieta is one of the few California gunmen who fits the mold of figures such as Wyatt Earp who engaged in multiple gunfights, even if we have almost no details of them. The most notable shoot-outs in early California, in fact, were one-off affairs. Armed with a rifle, a lawman named Steve Venard killed three outlaws with four bullets on the South Yuba River in 1866; he got an article in a national magazine, *Harper's Weekly*, and a future in obscurity.

The most eye-opening California gunfight was lost to history until rediscovered by Secrest and Boessenecker. In 1854, on a miner's trail in El Dorado County, an army veteran named Jonathan R. Davis and two pals were ambushed by a fourteen-man outlaw gang. Its first bullets killed one of them and badly wounded the other. A crack shot armed with two Colts and a bowie knife, Davis took cover and returned fire, picking off seven of his assailants. When four more rushed him with bowie knives, Davis drew his own, stabbed one to death, and lopped off another's nose. Two more had been wounded but gamely hobbled up anyway. Davis stabbed them to death. The remaining three bandits wisely ran off.†

---

*According to Boessenecker, the head toured the mining country for a period of time before coming to rest in a San Francisco gun shop, which was destroyed, presumably along with the head, in the earthquake of 1906.

†That Davis survived—he found six holes in his hat—was hard to believe. The poor guy actually had to go to court with witnesses to prove it all really happened.

By the Civil War, California had calmed considerably, the march of law and order ending the worst of the chaos. Gun violence continued, of course, especially in the mining towns of the High Sierra, and there was a nasty feud or two as late as 1871. One boomtown of the 1870s and '80s, Bodie, was sufficiently violent that it spawned a mythical figure, "the Bad Man from Bodie." By then, though, the days of the California gunfighter were passing. The state's best-known postwar outlaws were both gentlemanly stage robbers: Charles E. Boles, aka Black Bart, who left behind more poems (two) at his stickups than dead men (zero), and Bill Miner, often credited with popularizing the standard outlaw greeting "Hands up!"*

Maybe it was their distance from the eastern press, maybe the narrative power of the intervening war years, but almost all of early California's gunfighters, with the exception of Murrieta, were forgotten. When mainstream writers rediscovered the Old West in the 1920s, those with memories of the Gold Rush were mostly gone. The resulting literature all but ignored them. The legacy of California gunfighters, both in fact and in fiction, is thus minimal; no one in the 1920s much less the 2020s would speak of Cherokee Bob Talbot or Steve Venard in the same breath as Doc Holliday or Wild Bill Hickok. The early California shootist proved to be the Neanderthal line of the gunfighter lineage, a genealogical and narrative dead end.

ANOTHER SPAWNING GROUND FOR THE EARLIEST GUNFIGHTERS WAS found in the rugged mining towns of Nevada and Montana, remote

---

*Boles was active between 1875 and his arrest in 1883. Paroled from San Quentin five years later, he disappeared. Miner may have had the longest criminal career of the Old West, lasting almost fifty years, from the end of the Civil War to the eve of World War I. After three stays in California prisons, he went on to rob trains in Canada, eventually escaping from a prison there in 1907. He died in a Georgia prison six years later. If you haven't seen the great Richard Farnsworth portray Miner in the 1982 biopic *The Grey Fox*, check it out. It's terrific.

camps where a man who killed was not only tolerated but, in certain cases, venerated. By the 1860s, places like Carson City and Virginia City exhibited a kind of murder culture: the more men you killed, the more respect you earned.

In Virginia City, the most feared gunman was anointed "the chief." Mark Twain, who worked there as a young man, vividly described this phenomenon in his 1872 memoir, *Roughing It*. It's one of the best—and maybe the earliest—accounts of an emerging gunfighter mystique, one that echoes so many scenes and themes from Western movies it's jarring to realize it happened in real life. Twain describes a dawning fascination with gunfighters, which, at least initially, sprang less from eastern city dwellers than their fellow westerners. He writes:

The first twenty-six graves in the Virginia cemetery were occupied by murdered men. So everybody said, so everybody believed, and so they will always say and believe. The reason why there was so much slaughtering done, was that in a new mining district the rough element predominates, and a person is not respected until he has "killed his man." That was the very expression used. . . . It was tedious work struggling up to a position of influence with bloodless hands; but when a man came with the blood of half a dozen men on his soul, his worth was recognized at once and his acquaintance sought. . . .

The desperado stalked the streets with a swagger graded according to the number of his homicides, and a nod of recognition from him was sufficient to make a humble admirer happy for the rest of the day. The deference that was paid to a desperado of wide reputation, and who "kept his private graveyard," as the phrase went, was marked, and cheerfully accorded. When he moved along the sidewalk in his excessively long-tailed frock-coat [and] shiny stump-toed boots . . . hat tipped over left eye, the small-fry roughs made room for his majesty; when he entered the restaurant, the waiters deserted bankers and merchants to overwhelm him with obsequious service; when he shouldered his way to a bar, the shouldered parties wheeled indignantly, recognized him, and—apologized. They got a look in return that froze their marrow. . . .

The best known names in the territory of Nevada were those belonging to these long-tailed heroes of the revolver. Orators, Governors, capitalists and leaders of the legislature enjoyed a degree of fame, but it seemed local and meagre when contrasted with the fame of such men as Sam Brown, Jack Williams, Billy Mulligan, Farmer Pease [sic], Sugarfoot Mike, Pock-Marked Jake, El Dorado Johnny, Jack McNabb, Joe McGee, Jack Harris, Six-fingered Pete, etc., etc. . . . They were brave, reckless men [who] . . . killed each other on slight provocation, and hoped and expected to be killed themselves—for they held it almost shame to die otherwise than "with their boots on."[12]

By far the most celebrated of these early gunmen was a stagecoach-line supervisor named Jack Slade.* Sometimes called the first gunfighter, Slade managed the Central Overland's stations along a five-hundred-mile route from the Rockies to the western Nebraska settlement of Kearney on the eve of the Civil War. In his late twenties, described as five eight, 160 pounds, dark hair, thin mustache, and businesslike except when drunk, when by all accounts he became a bit of a madman, Slade killed his first man in 1858, a freighter en route to Salt Lake City

---

*The book to read is *Death of a Gunfighter: The Quest for Jack Slade, the West's Most Elusive Legend*, by Dan Rottenberg. It's easily a cut above most books in the genre.

he shot either because the man laughed at him or because he was delaying the caravan.

To rid his territory of the odd outlaw, it's said he strung up many more. The English traveler Richard Burton heard the number was three. Twain, who said three to six, was floored by the renown of a man who, years before order came to the region, was known as "the law west of Kearney." "Really and truly, two thirds of the talk of drivers and conductors had been about this man Slade," Twain wrote of his stagecoach trip across the Rockies in 1861. "There was such magic in that name, SLADE! Day or night, now, I stood always ready to drop any subject in hand, to listen to something new about Slade. . . . [He] was at once the most bloody, the most dangerous and the most valuable citizen that inhabited the savage fastnesses of the mountains."*[13]

---

*Much of Slade's legend rests on an incident involving a former station agent at Julesburg, two hundred miles northeast of Denver, a belligerent French Canadian named Jules Beni. Beni had been dismissed after billing the company for "rewards" he paid to recover "stolen" horses. He stayed on to run the rancid bodega beside the station. Relations between the two men deteriorated after Slade hired away Beni's houseboy, retrieved some "stolen" horses from Beni's corral, and during a visit to Beni's "restaurant," ordered a plate of oysters. Whether because of cross words or the state of the oysters, Slade ended up tossing the entire tray in Beni's face.

Afterward, Slade heard Beni had sworn to "fix" him. If so, Slade swore, he would kill the man, a remark relayed to Beni. Still, when Slade and a pair of his men returned to Julesburg, no one was expecting trouble. Slade wasn't even wearing a gun. As he approached the bodega, Beni emerged with a revolver and, without a word, fired between three and six bullets into Slade, who sagged to the dirt. Beni returned inside, reemerged with a shotgun, and fired a load of buckshot into Slade's prostrate form. At which point he turned to his stunned companions and, in one of the better après-shootout quips in the literature, gestured to one side. "There are some blankets and a box," he said. "You can make him a coffin if you like."

Incredibly, thanks to an army surgeon's eighteen-hour ride to tend him, Slade lived. By 1861 he was back on duty. Beni, meanwhile, after lying low, was roaming the region boasting he would kill Slade yet. A biographer insists Slade was in no hurry to confront Beni, but that his reputation—his honor—depended on it. "There was no other way out," one of his drivers said later. "Order in the (area) depended on Slade, and he could not enforce it while Jules was alive and defiant. You may not see it now, but it was plain enough then."

Slade put a reward on Beni's head, and two of his men captured him after a gunfight and brought him, wounded and bound, to Slade. For years afterward, westerners marveled at the barbarity of what happened next, how Slade shot Beni once, headed into a saloon for a drink, then returned and shot him again, then had another drink, a process he repeated until Beni was dead, at which point he cut off his ears, which thereafter he kept in his pocket as a watch piece. It's a great tale, if unlikely. According to Slade's biographer, Beni already appeared

Slade went down as a western legend, and thanks to Twain found a measure of literary fame, but his renown was based entirely on how unusual his behavior was. He stood out, in other words, because there weren't many in the early West we know like him. Compared with postwar gunfighters, Slade was a piker. He was involved in precisely two shootings we know of, which, had he done them in Texas, wouldn't have placed him on a list of the state's hundred most prolific gunmen.

---

dead when brought before him. "He's only playing possum," one of his captors insisted. Slade decided to check. He did so by walking over and cutting off Beni's ear. Only when Beni failed to stir was Slade satisfied. And then he cut off his other ear anyway. And then, yes, kept them both on the watch in his front pocket.

Things went downhill for Slade after that. He began drinking more heavily, and got into a series of fistfights in Denver and elsewhere. When he shot up the store at Fort Halleck, Wyoming, the army got him fired. By 1863 he was running a freight business in Virginia City, but his drinking was spiraling out of control. During a two-day bender in 1864, he wrecked a pair of brothels, rode a horse into a saloon and poured a bottle of wine down its throat, dumped a wagonload of milk, and took a judge hostage. During a subsequent binge, a crowd of fed-up miners collared him and, as he begged pitifully for a last chance to see his wife, proceeded to hang him from the crossbar of a corral.

CHAPTER THREE

The Cauldron

Texas, 1865 to 1871

Eighteen sixty-five was a year, like 1945, of new beginnings, many of them troubling. The South lay in ruins. America had been changed forever. More than three million men fought during the war— one in four white men, a far higher percentage among men under forty—and the war changed many profoundly, the more so because, absent modern media, most had no sense of the carnage they would endure. "Individuals," notes the Harvard historian Drew Gilpin Faust, "found themselves in a new and different moral universe, one in which unimaginable destruction had become daily experience."[1]

Thousands of men returned home scarred and broken. They were greeted, in many cases, with fear and trepidation. The Boston writer Nathaniel Hawthorne "predicted that New Englanders would surrender their bucolic towns to crude, drunken, and sinister men," in one author's words.[2] In Tompkinsville, New York, two soldiers, taunted by civilians, fixed bayonets and charged. Unfed and unwanted, members of the 105th Illinois did much the same when a Chicago saloon patron uttered the words "Damn Sherman." The ensuing riot, in which veterans assaulted scores of civilians with clubs, lasted hours.

Unemployed and often drunk, veterans rampaged through city after city in the summer of 1865. "Records of murders, garrotings, burglaries, and rapes are laid on every breakfast table," a Connecticut paper complained. "From day to day, and week to week, in every direction, the terrible circle seems to spread."[3] Cities such as Baltimore and Harrisburg, Pennsylvania, issued regulations forbidding veterans to buy alcohol. It was no use. By 1866 the nation was engulfed in a full-blown crime wave, much of it fueled by idle or troubled veterans. No doubt many suffered from what is now understood as post-traumatic stress disorder. Some veterans found solace in sanatoriums, but most went untreated in an age where depression and associated maladies were typically chalked up to "low character."

Any number of noted gunfighters fought in the war, from Jesse James and Hickok to lesser-known figures such as the Texan Jim Courtright and Wyatt Earp's brother Virgil. None, so far as we know, blamed their penchant for violence on wartime trauma, though in a handful of cases, its influence may be inferred. One of the most erratic of gunfighters, New Mexico's Clay Allison was discharged from the Confederate army for what his biographer Chuck Parsons calls "intense mood changes—moods ranging from mania to intense despondency." According to a doctor's opinion in a set of discharge papers Parsons uncovered, "emotional or physical excitement produces paroxysmal of a mixed character, partly Epileptic & partly Maniacal."[4]

If its influence on gunfighters' mental health must remain speculative, the war had a clear impact in the thousands of firearms soldiers brought home afterward. The government auctioned off 1.3 million surplus guns. Memoirs from the day are dotted with startled sightings of men openly wearing them.* In much of America, especially in frontier and rural areas, a revolver strapped to the waist became as accepted a part of a man's wardrobe as spectacles or a watch. And, sartorial implications aside, it forever changed the way Americans fought. The eye-gouging, ear-chomping brawls of the early frontier gave way to exchanges of gunfire lasting seconds. "Fist and skull fighting has played out here," a Missourian noted in 1866. "They now do that business in a more prompt manner."[5]

Nowhere was this more evident than in the South, where Reconstruction ushered in a decade of internecine warfare, much of it initiated against freed Blacks, occupying soldiers, and their allies. This was the dawn of the Ku Klux Klan, of night riders burning and pillaging, of race riots and deadly feuds. One study says murder rates in the postwar South were eighteen times higher than in the North. A 2022 study suggests attitudes that rose in the postwar South marked a turning point in how Americans viewed guns. Before the war, they had been seen as utilitarian, used mostly to kill varmints. Afterward, when the freeing of enslaved Blacks caused white Southerners to fear for their safety, they were increasingly viewed as items of self-defense and intimidation.[6] Some suggest gun use allowed defeated Southerners to reclaim a measure of their wounded masculinity.

Perhaps coincidentally—or perhaps not—the early postwar years are also the beginning of the era when those who killed could become celebrities. In fact, the first to become famous emerged in Southern and border states. The largest group by far rose from the wreckage of postwar Texas.

---

*This practice was not entirely new. As we've seen, it had been evident in areas of the South for decades, even before the introduction of revolvers. Travelers in Georgia remarked upon what's now called "open carry" as early as the 1700s. An easterner visiting frontier Arkansas observed much the same in 1837. Even so, the weight of anecdotal evidence suggests it became far more prevalent after the war.

ANTEBELLUM TEXAS MAY HAVE BEEN THE BIRTHPLACE OF THE SIX-shooter, its frontiers the site of countless battles with Mexicans and Native Americans, but it wasn't especially notorious for violence among civilians. There were duels, sure, especially in the Texas army and navy. A Mississippi-bred officer named Felix Huston nearly killed the future Confederate general Albert Sidney Johnston in one in 1837. Rivalries between incoming Anglos and established Tejanos led to violence across South Texas for years, including San Antonio's 1857 Cart War, in which Anglos killed seventy-five Latino teamsters in an effort to monopolize trade. And there was a feud or two, notably a nasty bit of business in far East Texas during the 1840s called the Regulator-Moderator War. A tangled affair involving land fraud and cattle theft, it claimed the lives of thirty-odd men via ambush, lynching, assassination, and an actual pitched battle or two, the largest said to have featured more than three hundred people.*

All this, though, paled before the tumult that arrived with the approach of war in 1860, when a wave of slave-revolt hysteria swept the South. In Texas, after unexplained fires burned the town squares in Dallas, Denton, and Henderson, citizens formed vigilance committees, hanged a series of Black people suspected of setting the fires, then tracked down and executed abolitionists charged with arranging the fires as part of a supposed plot to destroy Texas businesses. The Texas Troubles gave way to widespread strife during the war. Confederate militias such as the Home Guard, the Heel Flies, and the Haengebande, most no better than outlaw gangs, terrorized Union sympathizers in Central and especially North Texas. Thirty-seven Fredericksburg

---

*The book to read is Bill O'Neal's *War in East Texas: Regulators vs. Moderators.*

Unionists trying to flee to Mexico were run down and killed by troopers. Forty-two were hanged near Sherman in 1862.

And this was a mere prelude to what happened after Appomattox. In a matter of weeks, the state government melted away; the governor and his top men fled to Mexico. Mobs rampaged through the streets, looting stores and overrunning state commissaries and warehouses. The chaos reached its peak in June 1865 when a crowd ransacked the treasury in Austin, making off with more than half of the state's cash reserves.

In short order a federal military administration arrived and freed the slaves; more than two hundred thousand Black people were left to wander, unsure where to go, until troops herded many into refugee camps. It's difficult to overstate the deep-seated horror this provoked among Texans, a dismayingly proud populace whose victory over Mexico had introduced a strain of what's been called "Texas exceptionalism." Yet here they were, having lost no major battle on their own soil, a conquered people. The economy lay in ruins; without enslaved Black people, the only serious business, cotton, withered and died. Almost all money and savings were wiped out. And now blue-coated soldiers, many of them Black men, were suddenly everywhere. When Texans spied a soldier on the street, many glared and crossed to the far side, or spat at him.

The simmer soon reached a boil. What erupted in Texas was a kind of American dirty war, an orgy of murder, rape, and lynching, initially focused on Black people but soon morphing into attacks on anyone who might support them. This was more—much more—than Klansmen and night riders stringing up and burning former slaves, though Klan-like groups sprouted everywhere; by one count, thirty-nine Texas counties hosted some kind of terroristic organization focused on harassing and killing Black people.

A Cincinnati journalist who toured East Texas in 1869 reported:

You cannot pick up a paper in East Texas without reading of murder, assassinations, and robbery . . . and yet not a fourth part of the truth has been told: not one act in ten is reported. Go where you will, and you will hear of fresh murders and violence. . . . The civil authority is powerless.[7]

Reconstruction was violent across the South, but the violence in Texas, scholars agree, was on a different level. One academic study deems it "the most violent place in all the former Confederate states."[8] Another otherwise sober author says, "Texas literally ran with blood."[9]

If Missouri-born Jesse James is seen as the embodiment of the Reconstruction outlaw, the die-hard rebel who refused to stop fighting the war, Texas produced far more such figures than any other state.[*] Be warned: these folks are not a pretty bunch. While James robbed banks and trains, his Texas peers were stone killers who murdered Black people, soldiers, and "carpetbaggers," often without consequence. As loathsome as their aims, these men may be viewed among the first postwar gunfighters. In 1868 the state's military commander offered rewards for the three worst of them, each operating in chaotic North Texas. Unfolding in a remote area where news was reported spottily if at all, their stories are laden with as much folklore as fact.

Of the three, the best known is Cullen Baker, the "Swamp Fox of the Sulphur,"[†] a troubled drifter before the war, an avenging quasi-

---

[*]Outside Texas, there actually aren't that many postwar Southern outlaws of note. A list might include North Carolina's multiracial Lowry Gang, led by Henry Berry Lowry (sometimes Lowrie), a Lumbee Native American, which committed a series of murders and sensational robberies in and around Robeson County until Lowry disappeared in 1872; and Tennessee's Farrington brothers, onetime Civil War guerrillas who robbed two trains in 1871. Though not exclusively Southern, one might also mention the Reno Gang of southern Indiana, which robbed trains and banks in Missouri, Iowa, and Indiana; most of its members were arrested or lynched in 1868.

[†]"Sulphur" refers to the Sulphur River, which flows eastward 183 miles through far East Texas and empties into the Red River in Arkansas.

Klansman after, a drunk whose infamy beyond Texas rests on the bogus notion that he pioneered the fast-draw duel; Louis L'Amour titled his 1959 novel based on Baker *The First Fast Draw*. In his heyday, many in Texas cheered him on, as did early biographers. As one federal agent put it at the time, "There are many that admire and laud him as a brave man as 'he only kills yankees and n——rs.'"[10] Ordered to stop him, army officers and agents of the Freedmen's Bureau, the agency tasked with protecting Black Southerners, considered Baker a racist multiple murderer, an image his modern biographers endorse.*

Five nine, pale, with sandy hair and blue eyes, Baker was born in Tennessee, likely in 1835, and as a boy moved to Cass County on the Arkansas border. Poor, mean, and difficult, maybe suffering the effects of an early blow to the head, he had already killed at least two men in arguments by the time he joined a cavalry outfit at the outbreak of war. After he mustered out sick in 1863, legend has him leading a marauding guerrilla band in Arkansas, killing and burning out anyone suspected of disloyalty to the Southern cause; you can find entire books packed with this stuff. Alas, as Baker's modern biographers make clear, there's not a shred of evidence to back up the legend.

Whatever he did, Baker came home in 1865, tried and failed to establish a ferry business, then sank into something like a depression upon the death of his wife. Biographers suggest a downward spiral from there. When he proposed to his wife's sister, she instead married a schoolteacher named Thomas Orr, at which point the two men fell into a feud—not with guns at first, but with, of all things, threatening letters. The one a local paper printed suggests Baker was seriously unhinged.† When townspeople sided with Orr, Baker took revenge,

---

*The book to read is *Cullen Montgomery Baker: Reconstruction Desperado*, by Barry A. Crouch and Donaly E. Brice. It's one of the primary sources for this section.

†The letter is basically incomprehensible. The better missive comes from Thomas Orr, who in a subsequent book quoted Baker saying, "If I could sink this whole country into hell by

riding to several farms and gunning down, bizarrely, every dog in sight, eight or nine in all. For good measure he shot a goose.

Shunned, he withdrew to the woods, emerging to shoplift provisions, snarling at one merchant when caught, "Charge it to the Confederacy."[11] Baker's war with the government begins in June 1867, when he was accused of killing a Black farmer. When a federal agent named William G. Kirkman responded with a squad of blue-coated troops, Baker and a group of men ambushed them. Kirkman escaped, but Baker followed him into the town of Boston, initiating a wild shoot-out. Baker killed a soldier. Kirkman shot him in the arm.

Then Baker went on the warpath. Two months later, he led a gang that attacked four soldiers in the town of Jefferson, killing two. Then they ambushed three more, killing two. On Christmas Day 1867, after a long day of drinking, Baker and his men attacked an Arkansas farmhouse where a Black family was living alongside the farmer's white daughters, anathema to the likes of Baker. They opened fire on the house, killing two Black people, tried to burn the place but failed, then rode off, Baker with a bullet wound in his thigh.

Living in fear for their lives, federal agents in the region pleaded for troops to subdue Baker; they believed he was now leading a gang of seventy-five men. Their requests for troops were rarely granted, never in numbers and never for long; several agents quit as a result. Baker disappeared for the next six months, even as violence spiked across the area. It's speculated he was behind a rash of killings of soldiers and Black people in counties to the west, but there were so many Klan-adjacent groups at large by then it's impossible to know.

In October 1868 Agent Kirkman's fears were realized. Working after midnight in Boston, he heard a noise outside his office. When he

stamping upon the ground, I would stamp with all my power, and send it and every living creature, with myself, into the infernal regions" (Crouch and Brice, *Cullen Montgomery Baker*, p. 67).

stepped into the night air, he was struck by a fusillade of sixteen bullets and died instantly. Afterward, Baker told any number of locals he intended to wipe out every Union man in the area. It certainly appeared he was trying. He was believed to be behind almost every act of violence in the region for weeks, notably the massacre of seven Black people at a Cass County farm that same October, followed by the triple murder of a federal agent, a sheriff, and a local planter across the Arkansas border. The Arkansas governor declared martial law.

Matters came to a head in January 1869, when Baker and a pal began going farm to farm around the Arkansas town of Draw Bars looking for his rival, Thomas Orr. On the morning of January 6, when Baker appeared at his former father-in-law's farm, Orr slipped out the back and rounded up neighbors who agreed to confront Baker. When the group returned later that morning, they found him and his crony asleep in the yard, passed out drunk. Fifty years later a boy living at the farm claimed their whiskey had been spiked with strychnine. Maybe. Whatever they drank, the posse crept into the yard and shot Baker and his pal in the head as they slept. Neither, it's said, moved a muscle.*

Baker had gotten a little famous in his day—a clipping from a Kentucky paper was found on his body—but his legend blossomed as the posthumous darling of Southern apologists, who cranked out a new biography or history every decade or so.† Into the 1980s almost all of them praised Baker for protecting Southerners from evil Yankees. A 1939 book extolled Baker and the Klan for guarding families from

---

*Baker was a walking arsenal. On or around his dead body a shotgun, four revolvers, three derringers, and five or six pocketknives were found.

†There's often a yawning gap between the number of men a noted gunfighter is said to have killed and those that can be proven. Baker's "gap" has to be among the largest of all. His keenest biographers, Barry A. Crouch and Donaly E. Brice, put the total number of killings attributed to Baker at a startling seventy-six men, of whom fifty-four were Black. Crouch and Brice, while acknowledging that many killings were never reported in the press, estimate the number of Baker's likely killings at fifteen. Me: I suspect it's probably twice that.

"unscrupulous carpetbaggers, undesirable men and vicious negroes."[12] As late as 1992, a local essayist's piece on Baker decried the "hated Carpetbaggers" who arrived "like flies on fertilizer" and "slithered into political puppet power." Yikes.

Those who admired Cullen Baker for murdering "vicious negroes" would probably canonize his lesser-known but far more brazen contemporary Ben Bickerstaff, second of the wanted Reconstruction trio, a gang leader who not only survived multiple gun battles with federal troops but also once besieged an entire army garrison for weeks. Smallish, maybe five six, 135 pounds, Bickerstaff, like Baker, had been born in the South, in Mississippi, and as a boy moved to Titus County, Texas, west of Baker's Cass County. The Bickerstaffs, though, were successful farmers. Ben ended up owning a seven-hundred-acre farm.

He returned from the war determined to keep fighting and soon gathered the supporters to do it. Even discarding its folkloric elements, Bickerstaff's reign of terror across several Northeast Texas counties in 1866 and 1867 surpassed Baker's, an exhausting litany of robbery, murder, lynching, and torture aimed at Black people, Union sympathizers, and suspected traitors. When one or two brothers named Starr quit his band, it's said Bickerstaff tracked down and killed all five men in the family. His favorite tactic during a robbery, we're told, was burning a victim's feet until he produced his valuables.

The full story of Bickerstaff's campaign of terror is too long to relate here. Northeast Texas was shortly swarming with soldiers, and Bickerstaff relocated to Central Texas, where he bought a farm outside Waco. He was soon raiding across a swath of counties south of Dallas, murdering Black people and demanding extortion money from businesses. The turning point came on March 29, 1869, when Bickerstaff's gang hurrahed the courthouse in Cleburne, dispersing a grand jury poised to indict them. For weeks the rebels had been shooting up the nearby town of Alvarado, and a Cleburne judge warned Alvarado's leadership he was likely heading their way.

They were ready. Just before sunset on April 5, Bickerstaff and another rebel rode into town, apparently in need of flour. When he saw men scurrying into stores, he raised his hat and shouted, "Rats to your holes! Damn you all!" A moment later came the response, bullets exploding from a shoe store, followed by waves of buckshot from others. Shot in the face, Bickerstaff fell from his horse, as did his colleague. He raised himself onto an elbow and returned fire, but townsmen were pouring into the street, shooting. Bickerstaff gave up, dying two hours later, twenty-six bullet wounds in his body. His last words were "You have killed as brave a man as any in the South."

While Cullen Baker and Ben Bickerstaff were extreme cases, there were hundreds, probably thousands, of men like them in postwar Texas, aggrieved men, angry men, vengeful men, suspicious men, men comfortable with a gun, comfortable using it to settle a dispute and quick to take offense, especially when it involved a person of color or a "Union man." From their experiences a new kind of violent ethos began to emerge and, later, spread across much of the frontier. Early Western writers and academics, those active from the 1920s, heard about it from aging frontiersmen. They called it the Code of the West.

IF YOU THINK OF POSTWAR TEXAS MASCULINITY AS A BUBBLING CAUL-dron, its roux was the Southern honor code, but other ingredients were crucial as well: the tumult of war, the persistent and ongoing risk of Mexican and Native American raiders, the rigors and isolation of frontier life, the searing hatred of northern dominance, and the bloody chaos of Reconstruction. From this combustible brew rose a stridently martial way of experiencing the world, tribal, heavily armed, hypermasculine, hyperviolent, and acutely sensitive to slight. One foremost chronicler of early Texas, T. R. Fehrenbach, has described this "notorious Texas chauvinism" as the product of an "armed society with its almost theatrical codes and courtesies, its incipient feudalism, its touchy independence and determined self-reliance, its . . . individual self-importance, and its tribal territoriality."

One can see in postwar Texas a kind of template for what's been called the Code of the West, a set of behaviors that, for many on the frontier, came to define a man's honor and his duty to defend it. The idea of such a code, it should be said—the term itself was popularized in a 1934 Zane Grey novel—can be a polarizing subject. There are those who insist it never existed; no less an authority than *True West* magazine has said it originated with "the silver screen cowboys." It clearly didn't. A bit like Texas chili recipes, no two explanations of what the Code of the West actually was list the same ingredients.

All available evidence suggests that there are actually two distinct codes of behavior that have been called the Code of the West. One deals with cowboy etiquette, emphasizing honesty, courtesy, and horse care; it's sometimes called the Cowboy Code; you can find discussions of it sprinkled across the internet. The second Code of the West is a darker thing. This code is all about defending one's honor, emphasizing pride, courage, and the necessity never to back down from a fight and to avenge every insult, no matter how small. This version might be called the Gunfighter's Code. One of the better descriptions of this code comes from the western historian Robert M. Utley: "Among the young bravos who flocked to the frontier, the code governed male relationships. . . . Demanding personal courage and pride and reckless disregard of life, it commanded practitioners to avenge all insult and wrong, real or imagined; never to retreat before an aggressor; and to respond with any degree of violence, even death."[13]

Utley's views were shaped by the work of the mid-century Texas historian C. L. Sonnichsen, who was renowned for tracking down and debriefing aging veterans of the Old West and their children.* In his classic 1951 history of Texas feuds, *I'll Die Before I'll Run*, Sonnichsen explained the state's bloody rivalries as a product of the "code of honor, the most powerful set of compulsions in the Southerner's life." He goes on:

> In Texas the folk law of the frontier was reinforced by the unwritten laws of the South and produced a habit of self-redress more deeply ingrained, perhaps, than anywhere else in the country. . . . The Texan's code which demands immediate and active resentment of an insult has produced the story which says you can tell where a man is from by the way he acts when you call him a liar. . . . If he is from up around Ohio he waves his fists and shouts, "You're another." If he is from New England he spits on a grasshopper and remarks calmly, "Well you can't prove it . . ." If he is from Texas he shoots you.[14]

The behaviors that emerged in Texas were not simply an extension of the older code. There were clear differences. The western code eventually did away with the niceties of arranged contests; contrast a Southern-style duel, even the Hickok-Tutt showdown in 1865, to almost any of the gunfights in Billy the Kid's New Mexico fifteen years later. The Code of the West produced violence that was more feral, more instantaneous, and often more deadly.†

---

*Charles Leland Sonnichsen (1901–91) was a Harvard PhD who served as chairman of the English department at what is now the University of Texas at El Paso for twenty-seven years. During the 1930s and '40s he interviewed scores of onetime frontiersmen and, among his other writings, all but single-handedly exhumed the lost history of the state's great postwar feuds in a pair of books published in the 1950s. His work is superb.

†Two other influential historians of early Texas, T. R. Fehrenbach and the folklorist J. Frank Dobie, have cited the code's Texas origins in their work and agree it appears to be an outgrowth of the Southern code. Dobie, who probably interviewed almost as many frontiers-

––––––––

AMONG THE FIRST ARENAS WHERE ONE SEES THIS CODE IN PRACTICE was the series of bloody feuds that racked Texas after the war. The worst feuds in U.S. history took place in the Old West, and most of the worst occurred in Texas. According to one entirely unscientific internet list, nine of the fifteen deadliest feuds played out there between the 1840s and early 1900s, including the second- and third-deadliest of all. (The Hatfields and McCoys come in a disappointing fifth. Amateurs!)[15]

The first postwar feuds in Texas were rooted in passions stirred by the war. The Early–Hasley feud in Bell County, in Central Texas, was typical: a returning Confederate seeking revenge on a Union man who had roughed up his father. Once families got involved, there were a few shootings and a killing or two, but the notable thing is how it ended, in 1870. When two of the Union men, a judge and a doctor, fled the state, one was tracked down and killed in Arkansas, the other in Missouri. This is the kind of determined behavior Texans became known for. In San Antonio, after a rancher named Ben Franks was lynched for killing two cattle buyers during the war, his sons methodically tracked down and hanged several of those responsible, finding one in Louisiana.[16]

Probably the worst of these feuds, the Lee–Peacock affair in North Texas, by some ranks the second deadliest in U.S. history, revolved around one of Ben Bickerstaff's buddies, the third member of that

–––

men as anyone, was the more explicit. In his 1964 book, *Cow People*, he writes, "The six-shooter code of the West, especially in Texas, was derived mainly from the South." In his 1917 book, *West Is West*, the early Western writer Eugene Manlove Rhodes, a friend to several gunfighters, added his own twist to the western honor code with what he called the "code of the fighting man." It had six elements, including: never attack a rival at his table; never smile as you shoot a man; fight only upon "a fresh offense, openly given"; never shoot an unarmed man; and never stage an ambush.

wanted Reconstruction trio, a passionate rebel named Bob Lee, sometimes called the "Man Eater," who claimed to have killed forty-two men after the war. Raised near Sherman, an area with the state's largest concentration of Union sympathizers, Lee rode to war in 1861 a private and returned as "Captain" Lee, wearing a cavalier's plumed hat, his pockets stuffed with gold. Records suggest he was at best a sergeant, a likely war criminal who murdered hostages, rifled their bodies for valuables (hence the gold), and later deserted.*

Once home, Lee was aghast to find Union sympathizers feeding Black people. He refused to free some of his own slaves. Yet initially, Bob Lee was clearly also wronged. The feud began after local members of the Union League, a national pro-government organization, targeted him and his purported gold for extortion. Their leader, a big blond wheelwright named Lewis Peacock, led a group that "arrested" Lee, robbed him, and, it's said, forced him to sign a promissory note. Lee may have filed suit afterward. Whatever happened, by mid-1866 he had all but gone underground, gathering a force of twenty or thirty men and taking refuge in a tangled woods known as Wildcat Thicket.

He came out to drink, though, and during one such excursion to the town of Pilot Grove argued with a Union man, took the discussion outside, and was wounded in the ensuing gunfight. Lewis Peacock's men showed up at the doctor's home where Lee was being treated, and another gunfight broke out, a Lee sympathizer dead. The rebels took revenge, killing the killer. The Union men, for whatever reason, murdered the doctor.

Tit-for-tat killings raged for the next two years, that much is clear, during which Lee's rebels slowly gained the upper hand. Somewhere between thirty and sixty men seem to have died. And that's just counting

---

*The book to read is *Murder and Mayhem: The War of Reconstruction in Texas*, by James M. Smallwood, Barry A. Crouch, and Larry Peacock.

the two camps of white people. As Klansmen gathered to Lee's banner, dozens of Black people began showing up dead as well, including a pregnant woman who was mutilated; other Black women were gang-raped in front of their families. A Lee man killed a Black child because "he had his hands in his pockets and didn't stand at attention" when he rode past. Lee's pals bragged of the killings, one saying Black people needed to be "thinned out."[17] Lewis Peacock, meanwhile, survived repeated assassination attempts, ambushes in his fields, at his home, everywhere. Wounded at least twice, Peacock prevailed on the state to put a price on Lee's head.

The Unionists only regained the upper hand after the army sent a force of a thousand men into the area, killing, arresting, or scaring off many of Lee's men. Lee himself withdrew into Wildcat Thicket. Finally, in May 1869, a rebel who had been horsewhipped by one of Lee's sons agreed to guide soldiers into the thicket. By May 23, amid drenching rains, fifteen of them had taken up positions at every exit. Lee actually spent that night at his home, ignoring his family's pleas to escape to Mexico. At dawn, he took a rifle and four Colts and rode down a trail toward the thicket, bringing food to his men. Presently, a voice called out for his surrender. He went for a gun. The woods exploded. Lee fell dead, shot at least eight times.*

It should have ended there. It didn't. Violence continued into 1870 as Peacock's people and Union soldiers pursued Lee's lieutenants, chief among them three brothers surnamed Dixon and their half brother, a man named Dick Johnson. After several shoot-outs with soldiers, one Dixon was shot and killed in Central Texas; Peacock's men eventually got the other two. They didn't find Dick Johnson.

Around dawn on June 14, 1871, Lewis Peacock, reportedly dressed

---

*As late as the 1930s, it's said, members of the Lee family still displayed his bloodstained death shirt with pride.

in red long johns, stepped out his back door, apparently heading to the outhouse. He was met in the yard by Dick Johnson, two of Johnson's pals, and their three double-barreled shotguns. The first blasts killed him, though the trio then drew pistols and shot Peacock's fallen body repeatedly.* Hearing the shots, a weary neighbor, Martin Gentry, turned to his wife and said, "There, they've got Peacock, I figure."[18]

The deadliest feud in Texas history was finally over. As many as two hundred people, white and Black alike, lost their lives. Which is probably a good moment to introduce one of Bob Lee's young kinsmen, a troubled teenager who some believe may have been one of Peacock's assassins. He would go down as maybe the most prolific killer in Old West history, and certainly the purest incarnation of the violent Texas ethos that rose after the war. His name was John Wesley Hardin.

---

*None of Peacock's killers were brought to justice. Dick Johnson, it's said, moved to Missouri, where he lived into old age.

CHAPTER FOUR

The Killing Machine

John Wesley Hardin's Texas, 1868 to 1874

History has been kind, almost certainly too kind, to Wes Hardin, a homicidal Dixie diehard who shot his way across postwar Texas and as far afield as Kansas and Florida.* The spiritual heir to men like Cullen Baker, Hardin too was long lauded by Southern partisans as a crusading Last Confederate, taking the good fight to Yankees and carpetbaggers. Any number of modern storytellers have scrubbed the in-your-face racism from his story, rendering it unrecognizable. In the 1953 film *The Lawless Breed*, Rock Hudson played him as a farm boy who turned to violence after the death of his girl. Please. Johnny Cash issued not one but two songs about him; "Hardin Wouldn't Run" is the better. Bob Dylan named an entire album after him.† The title track terms Hardin "a friend to the poor" who "was never known to hurt an honest man," neither of which is remotely true.

---

*I'm calling Hardin "Wes" because that seems most common in the literature, but others have called him John, Johnnie, and even Jack. In letters his parents tended to go with John or John Wesley.

†In both the album and its title song, Dylan chose to misspell Hardin's name as "Harding."

69

The real Hardin was the archetype of the roving gunfighter, an American knight-errant, a troubled soldier in his own private war, Kwai Chang Caine with a Colt .44. But while David Carradine's *Kung Fu* character wandered the West righting wrongs and besting villains à la Galahad and Gawain, Hardin ranged the Texas backcountry shooting men in the face. The original rebel without a cause, he killed just about anyone who irked him in any way, from Black men he found disrespectful to white men who beat him at cards or jostled him in a crowd; most famously, he probably killed a man for snoring. He may have been the first "great" gunfighter, but it's also clear he was a maniac.

Gunfighter, in fact, is too tame a term for Hardin. He was literally a serial killer, though there's no suggestion he killed for sexual or emotional gratification. One biographer declares him a victim of narcissistic personality disorder, defined as a person with "a long-term pattern of exaggerated feelings of self-importance, an excessive craving for admiration, and struggles with empathy."[1] Me, I think he was more likely a psychopath, a person marked, as *The New York Times* has defined it, by "fearless dominance, meanness and impulsivity. The psychopath does what he or she wants, without anxiety, regret or regard for the suffering of others."[2]

How many did he kill? He claimed forty-two. Most chroniclers put the actual number closer to twenty-five. The most conservative estimate is probably eleven.[3] Perusing any account of his life, you're struck by how routine death becomes for him. There are years where Hardin literally shot a man every month on average; he was a killing *machine*. There is no one else in the Old West like him. He became famous in his day, at least in Texas, but never Billy the Kid famous. He never acquired a champion like Mark Twain nor any kind of national following. He rose in the dark years when Texas's few newspapers strained to keep up with the state's spiraling death toll.

Born in 1853 outside Bonham, just below the Oklahoma border, Hardin was weaned in the heart of North Texas feuding country and came of age at the fighting's zenith. His father was a Methodist preacher and his mother's people included any number of Bob Lee's guerrillas. He encountered violence early and often. When he was seven his family moved to Southeast Texas, where he witnessed a fight in which a man bled to death after his opponent severed his jugular vein with a bowie knife. From an early age, Hardin threatened deadly violence enough that others took him seriously. A boy named William Teagarden recalled how he protected him from an angry teacher. Hardin, he wrote, "stepped out into the aisle of the large school room, with open knife in his hands, and met the irate teacher coming with the hickory in hand to whip [me] unjustly, and told him he would kill him if struck [me] with that stick. The teacher retreated. . . . [E]verybody in the school room knew that John meant what he said."[4]

Maybe it was his father's Methodism, but as this story suggests, Hardin developed a keen sense of right and wrong at a young age, one that in time turned grotesque. In 1867, when he was thirteen or fourteen, he objected when a bully said something about a girl he favored. When words were exchanged, the bully approached Hardin's seat, struck him, and pulled a knife. Hardin pulled his own knife and stabbed the boy in the chest. By his own telling, the attack was ruled self-defense.

Then, in November 1868, came the moment that set Hardin on his path. Like Doc Holliday and several other Southern gunfighters, he killed a Black man. It started at a family gathering at an uncle's plantation, when Hardin and another boy were egged into wrestling a one-time slave named Maje Holshousen. In his autobiography, Hardin claimed Holshousen got mad when the boys threw him. Whatever happened, tempers flared. Holshousen was ordered home. The next day, Hardin found him walking on a wooded road. Obscenities were exchanged. Hardin drew his Colt and shot Holshousen five times. He died a few days later.

The killing was reported to Freedmen's Bureau agents, and suddenly, at fifteen, Hardin found himself a deeply resentful fugitive—"not from justice," he wrote later, "but from the injustice and misrule of the people who had subjugated the South."[5] This becomes the dominant theme of Hardin's adult life, his "oppression" at the hands of dastardly Yankees, Black people, the government, and especially the carpetbagger authorities of postwar Texas.

He hid for six weeks, he tells us, until hearing three soldiers were in the area searching for him. Armed with a shotgun, Hardin says, he ambushed them at a creek crossing, killing two and demanding the third, a Black man, "surrender in the name of the Southern Confederacy." When the soldier fired instead, wounding Hardin in the arm, Hardin killed him. "I had no mercy on men whom I knew only wanted to get my body to torture and kill," he explained.[*6]

So began his wanderings. Hardin was a fugitive, but given the patchy state of Texas law enforcement in those years—there was no statewide police agency before 1870—he was rarely in danger of arrest and lived more or less openly, occasionally using an alias. His father first spirited him to Navarro County, south of Dallas, where an aunt taught school in a log cabin. The family hoped a cousin might help him leave the state, but Hardin decided to stay, actually teaching for a time before signing on as a cowboy with an uncle's outfit. There he discovered the pastimes his coworkers favored, playing cards, betting on horses and cockfights— he was soon an inveterate gambler—and liquor, which became a problem. Many of Hardin's killings happened when he was drunk.

---

*Hardin's most thorough biographers, Chuck Parsons and Norman Wayne Brown, citing a local tradition in the area, tend to think this actually happened.

Hardin remained in Navarro County for a year, during which, among other misadventures, he claims that he joined a cousin—one of Bob Lee's last lieutenants—during several gunfights with soldiers in Central Texas. Whatever happened, his relatives suggested it was probably time to move on. This was in late 1869. At the time Hardin was still all of sixteen, five nine, maybe 140 pounds, dark hair, wide-set brown eyes, a cleft chin, and sometimes a patchy starter mustache. There's no sign he had any kind of plan beyond playing cards and drinking.

Over the next year he wandered Central Texas, killing at least three men we can confirm: a gambler he shot over a card game in Hill County, a man who jostled him at a circus in Union Hill, and a pimp who tried to rob him at a prostitute's home; when the man leaned over to pick up cash Hardin threw on the floor, he shot him. After a pair of long visits with relatives, he rode east after Christmas, into the East Texas pines, thinking he would visit family in Louisiana. Stopping in Longview, he was finally arrested, ironically, for a murder he did not commit, the barbershop killing of Waco's city marshal. The arresting officers turned out to be members of the new Texas State Police. Controlled by the Republican "carpetbagger" governor, its two hundred or so officers had little training, and a full 40 percent were Black, which earned them the hatred of racist Southerners such as Hardin, who referred to them as "the n——r police."

Tossed into jail in Marshall, Hardin discovered that a cellmate had managed to retain a loaded pistol, which he purchased. A cold front had blown in by the next evening, January 21, 1871, and snow lay on the ground as Hardin was marched out for the trip to Waco. The officers searched him, but he was wearing a heavy coat, and they failed to find the gun strapped beneath his left armpit. Roping Hardin to a pony, two officers and a local man led him out of town.

That night, they camped outside the town of Fairfield. When two of the men went in search of food for the horses, Hardin made his move, drawing his pistol and shooting the remaining officer, James Smalley, in the back. Hardin took a horse and rode into the night.

The murder of a state policeman, a crime one might expect to make statewide headlines, generated only one local news item and a single reprint. And no paper would report Hardin's next exploit, leading many to question whether it happened. If true, it probably occurred a few nights later. Without giving details, Hardin said he was arrested again, this time while asleep, by three "men calling themselves" policemen, whom he suspected were bounty hunters.

As Hardin told it, they camped one night outside Belton. They took turns watching him, but when one dozed off, Hardin grabbed one of their guns. In his book he called his captors Smith, Jones, and Davis. "I picked up Davis' shotgun and Jones' six-shooter," he wrote. "I fired at Smith's head and then turned the other barrel on Jones at once. As Davis began to arise and inquire what was the matter, I began to work on him with the six-shooter. He begged and hollered, but I kept on shooting until I was satisfied he was dead."[*7]

Whatever happened, seventeen-year-old Wes Hardin saw it was time to get out of Texas. He decided to flee to Mexico, where he could hide until the carpetbaggers were voted out of government and he could get what he saw as a fair trial. Visiting his father long enough to say goodbye, he rode south, then stopped in Gonzales County, east of San Antonio, to see a set of cousins, the Clements family. It was a fateful choice. The four Clements brothers, led by the intense, dark-eyed Mannen, would form the basis of the support network Hardin so obviously needed. They were cattlemen. Hardin became one too.

It was early 1871. That spring the Clements boys were planning to join a cattle drive to Kansas, and Hardin, likely in a bid to dodge the

---

[*]No news item described such a triple murder, but then the nearest newspaper office was a good seventy miles away. Six years later, Hardin boasted of the killings to a Dallas reporter; he had no reason to lie, and most biographers believe his claim.

state police, signed up. What ensued was one of the Old West's epic killing sprees, one that brought Hardin face-to-face with the country's most famous gunman. It's a story all its own, told in the next chapter. By the time Hardin returned to Texas, probably that August, he had killed at least seventeen men and conceivably as many as twenty-four. He had just turned eighteen.

BY THE FALL OF 1871, HARDIN WAS BACK IN GONZALES COUNTY, WHICH became what passed for his new home. Presumably he lived among the Clements family. By then he had probably begun dating a rancher's fifteen-year-old daughter named Jane Bowen; they would be married the following February. The state police were still looking for him. Hardin later told of several raids he managed to dodge.

Then, on October 19, two rookie officers surprised him inside a store in the hamlet of Smiley. As Hardin told it, the first hint of trouble was a voice behind him: "Throw up your hands!" He turned, hands raised, to see a Black officer named Green Paramore pointing a cocked pistol at him. The second officer remained seated on a mule outside. Hardin stayed cool. "Look out," he told Paramore, "you will let that pistol go off, and I don't want to be killed accidently."

Officer Paramore demanded his guns. Slowly Hardin offered them, butts forward. It was then, Hardin claimed, that he spun one of the guns in his hand and shot Paramore dead. It was a maneuver known as the road agent's spin, or the border roll. Outside, Officer John Lackey began firing into the store. Hardin's first shot struck him in the mouth. Bleeding badly but alive, Lackey galloped off. Hardin gave chase, but Lackey escaped—and survived—by diving into a lake.

The murder of a second state policeman is the moment Hardin begins to become a public figure in Texas. The governor put a bounty on his head. Hardin's name began to appear in newspapers. The police and press attention drove Hardin from Gonzales County for several months; he seems to have spent it zigzagging between relatives' homes, returning for his wedding. By May 1872, seven months after the Paramore killing, Hardin was likely breathing easier. Reunited with his wife, Jane—they appear to have had a house of sorts by this point—he raised a small herd of horses and hired two men to drive it to Louisiana. Hardin rode ahead to Hempstead, outside Houston, where between gambling binges he found still more trouble with the state police.

It was a stupid thing. Hardin saw a boy arguing with a state policeman named Sonny Speights in front of the courthouse. When the officer slapped the boy—Hardin's version—Hardin objected. Speights threatened to arrest him and drew his gun. Hardin whipped out a derringer, shot him in the shoulder, and rode away.

Two months later, visiting relatives in nearby Trinity County, he got into an argument with a man named Philip Sublett at a bowling alley; apparently, Sublett thought Hardin's skill at tenpins was somehow suspicious. Sublett stormed off, then returned with a shotgun, called Hardin a "goddamned son of a bitch," and shot him in the stomach. It was a serious wound. After chasing Sublett away, Hardin spent the next two months in a grueling recovery; it's said he nearly died. As rumors flew the state police were closing in, he was shuttled between the homes of friends and relatives across Southeast Texas.

There are multiple versions of how he came to surrender. By most accounts, fearing a state police that was fast developing a reputation for abusing and even murdering suspects in custody, Hardin got a message to one of his father's friends, an East Texas sheriff named Richard B. Reagan, who took him into custody, maybe after another gunfight, maybe not. However it happened, Hardin was brought to the town of Rusk, where he was tucked into a hotel bed. When he was well enough to travel, he was taken to Austin and put in the Travis County Jail.

His arrival prompted his first major headlines. One, reporting the claim Hardin had killed twenty-eight men in Texas and Kansas, termed him "the most bloody desperado we ever heard of."[8] A squad of state police ferried him back to Gonzales to face murder charges. Here, though, he had friends, including, it appears, the sheriff. Someone slipped him a saw, and on November 19, 1872, after using it on his cell door, Hardin disappeared into the bosom of family.

HARDIN'S ESCAPE FROM JAIL IS A TURNING POINT, WHEN HE BEGINS TO be drawn into the longest-running feud in Texas history, the Sutton–Taylor affair, centered in DeWitt County, ninety miles east of San Antonio. It has all the elements of a classic family feud, a byzantine contest pitting the Suttons and friends versus the Taylors and friends. It was also a struggle between two deeply unpleasant groups, the Taylor clan's sprawling Dixie crime ring, which demonized just about anyone in authority, and a murderous police apparatus peopled by Suttons.

Nobody can say exactly how it began. What we know is that in the first years after the war, the extended family of an old-timer named Creed Taylor formed a criminal network—"gang" is too limited a word here—that stole livestock, then intimidated and sometimes killed those who objected. Rabid Southern partisans like Hardin, the Taylors also murdered Black people, at least four we know of, and it was in here somewhere—maybe over a murder, maybe over a theft—that they ran up against a determined deputy named Bill Sutton.

Sutton killed his first Taylor, a horse thief, in Bastrop in March 1868. Some date the feud's onset to the following Christmas Eve, when a Taylor cousin, Buck Taylor, spied Sutton dozing in a saloon and whispered in his ear, "If the sun goes down on you in DeWitt County, we'll kill you." When Buck turned to leave, Sutton opened his eyes and supposedly said, "Why wait until sundown?" Sutton, a pal, and Taylor all drew and fired. Taylor ended up dead on the saloon floor.[9]

Afterward Bill Sutton brought in the roughest elements of the state police, led by one of Texas's fabled gunmen, a captain named Jack Helm. A big man, stocky, with black hair and eyes, Helm was a killer's killer, known in East Texas for organizing a lynching of five men. Together he and Sutton brought an unprecedented reign of terror upon the Taylors, arresting a string of them—twenty, by one credible account—and shooting each as they tried to "escape." Helm was fired as a result but was then elected sheriff of DeWitt County, where he remained active in the feud. His signature act of bloodshed came one night in 1872, when he led a group that enticed an elderly Taylor, Pitkin, from his home by ringing a cowbell, then shot him. He died not long after.

Pitkin's son, Jim Taylor, swore revenge. It was he, it appears, who helped recruit Hardin, whose cousins, the Clements brothers, were allied with the Taylors. We're told he initially tried to remain neutral, imagining the Suttons' allies in Austin could make his legal problems go away. That became difficult after December 1872, when his wife's brother, a moron named Brown Bowen, shot and killed a sleeping man he suspected was a Sutton spy. Bowen was slumped in the Gonzales jail three months later when Hardin rode up with twelve Taylor men and persuaded the jailer to free him. (By this point it's possible you've begun having questions about the professionalism of frontier jails. It gets worse.)

Probably suspecting what a game changer Hardin was, Jack Helm tried to lure him to the Sutton side, apparently promising to resolve his legal situation in a meeting that spring. Afterward, Helm waited for an answer. He got it when Hardin walked into a Cuero saloon on April 4, 1873, and shot one of Helm's deputies in the eye.

That did it. Helm gathered a posse and went hard after Hardin, but only succeeded in offending his wife, likely during an inopportune visit, which incited Hardin—not a wise move. Hardin responded by recruiting every available Taylor ally and mapping out a campaign to annihilate Helm and his three top lieutenants, including Bill Sutton. After two months of planning, the Taylors struck in midsummer. On July 16 they ambushed a column of Helm's men, killing two of the lieutenants, slicing one's throat in what appeared a coup de grâce.

Two days later, Hardin appeared for a meeting with Helm in the hamlet of Albuquerque to discuss a peace. Helm was at a blacksmith's shop, working on an invention, a "cotton worm destroyer." Inexplicably, he was armed only with a bowie knife. According to one version of what happened, another man, almost certainly Jim Taylor, walked up behind Helm as they talked, pulled a pistol, and fired. It misfired. Helm turned. A second shot struck him "in the breast." Helm lunged at Taylor. They grappled. Hardin pulled a shotgun and shot Helm in the arm. Badly wounded, Helm staggered into the blacksmith shop. Taylor fired several more shots, finishing him off.

The Suttons sued for peace. On August 12, 1873, eighty-seven men signed a treaty declaring the feud at an end. It wasn't. Jim Taylor still wanted revenge against Bill Sutton for the death of his father. Yet Sutton seemed unkillable. The Taylors had already tried at least three times, twice shooting his horse instead; the third time, Jim Taylor ambushed him in a Cuero saloon but managed only to wound him.

That winter, Hardin fielded a tip. Sutton, he learned, was leaving on a business trip from the port of Indianola. They needed his travel schedule, but Hardin and the Taylors were too well known to do the snooping. Instead, they sent for Hardin's brother Joe, an attorney specializing in real estate swindles, in hopes he could strike up a conversation with Sutton, perhaps in a saloon. This he apparently did, because on March 11, 1874, Jim Taylor and a cousin were waiting at the ticket booth when Sutton, his pregnant wife, Laura, and a young man named Gabriel Slaughter went to board a steamer at Indianola.

Sutton saw the two men as they drew. He gasped. "Hell is in the door, Gabe," he said to Slaughter. "Yonder comes Jim Taylor."[10]

The Taylors opened fire. Both Sutton and Slaughter fell dead. Laura Sutton was left wailing. It was a triumphant moment for the Taylors, a crushing blow for the Suttons. A reward now on his head, Jim Taylor joined Hardin in the Central Texas town of Comanche, where they were assembling a herd to drive north.* There they had a joyful reunion with almost all of Hardin's family.

On May 26, 1874, Hardin's twenty-first birthday, everyone celebrated a day at the horse races. Hardin won heavily, and that evening went from bar to bar, drinking heavily too, at one point throwing out twenty gold pieces to buy the house a round. By night's end, Hardin was deeply drunk, and as he waited outside the Jack Wright Saloon with friends and family, a pair of easygoing deputies sidled up. One suggested he head to bed. But Hardin wasn't quite ready. "Let us go in and get a cigar," he announced, "then we will go home."[11]

As they headed inside, one of the deputies said, "Here comes that damned Brown County sheriff."

It was actually a deputy from that neighboring county, a twenty-five-year-old named Charles Webb. No one ever figured out why Webb was in Comanche that night. Some said a girl, others the races. Hardin and his partisans always insisted he came to arrest Hardin and Jim Taylor, but in all likelihood their encounter was accidental.

---

*By the time the newly re-formed Texas Rangers swooped in and stomped out the feud's final embers in 1877, it's estimated between forty-five and sixty men had died. Only a few faced justice. One was Jim Taylor's cousin Bill, arrested for the killings in Indianola. He was eventually convicted of murder, but the conviction was overturned.

As Webb, wearing two pistols, his hands clasped behind him, approached the group, Hardin suddenly asked if he had papers for his arrest. Webb, probably puzzled, said no, he didn't know Hardin.

"Well," Hardin announced, clearly trying to provoke him, "I have been informed that the sheriff of Brown County has said that Sheriff Karnes [*sic*] of this county was no sheriff or he would not allow me to stay around Comanche with my murdering pals."[12] For a man wanted in multiple jurisdictions, this was not the savviest thing to say.

One of the local deputies, hoping to avoid trouble, introduced the two men. Hardin, suspicious, asked what Webb was holding behind his back. Webb produced a cigar. At that, Hardin seemed to soften, asking Webb into the bar for a drink. "Certainly," Webb said.

But the moment Hardin turned to enter the bar, one of his cousins shouted, "Look out!" Hardin swiveled. Webb was pulling a pistol. Hardin jumped to one side and drew as well. Webb fired, the bullet striking Hardin in the side. Hardin's hit Webb in the face, killing him. When the sheriff appeared, the wounded Hardin and his group turned over their guns.

This wasn't to be just another killing without consequence. Charles Webb had briefly served as a Texas Ranger, and that year the Rangers, after being disbanded before the war, were being revived to replace the troubled Texas State Police. They were forging something new on the western frontier, a reputation for professional, and deadly, efficiency. When a squad of Rangers appeared in Comanche, Hardin for once did the sensible thing. He vanished.

HARDIN'S KILLING OF CHARLES WEBB WAS BUT A SINGLE DATA POINT in the sprawling algebra of Texas violence during the 1870s, a period that saw a second round of furious feuds erupt in a belt of counties mostly north of Austin. These conflicts display the final crucial ingredient to

the developing Code of the West. They were less about wartime griev-
ances than about a booming new business, one that would transform
much of the state and, in time, the western frontier: cattle.

Forget those nice cows you see grazing by the interstate. This was
something entirely different, open-range cattle ranching, millions of
cattle roaming free across millions of acres, originally in South Texas—
and only in Texas. And not just any cattle but nasty, untamed Texas
longhorns, many practically the size and temperament of a World War
I tank, with slashing horns that could spread six feet or more. If by
chance you were out walking in the brush and stumbled on one, you
ran. Longhorns, whether raised or lassoed off the range, were a business that during the first years after the Civil War forever changed
Texas commerce and culture. The animals, a Spanish breed that came
to the New World on Columbus's second voyage in 1493, had been a
staple of Spanish and Mexican ranches below San Antonio for a century or more, until the Texas revolt, when the owners either fled or were
chased into Mexico, at which point the incoming Anglos took over.

That's half the story. While Spanish terms and techniques—from
the lariat to the rodeo—remained in use, the longhorn phenomenon
was also a product of the bustling open-range cattle business of the
Old South. American cattle ranching, like vigilantism, first rose in
South Carolina during the 1700s. It spread from the coast near Charleston to the Gulf Coast and then west into Texas, where American-bred
cattle were first merged into herds of longhorns. By the 1700s, there
were a few thousand or so in the South Texas scrub, though most were
run off by Native Americans during the chaos of the 1810s. The Southern cattlemen who began immigrating to Texas in the 1820s and '30s
rebooted the trade. What's important here are the traditions the
Southerners introduced, those descended from herding societies from
the British Isles to Asia. Because they roamed free, open-range cattle
were uniquely susceptible to thieves, aka cattle rustlers. As we've seen,

herding societies through the ages were notorious for the draconian methods they used to deter theft.

Texas cattlemen proved zealots to the cause. During the 1870s the killing of livestock thieves became epidemic, especially as ranchers spread north into Central Texas, tempting people who hadn't yet learned not to mess with them. Any number of counties between San Antonio and Fort Worth saw incidents of lynching skyrocket. Most were done quietly, a body found swinging from a tree limb on a Sunday morning. There were hundreds like that. Especially motivated vigilantes, though, sometimes wanted to send a louder message. In 1877 masked men seized four suspected rustlers at a dance at McDade, east of Austin, and hanged them from a single limb. Night riders in Shackelford County, west of Fort Worth, went on an epic killing spree, lynching more than twenty, including seven at once. "Shall horse thieves rule the country?" a note pinned to one read. "He will have company soon."[13] Out-of-state newspapers were aghast. One in Cincinnati noted, "The trees in Texas sometimes bear other fruit than horse thieves."[14]

An early poster boy of tetchy Central Texas cattlemen was Isom Prentice "Print" Olive. A small, slender man, with what appears to be a monster comb-over and a bushy black goatee, Olive was a Confederate veteran who with his three brothers ran a large cattle operation in Williamson County, north of Austin. ALL CATTLE AND HORSE THIEVES PAY ATTENTION, read his signs. ANYONE RIDING AN OLIVE HORSE OR DRIVING AN OLIVE COW WILL BE SHOT ON SIGHT.

Maybe he wasn't clear. Because animals soon began disappearing, replaced by dead bodies. Print and his brothers had been accused of murdering rustlers a time or two before; the cases had been dismissed. But now, in 1876, at least twelve bodies were found on and around the Olive spread, including two men killed in an unusually gruesome way, an old Spanish method of torture called "death of the skins." They had been wrapped in fresh cowhide while alive and left in the sun, where the hides shrank, squeezing them to death.

The local rustling chapter was not amused. A gang of fifteen or so attacked the Olive ranch, riddling Print's brother Jay with twenty-two bullets, burning the main house, and leaving at least one other man dead. Print was eventually put on trial for murder and acquitted.

As the Olive incident shows, when rustlers got organized and fought back, a full-blown feud could break out. During the 1870s as many as a half dozen of these nasty spats flared across Central Texas at any given time. Two give you the flavor, the first in Lampasas, eighty miles north of Austin, home to the Horrell clan, five blond brothers— Sam, Mart, Tom, Ben, and Merritt—who proved unusually volatile even by Texas standards.* The Horrells were small-time ranchers, not averse to sampling their neighbors' beef. The trouble began in January 1873, when one of their pals killed the sheriff and the Horrells blocked a posse's pursuit.

Sent to restore order, a squad of eight state policemen rode into Lampasas on March 14. Captain Thomas Williams, a Black man, noticed a cowboy wearing a pistol in front of a saloon. A dozen cowboys were lounging inside, including several of the Horrells. All we know for sure is that when Williams attempted to disarm this gent, all hell broke loose. When the smoke cleared, three policemen were dead.

Mart Horrell was wounded and, with others, was arrested and taken to the jail in Georgetown, from which he promptly escaped. Rather than face more arrests, the entire Horrell clan lit out for New Mexico, where they triggered a conflict known as the Horrell War, leading to the death of one brother and a dozen Latinos. By 1877 they were back in Lampasas, where their penchant for rustling got them

---

*Originally from Arkansas, the Horrells seemed to have known violence from an early age. Their father had been killed by Native Americans, a brother had been killed by another cowboy in a dispute over pay, and another brother had died during the war.

into still more trouble, this time with the wrong man, a long, lean rancher named John Pinckney Calhoun "Pink" Higgins.

Print Olive would've adored Pink Higgins. There's a story often told of him, how after stumbling upon a rustler butchering one of his steers, he shot him, stuffed his body into the disemboweled animal, then rode into town to tell the sheriff he should come see a miracle, a cow giving birth to a man. (You probably had to be there.)

Somehow Higgins became irked with Merritt Horrell. Later some said Merritt was paying a tad too much attention to Pink's wife, but most accounts agreed this was about rustling. On a frigid Saturday, January 20, 1877, Higgins walked into a downtown saloon, where Horrell was standing by a fire, spoke his name, and without another word raised his Winchester and fired a bullet into his chest, another as he fell. And walked out. The Horrells formed posses to find him but couldn't. Mart and Tom Horrell rode into an ambush instead. Both were badly wounded. Higgins ended up surrendering to the Rangers, posted bond, and was released.

The Rangers managed to keep the peace, at least until June 7. That morning the last three Horrells and several pals were standing in the Lampasas square when they spotted Higgins and three friends riding in; everyone involved, it turns out, had business at the courthouse. The Horrell group rushed to cover and opened fire. Higgins and one of his men wheeled away and left to get reinforcements, leaving Pink's beefy wingman, Bill Wren, and a cowboy named Bob Mitchell to face the Horrells alone. Wren was hit in the hip. Mitchell helped him into a store, where they were joined by Mitchell's brother Frank, who stepped outside to see what was what. When Mart Horrell and a man named Jim Buck Miller raced around an alley trying to outflank them, Frank shot Miller in the chest; he would die the next day. Return fire struck Mitchell, who staggered back into the store and died.

When Higgins and a dozen gunmen rode in, the Horrells "forted up" inside a stone building. After an hour or two of desultory sniping, it ended. The Rangers rode in a few days later, surrounded the Horrell ranch, took everyone into custody, and by August had forced both sides to sign a peace treaty in which they proclaimed the feud, in a nice turn of phrase, "a by gone thing."*

Probably the strangest cattle feud was Mason County's Hoodoo War, named after the local slang for masked vigilantes. By 1874 rustling there was so out of control the county judge appealed in vain to the governor for troops. The serious trouble began in February 1875 when a mob stormed the jail, removed five accused rustlers, and badly botched their hanging: two of the prisoners died, one survived, one ran off, and the last they lost patience with and just up and shot. The tipping point, though, was the arrest of a suspected rustler named Tim Williamson. En route to the jail, twelve masked men materialized, shooed off the sheriff, and shot him dead.†

Then things got weird. One of Williamson's friends, a cowboy and onetime Ranger named Scott Cooley, arrived in town, vowing to avenge his murder. Cooley is one of the Old West's scarier figures. He was certainly one of the angriest. Raised on the North Texas Comanche frontier at its worst, he had grown up devoting as much time and energy to fighting, killing, and scalping Native Americans as my kids did to Nintendo. In Mason County he gathered a rough crew—its

---

*Not a soul did serious time for any of this. The following year, Tom and Mart Horrell were accused of murder in Bosque County. A mob broke into the jail and shot them repeatedly through the bars of their cell. The last Horrell, Sam, wisely moved to Oregon. He died in 1936. Pink Higgins was acquitted of the murder of Merritt Horrell and went on to a long career as one of the state's storied gunmen. Upon his death in 1913 from a heart attack at the age of sixty-two, he was credited with killing fourteen men in various gunfights over the years.

†I don't want it to appear like I'm picking on Texas Tech—again, lovely people—but the university's mascot is a masked rider on a black horse who gallops around football stadiums yelling "Guns Up!" I'm not saying there was some intention here to invoke Texas lynch mobs of yore, but, I mean, if it walks like a vigilante . . .

best-known member the future Tombstone rowdy Johnny Ringo—assembled a hit list, and in August 1875 commenced killing people.

His first victim, a deputy sheriff named John Wohrle, he found working down a well. They talked for several minutes about something, the weather maybe. As Wohrle climbed out, Cooley suddenly asked, according to a newspaper account, "Why did you kill Williamson?"

"Because I had to," Wohrle replied.

"For the same reason, I am killing you," Cooley said, at which point he shot Wohrle in the back of the head. He then proceeded to shoot the corpse six times, stab it four more, and scalp it.

A month later Cooley shot and killed a gent named Jim Cheyney in his kitchen. At breakfast afterward, he told a man to inform the restaurant's owner "there is some fresh meat up the creek."[15] Four days later they ambushed three more in town, in broad daylight, killing one. After a wild gunfight, everyone rode off, leaving the town shocked. "The terror that gripped Mason in the fall of 1875," one historian notes, "is almost impossible to comprehend."[16]

The Rangers were sent in but never found Cooley, possibly because several of them were his friends. The bodies, meanwhile, kept piling up, nine or ten in the next few months. The killings only ended, most of them anyway, with Cooley's mysterious death outside Fredericksburg in June 1876. He had eaten a meal and bought a bottle of whiskey, ridden out of town, and stopped at a farmer's house, where he dismounted, lay down, and just died. Some papers said it was "brain fever," others suggested poison. To this day no one knows.

ALL THIS—THE LYNCHING, THE FEUDS, THE SEEMINGLY ENDLESS murders—proved to many that Texas cattlemen of the 1870s were living by their own rules, a new frontier code of conduct. As Walter

Prescott Webb noted in his pioneering 1931 study, *The Great Plains*, "The cattle kingdom worked out its own means and methods of utilization; it formulated its own law, called the code of the West, and did it largely upon extra-legal grounds."[17]

The violence this brought to Texas was of historic, and underappreciated, proportions. How bad was it? In a 1975 survey of extrajudicial violence in America, the University of Oregon's Richard Maxwell Brown crunched the numbers on killings astride an axis from Dallas to San Antonio. Brown judged postwar Central Texas the *single most violent region in American history*. Worse than Klan-plagued Mississippi, worse than Gold Rush California. "It was a land without surcease from killing," he wrote, marked by "an ethic of individual violent self-defense and self-redress."[18]

All of which might have gone down as merely local history, except the violence in Texas didn't remain there. In the early 1870s, as cattlemen sought new markets and grazing lands, it began exploding outward, west into New Mexico but also north, especially to the state where hundreds of cowboys soon began driving their herds:

Kansas.

CHAPTER FIVE

Gunfighters of the Cattle Kingdom

Kansas, 1871

Texas shot not only a business but a form of culture across the American West.

—T. R. FEHRENBACH[1]

An outsize portion of the marquee gunfighter violence in the Old West was spawned by the explosive growth of the frontier's first great business, the rambunctious Texas cattle trade, which in a scant fifteen years rose from the coastal scrub below San Antonio to overspread the Great Plains. It expanded west as well, all but colonizing vast swaths of Arizona and New Mexico, before pushing into the Mountain West, spreading herds across Montana and Wyoming.

It is hard to overstate the level of mayhem that cattle—and the Texans who came with it—brought to the already violent culture of the western frontier. This was a business where from the 1870s deep into the 1890s, robbery and murder—and worse—could seem almost commonplace, where thieves real and imagined were routinely dispatched with a bullet or a noose far from any courtroom, where rowdy workers—cowboys—regularly shot up flyblown towns, where millionaire ranchers deployed battalions of gunmen and silent assassins against rustlers, sheepherders, and homesteaders. Without the Texas cattle business, it's doubtful the gunfighter legend ever takes flight.

This Texas diaspora triggered an epochal shift, a commercial and cultural big bang that transformed much of the West. As Native American tribes were forced from their homelands, Texans spread longhorn herds into vacated lands as far afield as Utah, the Dakotas, Colorado, and Wyoming. The author of a ranching history in the latter two entitled his chapter on its origins "The Texas Invasion."[2] In some places the Texas footprint was fleeting, in others deep and lasting. Texas families still own ranches today that they founded in Montana and North Dakota in the 1880s. Some still call the southeastern quarter of New Mexico "Little Texas." And it happened with breathtaking speed. The historian Terry G. Jordan has called it "one of the most rapid episodes of frontier advance in the Euroamerican occupation of the continent."[3]

And wherever Texas longhorns went, whether it was a herd driven to railheads in Kansas or grazing one of the new ranches straddling the Continental Divide, a new American archetype, the Texas cowboy, arrived as well. The phrase "Texas cowboy," in fact, was redundant for the longest time; in those early years, there was no other kind. Clear your mind of Gene Autry and Audie Murphy and Rock Hudson and dreamy celluloid buckaroos. Until their reputations were rehabilitated by Buffalo Bill Cody and Hollywood Westerns, the Texas cowboys of the 1870s were viewed—with reason—as menacing figures, quick to offend, quick on the trigger, a kind of American Cossack.

Some were veterans of the Texas feuds. A veteran Shackelford County feudist named John Selman ended up wreaking havoc in New Mexico before gaining a measure of immortality by killing maybe the deadliest gunfighter of all, as we'll see. Print Olive would end up in Nebraska, where he fell into a feud with two neighboring ranchers. When his brother was shot and killed, Print hunted down the two men responsible and hanged them before setting their bodies on fire, earning him the nickname "Man Burner."*

Most, though, especially the cowboys who drove herds north, were just spirited country boys raised in the violence-plagued areas of Central and South Texas, sometimes away from home for the first time, looking to blow off steam after weeks or even months managing cattle in the wilderness, often with little experience of hard alcohol or women. Many were eager to prove their manhood, which often involved a gun. You can see it in the photographs they posed for, holding revolvers, knives, Winchesters, and whiskey bottles. The Texans became renowned for shooting a man for the smallest infraction: cutting in on a dance, name-calling, bumping shoulders, being refused a drink. One, the memoirist Teddy Abbott, wrote of "itching to shoot somebody in order to prove himself."[4] In one way, the Texas cowboy's dealings with sedentary Americans can be viewed as a classic clash of cultures, the unruly plainsman versus the mannered townsman, a paradigm that rings through history.

Among the first and most famous points of contact came on the plains of Kansas, where a series of dusty towns sprang up to buy and ship Texas cattle while entertaining the boisterous cowboys who risked their lives driving them north. The first venue where Texas-style violence was put on display for startled out-of-state newspapermen, the Kansas cow towns would go down as the Madison Square Garden of the Gunfighter Era, the single place any number of marquee gunmen, from Wes Hardin to Wyatt Earp, not to mention less-remembered shootists such as Clay Allison and Luke Short, made their marks. On one side of nearly every marquee gunfight was a Texan.

All this came about to solve a peculiar postwar problem: stranded

---

*Olive is one of the more fascinating footnote characters of the Old West. I could write another book just about him. He ultimately went broke. He was shot and killed in a Colorado saloon in 1886.

cows. Before the war, Texas dominated the beef cattle business; it really had no serious challenger. There had been maybe 1.2 million cows there in 1860. Most were sold locally, some herded into neighboring states. The war froze the trade as if in amber; Texas markets shut down, and while a few herds were pushed east to sell to Confederate quartermasters, the business atrophied. So the longhorns of Texas did what cattle did; they ate, bred, and multiplied. By 1865 there were 5 million of them—one of every four beeves in the country—roaming South Texas waiting to be roped and sold.

Everyone knew what had to be done. With the South in ruins, there was little demand for beef in New Orleans and Shreveport. A few herds had been driven to Denver and California before the war, but now cattlemen began looking north. In 1866 a handful tried to reach the railroads in Missouri but were turned back, sometimes at the point of a gun. There were widespread rumors longhorns carried a deadly tick fever. There were actually laws banning them from several states.

The stockyards in Chicago opened that year, and northern buyers wanted Texas cattle almost as badly as Texans wanted to sell them. As the railroad companies thrust west onto the plains, they urged the state of Kansas to do something. In early 1867 the legislature went along, passing a law allowing Texas cattle to enter the state, where they could be loaded onto railcars and shipped to Chicago. The opening of Kansas inaugurated the era of the great cattle trails north from South and Central Texas, not only the Chisholm Trail into Kansas itself but also the Goodnight–Loving Trail through West Texas and New Mexico to Denver, the Texas Trail on to western Nebraska, and a plethora of lesser paths.

It was the dawn of a new age not only in business but also in culture and behavior. The cattle trails functioned as superhighways through which the hyperviolent ethos of postwar Texas began to flow across the frontier. "These routes through central Texas," Richard

Maxwell Brown wrote in 1975 of cattle trails, "are among the most significant lines of cultural diffusion in our frontier history. By them knowledge of the range-cattle industry was sent outward from Texas. Exported to the north and west along with the techniques of the ranching livelihood was the violent subculture of . . . Texas."[5]

A common way to explain the violence Texans brought north was as a product of Civil War antagonisms, and that was no doubt a part of it. As the cowboy memoirist Teddy Abbott put it: "Those early-day Texans was full of that stuff. . . . They were bitter. That was how a lot of them got killed, because they were filled full of the old dope about the war and they wouldn't let an abolitionist arrest them. The marshals in those cow towns on the trail were usually Northern men, and the Southerners wouldn't go back to Texas and hear people say: 'He's a hell of a fellow. He let a Yankee lock him up.'"[6] That was part of it, certainly, but the deeper cause, one suspects, was the old Southern honor codes, inflamed by the war certainly, but stirred to a particular boil in Texas.

Among the people who made it happen was a sharp-eyed Illinois cattle trader named Joseph G. McCoy, who went looking for a spot where he could welcome and purchase all those cattle and found it in a collection of mud huts on empty land in the middle of Kansas. They were calling it Abilene. Just weeks after the Kansas law passed, McCoy bought 250 acres on the edge of town and opened holding pens. He sent men south to tell Texas trail bosses already bound for uncertain welcomes in Missouri that it was safe to come to Abilene, and in short order they began to arrive, a trickle at first. But McCoy's designs were grand. When the first herds rumbled into the fields around town in the spring of 1868, the Texans were amazed to find McCoy had built a three-story hotel, the Drover's Cottage.

More Texans arrived that summer, even more the next, and by 1870 Abilene had become a classic boomtown, albeit a unique one, a kind of

Texas-themed adult amusement park lined with raucous bars, dance halls, and gambling dens designed to make men from Belton and Victoria and Bastrop feel at home. The main drag was Texas Street, its centerpiece tavern the luxurious Alamo, whose forty-foot veranda around the corner on Cedar Street dwarfed bars like the Longhorn and the Lone Star. "Abilene . . . might be called a Texan town," a reporter marveled, "so much of the Texan being apparent on the surface."[7]

The permanent population of maybe five hundred mushroomed to seven thousand or more once the herds began arriving each spring, Texans mostly, but also the prostitutes and gamblers who came to serve them. In those first few seasons, Abilene was calm by boomtown standards, thanks in part to a stern city marshal, a man named Tom Smith. Smith preferred using his fists to his Colt, and after making an example of several uppity cowboys had little trouble controlling the streets. Ironically, his death in 1870 came not at the hands of a Texan but a homesteader who shot him as he made a routine arrest.

Which generated little notice outside Abilene. A nobody sheriff killed in nowheresville. Ho-hum. But then suddenly, in the spring of 1871, a series of events began that would transform into American legend what by all rights should have been a few more meaningless killings in the exact same corner of rural Kansas. What changed? What changed was the man town fathers hired as Abilene's new marshal—a man who happened to be the most famous gunfighter in America. In fact, the only gunfighter most Americans had ever heard of: Wild Bill Hickok.

WHAT HISTORIANS AND HIS BIOGRAPHERS HAVE PROVEN BUT NEVER come out and actually say is this: James Butler Hickok was a titanic fraud, the creation of his own propaganda and a series of credulous journalists. The big lie he embraced is the main reason you know his name. It made him the first celebrity gunfighter. Before anyone had ever heard of Wyatt Earp or Billy the Kid or Wes Hardin, Hickok was the fake patient zero of the gunfighter myth, the man who invented the role, an itinerant figure who lived a nineteenth-century version of reality TV, known to all and no one at the same time.

Yet here's the striking thing about Hickok: over time he became that rarest of frauds, one who grew into the image he built, who by hard work and circumstance actually became a lawman and gunfighter of note—until he shot the wrong man and spiraled into a boozy twilight existence that ended in a manner that buoyed all those who ever doubted him.

He was born a farmer's son in Illinois in 1837, and his early years, like Hardin's, can be viewed only as flashes in the prewar darkness. Tall and thin, with reddish hair he wore to his shoulders and that ski jump of a nose, by all accounts he was a skilled marksman even as a boy. All his life, he took regular target practice; there is no denying his skill. At eighteen, after a fight in which he mistakenly believed he drowned another teen when both fell into a canal, he fled to Kansas, where he may or may not have been bodyguard to a leading Unionist during the troubles there, briefly served as constable of the town of Monticello, probably did some farming, and definitely took a job driving wagons to Santa Fe until he was mauled by a bear.

As a gunfighter, Hickok's origin story has been told as often as Spider-Man's. It centers on a shooting, naturally, one of the more combed through in western history, during which Hickok, in a maze of accounts offered through the years, killed either one, two, three, or ten men. His biographers Joseph G. Rosa and Tom Clavin agree that the answer is technically one, although three men died. Much of the confusion originated with Hickok himself, who all his life amused himself regaling strangers with inflated versions of his exploits.

It happened on July 12, 1861, at the Rock Creek stagecoach station in southeast Nebraska, where the twenty-four-year-old Hickok had been sent to convalesce following the bear mauling. He was an assistant stock tender, meaning he looked after the horses. His superintendent, a man named Horace Wellman, had gotten into a row with the station's former owner, a bellicose Southerner named David McCanles. McCanles wanted money the company owed him, and that day he showed up outside Wellman's ranch house with a shotgun and loudly demanded it. With him was his twelve-year-old son and a pair of slouching henchmen.

At the door, McCanles berated Wellman, and not for the first time. When Wellman tired of this, he stepped aside and allowed McCanles to berate Mrs. Wellman. When Mrs. Wellman tired of it, Hickok loomed in the doorway. He and McCanles did not get along. Legend has it they had quarreled over a woman. Maybe. McCanles was cheering on the Confederacy; Hickok came from a family of abolitionists. Also, we have a clear sense that McCanles was, in modern parlance, an asshole. It was he, we're told, who first called Hickok "Duck Bill."

Standing there on the porch, McCanles spat that this was none of Hickok's business. "Perhaps 'tis" was Hickok's laconic reply, by one account I'd like to believe. "Or 'tain't."

Hickok, wearing a Colt, stepped back inside. McCanles followed and again berated poor Wellman. At one point, when McCanles made some kind of gesture with his shotgun, a shot rang out. McCanles fell dead, a bullet through the heart. His son fell to his side in tears.

When one of the henchmen outside, James Wood, burst into the house, Hickok shot him too. Badly wounded, Wood staggered out and collapsed in the yard. Hickok then shot the third man, James Gordon, who managed to limp off into a thicket. Mrs. Wellman, clearly no shrinking violet, emerged from her home and dispatched Mr. Wood with a garden hoe. Mr. Gordon was concluded with a shotgun.

Three men dead, a boy orphaned. Was any of this justified? We honestly don't know. A prosecutor reviewed the matter, it's said, but dropped it when the boy was ruled too young to testify. The incident made a single newspaper, then was utterly forgotten, until Hickok achieved national fame and it came to be viewed as kind of his Rosebud moment, pored over by generations of Western writers.

For the moment, he remained a nobody. He spent the war years as a wagon master and then a prized scout for Union outfits in Missouri and Kansas, emerging at war's end in 1865 with a wealth of colorful tales of spying and intrigue. Then, following the shoot-out with Davis Tutt in Springfield and a drubbing in his attempt to be elected town marshal, Hickok was approached by a writer named George Ward Nichols, a former member of General William Tecumseh Sherman's staff who, after authoring a perceptive profile of Sherman, had gotten a job writing for a top magazine, *Harper's Weekly*.

It was the moment that changed everything. No one knows how Nichols stumbled on Hickok, but in the weeks after the Tutt killing he interviewed him extensively. We'll never know if Nichols set out to concoct a legend—though the evidence suggests he did—or naively believed Hickok was the man he described. But when the article finally appeared in January 1867—this was how the Davis Tutt gunfight first became so well-known—it was a jaw-dropping exercise in mythmaking that, on the strength of little beyond the two men's conversations, portrayed Hickok as the deadliest gun in the West, a legendary figure on the order of "Jack the Giant Killer or Sinbad the Sailor."

All across the frontier, Nichols wrote, "I heard of Wild Bill and his exploits," which is clearly a stretch. Upon meeting him, he said, "You would not believe that you were looking into the eyes that have pointed the way to death to hundreds of men. Yes, Wild Bill with his own hands has killed hundreds of men. Of that I have not a doubt."

At this point, not counting men he conceivably shot in wartime, Hickok is known to have killed precisely two people, four if you count those henchmen. This was character invention on a monumental scale. Quoted throughout in a bizarre country dialect Nichols seems to have invented to underscore his backwoodsiness, Hickok doesn't claim to have killed hundreds of people—that comes later—but he doesn't deny it either. Nor does Nichols call Hickok a "gunfighter"; the term was not yet in use. But out of the clear blue sky the article gives birth to the archetype.

It was probably the most consequential thing ever written about an Old West figure during his lifetime. It turned Hickok from an anonymous, unemployed war veteran into one of the most famous men in the West. Easterners ate it up, of course, but the telling reaction came from the handful of Missouri and Kansas towns where Hickok was known. You can see editors there scratching their heads: Bill Hickok a deadly gunman, a hero? *Our* Hickok? Really? The Springfield paper had the best line, noting that some in town "are excessively indignant, but the great majority are in convulsions of laughter."[8]

That Hickok savored his newfound fame is illustrated by the follow-up interview he gave to a New York reporter, Henry M. Stanley, who four years later would make headlines discovering a missing African missionary with one of history's signature questions: "Dr. Livingstone, I presume?" Stanley tracked Hickok to Fort Riley, Kansas, and asked point-blank "how many white men" he had killed. Hickok chewed a moment and, maybe to amuse himself, maybe to tease the tenderfoot, probably because he liked mattering, replied, "I suppose I have killed considerably over a hundred." When Stanley gaped, Hickok insisted he "never killed one man without good cause."

The amazing thing is he got away with it. For the rest of his life there is no sense anyone ever seriously challenged his claims. It's hard to say how fame changed Hickok. He remains inscrutable. He was never a bad seed, just a nobody who warmed to being a somebody. He was prone to small kindnesses, it's clear, buying popcorn for children, that kind of thing. His fame was most noticeable in the eye-catching wardrobe he adopted, Prince Albert coats and the occasional silk cape, and his vigilance; what many noticed was how careful he got, especially once he became a lawman, sitting with his back to a wall, walking down the middle of streets to avoid anyone lurking in shadow. Where his fame became tangible was in the eyes of others. It's easy to imagine the reaction in small-town Kansas and Missouri, the pointed fingers in the street, the dropped jaws, the startled whispers: "That's Wild Bill Hickok." The first dime novel appeared soon after Nichols's article. It wouldn't be the last.*

If fame didn't make Hickok rich, it did open doors. After the article's publication, he served as an army scout for units battling Plains tribes led by Philip Sheridan and George Custer, then worked as a deputy marshal tracking army deserters in western Kansas and Nebraska, then in August 1869 was named marshal of the town of Hays, beside the army's Fort Hays in central Kansas, one of the state's tougher towns.

In Hays people noticed his unhurried cool, his steady gaze, and the unusual way he wore his two Colts. It was notable enough just to wear two guns—not many did—but unlike those who wore a pistol low or strapped to a thigh, Hickok wore his high, around his waist, with the butts facing forward. In the common wearing, a man needed to lift and point a pistol to shoot it. In Hickok's, he used his right hand to draw his left-side gun, and vice versa, a "cross draw" that, given his practice regimen, may have allowed him to fire his pistol a touch faster,

---

*Almost every retelling of Hickok's life after the *Harper's Weekly* article includes any number of wild, unconfirmed incidents, even a gunfight or two: facing down an angry saloon crowd in Kansas City, a wild gunfight in which he killed two men in Nebraska. They just go on and on. Many appear folkloric. I've tried here to include only those episodes that have been confirmed by historians. If you'd like to know more, there are two biographies of Hickok you can read. For the hardcore, try Joseph G. Rosa's exhaustive 1974 *They Called Him Wild Bill: The Life and Adventures of James Butler Hickok*. For an easier read, consider Tom Clavin's 2019 *Wild Bill: The True Story of the American Frontier's First Gunfighter.*

though Hickok, like Earp and others, always downplayed the need for speed. Accuracy, they agreed, was far more important.

Within six weeks of taking office in Hays he was involved in two killings. In the first, a drunk named Bill Mulvey went on a rampage, shooting up several bars. When Hickok appeared, Mulvey was on horseback, cradling a cocked rifle. Hickok shouted, "Don't shoot him in the back, he's drunk." When Mulvey turned to see who might be considering this, Hickok shot him through the temple—which, depending on your take, was either a dirty trick or genius.

A month later, a group of cowboys led by a notorious tough named Samuel Strawhun was wrecking another saloon, tossing glasses into the street, when Hickok arrived. He picked up several glasses, carried them inside, and announced, apparently referring to a beleaguered barkeep, "Boys, you hadn't ought to treat a poor man in this way."

Strawhun appeared offended. He said he'd throw more glasses if he wanted. "Do," Hickok said, "and they will carry you out."[9]

When Strawhun made some kind of move, Hickok shot him in the neck. The other cowboys stared at the ceiling, then left. A coroner pronounced both killings justified, but I have my doubts. Why use deadly force here? No account suggests either man drew a gun. One imagines a lawman such as Tom Smith defusing both situations without gunplay. Was it inexperience? Hickok had been a marshal barely a month at this point. Or could it be he was acting the part of deadly gunman to justify his legend?

Whatever the reason, and despite positive feedback from townspeople, Hickok was defeated in an election barely six weeks later. Five months after that, the town of Abilene came calling.

IN THE GUNFIGHTER CANON, WILD BILL HICKOK'S TIME AS ABILENE'S marshal in 1871 is uniformly the first theater of note. What came before—from Joaquin Murrieta and Jack Slade to Cullen Baker and Bob Lee—either played out too far from curious newspapers, got drowned out by the din of war, or reached the rest of the country as the dimmest of echoes. Abilene, though, featured the nation's most famous gunman in an accessible railroad town within earshot of a dozen alert Kansas newspapers, not to mention those in St. Louis and Chicago that were stunned to suddenly find lawmen and rowdy Texans shooting each other just a few hours away. So while the flamboyance of its gunfights frankly pales before what places in Texas and California had already experienced, and though they seldom made anything like national news, Abilene did generate a public record that was easily referenced by those who would come later looking to tell gunfighter stories.

For them, the main draw was its unprecedented star power, not just Hickok, but the two men who became Texas's best-known gunmen, eighteen-year-old Wes Hardin and the dapper British-born gambler Ben Thompson. Much of the drama revolved around Hardin, whose career was at its homicidal zenith. He'd had an eventful trip north. Along with his Clements cousins, he had left South Texas in early March, driven their herd past Austin and then Waco, then crossed the Red River into Indian Territory, which is when Hardin began killing people, including a Native American who shot an arrow toward him (probably), and another who may have tried to steal a cow. Finally, on the open prairie just a few days' ride below Abilene, Hardin took part in a wild, running gunfight in which he and one of his cousins appear to have killed six Mexican vaqueros who had driven a herd into theirs.

Hardin's account of the battle is loosely confirmed by a single article in *The Wichita Tribune* and the memory of another cowboy, though the details are Hardin's.[10] It happened in three phases on a Sunday, May 28, 1871. In the first, Hardin exchanged insults with the lead vaquero, who shot at him from a distance. Hardin shot back, wounding the man. After emissaries agreed to peace, a group of six vaqueros on horseback attacked Hardin and a group of cowboys anyway. As Hardin tells it, he and the wounded leader charged at each other, firing at long range in a kind of Old West joust, until one of Hardin's bullets struck home. The remaining five vaqueros descended on Hardin and his cousin Jim Clements. We don't have details of this final phase, but according to the *Tribune*, all five ended up dead.*

The site of the battle was near the Little Arkansas River, and by the time Hardin reached Abilene he had a new nickname: Little Arkansas. A man with a price already on his head, Hardin, like most Texans that year, was keenly aware of the new marshal's reputation. If Hickok tried to arrest him, he swore, he would shoot him dead.

HICKOK CUT A MEMORABLE FIGURE IN THE STREETS OF ABILENE: SIX one, 175 pounds, in a uniform of sorts, a wide-brimmed black hat, checkered trousers, a Prince Albert coat, and occasionally a silk cape. His official duties were less flamboyant. They included attending city council meetings—he was once obliged to retrieve a missing member by carrying him over his shoulder—and shooting stray dogs, for which the council paid him fifty cents a head. Most evenings he could be found at his unofficial office, the Alamo, watching the street over a glass of whiskey while his three deputies handled foot patrols.

Hickok was sworn in on April 15, a few days after Ben Thompson arrived in town.[11] Thompson and another Texas gambler, Phil Coe, took over the Bull's Head Saloon on Texas Street. For much of what ensued the only source is Hardin; while many of his stories can be confirmed, others, including his interaction with Hickok and Thompson, can't.

---

*In his autobiography, Hardin says he and Clements compared notes afterward and agreed Hardin had killed five of the six dead men.

Hardin had met Thompson in Texas. Walking into the Bull's Head, he found him livid at Hickok. The saloon's sign had featured a bull's erect penis, which offended many in town. When Thompson had refused to take it down, Hickok had brought in a painter and stood by, holding a shotgun, as he painted it over. According to Hardin, Thompson railed against Hickok, calling him a damn Yankee who hated Southerners, especially Texans. He asked Hardin if he would kill him. Thompson "tried to prejudice me every way he could against Bill," Hardin wrote. "[I said,] 'If Bill needs killing why don't you kill him yourself?'"

At the time, Hickok was giving Hardin his space. He must have known he was wanted but declined to arrest him; lawmen in frontier towns generally refrained from taking on the added work, and risk, of detaining those sought elsewhere. According to Hardin, the two men had introduced themselves. Hickok warned him to stay out of trouble. Hickok had posted notices reminding Texans that guns weren't allowed in town, but usually declined to enforce it. Hardin, like most, wore his openly.*

One morning, likely in June, the young Texan and a group got noisy playing tenpins in a bowling alley. Hickok appeared and, after a testy exchange, pulled a pistol and demanded Hardin's guns. It was a tense moment. According to Hardin, he handed them forward butt first. But as Hickok reached for them, he whirled them in the road agent's spin. Suddenly it was Hickok facing a gun. According to Hardin, he

---

*It's one of the ironies of the Gunfighter Era that gun laws were far more restrictive in many Old West towns than they are today. The restrictions were typically municipal ordinances rather than state law. Dodge City and other Kansas cow towns all forbade the wearing of firearms within city limits, as later would Tombstone, Arizona. In many towns, people turned in their guns at sheriff's offices or saloons, took a token or claim check, and returned with it later to retrieve their property. The problem, of course, was enforcement, which seems to have varied widely. From contemporary accounts, you get the sense the default behavior for many lawmen, as with Hickok in Abilene, was to ignore an openly carried firearm unless its wearer acted up.

ordered Hickok to holster his weapon, which he did, and "cursed him for a long haired scoundrel" for planning to kill him.

"Little Arkansaw," Hickok replied, "you have been wrongly informed."

"This is my fight," Hardin shouted to his pals, "and I'll kill the first man that fires a gun." At which point, Hardin goes on, Hickok suggested they relax. He offered Hardin a drink. Oddly, Hardin agreed. And that was that: gunfight avoided. That same day, though, Hardin, conceivably frustrated by Hickok's silky disarming, claims he was involved in an entirely separate confrontation. Drinking with a one-armed cowboy he names "Pain," the two heard a drunk who was insulting Texans.

"I'm a Texan," Hardin announced. When the drunk pulled his gun, fired, and hit Pain in his remaining arm, Hardin shot him as he ran for the door, the bullet striking behind his left ear, exiting through his mouth, and leaving, in one biographer's delicate phrasing, "teeth scattered all over the street."[12] Possible, though no such killing was reported in the press.

The next one was, though. Much of Hardin's outfit had returned to Texas, but others remained in camp outside town. In late June two of them, a twenty-two-year-old Texan named Billy Cohron and a vaquero named Juan Bideno, got into an argument. Bideno killed Cohron with a shot to the back, then quickly rode out of town. The cowboy was given one of the larger funerals in Abilene's short history. Hardin and three Texans, meanwhile, rode south in search of Bideno, who they assumed was riding for Texas.

They found him at the Southwestern Hotel in Sumner City, thirty miles south. Bideno was seated at a table, a cup of coffee to his lips. He apparently had no time to react when Hardin entered and drew his Colt. The shot struck Bideno in the forehead, killing him. Hardin's version has been confirmed in two contemporary newspaper accounts. According to one, he gave the proprietor five dollars to clean up the mess.*

Back in Abilene, Hardin found himself feted as a hero. Cattlemen and cowboys, he claims, showered him with gifts and rewards. Hickok left him alone, at least until August 6, when a rancher named Charles Couger was murdered in his room at the American Hotel. Hardin did it, and it's probably the most notorious of his killings. The question has always been why. Years later, Hardin claimed he shot an "assassin" sneaking into his room. Doubtful. In fact, the lone news account says Couger was reading in bed when he was shot by four bullets fired through a wall.

The version that's gone down in lore is that Hardin killed the man for snoring, apparently while drunk. Late in life, Hardin would admit to the killing, but never mentioned anything about snoring. Nor did anyone at the time. One biographer, Leon Metz, traces the tale to a story told by a Texas detective who pursued Hardin six years later, in 1877. The story does make a weird kind of sense. Why else would you shoot someone through a wall in the middle of the night? Metz says Hardin yelled for Couger to "roll over" and speculates that, when the snoring persisted, he fired the shots for emphasis, not trying to kill anyone.†[13]

Hickok was on the scene within minutes. Hardin and a cousin jumped from a low roof as he entered the hotel. Hardin hid in a haystack till morning, stole a horse, then surprised and disarmed a group of deputies when they rode into his campsite. Hardin and his cousin

---

*The paper named the killer as "Conway," almost certainly a name Hardin conjured on the spot because otherwise the two versions agree on almost every detail. Hardin even remembered giving the proprietor money, though he remembers it as twenty-five dollars.

†I have an ex-wife who, given my own nocturnal racket, would gladly have shot me in the night. So yes, I believe it.

then rode hard to Texas, reaching it in a few days. He had spent two months in Kansas and killed at least seven men. He was eighteen.

THE CATTLE SEASON'S FINAL GUNFIGHT WAS HICKOK'S, AND IT WAS A tragedy. On the night of October 5, a crowd of noisy cowboys was engaged in a farewell pub crawl, weaving from bar to bar, when Hickok, standing outside the Novelty Theater with his deputy Mike Williams, heard a shot around the corner, near the Alamo. "Be right back," Hickok said. He circled around to the back of the bar, strode through it, and emerged onto the veranda to confront the crowd.[14]

Hickok demanded to know who fired the shot. The Texas gambler Phil Coe, described as a large, belligerent man, six four with a black pompadour, confessed. He was shooting at a dog, he said. There was ill will between Coe and Hickok, we're told, either over a prostitute they both favored or because Hickok claimed Coe's games were fixed. According to one story, Coe had promised to kill Hickok "before the frost."[15]

Hickok upbraided the crowd, then told the cowboys to disarm and leave town. With no warning we know of, Coe suddenly drew his pistol. Hickok pulled both of his and fired, two bullets striking Coe in the midsection, mortal wounds. A moment later Deputy Williams raced around the corner, pistol drawn. Hickok wheeled and fired two shots, killing him instantly. The crowd gasped.

It was a horrible accident, entirely avoidable, yet understandable for a man who fired his guns so freely. What Hickok felt, we can only guess. His lone recorded comment was to the mob: "If any of you want the balance of these pills, come and get them."[16] Once the crowd dispersed, Hickok carried Williams's body into the Alamo and laid it across a poker table. He then strode from bar to bar telling Texans to leave town or die. The next day Hickok sent word to the deputy's family. Later, we're told, he paid for the funeral.

The shootings that night are among the most famous in frontier history. Much of it was simply Hickok's renown—a famous gunfighter guarantees a famous gunfight. And too there were all those witnesses; this is among the first marquee gunfights that would be described in detail for reporters the next day. The final ingredient was the reaction in Texas, where Coe was a well-known bar owner and gambler. Newspapers there were soon up in arms, painting Hickok as a bloodthirsty Yankee murderer.

The upshot was a place in history. The gunfights in Abilene that season, especially this one, put these new Kansas cow towns on newspaper radars across the nation's midsection, which tended to make future Kansas gunfights more newsworthy, padding the record that would later attract writers and historians.

THUS ENDED ABILENE'S REIGN AS A CATTLE TOWN AND AS A THEATER of gunfighter violence; that winter, city fathers announced they'd had enough of Texans, saying they would "no longer submit to the evils of the trade."[17] As for Hickok, his best days were now behind him. Abilene dismissed him that December. Some say he never got over shooting his deputy. Others point to some kind of degenerative eye disease he developed.* Bright lights and sun glare began to bother him; for the rest of his life, he often wore blue-tinted glasses.

Hickok spent much of the next three years crisscrossing the Northeast in Wild West shows, first a desultory one he helped assemble, then

---

*To this day no one can be sure what afflicted Hickok. A contemporary newspaper report called it "ophthalmia," recognized today as a catchall term for all manner of vision ailments. Some thought it linked to a venereal disease, glaucoma, or trachoma.

his friend Bill Cody's more famous production. The lights hurt his eyes; at least once, legend has it, he shot one out. The performances—pretending to kill bison and Comanche, spouting florid speeches—he found soul killing. Buoyed by whiskey before and during every performance, he began complaining and flubbing his lines. Finally, in late 1874, in the middle of a show in Rochester, New York, he tore off his buckskins, put on street clothes, and to Cody's dismay, walked out of the theater and quit. At his lowest point Hickok stormed onto a stage in Binghamton and slugged an actor who replaced him.

By early 1875 he had returned west. Believing, probably with reason, there were men who bore grudges in his old Kansas haunts, he decided to try Cheyenne, Wyoming, settling down to a quiet life as a gambler. A memoirist recalled seeing him there without his guns, dressed plainly for once: he "might easily have been taken for a Quaker minister," she wrote.[18] Hickok was only thirty-eight, but he developed rheumatism in his knee and had begun walking with a cane.

At one point he wed a Cincinnati circus promoter he'd met back east, but they never lived together. Had he settled down, or remained in Wyoming, things might have ended differently. But a marshal disliked him and arrested him for vagrancy, a charge often levied against unwanted gamblers. At least once he was warned to leave town. When gold was found in South Dakota, Hickok's gaze drifted there.

Another boomtown was rising, Deadwood. He tried organizing a wagon train of Missouri settlers, but the idea fizzled, so in 1876 he joined one leaving from Cheyenne. He reached Deadwood that July. Camping outside town with some pals, he began each morning with target practice and a shot of whiskey, then passed the day at Saloon No. 10, alternately playing poker and sitting at the bar regaling people who bought him drinks with embroidered versions of his stories.

They say Hickok had a premonition he would die in Deadwood, and maybe it's true. On August 1, dressed in his favorite frock coat and black sombrero, he was playing poker at the saloon. A drunk named Jack McCall was losing big. Hickok encouraged him to take a break and slid him money for a meal. The next afternoon McCall returned, circled around where Hickok was playing, placed a Colt .45 beside his temple, and with the words "Damn you! Take that!" pulled the trigger. Hickok died instantly. No one ever understood why McCall did it, but he did, and he hanged for it.

Hickok was America's first celebrity gunfighter. It's his only real legacy. Books about him, mostly fanciful dime novels, spread in the 1880s, and he was rediscovered in an imaginative 1926 biography, then got a decent Gary Cooper movie in 1936, a TV show in the 1950s, and a meh Jeff Bridges biopic in 1995. Yet he has never drawn the kind of adoration Wyatt Earp or Billy the Kid enjoyed. His career has no easy narrative arc, nor any discernible moral component, none of the things that tend to draw fans. He was good with a gun, if too often trigger-happy, a serial fabulist who seldom fought for anyone but himself. But by telling a tall tale, he essentially created the idea of the Old West gunfighter, which is an achievement of sorts.

The gunfights of the eighteenth-century American frontier evolved from the personal duels popular in the antebellum South, top. The first nationally recognized gunfight after the Civil War, Wild Bill Hickok's killing of Davis Tutt in 1865, bottom, was probably the purest example of this transition, a duel much like hundreds before it, only with modern revolvers. In this illustration, Hickok has just dispatched Tutt and has turned on his cronies, warning them not to respond.

The honor codes of the Old South morphed into something far more explosive in post–Civil War Texas, where resistance to the federal government triggered unprecedented levels of civilian violence, including several of the deadliest feuds in American history. A number involved cantankerous cattlemen, including Pink Higgins, top right, a key figure in feuds that wracked Lampasas County, and Print Olive, top left, who is believed to have killed two rustlers by sewing them inside green cattle hides that, when shrunk in sunlight, squeezed the men to death. The poster boy for Texas-style violence was the homicidal young racist John Wesley Hardin, at left and on facing page, who may have killed more men than any other Old West gunfighter.

J. W.

The kind of manic violence unleashed in postwar Texas erupted across much of the western frontier with the spread of the state's open-range cattle business, first via the Chisholm and other cattle trails to Kansas towns such as Abilene, Wichita, and Dodge City. Above, the aftermath of one shoot-out. Inset, a band of Texas cowboys on the Chisholm.

The first nationally recognized gunfighter was James Butler "Wild Bill" Hickok, photos at left and on facing page, a onetime Union Army scout who burst into public view in 1867 when *Harper's Weekly* magazine declared him the killer of more than a hundred men. The precise number at the time would appear to have been two—four if you squint; whatever the number, Hickok was a colossal fraud whose tall tales gave birth to a new American archetype. Later, as a lawman in two rough Kansas towns, he killed four more men, two he didn't have to, and another, his own deputy, in a tragic error.

The Kansas cow towns are dominated by the memory of Wyatt Earp, top left and on facing page, who cut his teeth in Wichita before rising to (largely posthumous) fame in Dodge City, above. Few, least of all his bosom pal Bat Masterson, top right, knew Earp was in fact an escaped federal fugitive and, along with his brothers, a onetime pimp.

S everal renowned gunfighters emerged from Wyatt Earp's orbit, including Bat Masterson, above and at right, whose fame probably topped Earp's in life but whose late-life writings as a New York newspaper columnist helped enshrine his friend's legend. Maybe the most feared gunfighter of all was New Mexico's Clay Allison, on facing page, whose erratic behavior, including once riding nude through a Texas town, may have been spurred by post-traumatic stress disorder as a result of fighting during the Civil War. Exactly what happened during Allison's 1878 face-off with Earp in Dodge City still inspires debate among historians.

Disputes at the gambling table produced an outsize number of marquee gunfights. Counterclockwise from top left: a faro game in Bisbee, Arizona, circa 1900; John Henry "Doc" Holliday, feral and quarrelsome, was perhaps the frontier's unlikeliest gunfighter; a faro game underway in Tombstone; a favorite of aficionados, "Mysterious" Dave Mather survived multiple shoot-outs in New Mexico and Kansas before disappearing; Luke Short, in top hat, was a Texas cowboy who became one of the West's best-known gambler-gunfighters.

The first American criminal to become a household name, Jesse James, top left and on facing page, was never an Old West gunfighter. He was instead a midwestern bank and train robber with little interest in gunplay; his killings were inevitably cold-blooded murder. James was assassinated by a craven nobody named Bob Ford, bottom left. Bill Longley, bottom right, was long considered Texas's second-most prolific gunfighter, after Wes Hardin; only in recent years has he been unmasked as a fraud. Sam Bass, top right, an illiterate cowboy who pulled off what might have been the frontier's richest train robbery, remained a Texas folk hero for generations.

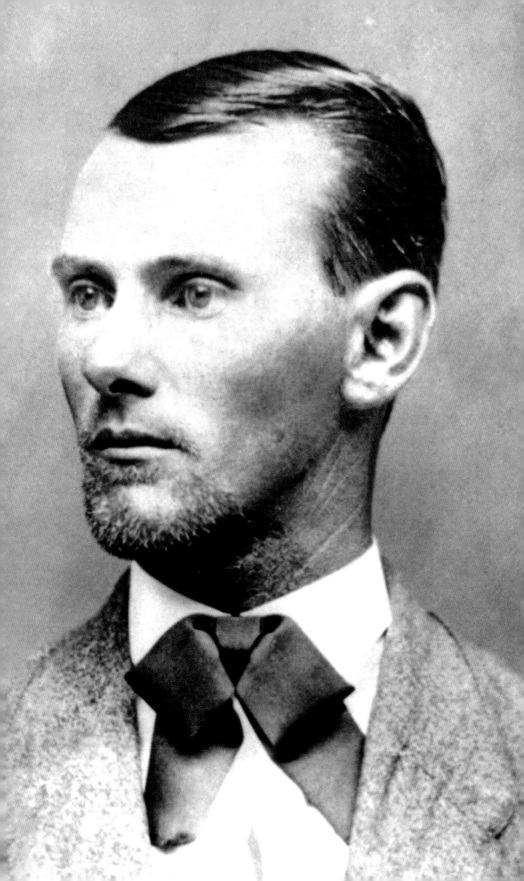

For a moment in the late 1870s, the Texas gambler Ben Thompson
may have been the frontier's most famous gunfighter, in part
because he assiduously courted newspaper reporters, politely explaining
the unwritten rules of gunfighting. Alcohol eventually overcame him,
though, leading to a series of increasingly bizarre shootings in his
hometown of Austin, climaxing in a storied shoot-out down the road
in San Antonio. In terms of conspiracy theories, Thompson's death
remains the Old West's equivalent of the Kennedy assassination.

CHAPTER SIX

"Get Your Guns, You Texas Sons of Bitches, and Fight"

The Rise of Wyatt Earp and Ben Thompson, 1871 to 1876

A drunken Texas cowboy was a nuisance, but an angry crowd of them was a thing to behold. Much like Atticus Finch facing down a lynch mob, any number of frontier lawmen had stories of confronting an outfit of seething Texans. One of the better ones, in Wichita, features Wes Hardin's cousin, a whorehouse piano, and a stern twenty-six-year-old deputy named Wyatt Earp.

It happened in the summer of 1874, when a struggling Wichita madam fell behind on payments on the piano in her parlor. When Earp was sent to repossess it, he chastised a group of cowboys inside for failing to help pay their hostess's debt. When the Texans reluctantly ponied up, passing a hat among them, Earp wryly warned them, in one biographer's words, "not to head into something they couldn't buy themselves out of."[1]

In a vivid display of how Texans sought to avenge even the slightest affronts, a mass of cowboys camped outside town vowed to teach the sassy Earp a lesson. It's said that Hardin's cousin Mannen Clements led a formation of sixty mounted Texans to the bridge into Wichita, where Earp awaited with a force of townspeople. Earp called for Clements to disarm his men and leave. Clements refused.

"Mind me now, Mannen, put up those guns and go on home," Earp warned. Clements studied the deputy a moment, presumably deducing his resolve, then holstered his gun and led the cowboys away.[2]

During the 1870s five Kansas towns all but took turns hosting the Texas cattle trade, usually after tiring of confrontations like this. Abilene gave way to Newton, which gave way to Ellsworth, then to Wichita, and finally to the fabled Dodge City. Their story is dominated by the memory of Earp, though he was in fact a latecomer, and not an especially remarkable one at that.

Three years before Earp's first appearance as a lawman in Wichita, there was Newton, a railroad town that rose on a desolate patch of prairie in central Kansas in the spring of 1871, and by autumn had twenty-seven saloons, eight gambling halls, a round-the-clock red-light district, and later, once Abilene banned the cattle business, Joseph McCoy's new stockyard. That first season the town had no actual government. Grass still grew in what passed for streets. Newton was a place of distilled havoc; its gunfights make Abilene's look like bridge games. There were four killings that first July alone, all involving Texans. "The citizens of the town," as one records, "were helpless before the fierce, gun-toting Texans."[3]

The real trouble began that August, when a hard case known as Mike McCluskie was named a special policeman for the town's first election. Another was a Texas gambler known as Billy Bailey. One evening the two got into a fistfight at the Red Front Saloon, then "took it outside," where McCluskie promptly shot Bailey in the chest. He died the next day.

The Texans in town vowed revenge. A group of them, led by a cowboy named Hugh Anderson, found McCluskie in Tuttle's Saloon around 2:00 a.m. on August 20. All we know for sure is that Anderson shot McCluskie. After that it was chaos, dozens of shots fired, people screaming, Texans and bystanders falling. Legend has it a quiet consumptive named Jim Riley stepped forward and shot most of the Texans. There's no evidence such a man existed. If he did, he was never seen again.

In all, nine men, including McCluskie, died as a result of their injuries.* It went down in history as "Newton's General Massacre." Killings, including that of a new marshal, remained so common into the following year that one leading Texas cattleman, Shanghai Pierce, announced he was abandoning Newton, and did.†

In 1872 most herds moved on to Ellsworth, also in central Kansas. Formed five years earlier, Ellsworth's distinctive feature was a police force among the more corrupt in western annals. The marshal was the pockmarked John Norton, known as "Brocky Jack," a onetime deputy of Hickok's who had relocated after being shot by another deputy. His officers included "Long Jack" Delong, "High Low Jack" Branham, "Happy Jack" Morco, and the sadly un-nicknamed Ed Hogue, the force known to history as "Four Jacks and a Joker." (This lineup was shuffled repeatedly.)

The roughest was Morco, a West Coast refugee who upon arrival had been arrested for vagrancy and, in the spirit of the town, was

---

*A few years later, a New York newspaper carried a vivid story of how Hugh Anderson, who survived the fight, died in a gory gun-and-knife duel with McCluskie's brother. It's an episode mentioned in any number of western histories. In 2014 a researcher named Douglas Ellison investigated the incident and found the story was pure fiction, the concoction of a discredited newspaper stringer. Anderson, it turned out, went on to a long career as a rancher in Texas and later New Mexico. He died when struck by lightning in 1914 at the age of sixty-two.

†Newton's time as a cattle town lasted only one more season, but it probably set some kind of speed record for law enforcement casualties. A month after McCluskie's death, one of the town's new lawmen was shot with a derringer after disarming a drunk. His partner, Thomas Carson, was later charged with murder in Dodge City and disappeared after a jail break. The following year the new marshal survived three gunshot wounds in a shooting with several Texans.

promptly hired to help police it. Described as a drunk, swaggering braggart, he boasted of having killed twelve men. "Every man on the force was a bribe taker and a villain," another local memoirist wrote. "Every man on the force would kill on the slightest provocation."[4]

Brocky Jack and his men delighted in harassing the Texas drovers and especially the gamblers, arresting them for just about any infraction, real or imagined: carrying a weapon, disorderly conduct, disturbing the peace. Those arrested, typically amid the section of bars along South Main Street known as "Snake Row," would be escorted across a plaza into court to pay fines of between fifteen and thirty-five dollars, unless they slipped money to a deputy to avoid it. By one estimate, as many as thirty men a day made the trip.

The summer of 1873 was oppressively hot by Kansas standards, temperatures regularly rising above ninety degrees. Thanks to police harassment, temperatures were rising among the Texans too. As June gave way to July, there were murmurs of violence, and relief that none had broken out. On July 3, a headline in the paper came off as both hopeful and ominous. It was just three words: NOBODY KILLED YET.

Which of course meant the worst. And when it began, no one was all that surprised that the man who started it was one of the West's renowned next-tier gunfighters, the Texas gambler Ben Thompson.

SELDOM IN AMERICA HAS GAMBLING BEEN AS WILDLY POPULAR AS IT was in the Old West. Games and wagers went a long way toward relieving the boredom of a crude frontier without radio, television, or internet. And done well, gambling was one of the best-paying jobs west of the Mississippi. In towns where the only serious money was made by faraway investors and cattlemen, work on the ground didn't pay much. Store owners, cowboys, miners, prostitutes—none were getting rich. Gambling was not only an indispensable entertainment but the omnipresent gig work of the frontier, a chance to make extra money for most, a career for the few. "Gambling," Bat Masterson wrote, "was not only the principal and best-paying industry of the town at the time, but it was also reckoned among its most respectable."[5]

It was also, by any measure, among its more violent. Any reading of the literature suggests gambling and gunfighting became intertwined. Gambling disputes, after all, were among the single greatest causes of frontier gunfights. Almost all the best-known gunfighters— Hickok, Hardin, and Wyatt Earp among them—spent as much time playing cards as anything else, both as a pastime and a sometime job. Others, notably Doc Holliday and Luke Short, were professionals.

The reasons for bloodshed would seem simple to grasp. Stacks of money on a tabletop, half-empty glasses of whiskey or beer, a handgun on every hip, and little in the way of legal oversight: What could go wrong?

Yet none of this fully explains gambling-related violence, why people would disagree so often, and so heatedly, about a game whose results were as obvious as the cards thrown on a table.

What does, I suspect, are two unavoidable facts.

Number one: cheating was pervasive.

Number two: everyone knew it.

Which means that at pretty much every game of chance in the Old West, everyone involved was as keen to watch for cheating as to win the game itself. An accusation of cheating—and certainly proof of it— was viewed as an acute challenge to a man's honor, a legitimate reason to draw a gun or knife. "Every time a man sits down to a card table to gamble he takes his life in his hands and lays it down between him and his adversary," Ben Thompson told his biographer.[6]

The emergence of gambling as a blood sport seems to have been a newish phenomenon. Americans had gambled since Jamestown, but it was long a discreet affair. The Puritans passed the first anti-gambling laws, and by the 1800s their spread had forced most northern gambling underground. Not so in the South, where men gambled openly, even flamboyantly.* The *professional* gambler is considered a Southern invention, born in New Orleans, a city rich in French and Spanish gambling traditions, after the Louisiana Purchase in 1803.

These first pros ran crooked card games to fleece boatmen on the waterfront, then moved up the Mississippi to work the grimy riverside camps slouching below Natchez, Vicksburg, Memphis, and St. Louis. To call these "sharpers" gamblers is misleading. Their games—faro, monte, and a New Orleans innovation, poker—were inevitably fixed; it's more accurate to call them con men, their victims river travelers and the occasional errant Southern planter.

This changed after 1835, when the river towns, frightened by bizarre rumors of a gambler-led conspiracy to free slaves, chased the gamblers out. New Orleans all but shut down. The purge forced almost all gambling onto the riverboats that transported travelers and cargo up and down the Mississippi, giving birth to a new American archetype: the stylish riverboat gambler. He typically hosted a running game in a big boat's main salon, usually giving the captain and crew a cut of his winnings. The riverboat gambler flourished for twenty years, but the slow death of the boats during the 1850s with the coming of the railroads forced the professionals to find new homes.

Many headed onto the frontier, where in the years before many territories became states—and often after—an entirely new paradigm opened: wide-open, unregulated public gambling, in dedicated and sometimes palatial card houses, saloons, and every conceivable venue, from muddy tent camps in the Sierra Nevada to smoky back rooms

---

*George Washington, a Virginian, could play cards for rainy days on end—his records indicate he broke about even—while Thomas Jefferson's gambling debts drove him to the brink of bankruptcy. No president gambled more passionately than Tennessee's Andrew Jackson, on horses, cockfighting, cards, you name it. One of his two duels was over a gambling debt.

from Texas to Idaho. The pros arrived first in Gold Rush California; so many gamblers sailed around South America it became known as "the gambler's route." After San Francisco cracked down in 1856, many moved on to Denver, and gambling was soon a prominent business in almost every growing frontier town. Dallas was all but run by gamblers into the 1880s. By then, the natty professionals, still attired in the ornate vests and silk top hats they had adopted on the river, traveled a circuit—Texas, the Kansas cow towns, and Southern cities in the summer, northern cities and mining camps in the winter.

Something crucial changed in the transition from riverboats to the frontier, though. In 1843 a riverboat sharper named Jonathan H. Green published the first of a series of books exposing endemic cheating; he became a sensation on the lecture circuit. For the first time, millions of Americans learned of the tricks and devices used to cheat them: marked and trimmed cards, the false shuffle, and all manner of "holdouts"—straps, boxes, and even cord-and-pulley contraptions, hidden in a gambler's clothes, that held cards.

Not all professionals used them. Gambling had its codes too. Pros looked down on those who employed brazen cheats like holdouts and hidden decks. Yet they thought little of using nuanced cheats that required skill, such as stacking a deck, reversing a cut, or, in the case of the gambler Dick Clark, wearing a diamond ring that, when turned, produced a tiny mirror he used to see every card he dealt.

Men like Clark, who used their reputation as "square," or honest, gamblers to attract wealthy opponents, could get awfully huffy when their reputation, their honor, was challenged. Add this and the heightened fears of cheating into the mix, on top of all those whiskey bottles and handguns, and you begin to get a sense of how this new world of gambling on the frontier could so quickly turn deadly.

The presence of professional gamblers was also a factor in why some gunfights were remembered and others forgotten. Stepping off trains in Denver or Fort Worth wearing their silk top hats, men like Dick Clark were what passed for public figures in the towns where they worked. Reporters often knew them, and certainly knew of them. Any violence they touched off thus tended to be more newsworthy than, say, a knife fight between miners in some obscure Nevada camp. And, more often than not, it happened in public. Card playing, after all, was typically a semipublic event, a contest commonly enacted in a saloon as people watched, providing the witnesses that most marquee gunfights required.

AMONG THE ROVING "SPORTING MEN"—SPORTS—WHO SWARMED THE Kansas cow towns, one of the best known was Ben Thompson, a popular, press-friendly pro who rose to prominence in Texas after the war. Thompson had a striking mix of Southern gentility and hair-trigger temper, genial and jocular one moment, drunk and deadly the next. Bat Masterson, overestimating his record, judged him the greatest gunfighter of all (a stretch), killer of the most men (no), keenest marksman (unlikely), and most feared (if he says so).

What set Thompson apart was less his physical than his mental gifts. Masterson credited him with not only a "much higher order of intelligence" than his peers but a coolness under fire to match. A man with gentlemanly pretensions, Thompson was said to be a stickler for honor and decorum. Those he killed, Masterson wrote, echoing others, were dispatched "in an open and manly way."[7]

Chatty with reporters, Thompson probably did a better job than any other gunfighter of controlling his personal narrative. At the height of his fame in the late 1870s, he owned a sailboat he named after the editor of a New York newspaper. Much of the hair-raising backstory he unspooled was reported in Texas papers, and he later filled in the blanks for his lawyer, who published a posthumous biography in

1915. Some of his tales were clearly inflated, but the overall thrust appears largely accurate. Biographers haven't poked major holes in it.

He was born in England in 1843, and at eight immigrated with his family to the Texas capital, Austin, where his father was a fisherman. As a child, he told his lawyer, he was beaten bloody by a policeman and developed a "great hate against the brutal oppressors of poor men." It's clear he developed an explosive temper and thought little of drawing his gun to settle a disagreement. He shot his first man, another teenager, at fifteen. It's said the other boy mocked his ability to shoot, offered his rear end as a target, and dared Ben to hit it. Ben hoisted a shotgun and blasted him with bird shot. Convicted of aggravated assault, he was sentenced to sixty days in jail.

He became a printer's apprentice, first in Austin, then for a bookbinder in New Orleans, where his penchant for violent confrontation escalated. In his biography Thompson tells of a time he shot and wounded a man he caught stealing items from the bookbinder's shop. Another time he saw a Frenchman offend a woman on a trolley, rose to defend her, and stabbed the man in the tussle that ensued. The man later found Thompson and demanded a duel, during which, Thompson claimed, the two men fought with knives in a darkened basement. The Frenchman ended up dead, and when his friends vowed revenge, Thompson fled New Orleans for Austin.

Seventeen at the outset of war, he enlisted in the Confederate army and fought in Louisiana and Galveston. He later told of his first serious shooting scrape in December 1861, at a fort on the Rio Grande, in which he shot a sergeant during a disagreement, then fended off and shot an officer who attacked him with a sword. The version that the sergeant, an older soldier named Billy Vance, told a reporter was a smidge less dramatic. According to Vance, he and Thompson argued over a scrap of meat at chowtime. When Thompson drew his gun, Vance grabbed its muzzle. The shot went wild. Thompson was thrown in a stockade for four months. Something of his charm can be inferred from the fact that Vance dismissed this as boyish bravado; the two became friends.

The centerpiece of Thompson's origin story is another wartime yarn, a Peckinpah-esque narrative of gambling and gunfights on the Rio Grande in the war's final months. It introduces his brother, Billy, a drunk Thompson was forever bailing out of scrapes. The meat of the tale is a two-night monte game Ben held in Laredo, during which a dozen Mexican American soldiers bet and lost both their pistols and paychecks. When Thompson closed the game, he faced a roomful of angry losers. An officer stepped forward and menacingly demanded the guns.

When Thompson refused, a soldier opened fire. Thompson says he ducked low, shot and killed the soldier, then the officer. The room's two candles blew out, and in the gloom, he plunged into the crowd jostling at the door. Outside, another soldier shot at him. Ben dived into a cistern and emerged to find Billy waiting to flee. The story of their unlikely escape north to Austin features an attack by feral dogs and a climactic battle—cannons and all—in which the Thompsons and a Confederate regiment fight off a mob of angry Mexican American soldiers attempting to bring Ben to justice.

Was any of this remotely true? It's impossible to know, but Thompson's reputation as a gunman, at least around Austin, was made after two confirmed incidents late in the war. In 1864, while working for Confederate recruiters, Thompson and a pal named John Rapp ran into some kind of trouble with a tough named John Coombs. After Coombs knifed Rapp in a bar fight, Rapp staggered to Thompson's house for protection getting home. Thompson grabbed a pistol and the two left, only to be warned that Coombs was gathering a mob to come after them. Thompson crept into a darkened alleyway to investigate, at which point Coombs and a crowd of maybe twenty men emerged and opened fire.

Rather than run, Thompson rushed forward in the shadows, shot one man at close range, then wheeled and shot and killed another on horseback—apparently Coombs—at which point the mob, clearly in no mood for a gun battle, melted into the night. The next day Thompson turned himself in, was charged with murder, and went free on bond.

Nine months later, in the war's waning days, Thompson and another soldier noticed an Italian teamster named Alberto Algerio driving a team of horses bearing Confederate brands. Sensing they were stolen, they flagged Algerio down and tried to question him, but he spoke no English. Confused, probably thinking he was being robbed, the Italian hoisted a shotgun. Thompson drew his pistol and shot him dead.

In July 1865 Union forces assumed control in Austin and Thompson was jailed, probably on charges related to these killings. Two months later, on September 17, having slipped bribes to a pair of guards, he disguised himself as a Union soldier, escaped, and rode for Mexico. Another civil war was underway there, to defeat the French-installed emperor Maximilian, and for the next two years Thompson served in his forces, seeing action in a dozen battles. Once Maximilian was defeated in 1867, Thompson survived a bout of yellow fever and returned to Austin.

There he submitted to a trial for the murder of John Coombs and was found not guilty. By this point, Thompson had begun putting down roots; he had married, welcomed a child, and decided to become a professional gambler. The Texas sport Phil Coe—later shot by Hickok—granted him a concession at a barroom he bought, the Rawhide Saloon, even though Thompson's skill was maybe a little debatable. In his biography he admits to being so broke he had to pawn his pistol three times in his first years as a pro. Nearly a century later, the gambling historian Herbert Asbury wrote, "His talent as a sharper was mediocre—he was clumsy at short cards, and usually dealt Faro honestly because he wasn't clever enough to deal it otherwise."[8]

Still, as bright as his prospects were, Thompson's temper soon got him back in trouble, and this time it was serious. It involved his temperamental brother-in-law, James Moore. After some kind of family argument in September 1868, Thompson was asking a justice of the peace for a protection order against Moore when a man rushed in to say that Thompson's pregnant wife had been attacked. He raced home and found Moore had struck her with a pistol. Thompson tracked Moore down and shot him in the side.

Moore survived, but Thompson was again thrown into jail. With his previous shootings clearly in mind, a military tribunal sentenced him to four years' hard labor at the state prison in Huntsville. A local paper diplomatically termed Thompson "somewhat notorious for murders and assaults," noting that the tribunal had gotten involved because "no one dared appear against him" in civil court. One gets a sense of Thompson's fury at all this from the same news account, which notes that he "saw fit to inform the magistrate who issued process against him that he intended to kill him at his earliest convenience."[9]

Prison clerks measured Thompson as five eight and a lean 117 pounds, with blue eyes and wavy brown hair. His prison file is otherwise meager, given that two years after arrival he received an official pardon from President Ulysses S. Grant. That's right, a presidential pardon, for which, to this day, there has never been a full explanation.*

---

*Though, according to one biographer, Thompson was quoted late in life saying a law involved in his conviction was found unconstitutional.

One day he was in prison, the next back in Austin, where Phil Coe and his partners welcomed him and told of a new business venture they had planned for the following spring: they were opening a bar for Texas cowboys in Kansas.

TO THIS POINT, BEN THOMPSON COULD BE DISMISSED AS ONE MORE VI-olent Texas thug. Yet his behavior clearly softened after prison. Maybe the experience chastened him; maybe it was his growing family; maybe he just grew up. In any event, during the 1870s he emerged as one of the Kansas cow towns' best-known sports, popular among the Texans and, his spat with Hickok aside, friendly with lawmen; in Dodge City, he and Bat Masterson became close. He avoided the mayhem in Abilene by a bit of bad luck. Missing his family, he met them in Kansas City, and a buggy in which they were riding overturned, severely injuring Thompson and his wife. She had her arm amputated, and he was laid up for months with a broken leg.

By 1873 he was sufficiently recovered to join the gamblers descending on Ellsworth and its corrupt police force. Thompson and his brother, Billy, were known as hell-raisers, and Billy was arrested twice, the first time for firing his pistol in the air; he spent a week in jail. On July 31, when the notorious deputy Happy Jack Morco arrested him again for public drunkenness, Billy tried to resist. He was fined. The Texans protested this kind of thing repeatedly, and Billy's arrest seems to have become a talking point in a municipal debate over how zealously to police them. Morco ended up getting fired, then rehired, and he apparently blamed the Thompsons for his travails. Tensions between the Texans and the police were running high.

The shooting began on a sweltering Friday morning, August 15. Ben was in Brennan's Saloon, watching a monte game between two

Texas cattlemen. When one bet more than the other wanted to handle, Thompson was asked to find someone to cover the man's overbets. He turned to a gambler named John Sterling, a Medal of Honor recipient, who agreed to cover the bets and split any winnings with Thompson.

Sterling ended up joining the game and winning something like a thousand dollars, a major haul. Thompson had left by that point, and Sterling showed no inclination to pay him. When Ben heard this, he went in search of Sterling and, finding him in another saloon, asked for his money. Sterling, said to be deeply drunk, slapped him. Ben, from all accounts, was pretty close to drawing his gun.

Happy Jack Morco was in the saloon and drew his gun first, warning Ben not to escalate the fight. Furious, Ben stormed out and returned to Brennan's, where he buttonholed one of the cattlemen, probably to enroll him as a witness to Sterling's promise.

As they spoke, Morco and Sterling appeared at the door. Morco was holding two pistols, Sterling a shotgun. One of them, probably Morco, yelled, "Get your guns you Texas sons of bitches and fight!"

Thompson, unarmed, demanded someone hand him a gun. When no one would, he stalked out a back door to the saloon where he had checked his guns. Grabbing his pistol and a Winchester, he circled back to the plaza, where Billy, drunk and holding a balky shotgun, offered his aid. Ben shooed him away, then hollered to a crowd forming along Snake Row: "If you damn sons of bitches want to fight, here we are!"

It was the moment that cemented his legend, a story told for years up and down Kansas and beyond. As it happened, his challenge was met only by the county's kindly sheriff, Chauncey Whitney, who strode up and suggested everyone join him for a drink and calm down.

Ben, simmering, agreed. They were reentering Brennan's Saloon when someone shouted, "Look out, Ben!" Thompson turned to see Morco and Sterling duck into stores down the street. He raised the

Winchester and fired. Ben had just begun striding toward where the two men hid when the sound of a shotgun blast exploded behind him.

He whirled, only to see Sheriff Whitney standing with a stricken look on his face, Billy a step or two behind him, the shotgun in his hands. It had gone off accidentally.

"My God, Billy," Whitney rasped. "You have shot me."

"My God," Ben barked, "you have shot our best friend!"

An angry crowd gathered. Ben managed to get his brother onto a horse and persuaded him to leave town before they were lynched. By afternoon a hundred Texans were milling in front of Ben's hotel, making sure no one did. The sheriff died. Billy, charged with murder, became a fugitive. Ben was briefly detained, testified at the inquest, then boarded a train to safety. The violence that day, and afterward, was news all the way to Chicago; Ellsworth made Thompson's name.

As he feared, the violence was only beginning. A vigilance committee was formed. The police clearly wanted revenge for the sheriff's killing. The following week, with rumors swirling of individual Texans marked for death, an officer named Edward Crawford argued with one of the original cardplayers, the cattleman Cad Pierce, shot him inside a store, then leaned down and beat him with a revolver until his brains spilled onto the floor.

The next day, August 21, Ellsworth emptied; dozens of gamblers and cattlemen boarded trains east. Happy Jack Morco, fired yet again, left town for a time, but then, defying all warnings, returned in early September. When a new lawman, Charles Brown, demanded his revolvers, Morco drew on him. Brown shot him through the heart. Edward Crawford too refused to leave. He was shot and killed in November.

So ended Ellsworth's days as a cattle town. Texans, for the most part, wanted nothing more to do with the place. Years later a story was told, its accuracy still debated among Western enthusiasts, of an obscure

Ellsworth deputy who displayed conspicuous bravery that day Ben Thompson allowed himself to be arrested.

His name was Wyatt Earp.

IF, LIKE A LOT OF PEOPLE, YOU ONLY KNOW WYATT EARP FROM THE movies with Kevin Costner and Kurt Russell, you may have little sense of how controversial he was. Much of the controversy revolves around events after the Old West's most famous shoot-out, beside Tombstone's O.K. Corral in October 1881. The crux of it, as detailed in articles and books that date to the 1890s and continue to this day, is how to interpret the violence Earp unleashed on outlaws who killed his brother Morgan and badly wounded his brother Virgil. Some find it justifiable; others, especially those of a conservative bent, view it as an early episode of government's bloody overreach, à la Waco or Ruby Ridge.*

Then too there is the question of how Earp and his brothers made their livings, as lawmen sometimes, yes, but also as gamblers and, especially in their early years, as pimps and petty criminals. You can find writers who allege Earp was everything from a con man to the keeper of a secret Templar treasure. What turns out to be true is the fact that for the length of his career, Wyatt Earp was actually an escaped federal prisoner.

There's no denying that today, even as the memory of men such as Wild Bill Hickok and Wes Hardin has dimmed, Earp is the only gunfighter whose legend has grown. Much of it is the abiding fascination with the O.K. Corral shoot-out and its aftermath. What took Earp's fame to the next level was the fact that he and his friend Bat Masterson lived long lives, Earp into his eighties, into the 1920s, by which

---

*Much more on this in chapters 14 and 15.

point he had been debriefed by biographers and begun to appear in a series of bestselling books. Masterson, meanwhile, went on to a second career as a New York writer, praising Earp at every turn. Much of what is known about Earp's experiences as a lawman emerged fifty years after they happened. Much of what you know probably comes from the movies that resulted.

Accessibility, however, does not explain the pull he exerts on the American imagination. What does, I think, is the clear sense that Earp, in contrast to men like Hickok, not only fought for something—his family, the rule of law, justice—but stood for something. In a Wild West where thievery and murder and the worst imaginable crimes can seem routine, Earp is the moral center the legend requires. There are few major figures from the era who enjoy anything like his moral authority. If the Old West is to stand as America's creation myth, it needs Wyatt Earp. We need him to fill that void.

This is where you're probably expecting me to begin tearing him down. This is a man, after all, who had been a pimp and an escaped federal prisoner. And for all his skills with a gun, there are maybe two men we are pretty sure he actually killed. Two. A handful of others we believe, but nothing that will ever be confirmed. But tear Wyatt Earp down? Sorry, I can't do it. The fact is, if you've read everything out there, you know in your bones he was the real deal, an upright if imperfect beacon of rectitude in an era of workaday barbarism.

But yes, he sure didn't start out that way. Wyatt Berry Stapp Earp—he was named after his father's commanding officer during the Mexican War—was born, like Hickok, in small-town Illinois in 1848, the fourth of eight children sired by Nicholas Earp, a wandering jack-of-few-trades who took his family to Southern California and back during the 1860s. There were six Earp sons, including Wyatt's older brothers James and Virgil, and two younger, Morgan and Warren. All would inherit their father's wanderlust. None was exactly a choirboy.

Virgil in particular, at least in his early years, was a bit of a thug. A Union cavalryman during the war, he drifted through Illinois and Iowa afterward, drawing a string of arrests—one for arson—getting shot by a prostitute, and working as hired muscle for a gang of Omaha con men. By late 1871 he was tending bar in Peoria, where he was reunited with his brother James, who had compiled his own record of colorful arrests across the Mountain West, at one point escaping from a Montana jail, and had washed up in Illinois working as a pimp.

Wyatt's early years were just as troubled. Coming of age in California, he grew to be a sinewy six-footer, dirty blond and tough; hating life on the family farm, he worked on wagon trains between San Bernardino and Arizona. When the Earps returned to the Midwest in 1868, soon settling in the Missouri town of Lamar, his even temper and determination got Wyatt named to replace his father as its part-time constable. He was twenty-one.

For a year, everything appears to have gone well. Wyatt got married, bought a house, and won reelection. Then, for reasons no one has been able to explain—only the thinnest paper trail remains—he went off the rails. Likely it was his wife's death, from either typhus or childbirth. It's been speculated her brothers somehow blamed Wyatt, which could explain the street brawl that erupted between a group of them and their friends and Wyatt, Virgil, and Morgan. Whatever happened, by early 1871 Wyatt had left Lamar, never to return.

Soon after, two lawsuits were filed against him, each alleging he absconded with city funds, which might also explain his disappearance. What we know now, thanks to recent discoveries, is that Wyatt headed southwest into Indian Territory, where in March 1871 he and another man were arrested and charged with stealing a pair of horses. Wyatt was shoved into a jail in nearby Van Buren, Arkansas, to await trial.

This was serious business; he faced years in prison. So, on the night of May 3, 1871, as Wes Hardin was approaching Abilene, Wyatt joined a group of seven prisoners who knocked a hole in the jail's roof and escaped. Though few knew it, and Wyatt never spoke of it, for the rest of his days he would remain a federal fugitive.

He headed to Peoria, reuniting with his brothers, where from all evidence he too became a pimp. He and Morgan were arrested in early 1872 for "keeping and being found in a house of ill fame." After Wyatt was arrested and fined again, this time at a riverboat brothel, the local paper termed Wyatt "the Peoria bummer," slang for bum. It's at that point that all the Earps appear to have scattered.

The next two years Wyatt disappears from history. It appears he returned west, this time to the Kansas plains. Late in life, he told a biographer he was a buffalo hunter one year and worked on a government surveying crew the next. He claimed he returned to law enforcement in Ellsworth in 1873, further claiming that it was he who arrested Ben Thompson that August day. That's unlikely, and speaks to his shaky grasp of facts late in life. Because while Wyatt could have served briefly in Ellsworth, Thompson's arrest is well documented, and Wyatt's name appears nowhere in Ellsworth's public record.

What we know for sure is that Wyatt surfaced next in Wichita, in 1874, where he reunited with his brother James, who had opened a brothel there with his wife. Wyatt may have been their partner for a time, but by that summer he was also serving as a part-time policeman. This was the period, thinly documented, when memoirists remember him facing down that Texas mob. Which serves to remind us that, as large as Earp looms over the story of the Kansas cow towns, he never found anything like fame there. Other than one mention in the pulpy *National Police Gazette*, he was unknown outside the places he served.

He was skilled at his job, that much is evident. The two years he worked in Wichita leave us a snapshot of an honest, disciplined lawman who went out of his way to avoid violence. Promoted to deputy, he was the low man on the force, responsible for not only keeping the peace when the Texans got rowdy but also inspecting chimneys, sweeping and repairing the wood-plank sidewalks, and shooing and probably shooting the wild dogs that infested the town. He engaged in nothing remotely like a gunfight. The only time we know his pistol actually fired, in January 1876, it was because it fell from his holster and discharged accidentally; the bullet, it's said, went through his coat.

Wyatt's time in Wichita came to an abrupt end three months later, when a disagreement with a candidate in the town marshal's election resulted in fisticuffs. At a time when citizens were growing impatient with the town's vice trade, the candidate, Bill Smith, seems to have made an issue of the fact that Wyatt had a brother and sister-in-law running a brothel. He was told to stay clear of Smith but didn't. The fistfight ensued. They say Wyatt had to be pulled off the man.

He was fired. The newspaper sighed: "It is but justice to Erp [*sic*] to say he had made an excellent officer, and hitherto his conduct has been unexceptionable."[10] When a pal won the election, he tried to rehire Wyatt, but the move bogged down in a dispute over back pay. Wyatt, who had a self-righteous streak, up and quit town.

He wasn't unemployed for long. The Texas cattle business was already moving to a rugged village in the state's southwest quarter, a remote spot that would go down as ground zero of the Gunfighter Era:

Dodge City.

CHAPTER SEVEN

Legends in the Making

Dodge City, 1876 to 1883

D*odge City.*
    The name conjures up every stereotype of the era—tense men facing off in a sandy lane, fingers twitching over their holsters, drunken Texans hurrahing the town, canny gamblers, dowdy whores, and straight-arrow sheriffs—a panoply of western myth. The actual Dodge City, it may not surprise you, doesn't quite live up to the legend.

While "the Queen of the Cow Towns" was indeed infamous in its day, it was Wyatt Earp's rise in popular culture that's made it iconic, the preeminent platform for frontier gunplay, a notion enshrined by *Gunsmoke*, the 1950s radio show that morphed into a long-running television drama. Yes, the order to "Get out of Dodge" refers to Dodge City; it's probably a *Gunsmoke* thing. Yes, there was a Boot Hill, so named as a graveyard for those who "died with their boots on," but it wasn't the first Boot Hill, nor the most famous.*

---

*The first was in Hays, Kansas. The most famous would have to be the Boot Hill in Tombstone, Arizona.

And no, Dodge City was never really *Dodge City*. Of all the places gunfighters trod, it's odd that this bustling cattle town on the plains of southwest Kansas has gone down as the deadliest. Because it wasn't; far from it. Even today writers keep extolling it as this great, bloody citadel of sin. A 2017 history terms Dodge "the most depraved and criminal town in the nation . . . the most violent and turbulent town in the West," which is ridiculous.[1]

Dodge had been "founded," if that's the word, as a tent or two thrown up on the prairie to sell liquor to buffalo hunters and, as the railroad approached, to construction workers. Its image problem was rooted in its one period of genuinely startling (if thinly documented) violence, its first year as an unorganized village in 1872 and 1873, when eighteen men were killed. Newspapers across Kansas had a field day; one limned a town "infested principally with gamblers, horse thieves, prostitutes and murderers, who look upon the law as a huge joke."[2] The odd story even floated into the eastern newspapers.

Kansans were not amused. In a fast-maturing state where several towns had already rejected the excesses of Texas cowboys, Dodge was viewed as a final hurdle in the march of civilization, an abhorrent anachronism. In Kansas, its name became a synonym for savagery, never mind that not a soul was killed there in the next two years.[3]

And it didn't get much more "depraved" after that. In the eventful years Western writers tend to focus on, 1878 and 1879, when Wyatt Earp and Bat Masterson and Doc Holliday walked its streets, Dodge suffered precisely seven killings, less than the number killed on a bad Saturday night in Newton. It was a boomtown, sure, with dance halls and brothels and gunfights, but thanks in part to Earp and Masterson, it was fairly well-behaved by Old West standards. "Three dancehalls in full blast on the South Side, stables jammed full, hundreds of cowboys perambulate daily, but two cases in police court? Who says we aren't a moral city?" a Dodge paper asked in 1878.

That its notoriety endures is due in part to latter-day civic boosters, who judged that Dodge's history as "Sodom of the Plains" might draw more tourists than, you know, wheat. What Dodge did have, though, even more than Abilene, was star power. As the principal Kansas town still accepting Texas cattle in the late 1870s, it drew a who's who of gunfighters, cattlemen, and gamblers, not just Earp, Masterson, and Holliday, but Dick Clark, Luke Short, Rowdy Joe Lowe, Mysterious Dave Mather, and Billy and Ben Thompson—not to mention the man who may have been the most feared gunfighter of his day, Clay Allison.

In 1876, when it accepted the cattle baton from weary Wichita, Dodge City was a jumble of saloons, ramshackle houses, and a hotel or three on a bluff overlooking the Arkansas River. The town marshal was mostly an administrative position; the actual policing fell to the assistant marshal. There's little to document that first cattle season, but it's been suggested the first wave of invading Texans scared off the incumbent assistant by hurrahing the town. City fathers hired Wyatt as his replacement and must've been pleased. There were no gunfights that first season, no serious drama at all, in fact.

Part of it was Wyatt's approach to order. As a lawman, he always de-emphasized guns in favor of fists. When challenged by a drunk, Wyatt would often draw his pistol and brain his opponent, a practice that came to be known as "buffaloing." Dodge was run by merchants who understood that shooting people could be bad for business. Wyatt had the discipline, and the fistic abilities, to make the policy work.

He was responsible for policing a town halved by the railroad tracks that ran along Front Street. To the north lay respectable Dodge. To the south lay the vice district, which Wyatt and his men oversaw with a firm hand; carry a gun, pee in public, or cause a ruckus and you could expect an arrest and a fine, or the butt of a pistol. As in Ellsworth, the Texas cowboys constantly carped about these heavy-handed tactics, but no one much listened. Why should they? Wyatt's tactics worked. There weren't any gunfights in 1877 either.

As effective as he was, at this point there's not much to justify Wyatt's place in the Western pantheon, or even Dodge City's. This began to change once he renewed acquaintance with William Barclay "Bat" Masterson, an avuncular Canadian who became a legend in his own right. Remembered today mostly as Wyatt's sidekick, Masterson in his prime was considered a premier gunfighter, among the most famous in the West. The countless books and articles that claim to tell his story credit him with as many as thirty-eight killings; the actual number would seem to be three. He was also a natural storyteller, and in later years wrote his stories down, emerging as an indispensable Boswell for the striking number of gunmen he encountered. A hundred years after his passing, Masterson remains a primary source on a dozen or more marquee gunfights.*

His family immigrated when he was a boy. Bat grew up near Wichita with brothers who would follow him to Dodge. As a teenager he left home and became a buffalo hunter, meeting Wyatt somewhere along the way. He found his first measure of fame in 1874 as a defender at the Battle of Adobe Walls, where seven hundred or so Comanche and Kiowa besieged twenty-eight buffalo hunters at a remote trading post in the Texas Panhandle. When they finally withdrew six days later, four hunters and dozens of tribesmen were dead, and twenty-year-old Bat Masterson was able to ride back into Dodge a minor celebrity.

---

*Masterson's importance as a witness to the careers of men such as Earp, Holliday, Clay Allison, and Luke Short raises a chicken-or-the-egg kind of question: Was it simply serendipitous that he was drawn into the lives of so many significant gunmen? Or were their reputations a product of Masterson's witnessing? In other words, did Bat Masterson create the legends around Wyatt and others? While he certainly contributed, I tend to think not. The later events in Tombstone all but guaranteed Wyatt and Holliday places in western history, while Allison and Short were involved in enough shootings that they became public figures long before Masterson wrote about them.

After a year serving as a civilian scout for the army, he returned to buffalo hunting, spending much of the winter of 1875–76 at the isolated Panhandle settlement of Sweetwater, today's Mobeetie, which had sprung up beside the army's Fort Elliott.* The soldiers there were a rough bunch, and the roughest, it's said, was a notorious twenty-eight-year-old corporal named Melvin A. King (real name: Anthony Cook) who bragged incessantly of men he had killed in saloon gunfights.

There are multiple versions of their encounter, but the most credible agree that late on the night of January 24, 1876, Masterson borrowed a key to the Lady Gay Saloon and snuck in for a tryst with a prostitute named Mollie Brennan, who had earned notice in Kansas as Billy Thompson's boon companion. Corporal King, who also favored her, learned of this and, wildly drunk, headed for the dance hall.

In version one, related sixty years later by Masterson's brother, King banged on the door. When Bat opened it, thinking it was someone else, King stepped inside and drew his Colt, at which point Brennan screamed and jumped in front of Bat. When King fired, his bullet went through her, killing her instantly, and struck Bat in the pelvic region. Bat fell, drew his own gun, and managed to get off a shot before King could fire again. It struck King in the heart.

In version two, related by Bat himself in testimony for a lawsuit in 1913, King shot him without warning at the door. The bullet struck him in the stomach and knocked him back five or six feet, where he fell. When King fired a second time, his round struck and killed Brennan. As it did, Bat drew his own gun and shot and killed King.[4] This is easily the most likely account, at least to my thinking.

The most famous version, though, the one you can read in many older accounts, was the one Wyatt told late in life. In it, King stalked

---

*The fort actually acquired its name later that winter. At the time of Masterson's altercation in January 1876, it was still known as "Cantonment Sweetwater."

into the Lady Gay while a dance was in full swing. Outraged to find Bat sashaying with Mollie Brennan, he drew and fired, killing her and wounding him. Bat then pulled his pistol and shot King dead.

What's remarkable about this version is that, as a crowd of King's incensed army pals readied to take revenge, who should jump up on a faro table, pull his own Colt, and cover Bat's exit?

Ben Thompson!

Okay, I grant you, this is a lot to process. Suffice it to say, credible biographers roll their eyes at the Thompson tale; it speaks to the elderly Wyatt's unreliability, especially for events he didn't witness firsthand. The odd thing is there's evidence the Lady Gay was owned or co-owned by Ben's no-account brother, Billy. If anyone saved Bat's life that night, it was probably Billy Thompson, not Ben. In all likelihood, no one did.

Two things are indisputable, though. The incident at Sweetwater was described around Dodge City so often it earned Masterson a reputation as an accomplished gunfighter, fairly or not. The second is that Bat was badly wounded. It's said he recovered back at the family homestead outside Wichita, but he walked with a cane the rest of his life; it became his trademark. When he and his brother Jim took jobs working as Wyatt's deputies on the Dodge City force in 1876, we're told he used the cane to buffalo any number of Texas cowboys. The following year, Bat ran for sheriff. He won by three votes.

Bat and Wyatt became close, even though, or maybe because, they were a mismatched pair. Wyatt was lean, taciturn, unsmiling, and tightly wound. Bat was five years younger, thickly built, dark and garrulous, someone to drink with. Wyatt was the polarizing one; people tended to love him or hate him. Bat was the one who made friends easily. In Dodge they became a strong team. On a frontier where too many lawmen were corrupt, drunkards, or both, they displayed discipline, professional pride, and a work ethic. Theirs became one of the most famous friendships in the Old West. The most famous of all also involved Wyatt, and it began at just about the same time.

FOR WYATT IN KANSAS, BEING A LAWMAN WAS SEASONAL WORK. BY OC-tober 1877 he had left Dodge to pursue a pair of train robbers, either on assignment from the railroad or as a bounty hunter. The pursuit drew him down into North Texas, where he lingered in the rugged town of Fort Griffin. A bartender suggested he talk to a strange, thin man at a gambling table. His name was John Henry Holliday. His day job was dentistry, hence his nickname: Doc.

Thus began a legendary friendship. Doc Holliday has since gone down as the Old West's great oddball, a boozy, cantankerous Georgia consumptive who fled to the frontier in hopes the climate might help his tuberculosis. His illness left him weak, sometimes even unsteady— Masterson joked a child could beat him up—yet Holliday radiated a feral intelligence. No doubt aware of his weakness, he resorted to weaponry more readily than most. He was lethal with a Colt, a der-ringer, and the massive knife he carried, which he dubbed "the Hell Bitch." He was perhaps the unlikeliest gunfighter of all.

Born in 1851 into a well-educated north Georgia clan that fled Sherman's March to the town of Valdosta, Holliday received training in rhetoric, mathematics, and languages, including Latin and Ancient Greek. A turning point came in 1866, when he was fifteen. His mother died of tuberculosis, as did his adopted brother. When his father re-married a neighbor's daughter, it's said, Holliday began to act out a bit. When an angry classmate challenged him to a mock duel, Holliday in-sisted on using a loaded gun. His friends had to explain it was just a joke.

At nineteen he went to Philadelphia for dental school; afterward he joined a practice in Atlanta. But then something happened. Exactly what, people debate to this day. Years later, Masterson wrote that, much like Wes Hardin, Holliday was obliged to flee Georgia after murdering two Black men at a swimming hole; when this story made the rounds decades later, his relatives insisted Holliday only fired over their heads. While the details are debatable, not so the other reason he left the state. In 1873, at twenty, he too was diagnosed with tuberculosis. Given weeks to live, he headed west, to Texas.

In Dallas he opened a dental practice and not only lived but thrived for a time, even co-winning a set of dental awards ("Best set of teeth in gold!"). But the hacking cough he had acquired did not help his business. He had begun drinking, meanwhile, probably to ease tubercular pain, and when drinking he liked to gamble. In the next two years, while shuttling between Dallas and nearby Denison, he generated an impressive record of gambling arrests. After his first gunfight—a bloodless affair with a saloon keeper known as "Champagne Charlie"—he decided to explore the frontier.

Holliday was drawn anywhere there were gamblers. He left behind a trail of tales that suggest his innate orneriness was morphing into a taste for violent confrontation. He may have killed a Black soldier at Fort Griffin. He may have used the Hell Bitch to slash a Denver gambler's throat. Or he may just have wandered, to Cheyenne, to Deadwood, then a long tour along the Rio Grande, where by one account he tended the molars of a Mexican general. He got shot by a sharper while back in Dallas, and in time recovered.

Somewhat like Hardin, the poster boy of put-upon Southern masculinity, Holliday seemed unable, or unwilling, to avoid or smooth over many minor disagreements, especially at the gambling table. "He was hot-headed and impetuous and very much given to both drinking and quarreling, and, among men who did not fear him, very much disliked," Masterson wrote in 1907. "He would no sooner be out of one scrape before he was in another, and the strange part of it is he was more often in the right than in the wrong, which has rarely ever been the case with a man who is continually getting himself into trouble."[5]

Much that we know of Holliday in these early years comes from the memories of the Hungarian-born prostitute he took up with along the way, Mary Katherine Horony, known to history as "Big Nose Kate." The sense one gets of him from Horony is of a lost soul, adrift, hard-drinking, argumentative, moralistic, sensitive to slights. Holliday was thin, wan, and clean-shaven, with reddish hair, a deep Southern drawl, and a .41-caliber derringer he kept tucked in his vest pocket. He was also apparently not a bad gambler. According to Herbert Asbury, Holliday was far more talented at cards than his peer Ben Thompson. "He dealt a very tricky game of Faro," Asbury writes, "and at short cards was regarded as a veritable wizard."*[6]

When Wyatt met him at Fort Griffin, Holliday peppered him with questions about Dodge City, which was growing fast. After they parted, Wyatt said later, Holliday got into an argument with a gambler he suspected of cheating, drew out the Hell Bitch, and stabbed him "just below the brisket." At which point Doc and Big Nose Kate decided Dodge might be worth a try. By the following June, when he advertised his new dental practice there, Holliday had firmly inserted himself into what would become one of the great narratives of the Old West.

THE RIOTOUS 1878 CATTLE SEASON WAS DODGE CITY'S SIGNATURE MO-ment, providing not only the defining episodes of Wyatt's origin story, but also a vivid reminder of the havoc Texas cowboys could still bring to a cow town. Bat's brother Ed Masterson, who had been promoted

---

*"Short cards" refers to the practice of surreptitiously removing cards from a full deck and dealing from it anyway; i.e., "short" of cards.

in Wyatt's absence, proved no match for the Texans. The *Ford County Globe* was already complaining about public drunkenness and petty theft on April 9, as the first longhorn herds were moving into the area.

That evening Ed attempted to disarm two cowboys outside a dance hall on Front Street and ended up grappling with one. Bat saw it from down the street. "Ed, shove him away from you!" he hollered.

There was a gunshot, and Ed staggered back, dying, clutching his midsection, his shirt afire. Both cowboys ended up shot dead, and in the ensuing chaos, people believed Ed had done it; not till years later would Bat admit it was he who had avenged his brother.

Wyatt was tracking a man in Joplin, it's said, when he got the telegram from Dodge's mayor. He was back on duty by mid-May. By most accounts, he made an immediate impact. Faced with emboldened Texans, Wyatt stole a page from modern New York's playbook by zealously policing minor infractions—drunkenness, carrying a gun—in hopes of bringing them under control. Unlike in Ellsworth, no one accused Dodge lawmen of taking bribes. They seemed to make enough playing cards.

Still, as in Ellsworth, tensions with the Texans grew, especially after an incident on July 13 when a cook for one of the Texas outfits shot and killed a visiting deputy U.S. marshal inside the Long Branch Saloon. The second murder of a lawman that season prompted Wyatt to crack down harder still. The next few weeks saw dozens of visiting cowboys streaming into the jail on all the usual charges. Among those who complained the loudest, it appears, were drovers who worked for a Texas rancher named Tobe Driskill.*

In old age, Wyatt recalled an incident involving the Driskill out-

---

*William Walter "Tobe" Driskill (1852–1922) belonged to one of the most prominent Texas ranching families moving longhorns north in those years. His father, Jesse Lincoln Driskill, is best known as the builder of Austin's landmark Driskill Hotel, which still stands. Its bar remains one of the capital's premier drinking spots; I highly recommend it. In the 1870s, when the younger Driskill had dealings with Wyatt Earp, the family was in the process of

fit that forged a lasting bond with Doc Holliday, who up to that point was likely just an acquaintance. Tobe Driskill himself and at least one other man had gotten drunk at the new Comique Theater, known to the Texans as the "Commy-Kew," and were apparently attempting to ransack its bar. Holliday was seated at a monte table, a bystander.

When Wyatt and a deputy responded, they began pistol-whipping the cowboys. A melee broke out. At one point, a Texan drew his gun and aimed at Wyatt's back. "Look out!" Holliday shouted, drawing his own gun. He fired what may have been a warning shot, freezing the cowboy. Other versions of the story say he drew down on an entire crowd. Whatever happened, Wyatt was able to regain control of the saloon. He would always credit Holliday with saving his life.

Wyatt's brand of two-fisted justice had its fans; one of the Dodge papers termed his work "splendid." But others weren't so thrilled. As Wyatt told it later, he managed to alienate the town's leading merchant and state representative, Bob Wright, by arresting a Texas trail boss for shooting at a fiddler. Wright thought this kind of thing bad for business. He threatened to have Wyatt fired. Wyatt's none-too-subtle reaction was to briefly toss both men into jail.

At this point, Wyatt began hearing whispers that Wright wouldn't mind him dead, a feeling that solidified after events in the early morning hours of July 26. At 3:00 a.m. Dodge was still rocking, Texas cowboys thronging the poker tables, bars, and theaters. At the Commy-Kew, a dance was underway as Bat Masterson dealt Spanish monte in a corner. Holliday was seated at his table. Wyatt and Jim Masterson were standing outside, leaning against an awning post.

Suddenly a group of mounted Texans, apparently from Tobe Driskill's outfit, rode up and opened fire, the 1878 version of a drive-by

---

opening new ranches in South Dakota and Wyoming, elements of which remain in the family to this day.

shooting. Inside the theater, Masterson, Holliday, and everyone else fell flat onto their bellies. One presumes Wyatt did the same. According to one eyewitness, several fusillades were fired. What seemed like hundreds of bullets ricocheted through the theater.

When the shooting stopped, the Texans turned to flee. Wyatt lunged at one of the horses but missed, the cowboys riding hard toward the bridge over the Arkansas. Joined by Holliday and the Mastersons, Wyatt fired as they did. In the distance, a young Texan named George Hoy fell from his mount, a wound in his arm. He died a few weeks later. No one knows whose bullet took him down, but the incident may have been the first time Wyatt Earp fired his gun at a man.

Wyatt believed the assault was an assassination attempt arranged by Bob Wright, a feeling that grew a few weeks later with some ominous news: Clay Allison was in town.

FROM *HIGH NOON* ON DOWN, WESTERN CINEMA AND LITERATURE ARE replete with themes of gallant sheriffs and townspeople fearing the arrival of a dastardly badman intent on violence. An iconic incident that fueled this worn trope occurred in August or September 1878, with the appearance in Dodge of Clay Allison, who may have been the frontier's most feared gunfighter in the late 1870s and was likely the most unstable. No one claimed to understand him. He was the kind of wild card who once rode through the streets of a Texas town wearing nothing but a gun belt. Why? No one knew.

A rancher in postwar Texas and New Mexico, Allison is one of those gunmen whose notoriety has dimmed over the years, which is a shame, because he earned it. He was six foot two and handsome, with a high forehead, lustrous black hair, dark blue eyes, a thick mustache, and a chin beard. Born in Tennessee, he fought for the Confederacy and may be the single gunfighter of note whose behavior could be traced to wartime trauma; rebel doctors granted him a medical discharge, citing epilepsy and manic episodes, which seemed more prevalent when he drank.

His early years are cloaked in shadow, though folklore suggests a man with a taste for extreme violence. After the war, Allison and his brothers tried ranching on the North Texas frontier, where an incident occurred that fired his legend. He got into an argument with a ferryman over the Brazos River, and to settle it, the men are said to have bound their left hands together and fought it out with knives, a rare and uniquely deadly version of the Southern duel.* Only Allison walked away.

By 1870, when he was about thirty, he had established a ranch near the northeast New Mexico town of Cimarron, between Taos and the Texas border. Legend has him leading a lynch mob that strung up a man suspected of murder; Allison, we're told, had the gentleman's severed head stuck on a pike outside a saloon.

His reputation was secured in a series of shootings during the mid-1870s. The most famous occurred on January 7, 1874, and made the New Mexico newspapers. It involved a Texas gunman named "Chunk" Colbert, who was purported to have killed seven men, though the actual number appears to be one or two. According to the Santa Fe *Daily New Mexican*, Colbert embarked on a bender in the town of Red River,

---

*In what's generally known as a handkerchief fight, or duel, combatants take ends of a handkerchief—in their hands, or their teeth—and fight at close quarters, typically with knives. The idea seems to have originated with a French dueling variant, the duel au mouchoir, in which opponents stood apart the length of a handkerchief. While there are several accounts of mouchoir duels in Britain, I have yet to find a documented account of such a fight in the United States, much less one where combatants grasped a handkerchief. Three different histories of U.S. duels do not mention the practice. The best-known example of the handkerchief fight may be in the 1980 movie *The Long Riders*, in which David Carradine's Cole Younger faces off with James Remar's Sam Starr. Great film.

shooting out the eyes of portraits in a saloon and wildly firing his pistol, wounding a man in the hand—what the paper termed "a general drunk with promiscuous shooting accomplishments."[7]

Allison and Colbert did not get along, though whether the cause was a disagreement over a horse race that day or Colbert's prominent assholishness we don't know.* Whatever the reason, they ended up dining across from each other at the Clifton House hotel, Allison's pistol on the table, Colbert's in his lap. At one point, when Colbert reached for a cup of coffee with his left hand—one account says he was grabbing for Allison's gun—he drew his pistol with his right and fired. Allison lunged to one side, drew his own gun, and fired once, the bullet striking Colbert above the right eye, killing him.

The story is told that when asked why he shared a meal with a gent he intended to kill, Allison replied, "Because I didn't want to send a man to hell on an empty stomach."

Colbert's killing was the kind on which reputations were built, and Allison's blossomed accordingly. He became the type of regionally famous gunman people pointed to and whispered about, much as Kansans did of Hickok. When he traveled, reporters sought him out. When one in St. Louis asked if he was the frontier's most famous gunfighter, Allison said he preferred the term "shootist," a word that, one decent John Wayne movie aside, never really caught on. "I never killed a man that didn't need it," Allison said, an echo of Hickok's quotes, soon a gunfighter staple.

His reputation soared during a bloody mid-1870s land dispute called the Colfax County War. Hundreds of ranchers and settlers, including Allison, had moved into northeastern New Mexico believing the land they claimed was public, when in fact it was subject to an old

---

*The most intriguing explanation of their enmity is the suggestion that Colbert was related to the Texas ferryman Allison had killed years earlier.

Mexican land grant. In 1870 the titular owner sold it to a British mining company that was allied with a corrupt cabal of politicians known as the "Santa Fe Ring." Allison and everyone else faced eviction. They organized themselves and vowed to resist.

Among the most vocal resisters was a minister named Frank J. Tolby, who was suspected of coauthoring letters critical of the ring to *The New York Sun*. In September 1875 Tolby was found murdered near Cimarron. Suspicion fell on a laborer named Cruz Vega, who had substituted for the dead man's mail carrier that day.* Allison and a group of locals seized Vega and strung him from a telegraph pole, raising and lowering him as they fired questions. Before dying, Vega confessed to being involved but named another man as the killer.

Cruz Vega had friends, though, chief among them a rough character named Francisco "Pancho" Griego, a monte dealer said to be an enforcer for the Santa Fe Ring. Griego had his own reputation as a gunfighter, having shot two soldiers in the back, killing one, and knifing a third, after a disagreement over cards. The day after Vega's funeral, Griego confronted Allison at the front door of the St. James Hotel in Cimarron. According to the *Daily New Mexican*, the two shared a drink before repairing to a corner where, after a chat, there was a commotion and, suddenly, three deafening gunshots. Griego fell dead.

Afterward, in one of the great synopses of an Old West gunfight and its aftermath, the hotel's owner, Henry Lambert, wrote in his journal: "Pancho try to pull the pistol. Mr. Allison smarter. I tell all to go home. Close door and go to bed. [My wife] scared. Buried Pancho in morning. Blood stain floor. Compte rendu."[8]

A judge ruled the killing self-defense. The drama, if not the killings, lasted another year or two, during which Allison ransacked the

---

*I had no idea there were mailmen on the western frontier, though of course there had to be. There's a book there for someone, I bet: *Deadly Mailmen of the Old West*. Or not.

THE GUNFIGHTERS

offices of a pro-ring newspaper, destroyed its printing press, and in a sign the man had a sense of humor, took sheets of newsprint, signed them "Clay Allison's Edition," and passed them around town.

It all ended, anticlimactically, with a mysterious stagecoach ride in which Allison and New Mexico's governor made a kind of peace. Allison agreed to stand trial on seven charges, including three for the murders of Chunk Colbert, a missing witness to his killing, and Pancho Griego. A prosecutor, alas, could find no witnesses to the Colbert shooting, no proof the missing witness was dead, and no gumption to indict Allison for Griego's killing. He walked free.

AS WITH MANY WYATT EARP STORIES, THERE ARE TWO VERSIONS OF the Clay Allison episode, one that flatters Earp and one that doesn't. The incident only became public eighteen years later, in 1896, when Wyatt told the flattering version to a reporter in San Francisco. It's the one most still believe. As Wyatt told it, he was warned that Allison and a band of Texans had arrived in town, hired to avenge the cowboy George Hoy's death. His first day in Dodge Allison behaved. On the second, he was overheard making threats. Wyatt gathered Masterson and several pals, stationed them around town, then went in search of him. He found Allison on Front Street. The two coolly exchanged greetings as they leaned against a wall, taking the measure of each other.

"So, you're the man that killed my friend Hoy," Allison said.

"Yes, I guess I'm the man you're looking for," Wyatt replied.

Wyatt said he was gripping the pistol in his pocket as he watched Allison's hand reach down toward his own. He was prepared to grab the gun if Allison drew. Allison glanced around, and spied Masterson lingering nearby, conspicuously cradling a shotgun.

"I guess I'll go round the corner," Allison said.

"I guess you'd better," Wyatt said.

Suddenly the merchant Wyatt suspected was behind all this, Bob Wright, came running down the street. He was apparently having second thoughts after a visit from Masterson, who had promised him, "If this fight comes up, Wright, you're the first man I'm going to kill."

The armed Texans Allison had been promised as backup, meanwhile, had failed to materialize. Standing there, Allison seems to have shared a word with Wright. His will, it appears, was wavering.

"Earp," Allison finally said, "I believe you're a pretty good man from what I've seen of you. Do you know that these coyotes sent for me to make a fight with you and kill you?"

And with that, Clay Allison rode out of town. When he returned ten days later, perhaps on unrelated business, he sent an emissary announcing his visit and promised no trouble. And there wasn't.

That's Wyatt's version at least. The second version was raised by the range detective Charles Siringo, who in a 1912 memoir claimed he was one of the Texans recruited to provide Allison backup. Siringo, though, insisted it wasn't Earp the Texans were after; it was Masterson. According to Siringo, Allison and his posse searched Dodge for much of a day and couldn't find a single lawman to kill.

Siringo believed they were frightened and hiding. Masterson's biographer, Robert DeArment, points out that this visit could have coincided with a Native American raid whose response drew pretty much every lawman in western Kansas. The fact is, both versions could have happened since, according to newspaper accounts at the time, Allison visited Dodge at least twice that season. Whatever happened, the Allison–Earp nonfight remains, along with the Hickok–Hardin face-off in Abilene, one of the great what-if scenarios of the era.

BY THE TIME HE LEFT DODGE, CLAY ALLISON HAD TIRED OF FAME, AND for the rest of his life, while his travels still reliably generated news items—CLAY ALLISON IN TOWN!—he avoided the violence that inspired it. That is, with one eye-opening exception, related in a newspaper account. In 1886, after shipping a herd to Cheyenne, Wyoming, Allison developed a toothache and visited a dentist there. It didn't go well; a tooth broke. After another dentist fixed the damage, Allison returned to the first in a fury. In the words of New Mexico's *Daily Optic*, whose correspondent had recently interviewed Allison:

> [Allison] proceeded to the quack's office, seized a pair of forceps, threw him down upon the floor and in spite of the yells of the victim inserted the instrument in his mouth and drew out one of his best molars. Not content with this, he grabbed for another and caught one of the front teeth together with a large piece of the upper lip and was tugging away at it when the agonized shrieks and yells of the poor devil upon whose chest Allison was pressing his knee, drew a crowd and ended the matter. The story is said to be absolutely true and Allison admitted it.[9]

You can understand why people, and not just dentists, would leave such a man in peace, and thereafter they did. By 1880 Allison was quietly ranching in the Texas Panhandle, where he got married and sired a daughter. Cattle were good to Allison, and by 1886, well-to-do by frontier standards, he and his new family moved to Pecos, in West Texas, where he built a house in town and bought a ranch outside.

It was there, a year later, after picking up a load of supplies, that he fell from a wagon and was run over, his skull crushed, not at all the way people had expected he would pass. Western writers have since credited Allison with fifteen or more killings, depicting him as this crazed killer who terrorized his corner of the frontier. But while he was certainly notorious in his day, his biographer Chuck Parsons puts the actual number of men he killed at four or five.

Eulogists, in fact, remembered Clay Allison fondly. When he was sober, his Southern manners seem to have left a nice enough impression. The *Optic* called him "brave" and "true hearted," with a gunfighting career "perhaps unparalleled in the western country." A Dodge City paper noted: "Whether this brave, genteel border man was in truth a villain or a gentleman is a question that many who knew him never settled to their own satisfaction."[10] He was buried in Pecos, where a marker at his grave took the point of view you might expect:

CLAY ALLISON

GENTLEMAN

GUNFIGHTER

1840-1887

R.I.P.

CHAPTER EIGHT

"You Have Lived Long Enough"

Bat Masterson, Luke Short, and Beyond

The final act of Dodge City's 1878 season centered on another hell-raising Texas cattleman, although one of a different breed, a wealthy, entitled ranching heir named James "Spike" Kenedy.* Wyatt had snatched a pistol off Kenedy that summer; the Texan had paid a fine. A month later he was arrested and fined for disorderly conduct.

Kenedy did not take this well. Early that autumn, he confronted Mayor Jim "Dog" Kelley. When Kelley defended his men and warned him to behave, Kenedy threatened him, then rode out of town. By four in the morning on October 4 he was back. He rode up to Kelley's shanty behind the Western Hotel and fired four shots into it.

Wyatt and Jim Masterson arrived to find an actress from the

---

*Kenedy had earned a reputation as a gunman after an incident in Ellsworth in 1872 in which he shot the obstreperous Texas rancher Print Olive. The two had been playing cards at the Ellsworth Billiard Saloon earlier in the day when, according to a newspaper account, Kenedy accused Olive of what the paper calls "unfair dealing." When Kenedy returned around four, he produced a pistol, at which point Olive threw up his hands and said, "Don't shoot!" Kenedy fired four times, bullets striking Olive in the groin, thigh, and hand. Olive's life was saved by the intervention of his servant, James Kelly, who shot Kenedy in the hip. Everyone lived.

Commy-Kew sobbing outside. She pointed into the house, to the mayor's bedroom. There they found another actress, Dora Hand, dead in a bed. Mayor Kelley, it turned out, had taken ill and left town to see a doctor. He had allowed the women to use his house in his absence.

Wyatt knew of Kenedy's grievance. He stalked to the Long Branch Saloon, where he spotted him at a monte table. Wyatt asked the bartender how long he had been there. "For God's sake, don't say anything here," the bartender whispered, motioning him into a back room. There he told Wyatt the cattleman had left just before the shots rang out and returned shortly after, downing a large whiskey.

When Wyatt returned to the barroom, Kenedy was gone. So was his horse. Wyatt and Bat collared one of Kenedy's pals, pushed him into a cell, and started asking questions. The man admitted that Kenedy had done the shooting. By breakfast Bat was already assembling what one of the papers called "as intrepid a posse as ever pulled a trigger."*[1]

Assuming Kenedy was headed to Texas, the five men rode south. They found his trail, followed it for two days, then lost it in a rainstorm. Stopping at a ranch, they learned Kenedy had ridden through the day before. Again, they found his trail; again, they lost it in the rain. Finally, exhausted, they decided to rest their horses on the open prairie. As they did, one of them spied a rider in the distance. After a few minutes, they realized he was heading toward them.

"That's Kenedy," Bat breathed. "I know him by the way he rides, and besides, I know his horse."

The posse's own horses had wandered afield. The men lay flat behind a little mound. When Kenedy rode to within seventy-five yards, they rose and challenged him. He fired wildly and wheeled his horse

---

*There were five of them: Bat, Wyatt, Marshal Charlie Bassett, a deputy named Bill Duffy, and, most notably, Deputy Bill Tilghman, who would go on to a long, heralded career as perhaps the most decorated lawman in Oklahoma.

to ride away. Wyatt fired at the horse, which fell. Bat's bullet hit the cattleman in the shoulder. The horse landed atop him. When they walked up to free him, Kenedy snarled, "You sons of bitches, I will get even with you for this."[2]

He never did, though neither did he face justice. When his wealthy father arrived in Dodge, a quiet meeting was convened in the sheriff's office. Afterward, to Wyatt's dismay, Kenedy walked away with his freedom. Everyone suspected his father's money won it. The most eventful season in Dodge's short history was finally over.

And with it, the era of the Kansas cattle towns began to close.

By 1879 Dodge City was calming. The cattle business fell off that season as more settlers moved in, throwing up tents and sod huts in the fields where Texans fed their beeves. (Many Texas herds began heading north on the Texas Trail to Ogallala, Nebraska, another wide-open cow town.) Dodge, Earp was famously quoted saying late in life, "was beginning to lose much of the snap which had given it a charm to men of restless blood." Along with Doc Holliday and many of their peers, he cast his eyes west. Having crossed Kansas, the railroad was now inching into northeastern New Mexico, and Wyatt rode there first, and then farther, to the remote Arizona Territory and a sunblasted place called Tombstone, which would furnish all the snap he needed.

ONE OF THE FINAL MARQUEE GUNFIGHTS IN DODGE CITY FELL TO MAS-terson, who initially accompanied the Earps to Arizona. In 1881 he was summoned back to Dodge by an urgent telegram saying his brother Jim was in danger. Jim was running the Lady Gay Saloon and had developed a toxic relationship with a bartender, a bellicose type named Al Updegraff. His partner, Updegraff's brother-in-law A. J. Peacock, was siding with the bartender. Violence was in the air.

Bat stepped off his train in downtown Dodge on a Saturday, April 16, into a scene out of a Western. No sooner did his foot hit the dirt than he saw Peacock and Updegraff walking alongside the train. "Hold up there a minute, you two," he shouted. "I want to talk to you."

The pair took one look at Masterson and ran, ducking behind the jail. A shot was fired; no one ever understood by whom. Bat dropped behind a railroad embankment. Ahead, to his south, Peacock and Updegraff opened fire from behind the jailhouse. Their shots zinged past him and blew out windows behind him on Front Street.

Everywhere, people ran for cover. For a few minutes, Masterson and his adversaries sniped at one another in grim silence.

Then, bizarrely, their shots were subsumed in a hail of bullets seemingly emanating from every storefront. Those from in front of Masterson, in the South Side saloons, seemed to be firing at him. Those from behind seemed to be shooting at Peacock and Updegraff.

After a moment, Updegraff pitched forward, a bullet in his chest. He would survive. Soon both Masterson and Peacock ran out of ammunition. The mayor emerged, jogged toward Bat, and placed him under arrest. Bat went quietly. The "Battle of the Plaza" was over. Facing charges later that day, Bat paid a fine of eight dollars, recognized as a pittance even by Old West standards. As one paper commented: "It costs $8.00 to shoot a man through the lung in Dodge City."[3]

Masterson would go on to the most notable post-frontier life of his peers. In the 1880s and '90s, already among the most celebrated gunfighters, he shuttled between Denver and outlying Colorado towns, gambling, running saloons, and gaining an interest in boxing. He became a fixture at bouts across the country, sometimes serving as timekeeper. In 1902 he moved to New York, where *The Morning Telegraph* gave him a sports column, "Masterson's Views on Timely Topics," which he wrote three times weekly from 1903 until 1921. He emerged as a noted bon vivant and a friend to President Theodore Roosevelt, who shared his love for boxing and the frontier. Masterson is almost certainly the only gunfighter to stay overnight at the White House.

Along the way, he wrote about Earp and other gunfighters, most notably in a 1907 magazine series. He died of a heart attack at his desk in 1921. He was sixty-seven. Masterson's fame only grew after his death. From the 1940s, he was regularly portrayed in movies and then television, often as Earp's good-natured sidekick, earning his own NBC television series from 1958 to 1961; in it, Gene Barry portrayed Masterson as a roving, do-gooding dandy and ladies' man, complete with black derby, ornate vests, and a gold-topped cane—a stretch, to be sure, but for the cane. His pal Damon Runyon used Masterson as the basis for the rakish gambler Sky Masterson in his story (and the subsequent musical) *Guys and Dolls*. It was quite the life.

DODGE CITY HAD ONE FINAL MOMENT IN THE SUN, REVOLVING AROUND the frontier's third gambler-gunman of note, the enigmatic Luke Short. A small, illiterate cowboy turned card shark, Short, like Doc Holliday, roamed the frontier for years, a flinty little asteroid who regularly streaked across the Earp–Masterson galaxy. He was famous enough in his day to sit for a few interviews, but as with Wyatt, what fame endured had to be nudged along by Masterson, his longtime friend. "Modest" is the common descriptor. Quiet. Steady. Loyal. Polite. Controlled. In other words, the anti-Holliday.

Born in 1854 and raised in North Texas—his people ended up in San Angelo—Short, like Masterson and so many others, struck out onto the plains as a teenager. He started as just another Texas cowboy, taking several drives to Kansas, and kept at it for six years; Masterson suggests his riding and shooting were so advanced he qualified as a "white Indian." His skill with a pistol inspired one of the great tales of frontier gunmanship. Short, it holds, was dining in a Fort Worth restaurant when he was served a glass of milk in which a fly was "treading water." Short tossed the glass into the air, drew his Colt, and as the contents of the glass fell toward the floor, shot the fly.

What strikes you about Short, though, is his entrepreneurial streak, his head for numbers; he may be the only gunfighter ever described as an "autodidact." His first venture, it's said, was a Nebraska trading post where he sold whiskey to the Sioux. Run off by the army—according to Masterson, he was arrested and escaped—he found work as a cavalry scout and dispatch rider, surviving multiple skirmishes with Sioux tribesmen. Some claim he killed dozens.

By 1879, when he began transitioning to a gambler's life, Short was all of five foot six, slender, with thinnish black hair parted on the left and a mustache that drooped just past the edges of his mouth. Older men tended to underestimate him given his boyish appearance. A Southerner, and a Texan to boot, Short was not one to take such insults lightly. When he began his card-playing career in Leadville, the Colorado mining town, Masterson relates a tale of one rough-hewn opponent who warned Short not to make a particular bet and called him an "insignificant little shrimp." When Short ignored him, the man went for his gun. According to Masterson, Short drew his own gun first, pressed it against the gent's cheek, and fired. Somehow the man survived, albeit presumably cheekless.

Short's reputation as a gunfighter is based on three shootings. The first occurred after he began working the new gambling scene in Arizona, in Tombstone, unrelated to but smack in the middle of the violence the Earps encountered there. On the morning of February 25, 1881, Short was working at a faro table alongside Bat as a "lookout," something like a pit boss, when another prominent gambler, Charlie Storms, took offense at something he said and slapped him. Masterson, we are told, jumped between the two just as they went for their guns.

Bat escorted Storms back to his rooms and told him to sleep it off. He had just returned and was talking to Short inside the front door when Storms materialized in the doorway. Without a word, Storms went for his Colt. Once again, according to Masterson, Short was a touch too fast. He drew his own gun, pressed it against Storms's chest, and fired a shot into his heart; as he fell, he shot him once more. Later, after a hearing, a magistrate ruled it self-defense.*

After the shooting in Tombstone, Short returned to Dodge City, working there during the cattle season and shuttling among Colorado camps in the winter. By this point he had transformed himself into a true sporting man, commonly wearing an ornate vest and sometimes a top hat. He had learned to read and, according to Masterson, had become an avid letter writer and lover of the classics, able to quote Shakespeare, Byron, and Longfellow.

He was also talented at the tables; by early 1883, having played cards professionally barely four years, Short had amassed a bankroll large enough to buy an interest in Dodge's famed Long Branch Saloon. That's when his trouble began. A spirited civic debate had sprung up between those who favored an unfettered approach to vice and those who wanted to clean up the town. Two months after Short took over the Long Branch, a reform slate won every race in a town election.

The "reformers," as it turned out, exhibited a selective eye toward enforcement. A week after passing a pair of anti-vice ordinances, three young ladies who worked at the Long Branch were arrested for prostitution, despite Short's protests that they were dancers. The ordinances also forbade live music. Short fired his band.

The next night, though, he noticed that the mayor's saloon seemed

---

*Here one might note that placing a gun barrel against an opponent's body before firing is not only an unusual tactic—it's a challenge to find many such incidents in the literature— but an unusually effective one. It is, after all, difficult to miss. Why Short was the first to popularize this method of attack, and why others didn't try it more often, remains a mystery. At least to me.

to be hosting not only a series of comely women but a band. Short promptly rehired his musicians and then took the night off, only to be summoned when they were all arrested. He stalked off in search of the officer responsible and found him standing on the sidewalk.

The officer, Louis C. Hartman, seeing Short angry and armed, panicked and fired point-blank at him, missing. Short fired a shot or two in return, missing as well. Hartman slipped and fell. Short, believing he had killed him, barricaded himself inside the Long Branch, where he refused all efforts to surrender until morning, when he was jailed. Thus began what's known as the Dodge City War.

A vigilance committee sprang up, proclaiming Short part of a conspiracy of gamblers determined to take over the town. Five more gamblers were arrested; all were given the choice between a westbound or eastbound train. Short chose to go east, to Kansas City, and began attempts to reclaim his saloon. He wired Masterson in Denver. Together the two headed to Topeka, where they saw the governor, who expressed sympathy but little else. Sensing the need for more support, Masterson sent for Wyatt, who—this was after his years in Tombstone—was tending bar in Colorado. He promised to bring some friends.

Rumors of an army of all-star gunmen heading to Dodge was the biggest news in Kansas in years. A Kansas City paper reported, inaccurately, that Doc Holliday and Rowdy Joe Lowe had been recruited, though Earp was the headliner: Wyatt, it noted, was an expert "in the cheerful business of depopulating the country." In Dodge, meanwhile, vigilantes stopped and searched every incoming train. It was widely rumored that Short was to be shot on sight.

Wyatt, as planned, arrived in Dodge first, along with four tough-looking characters from Colorado. As he told it later, the district attorney was among those who met the train. "My God, Wyatt," he gasped, "who are these people you've got with you?"

Wyatt allowed himself a moment of levity.

"Oh," he replied, "they're just some bushwhackers I've brought over from Colorado to straighten you people out."

An emergency city council meeting was convened. Asked what he wanted, Wyatt demanded safe passage for Short and Masterson to come settle Short's affairs. The council caved. When Wyatt escorted the two into town, no one had the stomach for a fight; the trio was met not with bullets but handshakes. The Dodge City War was over before it started. The episode was memorialized in one of the most famous photographs of the Old West, Earp, Masterson, Short, and five other unsmiling men sitting for a celebratory portrait. *The National Police Gazette* ran it under the caption "Dodge City Peace Commission."

The publicity vaulted Short into the top ranks of American sporting men. Sick of Kansas, he moved to Fort Worth, where he bought a share in the White Elephant, one of the state's largest gambling parlors. Masterson got him interested in boxing, and Short was soon a staple at championship matches and horse races from New York to New Orleans. Unlike Masterson's, though, his gunfighting days weren't over.

In fact, he was soon embroiled in a dispute that led to one of the Old West's storied confrontations. It happened in Fort Worth, where Short ran afoul of a notorious blackguard named Jim Courtright. Courtright is one of the era's great villains, a mysterious Illinoisan who appeared in Fort Worth in 1876 and, in his late twenties, won an election for marshal. He cut a striking figure in the streets, sharply dressed, his blond hair long and a pistol on each hip, butts forward, Hickok-style. Courtright is credited with bringing order to the city's infamous redlight district, "Hell's Half Acre." He certainly acquired the kind of violent reputation that might have helped. The Texas newspapers reported he killed four men along the way.

But Courtright's primary interest, it's always said, was shaking down businesses for protection money. Those who refused him, it was whispered, ended up dead. In 1879 he lost a reelection bid and skulked away to New Mexico, where he was a town marshal and later a hired gun and was rumored to have killed several more men. He arrived back in Fort Worth in 1884, fleeing at least one murder investigation.

There he formed a detective agency, though everyone seems to have understood it was a front for Courtright's menacing attempts to reenter the protection business; he remained the most feared man in the city. It was probably a matter of time before he approached the White Elephant. When he did, Short politely tried to fob him off. Courtright threatened to have him shut down.

Events came to a head early on the evening of February 8, 1887, when Courtright appeared at the club and demanded to see Short on the sidewalk outside. Short was sitting in the billiard room having his shoes shined alongside the ubiquitous Masterson, who was visiting from Denver. Short sent word for Courtright to come inside. He refused. Short reluctantly rose and stepped outside.

They were seen strolling up the block in conversation, eventually stopping in front of a saloon called, of course, the Shooting Gallery. As Short told it afterward, he was standing with his arms crossed, thumbs in the armholes of his vest, when he dropped them, the better, he said, to adjust his clothes. "Well, you needn't reach for your gun," Courtright said, and promptly went for his.

This time Short was unable to draw first. Courtright did, but his revolver's cylinder failed to turn, and the Colt didn't fire. Short's first shot hit Courtright in his shooting hand, taking off his thumb. As Courtright tried to pass his gun to his other hand, Short fired four more times. Each struck home. Courtright fell into the street dead. A judge ruled it self-defense.

This encounter is among the best-documented incidents of two men standing face-to-face in what amounts to a quick-draw contest. By the way, that's something you'll start to notice about gunfights after 1880. Largely because of the spread of newspapers, a violent act that

once remained a rumor begins to be reported in detail. It's one reason
Wyatt Earp and Billy the Kid became so famous.

Luke Short was in his mid-thirties by this point. One imagines his
gunfighting career might be over. He began spending much of his
time in Chicago, where he tried promoting boxing matches. He had
become a gentleman. He wore the silk top hat. He had gotten married.
A sweet woman, they said. They were homeowners.

And yet. In April 1890, after attending an auction of racehorses in
Nashville, Short passed through Memphis, where he and several other
sports pooled their bets in a night of faro. Afterward, one of their number, a Fort Worth barman named Charles Wright, was entrusted with
their winnings. Rather than deposit the money in a hotel safe, as expected, Wright kept it in his room, and the next day claimed it had
been stolen. Short and the others were less than supportive and demanded their money back. Ill will ensued.

This time it was Short who arrived outside his rival's gambling parlor, the Bank Saloon on Main Street in Fort Worth. It was around 9:30
on the night of December 23, 1890. What he had in mind—talking,
shooting—he never said.

The Bank featured a second-story gambling hall, and after entering, Short drew a gun and pushed a Black porter up the steps toward
it. Upstairs, the hall was packed with gamblers. Short waved his pistol
and shouted, "Skin out of here, every one of you!"*

Chaos ensued. Patrons sprang to their feet, knocking over tables
and chairs, and poured down the stairs and out into the street. Told
that Short was upstairs waving a gun, a bar owner named Louis de
Mouche hustled inside and may have been the only witness to what

---

*The derivation of Short's demand to "skin out of here" is unclear. Its only mention in an in-
ternet search is for a Jamaican slang command involving a certain sex act, which I'm guessing is not what Short had in mind. I remained perplexed until finding the term used in
accounts of Billy the Kid's career. "Skin out of here" was clearly a way of saying "Get out of
here." Sadly, other than its apparent popularity in Jamaica, it has gone out of use.

happened next. According to de Mouche, he found Short standing alone in the empty gambling hall, the pistol still in his right hand.

"Come on away, Luke, or you will get hurt," he told him.

Short didn't move. Suddenly, maybe six feet away, the door to a storage room opened. A gun barrel—de Mouche insisted it was a pistol, history a shotgun—appeared. It fired just as Short did. Behind the door, Short's round struck Charles Wright in the right wrist. Wright's bullet, or buckshot, tore through Short's hand, taking off his thumb at the joint, before blowing a hole in his thigh.

Both men limped away, dazed. Both told reporters they never saw who shot them. The exchange was front-page news across Texas. Papers carried updates on Short's convalescence for days. His wounds were serious; he was bedridden for months. In fact, while he made a full recovery, Short didn't have long to live. By 1893 he was showing signs of a kidney disease known today as chronic nephritis. He retreated with his wife to a spa in Kansas, where he died that September. The papers said his funeral procession in Fort Worth stretched a mile or more.

THERE IS A KIND OF BLOODY SEQUEL TO THE DODGE CITY STORY. IT begins in 1879, just down the new Santa Fe Railroad line arcing into northeastern New Mexico, in the hair-on-fire boomtown of East Las Vegas. Wyatt passed through that season, lingering a bit, before heading to Arizona. Doc Holliday came too and ended up staying for a time.* A contingent of Dodge's unruly set moved in as well, occupied the major law enforcement positions, and oversaw a spasm of violence stretching into 1880. They were called the Dodge City Gang.

---

*Holliday's arrival seems to have followed his rushed departure from Trinidad, Colorado, where according to both Masterson and Earp, he had shot and wounded a "young sport" known as Kid Colton. If so, historians have yet to find a public record of it.

One of the town's early gunfights apparently involved Holliday, who with a partner had opened his first business venture, a saloon on Center Street. On the night of July 19, a well-traveled tough named Mike Gordon was shot under hazy circumstances outside it. A onetime army scout, Gordon was said to have been in Wichita during its heyday, then in Dodge, then Fort Elliott. He was easy to spot in a crowd, for he no longer sported a nose. It had been bitten off during a brawl.

That evening, in the precise words of Holliday's biographer, Gary L. Roberts, "Gordon was drunk and apparently had been for several days."[5] When a lady friend refused to accompany him to the next bar, he flew into a rage, swearing that, in the words of the *Las Vegas Gazette*, "he would kill someone or be killed himself before morning."[6]

He got his wish. According to the *Gazette*, Gordon fired a shot, which went through a Mexican gentleman's pants leg. Here accounts get fuzzy; presumably this was not the kind of town where people prized public testimony. Several more shots were heard, then silence. Gordon vanished. An hour later he was found lying outside a downtown tent, bleeding from a bullet wound in the chest. He was dead by dawn.

It took several years before Holliday was implicated, first in a local newspaper, later by Bat Masterson. Masterson was the only source to provide details, presumably learned from Holliday. According to this account, one of Gordon's shots had been fired into Holliday's saloon, whizzing just past the gambler's head. When a startled Holliday drew his revolver and stepped to the door to see who fired it, Gordon was standing outside, his gun still raised. Before he could fire a second time, Holliday shot him in the chest.

That Holliday was never identified, much less prosecuted, was likely a favor from the justice of the peace, Hyman G. Neill, known to all as "Hoodoo Brown," a tall, thin con man who served as boss of the colorfully nicknamed Dodge City Gang, which counted among its members "Dirty Dave" Rudabaugh, "Slap Jack Bill" Nicholson, and "Bull Shit Jack" Pierce. The gang's depredations in 1879 alone included several men shot under mysterious circumstances, a train robbery, and a pair of stagecoach stickups, which brought in Wells Fargo detectives.

The gang's ineptitude as public servants brought them down long before Wells Fargo could. On January 22, 1880, the marshal, also a gang member, was shot and killed by four men in a saloon. A deputy named Mather dispatched one of the attackers and wounded the rest. Three days later, Mather killed a railroad worker waving a gun around. And then there was another killing, and another, and then a lynch mob grabbed the marshal's killers and went to string them up, but a crowd opened fire and killed them first. Then Hoodoo Brown got arrested, his pals tried to break him out, another marshal got killed, and, Lord, it just went on and on. Until finally, in April, the citizens rose up, formed a vigilance committee, and began indicting people. Within days almost all the gamblers and gunmen had fled.

East Las Vegas shone, if that's the word, for just that single season. In its moment, though, it was a kind of gunfighters' crossroads, hosting any number of gunmen washing their hands of Kansas and heading out into the raw new open spaces of New Mexico and Arizona. Wyatt passed through, as noted, and Masterson. Holliday soon followed; later, some would charge he and Wyatt had been part of the Dodge City Gang, which they weren't. Dirty Dave Rudabaugh would ride with Billy the Kid before ending up in Tombstone too.

East Las Vegas is also known for the debut of an especially inscrutable gunman, that deputy Mather, who would go down in western lore as Mysterious Dave Mather. Mather was born in Connecticut in 1851—it's said he claimed to be descended from the Puritan minister Cotton Mather—and, after a turn as a sailor, wandered onto the frontier, apparently making it to Dodge as a buffalo hunter. The lone surviving photo shows an intense, unsmiling fellow, with dark eyes and the period's signature drooping mustache.

Somewhere along the way, he earned his distinctive nickname; it seems Mather was not the chatty type. He first enters history in East Las Vegas, where he was briefly charged with that train robbery; the charges were dropped when the prosecutor failed to appear. From New Mexico Mather ricocheted across parts of Colorado and Texas, getting arrested in Fort Worth for stealing a gold ring from a madam.

All of which, naturally, qualified him to reenter the realm of law enforcement; he was hired onto the Dodge City force in June 1883. His work wasn't half bad; according to the papers, he led a posse that arrested a pair of train robbers and foiled a jail break. Even so, he lasted a scant nine months, until a new municipal administration replaced him with an old hand named Tom Nixon. There was already bad blood between the two men, though few understood why. Whatever the reason, Mather was incensed. Both he and Nixon had interests in local saloons, and their rivalry flared further when Mather, in one of the era's more unusual acts of retaliation, initiated a price war on beer, selling his for half that of Nixon and others. Nixon pressured wholesalers to cut off Mather's beer supply.

That kicked it off. On the night of July 18, 1884, the two men exchanged gunshots on a downtown sidewalk. Neither was hit, though it was reported that Mather suffered a powder burn to his face and, in a sign of the journalistic detail spreading across the frontier, a nasty splinter in his left pinkie finger. From "all appearances," one paper concluded, "the end [of the feud] is not yet."[7]

It wasn't. Three nights later, witnesses watched as Mather calmly descended the stairs of his second-floor Opera House Saloon and encountered Nixon on the sidewalk. "Oh, Tom?" Mather said.

When Nixon turned, Mather said something else. Later, a witness would say it sounded like "You have lived long enough."[8]

Whatever he said, Mather drew his pistol and shot Nixon through the left nipple. Nixon breathed three last words—"I am killed"—and crumpled to the ground. As he did, Mather shot him three more times. A ricochet struck a Texas cowboy in the knee. As he was arrested, Mather was heard to say, "I ought to have killed him six months ago."*

Mather hired a talented attorney, who somehow persuaded a jury that Nixon was the aggressor that night. Mather walked free.

Six months later he was in trouble once more. One evening in May 1885, Mather was in Dodge's Junction Saloon playing cards with a man named David Barnes for a dollar a hand. At one point, Mather scooped up his winnings, rose, and tossed his cards at Barnes, who seems to have had a contrasting view of the game's outcome.

"I want my money," Barnes said, rising himself.

Mather punched him. As it happened, the sheriff was watching the game. He stepped forward, braced Mather, and said, "Here, that won't do." As he did, someone yelled, "Look out, he is pulling a gun."

It was Barnes. His shot went through Mysterious Dave's hat. Several more shots rang out. Mather appears to have fired once, but his brother Josiah, who was also in the bar, shot three times. At this point Barnes's own brother—this was getting to be a real family affair—saw Barnes standing frozen at the door. "And then," he said later in a statement, "he fell down, easy like."[9]

David Barnes died on the spot. Though it wasn't entirely clear which Mather brother fired the fatal shot, both were arrested, but the case was never prosecuted, and both men left town. Not long after, it was reported that Mysterious Dave had been hired as the new marshal in the town of New Kiowa. It was the last anyone heard from him.

In later years, there were stories that Mather was killed in Dallas.

---

*You'll never guess who was among the first bystanders to kneel beside Tom Nixon's fallen body and give a sworn statement afterward: Bat Masterson. You can't make this stuff up. The guy was everywhere.

Someone quoted his brother claiming he was done in by moonshiners in Tennessee. The most persistent story, though, had him reemerging in the far north of Canada, working for the Royal Canadian Mounted Police. In the 1950s, a book claimed he was working there as late as 1922. The Mounties denied it. To this day, the disappearance of Mysterious Dave Mather remains an imponderable.

THERE IS ONE LAST IMPROBABLE TALE OF GUNFIGHTERS PASSING through East Las Vegas in 1879. You can actually read it in a few otherwise credible histories. New Mexico's Billy the Kid, it's said, popped into town, as he was in fact known to do, just long enough to share a fleeting dinner with the one man whose fame eclipsed that of all others, the single figure who was bigger than Billy, more famous than Wyatt. The story of the dinner is almost certainly a legend, yet it's the kind of thing you grapple with when telling the story of the most famous gunfighter—the most famous American criminal—of all: Jesse James.

CHAPTER NINE

The Trouble with Jesse James

The Midwest (Sigh), 1869 to 1882

Here we need to pull back from Dodge City, leave behind all that's happened in Kansas and Texas, and pan not only eastward but back in time a full fifteen years, to the restive days after the war, to the beginnings of the most notorious American criminal epic of all, the Southern-flavored saga of Jesse James, a man who began robbing banks when Wyatt Earp was a teenager and didn't stop until six months after the gunfight beside the O.K. Corral.

Was he America's first celebrity criminal? It's hard to find a serious challenger. He was already a household name for years before anyone heard of Earp, Doc Holliday, or the teenager who became Billy the Kid. And yet, much like Al Capone and Bonnie and Clyde, Jesse James has been spun through the washing machines of popular culture for so long, and in so many venues—dime novels, pulp magazines, comic books, awful movies, great movies, television, video games— that he's been bled of all reality, of any sense he was once a flesh-and-blood person, a man who lived, loved, and killed, mostly in the state of Missouri. He is bigger than the Gunfighter Era.

I confess, I'm ambivalent about including him here. Because in my eyes, he was never an Old West gunfighter. He was a midwestern bank and train robber. He struck targets in Kentucky and Minnesota and, for Pete's sake, Alabama. There's no serious suggestion he ever committed a single crime, much less shot a man, west of the Kansas-Missouri border. But I'm telling his story anyway, because all this feels like a technicality, because his career is at least gunfighter-adjacent, and, candidly, because you're expecting it.

But this is firmly not a story of the Old West. When Jesse, as I'll call him, fled the law, it wasn't to some New Mexico mesa or box canyon; it was to a horse farm outside Nashville. Other than bouts of gunplay, the one thing that binds his story to that of the early postwar gunfighters is his status as an inveterate Southern rebel. His criminal career, like that of Wes Hardin and Cullen Baker, is almost as much about politics as criminality.

In practically every other way, he is an outlier. Across the span of postwar outlawry, there is no one like him. No other figure has his pedigree; the wartime guerrillas in Missouri that produced the James Gang did not spin off other renowned gunmen, at least none who lived long.* Missouri may have been too settled, too civilized; the notable gunfighters who emerged there, Hickok and Earp, were lawmen.

And compared with a multitude of criminal peers who tended to be abject bumblers, the James Gang developed unrivaled acumen. They were probably the first to rob a bank during peacetime, and they stayed at it for more than ten years, amassing a record of blitzkrieg raids that overshadows anything in the annals of nineteenth-century crime. In the Old West, Butch Cassidy's record might rank a very distant second.

---

*These might include Jim Jackson, accused of murdering several Black men, who was hanged in 1865, and William McWaters, an itinerant gunman named as a suspect in several frontier murders, who was killed in prison in 1875.

Here's a fun factoid: For all the mythos surrounding Wild West bank robbers, bank robbery was in fact not only rare on the frontier but until the 1890s *it was almost unheard of.* Historians cannot find a single robbery in Arizona, New Mexico, Nevada, or Montana before 1896, and precious few elsewhere.[1] Why? Bank robbery was uncommon everywhere at the time—it only became a serious problem with the advent of the automobile—but on the frontier the main reason was that what meager commerce existed didn't produce tons of cash. In fact, the Old West was chronically short of hard currency. Beyond Denver and San Francisco, there weren't that many banks. (What got robbed were trains; that's where the money was.) Why the myth then? Probably the James Gang. Their exploits, both in reality and in a rash of dime novels set out west, suggested bank robbery was endemic.*

Jesse was born in 1847, the second of three children raised in a slaveholding family in Clay County, Missouri, east of Kansas City, an area settled by so many Southerners it was known as Little Dixie. His father died when he was three; his mother remarried twice, the second time to a kindly doctor named Reuben Samuel. When war came, fourteen-year-old Jesse remained on the Samuel farm while his brother, Frank, rode with guerrillas and Confederates fighting across the state.

What Texas endured after the war, Missouri suffered during it; it probably saw the most vicious fighting anywhere, massacre after massacre, prisoners executed, farms burned. The worst atrocities were carried out by Confederate irregulars known as bushwhackers, including William Quantrill's massacre of between 160 and 190 men and boys during the 1863 sack of Lawrence, Kansas, and "Bloody Bill" Anderson's killing of twenty-three unarmed federal soldiers at Centralia

---

*If you're wondering how the image of Jesse James morphed from that of midwestern bank robber to Old West gunfighter, there's an entire book on it, and it's a good one: *The Ghosts of Guerrilla Memory: How Civil War Bushwhackers Became Gunslingers in the American West*, by Matthew Christopher Hulbert.

in 1864. The atrocities tend to obscure the day in, day out horrors, the farmers found dead in their corn, the wounded Yankees dispatched with rifle butts to the face, the Union prisoners having their ears and noses cut off while still alive.

In 1863, at sixteen, Jesse joined Frank in the thick of it. He was a slender kid, with a lean, almost bony face, suggesting less than stellar nutrition, with straw-colored hair, alert blue eyes, and an upturned nose people remarked on. He was green, and in those first months he lost the tip of his left middle finger when he mishandled a Colt Navy he was loading. Going to war was less a duty than a passionate calling for the bushwhackers; there was a keen sense their way of life hung in the balance. This had been drilled into Jesse when Union militiamen looking for Frank roughed him up—choking, beating, or whipping him, depending on the account—and tortured his stepfather during a brutal raid on the Samuel farm.

What's notable about Jesse's wartime experiences is that while he was too young to be a true leader, he was not a nobody for long. He grew close to the teenager who emerged as Bloody Bill's right-hand man, Archie Clement, among the bushwhackers' most renowned killers. Both boys murdered prisoners at Centralia. Jesse's two years in the field are a litany of mayhem, raiding and burning farms and small Missouri towns, assassinating Union sympathizers, and the odd battle. He was shot twice, first in the chest by a farmer whose saddle he was stealing, the bullet hitting him near the right nipple and passing through his body; a doctor patched him up. The second was worse. In May 1865, while he was riding into the town of Lexington, Union soldiers opened fire; again, the bullet struck Jesse in the chest, inches from the first wound. He spent months recuperating alongside his cousin Zee, whom he would later marry. The bullet remained in his body.

As in Texas, the war in Missouri didn't end after Appomattox. Scores of bushwhackers still rode, taking revenge on Union men, murdering free Blacks, and, in Archie Clement's case, robbing a few banks. Unlike in Texas, though, the chaos in Missouri soon ebbed, especially after Clement was killed in a barroom gunfight in 1866. The violence went on, the bank robberies too, but after a year or two, most bushwhackers returned to their farms, leaving the politics to the politicians and the newspapers.

Exactly what Jesse did in these first years after the war is all but lost to history. In the cinema of Missouri political violence, he remained an extra for four years, a flickering presence who may or may not have joined in a half dozen bushwhacker bank robberies. Not until December 7, 1869, when he was twenty-two, does he step in front of history's camera. It happened in the town of Gallatin, in northern Missouri, where at 12:30 p.m. Jesse and Frank descended from their horses and stepped into the Daviess County Savings Association.

One of the two men inside, the bank's owner, John W. Sheets, took a hundred-dollar bill Jesse asked to change. As Sheets sat at his desk, Jesse stared at his face. After a moment, he pulled a pistol from beneath his coat and pointed it at Sheets. Then, with a curse, he called him "Cox" and, clearly under the impression he was another Gallatin resident, Samuel P. Cox, the Union officer whose troops killed Bloody Bill Anderson, announced he was there to avenge Anderson's death. And with that, Jesse fired into Sheets's chest. Before the man could fall, he fired once more, a second bullet striking him square in the forehead. When the second man in the bank lunged toward the door, Jesse shot at him twice, one bullet striking his right arm, at which point the man stumbled from the bank and began shouting for help.

Three possemen tracked them to the Samuel farm the next day, at which point a local deputy named John Thomason walked to the door while two Gallatin men hid nearby. At his knock, a servant boy emerged, darted to the stable, and threw open the door. Jesse and Frank galloped out, jumped a fence, and as the posse fired away, swung up the road.

Only Thomason gave chase. On the road he spied the pair in the distance. He leaped from his horse and squeezed off two shots. They missed. Thomason's horse then sprinted forward, leaving him alone. Up ahead, he saw the animal gaining fast on Jesse and Frank. When it drew abreast, one pointed his revolver and shot it dead. Afterward Jesse and Frank rode into nearby Kearney and announced they would never be taken alive and would kill any man who tried to bring them in. For the first time the name Jesse James appeared in the press. The public phase of his career was underway.*

WE KNOW LITTLE OF JESSE'S INITIAL MOTIVATIONS, WHETHER HE WAS primarily driven by his hatred of Yankee-backed banks and railroads or just wanted their money. Whatever it was, eighteen months later, in June 1871, his aborning gang hit their first bank, in Corydon, Iowa: Jesse, Frank, and two bushwhacker pals, Clell Miller and a tall, balding tough guy named Cole Younger. The town was all but deserted; everyone was at the churchyard listening to a visiting preacher's speech. After robbing the bank, the gang rode to the church, interrupted the speaker, and announced what they had done, cursing the "damn Yanks" as they left. When a posse found them two days later near Gallatin, they once again burst from a barn firing as they galloped away. In the exchange, Frank took a full load of buckshot and was laid up for months.

Once he recovered, the gang struck with regularity. A bank in Columbia, Kentucky, in April 1872. Another in Ste. Genevieve, in southeast Missouri, in May 1873. Then their first train robbery, near Adair, Iowa, two months later. In January 1874 they ventured south, robbing

---

*The book to read is *Jesse James: Last Rebel of the Civil War*, by T. J. Stiles. It's one of the best books ever written about an American criminal and is one of my favorites. I can't recommend it highly enough.

stages in Louisiana and Arkansas; at one, they grandly returned a watch to a Confederate veteran, saying Yankees had driven them to crime. They then struck a train at Gads Hill, in southeastern Missouri. When the St. Louis paper failed to give them credit, Jesse telegraphed an editor to make clear the James Gang was responsible.

All this was unprecedented. There were no other gangs in the Midwest, or anywhere for that matter, hitting such an array of targets at the time. These were the first train robberies west of the Mississippi. There was the uproar you'd expect, but what truly made Jesse a celebrity, what pushed him into the political realm, was the coverage he drew from a die-hard rebel named John Newman Edwards.

Edwards had served during the war as an aide to the Confederate general "Jo" Shelby; when Shelby marched his troops into Mexico at war's end, he went too. Returning in 1867, Edwards cofounded *The Kansas City Times*, a pro-Southern organ that attacked the state's military rule, denounced carpetbaggers, and in 1870 began publishing letters from Jesse, the first denying that he killed John Sheets. In the ensuing years Edwards befriended Jesse and began promoting him as the soul of Southern valor, a righteous warrior who might have "sat with Arthur at the Round Table," taking the fight to "corrupt, tyrannical" Yankees. One editorial he called "The Chivalry of Crime." Another was a twenty-page special edition devoted to glorifying the gang. Jesse basked in the glow. Edwards became his political mentor, to the extent that, in time, he actually came to believe this pablum.

The railroads and express companies, not so much. In 1874 one brought in Chicago's Pinkerton detective agency, best known for its work breaking labor strikes, to try to stop the gang. Three agents were sent on an initial reconnaissance. The one scouting Jesse and Frank turned up dead. Working with a former deputy, the two sent after Cole Younger and his three brothers got noticed. Jim and John Younger confronted them on a lonely Missouri road. In the ensuing gunfire,

John and the deputy were killed. One of the agents, struck twice, died three days later. Jim and the other agent got away.

Allan Pinkerton, the agency's founder, was incensed. Enlisting Union men in the area, he plotted an attack on the Samuel farm. On January 25, 1875, his agents tossed a makeshift Molotov cocktail through a window, starting a fire. Jesse's mother, Dr. Samuel, and their young children were inside. When his stepfather shoveled the burning blob into the hearth, it exploded. The next day Jesse's eight-year-old half brother died from his injuries. His mother's arm had to be amputated. The attack was national news. Amid the controversy, Pinkerton quit the case. A neighbor was soon found dead, likely killed by the James brothers as revenge for helping the Pinkertons.

Jesse and Frank could see Missouri was no longer safe. That summer they moved to houses outside Nashville, forty miles south of an uncle's Kentucky farm. Donning the alias "J. D. Howard," Jesse spent the next year playing cards and writing incendiary letters to the Missouri papers. Maybe the gang robbed a bank in West Virginia. Maybe Jesse and Zee moved to Baltimore for a time. The one thing we know for sure is that Jesse began planning his most audacious robbery yet. If he couldn't strike back at the Pinkertons, he could at the North.

ONE NOTABLE THING ABOUT JESSE JAMES IS THE RELATIVE SCARCITY of gunfights during his criminal career. He executed far more men than he killed in contested situations. Unlike for Hickok and Ben Thompson, there are no stories he took anything like regular target practice. In fact, he appeared to be something less than a crack shot. When a lone St. Louis policeman was sent to arrest him in 1874, Jesse and Jim Younger ambushed him on a wooded road. He rode right up to them. They emptied their guns at him—and every shot missed. One of the policeman's struck Jesse a glancing blow, knocking him from his horse.

The lucky policeman only survived when his own horse panicked and carried him away.

There was really no pressing need for Jesse to be a marksman. During robberies, the gang was after the money, and gunplay, which drew the curious, tended to jeopardize that goal. They killed a handful of men anyway; at the bank in Columbia, Kentucky, one of them, apparently Jesse, walked in, said "good evening," and inexplicably opened fire, killing the cashier and wounding another man. Typically, when the gang fired guns, it was to scare off bystanders who might interrupt their work.

The single momentous exception happened on a sunny Thursday afternoon, September 7, 1876, when the gang, after robbing a train in Missouri and a long ride north, dismounted outside the Minnesota town of Northfield. They'd come because Jesse wanted to deal a blow against a Yankee politician he had come to despise, Adelbert Ames, a onetime Union general and Mississippi governor who was a leading voice in Radical Republican efforts to reinvent the South. Ames owned a bank in this somnolent village forty miles south of Minneapolis.

The Northfield plan was in every way questionable, even hubristic. It was as if Jesse were playing the role of avenging Last Confederate that John Edwards had written for him. Putting aside their limited time to scout the bank, the town, and the state, just the distance to Missouri should've stopped him. Every bank robber, even early ones like Jesse, knew it was easier to rob a bank than escape afterward. Armed men would pursue them. They were almost four hundred miles from home. Even assuming they covered a hundred miles a day—a very big if—they were at a bare minimum four days from safety.

There were eight of them outside Northfield that day. Just before two o'clock, they split into three groups. Cole Younger's brothers Jim and Bob, along with a new man named Bill Chadwell, stayed behind, ready if needed. The lead trio, Jesse, Frank, and another new recruit,

Charlie Pitts, rode across a bridge into town, hitched their horses in front of the bank, and leaned against a dry goods box belonging to a hardware store.* At two, Cole and Clell Miller trotted across the bridge just in time to see Jesse and the others walk toward the bank. "They're going in," Clell murmured. The two rode on, stopping in front.

Stepping into the bank, Jesse's trio pulled revolvers and scrambled over the glass-topped counter, coming face-to-face with something they had never encountered: three exceedingly poised Minnesota bankers.

"Throw up your hands," one of them, likely Jesse, shouted, "for we intend to rob the bank, and if you hallo, we will blow your God-damned brains out." When he demanded to know who was the cashier, one of them replied calmly, "He is not in."

"You are the cashier," Jesse barked at the man, who was actually the acting cashier, Joseph L. Heywood, a bearded thirty-nine-year-old former Union infantryman. (The cashier was on vacation.) "Now open the safe you God-damned son-of-a-bitch."

Heywood replied, "It is a time lock, and cannot be opened now." This Jesse should've been prepared for. They had read about the new lock in a newspaper.

Jesse drew a knife and slid it across Heywood's throat. "Open that door or we'll cut your throat from ear to ear," he said.

The implacable Heywood pushed Jesse away and shouted, "Murder!"

Across the street, a merchant named J. S. Allen noticed Jesse's trio disappear into the bank, then stared as Cole and Clell rode up. "Who are those men?" he asked a friend. "I don't like the looks of them." Allen strode outside and marched to the bank. One of the bandits, probably Cole, had dismounted and was standing at the door. He grabbed Allen's collar and growled, "You son of a bitch, don't you holler." Another merchant, watching this, realized what was happening. As Allen ran

---

*Charlie Pitts's real name was Samuel Wells. Chadwell's was William Stiles.

to safety, he stepped into the street and shouted, "Robbers at the bank!" Cole fired a shot his way. "Get in there, you God-damn son of a bitch!" he yelled.

This was bad, though nothing the gang hadn't experienced before. At the Kentucky bank, Cole had fired to scare away first responders. Now, he and Clell began shooting in the air, ordering everyone inside. Hearing gunfire, the trio outside town came charging in, firing and cursing. All of which only stirred up these determined Minnesotans. People began grabbing aging rifles and bird guns. Up and down the street, they ducked behind doors and window sashes. Shots rang out.

A moment later, Clell took a load of bird shot to the face and toppled over dead. Cole leaped down to check him and was struck by a bullet to the hip. A moment later, Bill Chadwick was struck and killed. As more and more townspeople got involved, there was a seriocomic quality to their efforts. One man inside a store ran out of ammunition but kept yelling "Now I've got you!" to draw fire. Caught unarmed, the town marshal began throwing rocks. When an oblivious woman drove her carriage into the melee, Cole shouted, "Lady, get off the street, or you will be killed," at which point he wheeled and shot and killed a drunk staggering out of a saloon.

As the firing intensified, the remaining three riders, Cole and his brothers, gathered before the bank, where Jim and Bob Younger dismounted, using their horses as shields. The two shot out windows up and down the street until one horse fell dead. They then turned to see two men with rifles a block away, on their side of the street. One of the men turned out to be Adelbert Ames himself. Bob took a bullet in the arm.

Things were going no better inside. Jesse continued badgering and beating poor Heywood, at one point firing his pistol beside his ear. When he did, a twenty-six-year-old teller rose and lunged through the open rear door into an alley. Charlie Pitts followed and shot him through the chest. (He lived.) Outside, Cole realized they couldn't go on like this. He rode to the bank's front door and kicked it in. "The game is up!" he hollered. "We're beaten!"

No one argued. While the others hustled out, Jesse paused to place his gun against Heywood's head and fired, killing him. Outside, everyone jumped atop horses, Bob Younger hobbling behind. "For God's sake, don't leave me!" he yelped. Cole hauled him onto his horse.

As the gang thundered off into the Minnesota countryside, they left behind dead two of their own and two citizens. The ride south was a nightmare of cold, drenching rains, possemen everywhere, all three Youngers suffering from wounds. At one point, trying to shake their pursuers, they struck out on foot, creeping through the streets of Mankato late one night stealing fruit. Finally, after a week of this, suffering from exposure and lack of food—and still in Minnesota—Jesse and Frank left the others to be captured. After a gunfight in which Charlie Pitts was killed, they soon were.* The James brothers managed to steal a horse, taking a load of bird shot from a farmer as they did, later stole two more, and after another week of misadventures, made it safely to Missouri.

It was the end of the James Gang, a disaster from which Jesse never fully recovered. Maybe its most humiliating aspect lay back at the bank. It turned out Jesse had been badly outsmarted. The safe indeed had a time lock, but it wasn't being used that afternoon. Had he simply bothered to test it, the door would have swung open.

AFTER NORTHFIELD, JESSE AND FRANK ALL BUT VANISHED. FOR THREE years they lived under assumed names on a pair of Tennessee farms,

---

*All three Younger brothers drew life sentences at the Minnesota Territorial Prison in Stillwater. Bob died there in 1889, of tuberculosis. Jim and Cole were paroled in 1901. Jim committed suicide the following year. Cole lived on.

raising, racing, and betting on horses, sometimes ducking into Nashville to play cards. Frank was content, even happy. He married and had a son, joined the Methodist Church, read Shakespeare, and worked hard clearing his land. Jesse, though, seemed restless. He clearly missed the spotlight, the action. He was bored.

In early 1879 he stirred, moving his wife and now two children onto Frank's farm and traveling alone back to western Missouri, where he held court at the rebel general Jo Shelby's farm. There he gathered a circle of young acolytes, kids really, eager to form a new gang but hopelessly inexperienced; none had even fought in the war. Among them were one of his Kentucky cousins, Wood Hite, Clell Miller's brother Ed, and a horse thief named Dick Liddil. Soon Jesse was planning a job.

As sequels go, the James Gang 2.0 is a sad, low-budget melodrama, an aging outlaw trying to reclaim his glory days by recruiting from the Island of Misfit Toys. On October 8, 1879, the proto-gang made its debut in the hamlet of Glendale, east of Kansas City, stopping a train Jesse heard was carrying gold bullion. Everything went smoothly, no gold but a decent take, six thousand in cash. More disappointing was the reaction. Jesse issued a press release that clearly missed that old John Edwards zip: "We are the boys that are hard to handle and will make it hot for the party that ever tries to take us." Far from the buzz he might have expected, the papers mostly yawned. Edwards didn't even bother responding to Jesse's invitation to meet. Their war was over. Missouri, and America, was moving on.

Whatever itch Jesse had, this robbery seems to have scratched it. Afterward he spent months shuttling between Missouri and Tennessee, where he busied himself with cards and horses. Finally, in August 1880, he went back to work, initiating a strange crime spree. This time, the jobs were bizarrely small, most done east of the Mississippi without any kind of announcement. He and one of the Missouri kids robbed a stagecoach at Mammoth Cave, Kentucky, then a store in the town of Mercer, then another stage, before which he and Dick Liddil impulsively attempted to mug a pair of armed riders and ended up in a pointless gunfight. It was as if Jesse were doing it only for jolts of the old adrenaline rush.

It was during this period that his long-simmering paranoia began to surface. He first doubted an old bushwhacker friend named Jim Cummins, who then "disappeared." Next came Ed Miller. A cousin later said Jesse and Miller agreed to a duel in Kentucky. Miller's shot, it's said, went through Jesse's hat. Jesse's didn't miss.

Then, after the strangest robbery yet, the March 1881 stickup of a payroll supervisor on a canal-building crew in northern Alabama, the inevitable happened. One of Jesse's henchmen got drunk and boasted of his prowess as an outlaw to a bar patron outside Nashville; the patron turned out to be not only a county judge, but one Jesse and Frank had actually met in their new identities, at a racetrack. The day after the Nashville paper carried news of this man's arrest, Jesse and Frank packed up and fled Tennessee with their families, first to their uncle's farm in Kentucky, then to homes they rented in Kansas City.

What they found was a Missouri different from the one they had left. In January 1881 a new governor, a onetime Union militiaman named Thomas Crittenden, took office, devoting much of his inaugural address to ridding the state of "outlaws," meaning Jesse. That July, as if in reply, Jesse rose from his seat and opened fire inside a moving train east of Winston, killing the conductor and a passenger, which drew criticism even from once-reliable backers like *The Kansas City Times*; the gang made off with all of $600. Governor Crittenden responded by putting a massive $10,000 reward on Jesse's head—$300,000 today.

At a follow-up robbery, near Blue Cut in September, Jesse seemed curiously buoyant as they robbed the passengers, tipping the brakeman and quoting scripture; when a woman fainted, he wiped her brow.

Either he was energized by the new attention the governor's reward brought, or he was desperate to win back Missouri's good graces. "Good-bye," he said as they left. "This is the last time you will ever see Jesse James."[2]

This kind of showboating belied tensions growing behind the scenes. Jesse's paranoia had begun seeping into the youngsters who now surrounded him. The size of the reward was part of it; it was the kind of money that couldn't be ignored. The immediate problem, though it's not clear Jesse appreciated its severity, was friction rising between his cousin Wood Hite and Dick Liddil. Both favored a young widow, Martha Bolton, whose home served as a gathering place for the gang. After Blue Cut, Hite accused Liddil of stealing from the take.

It's not clear Jesse took this seriously, but Liddil did. When the gang convened in Kentucky to rob a train, he and Hite got into an argument, agreed to settle it with a duel, then missed every shot. Liddil stormed back to Missouri, aborting the robbery. Hite soon followed him to Martha Bolton's. On the morning of December 4, 1881, he came downstairs and found Liddil in the dining room. A frantic gunfight broke out. When it was over, Liddil had a nasty wound in his thigh. Wood Hite—Jesse's blood relative—was dead on the floor. This was something, Liddil knew, that Jesse would not forgive.

JESSE KEPT HIS FAMILY MOVING AMONG RENTAL HOMES IN KANSAS CITY until November, when he found a new place in St. Joseph, sixty miles north. On Christmas Eve, now calling himself "Thomas Howard," he moved again, this time to a house on a hill at 1318 Lafayette Street, just around the corner. When in town, he bought cigarettes at a drugstore on Sixth Street, sitting and joking with the owner. Much of the time, though, he traveled, sweeping through eastern Nebraska and Kansas in his relentless search for targets.

He was living his old life in a new world, though, and never grasped what that meant, never, despite his paranoia, sensed the conspiracy forming in his inner circle. The flash point was Dick Liddil's killing of Wood Hite. Afterward, certain that Jesse would kill him—in fact, Jesse never connected him to the shooting—Liddil sent the widow Bolton to meet with Governor Crittenden.

But the real risk lay in the conspiracy's third and fourth members, Martha Bolton's brothers, a pair of desperate nobodies named Charley and Bob Ford. With Frank more or less retired, Jesse was lonely. He ended up all but adopting Charley. He'd ridden with the gang, and it was Charley Jesse favored, Charley who rode with him on his trips and emerged as the only man he seemed to trust. Charley said to be careful around Bob.*

In fact, twenty-one-year-old Bob Ford had been mulling ways to collect the governor's reward since it was announced. Once the widow Bolton arranged things, he too slipped into Kansas City to see the governor. They made a deal: if he could deliver Jesse, he would get a pardon and the reward. Charley signed on too.

The turning point came when Jesse, planning his next robbery, asked Charley who they might recruit for help. He suggested Bob, who moved into the James home with them on March 23. Jesse was careful around Bob, but not careful enough. The Fords didn't dare challenge Jesse to a fair fight. He wore at least one pistol most of the time, so for ten days they watched, waiting for a moment he was unarmed.

Finally, after breakfast on a Monday, April 3, 1882, they walked

---

*I say this with no real enthusiasm for anything other than the story it tries to tell, but the movie to watch—because, frankly, I never read the novel—is 2007's *The Assassination of Jesse James by the Coward Robert Ford*, starring Brad Pitt as Jesse. I tried to rewatch it recently and, alas, found it even more boring than I had the first few times. How do you make a boring Jesse James movie? Endlessly ruminative, with a glacial pace, it's more like a tone poem than anything else. If I sat through one more shot of soft clouds or waving wheat, I was gonna scream.

with him to the stable and fed the horses. Afterward, complaining of the spring heat, Jesse took off his jacket, tossed it on a bed, and threw his belt and two revolvers down with it, worried someone would see them. The Fords understood this was their moment; one imagines them exchanging glances, maybe some kind of signal. Jesse walked into the living room, where he noticed a picture was askew. When he stepped onto a chair to straighten it, Bob pulled his pistol and shot him in the back of the head. He and Charley then dashed from the house, blurting to Zee that the gun had gone off accidentally.*

The century's most heralded criminal died the way he killed so many others, unarmed and unsuspecting. He is remembered as the greatest American bandit, but when I think of Jesse James, I think not of trains and banks and derring-do, but of John Sheets, shot at his desk at Gallatin; of the cashier he killed in Kentucky; the conductor and the passenger he killed at Winston; and Joseph L. Heywood, shot in the head for heroically doing his job at Northfield. Yes, Jesse James was a product of a violent time and place. Yes, he was no doubt scarred and desensitized at a young age during a terrible war. But you can't really call him a gunfighter. He was a murderer.

---

*Public opinion was sharply divided by the assassination. Many considered the Fords cowards or traitors. For a time, they went on the lecture circuit; eventually they were reduced to charging to pose for photographs at dime museums. Stricken by tuberculosis, Charley became a morphine addict and committed suicide in 1884. Bob moved west, opening a series of bars in Colorado. In 1892 a man named Edward O'Kelley walked up behind him, said "Hello Bob," and killed him with a shotgun blast. He never said why. Dick Liddil ran saloons in New Mexico during the 1880s and later became a horse trainer of some note. He died of a heart attack in 1901.

CHAPTER TEN

The Taming of Texas

Texas, 1874 to 1884

There have been more men killed in Texas in the last year than she lost during the late war.

—*GALVESTON DAILY NEWS*, DECEMBER 26, 1876[1]

The chaos that enveloped Texas after the war reached a tipping point in 1874, when a new governor reintroduced the Texas Rangers and tasked them with bringing order to the countryside. And whew, boy, did they. Rarely in history has the mobilization of a law enforcement entity had a more dramatic impact. In its first two years these new Rangers, under Captain Leander McNelly, focused on taming the southern border, where the Mexican kingpin Juan Cortina's bandits had raised havoc, stealing herds of cattle and horses after the U.S. Army abandoned the border during the war. Once Cortina's riders were defeated in a series of battles, the Rangers began targeting the outlaws and feudists who still plagued parts of the state.

First in their sights was King Fisher, a dapper rustler and gunman who in the 1870s ruled a swath of South Texas from the border town he dominated, Eagle Pass. A cocky, swaggering type, Fisher famously admitted to killing "only" seven men, though he always threw in the

187

winking caveat: "Not counting Mexicans." The Rangers surrounded his ranch in 1876. Fisher went peacefully. Leaving a life of crime behind, he became a deputy sheriff in Uvalde, where he killed two more men. Counting Mexicans.

One by one, the Rangers swooped in and ended the big Texas feuds, stamping out the embers of the Sutton–Taylor affair and arresting the Horrell brothers in Lampasas County. Though local dustups would continue into the 1890s, the era of the great conflicts was over.

AMONG THE FIRST TO FLEE THE RANGERS WAS WES HARDIN, WHO DISappeared in 1874 after killing the former Ranger Charles Webb. Hardin had taken his young family east to, of all places, Florida, where he bought a saloon in Gainesville. But, Hardin being Hardin, he was unable to avoid trouble. When a deputy arrested a Black man, a mob threatened to lynch the prisoner. Hardin intervened, threw a few punches, and ended up shooting someone, perhaps fatally. When the Black man was released, he was accused of raping a white woman and put back in jail. Hardin then helped burn down the jail, with the accused inside.

Calling himself "J. H. Swain," he sold the bar in early 1875 and moved to Jacksonville, where he opened a butcher shop. It failed. When he heard two strangers were asking about him—he had been recognized by two Texans in Gainesville—Hardin assumed they were Pinkerton agents and fled, promising to meet his wife and their two small children in Alabama. The men were probably bounty hunters; Hardin later claimed he and a pal killed them near the Georgia border.*

After settling his family in the Florida Panhandle, Hardin and his

---

*His biographers Chuck Parsons and Norman Wayne Brown provide evidence this story is probably true.

buddy turned to gambling, using a deck or two of marked cards to win big at games in Pensacola and Mobile. This lasted until they got involved in a massive brawl—I'm guessing over those cards—in Mobile. At least one policeman was shot, in the arm. It was Hardin's doing; he later claimed he killed the man. He was invited to leave town and did—without the cards.

No one knew why Hardin was like this. It doesn't take a genius to imagine his masculinity was somehow challenged. Some people have a short fuse. He had no fuse at all. If he could take offense, he always did. His wife, it's said, tried to talk to him. It was no use. He was who he was. And Texas had not forgotten. By 1876 the governor had increased the reward on Hardin to $4,000—$115,000 in today's money. The father of a man his brother-in-law Brown Bowen had killed, meanwhile, heard a rumor that Bowen was visiting Hardin in Florida or Alabama and wrote to both governors begging them to arrest the two. Nothing happened.

By early 1877 Hardin had settled in the south Alabama town of Pollard, where his wife had family, and Bowen had in fact joined him in some kind of dodgy logging business. Mostly, it appears, they drank and played cards. Bowen was a hothead too, and a stupid one at that. When a Black worker somehow offended him at a railroad stop outside Pensacola, Bowen chased him with a pistol until the superintendent, a man named William Chipley, grabbed his gun and brained him with it. The next day Bowen returned swearing revenge. While at it, he shouted to everyone in earshot that he was the notorious John Wesley Hardin. A *Jeopardy!* champion this guy was not.

That is where things stood when King Fisher was arrested in Texas. Afterward, one of the Rangers involved, John Armstrong, grew determined to get Hardin next. Armstrong brought in a Dallas detective named Jack Duncan to nose around Hardin's kin in Gonzales County. Posing as a laborer, Duncan managed to befriend Hardin's father-in-law and at some point saw or intercepted a letter he posted to a J. H. Swain in Pollard, Alabama—one of the two states where Hardin was rumored to be hiding.

Betting this was Hardin, Duncan and Armstrong boarded a train, reaching Montgomery, Alabama, on August 20, 1877. While Armstrong arranged warrants, Duncan headed to Pollard. Asking after Swain, he was told he was in Pensacola. Wiring ahead for information, the Texans caught wind of Bowen's tussle with William Chipley. Chipley came straight to Alabama, bringing along Pensacola's sheriff, William H. Hutchinson, and a judge. Together the five men began plotting Hardin's capture.

When they reached Pensacola the next day, August 23, they found that "Swain"—Hardin—had been located and was known to be traveling back to Alabama on an afternoon train. They decided to arrest him on board. When the time came, deputies at the station watched as Hardin and three buddies boarded, taking seats in the smoking car. Hardin lit up a meerschaum pipe. Sheriff Hutchinson, who regularly walked the train ejecting undesirables, was a familiar presence as he ambled through the car. When he and a deputy named A. J. Perdue greeted Hardin, Perdue asked if he couldn't stay in town a bit longer. Apparently, Perdue had lost money to him at cards and, with a smile, asked for a chance to win it back. Hardin demurred, saying he had affairs to return to.

"Business before pleasure," he said.[2]

The lawmen stepped out. The Ranger, John Armstrong, then entered the car behind Hardin, holding a Colt. A moment later, Sheriff Hutchinson, Deputy Perdue, and William Chipley jumped back into the car and lunged at Hardin, tackling him. As the four men fell to the floor in a scrum, Armstrong strode forward. When Hardin spied the Colt, he realized what was happening. "Texas, by God!" he yelped.[3]

Suddenly one of Hardin's traveling companions, James Mann,

pulled a pistol and shot at Armstrong, missing. Armstrong shot him in the chest; Mann staggered outside, where deputies finished him off.

Armstrong then stepped toward Hardin, who was still grappling on the floor, unable to draw a pistol he wore in a holster beneath his clothes. The Ranger told him to surrender or be shot. Everyone remembered Hardin's reply a little differently. The most likely retort was "Shoot and be damned. I'd rather die than be arrested."

Armstrong swung the heavy Colt down hard on Hardin's head. He went slack. They put him in leg-irons, threw him on another train, and had him locked in the Austin jail four days later.*

WHEN HARDIN WAS BROUGHT BACK TO TEXAS, HE FOUND HIS STATUS as its deadliest gunfighter being challenged by a newcomer who for more than a century to come would be considered his chief rival for the title, a twenty-six-year-old drifter named William "Wild Bill" Longley. A total nobody before his arrest in June 1877, Longley rocketed to infamy via a series of jailhouse interviews in which he confessed to gunning down thirty-two men.

The parallels to Hardin's career were unmistakable. Longley could have been Hardin's eviler twin, an unrepentant rebel who began his "career" murdering Black people before riding with Cullen Baker and spending seven years as an itinerant shootist, admitting to killings across Texas and as far afield as Kansas and Montana. His exploits would be retold in books and novels and, most notably, in a highly burnished television series that aired from 1958 to 1960.

Longley's is quite a story. Raised in Lee County, east of Austin, he was a thin six-footer with jet-black hair, a deep-seated racist who left

---

*Brown Bowen was arrested in Florida not long after. Returned to Texas, he was convicted of murder and hanged.

home at sixteen and was involved in his first killings a year later, in 1868, when three Black men were murdered near the Longley farm. He and his brother-in-law then went on a rampage, robbing and killing several more. Afterward Longley fled to the Arkansas border, where he rode for a time with Cullen Baker. In 1870, after a reward was posted for his capture, he fled north, joining the cavalry in Wyoming. He deserted, was briefly imprisoned, then deserted again in 1872.

Before and after returning to Texas the next year, there were adventures and gunfights galore, too many to recount. But as Longley told it, he surely ranked with Hickok and Hardin as one of the deadliest guns in the West. Near Fort Leavenworth, Kansas, for instance, he told of bristling when a Yankee soldier dared disparage Texas. "[He said] there was not an honest man nor a virtuous woman in the entire state," Longley told reporters. "Before the words were cold on his lips I had sent a bullet through his heart."[4]

Back in Texas, Longley wandered the backcountry much as Hardin had, dodging sheriffs and bounty hunters. He was arrested once but released. Along the way he shotgunned a cousin in 1875, killed a prospective outlaw partner near Uvalde, and while hiding out as a sharecropper in East Texas, shot his landlord to death over a woman. A sheriff tracked him down in Louisiana in 1877 and returned him to Lee County, where he was sentenced to hang for his cousin's murder. It was then he began telling his story to several awed reporters.

You know where this is going. The only surprise is it took so long for Longley's story to fall apart. In 1996 a retired Texas prosecutor named Rick Miller published a biography proving he had killed maybe five men, four shot in the back or in ambush, including the cousin, the landlord, and several Black men. But no record was ever found to confirm even one of those other shootings, or anything like an actual gunfight. The one in Kansas? Please. His time with Cullen Baker?

Baker was already dead. There's a difference between a murderer and a gunfighter. Longley was far more the former than the latter.

Like Hickok, he simply concocted a tale accepted by gullible journalists and perpetuated by three generations of Western writers, including a noted Texas author in a 1953 biography. That Longley clearly yearned to take his place alongside Hardin in the gunfighter pantheon speaks not only to its allure but to the unsteady foundations upon which any number of gunfighters built their legends; Hickok might be exhibit A. Rick Miller was the first, in fact, to seriously investigate Longley's story, a pointed indictment of a literary genre that passed on folklore as fact for too long.*

Longley was smoking a cigar and making jokes as they led him to the gallows in the town of Giddings on October 11, 1878. The crowd was estimated at two thousand. After he made a self-serving speech about all the men he was sorry he killed, a judge ordered him hanged until he was "dead-dead-dead," and a few minutes later he was-was-was.

IN THE SPRING OF 1877, JUST AS LAWMEN BEGAN CLOSING IN ON WES Hardin and Bill Longley, a twenty-six-year-old Texas drover in far-away South Dakota realized he had finally spent the last of the money he had earned driving a herd north. His name was Sam Bass, and his efforts to recoup his losses would earn him a place in western lore.

Texans have long held Bass in warm regard, many viewing him as a simple country boy lured into a spectacular crime spree. Born in 1851, he was an Indiana orphan who wandered south after the war, first to Mississippi, then to North Texas. Five eight, with a dogged

---

*Miller was a prosecutor in Bell County, Texas, where I grew up. He was one of the very first writers I consulted when considering whether to write this book. I am deeply grateful for his guidance.

five-o'clock shadow, he was quiet, stoop-shouldered, and illiterate, a friendly, unassuming kid who rarely looked anyone in the eye. In the town of Denton, he worked briefly for the sheriff and as a cowboy, but neither job took. In 1874 he finally seemed to find his calling, racing horses, buying a gray mare named Jennie that, once she began winning, became known around the state as the Denton Mare.

Then, while at the races in San Antonio, Bass had the bad luck to befriend a shifty cattleman named Joel Collins, who owned a saloon. For whatever reason, the two decided to sell the horse and the saloon and buy a herd (on credit) to take north, which they did, selling the cattle, depending on the story, in either Dodge City, Ogallala, or South Dakota. What we know for sure is that they arrived in Deadwood right after Hickok's death, flush with between five thousand and eight thousand dollars—and proceeded to lose it all, by investing in either a failed saloon, a mining claim, or the tables. Whatever happened, it was then that Bass, probably at Collins's urging, decided to sample the outlaw life.

Enlisting random henchmen, they first tried their hand at stage robbery, stopping a coach in a canyon outside Deadwood one night in March 1877. Someone panicked and shotgunned the driver, at which point the stage horses bolted and the gang scattered, left with nothing to show for their efforts but a dead man. They tried again six or seven times that summer but proved stunningly inept. The take from one robbery came to eleven dollars. During another, the driver, his treasure box empty, offered them a dozen peaches.[5] "Why, darn it," one member of the gang whined to a stageload of penniless passengers, "we fellows will starve if you don't get to doing better."[6]

Down to their last forty dollars, the gang decided to try a train instead, a scheme that at a glance didn't appear to match their skill set. Returning to Ogallala, they boarded an eastbound Union Pacific at a watering station west of town on the night of September 18, 1877, and miraculously managed to rob it, faces covered, pistols drawn, beating a clerk bloody, taking watches and wallets from passengers, finally using an axe to break open a box holding $60,000 in shiny new Gold Eagle coins from the San Francisco mint.

It was a monster haul—$1.7 million in today's dollars—among the biggest in Old West history, a full five times larger than the James Gang's most lucrative robbery, and it drew headlines nationwide. Afterward the gang rode hard for Texas, railroad detectives and army detachments fast on their heels. They split up in Kansas, where a posse killed Collins and one gang member. Another was killed near his home in Missouri. Bass made it back to Denton alone.

This is where the legend begins, because Sam Bass was only getting started. Gathering a revolving gang of old pals, he began robbing trains. The Texas Central at Allen Station north of Dallas in February 1878. The Texas Central again a month later, at Hutchins. The Texas and Pacific at Eagle Ford in April, then again at Mesquite. At each the gang made off with only a pittance, which raises the question: Why on earth was Bass doing this? His take in Nebraska was ten thousand dollars or so, enough for him to buy a row of saloons, even a corral of racehorses. Did he lose it somewhere? Had he hidden it? Whatever he did, treasure hunters have been searching for those Gold Eagles ever since.*

The robberies prompted an uproar unlike any Texas had seen. Train robbery was still a rarity, now suddenly there were four in a row, and not off in remote South or West Texas, but in the heart of the state, around Dallas. Every conceivable pursuer mobilized: Pinkertons, railroad detectives, bounty hunters, sheriffs and deputies, and a company of rookie Rangers, sent by the spitting-mad governor.

---

*They'll probably still be looking years from now. All available evidence suggests Bass spent all the money on horses, weapons, and food for his new gang.

Once Bass was identified, many of them descended on Denton, where the gang was hiding in the labyrinth of wooded arroyos and swamps outside town. On April 29 a posse exchanged shots with them across a canyon. The next day another spied their camp, firing in vain as Bass and his men disappeared into a marsh. The Rangers, meanwhile, swept the county, arresting six of those who had helped him rob one train or another. For the next six weeks Bass led lawmen on a merry chase, exchanging gunfire at least three more times. On June 12 a posse again stumbled onto their camp. In the ensuing gunfight, one gang member was killed. Bass and the rest scampered into a dense thicket. A Ranger ruled it too dangerous to follow. Once again, they got away.

While Sam Bass knew the Denton woods better than his pursuers, the Rangers belatedly realized an awful lot of folks had to be helping him. And they were, sharing meals and feed, horses, even barns for sleeping. A few were detained. But Bass had been popular in town. Many around Denton had little patience for fat-cat railroad presidents hounding a simple working man who hadn't hurt a soul, as far as they knew; by this point, lots of people were actually kind of rooting for him. By the time his story came to a close, that feeling would spread across Texas.

His fan club turned out to be Bass's Achilles' heel. It included a farmer named Henderson Murphy and his twentysomething son Jim. Both were detained. Jim Murphy offered a deal: if the Rangers let them go, he would join Bass's gang and betray it. The Rangers agreed. One night that June, when Bass swung by the Murphy place, Jim rode off with him. Others in the gang were suspicious; one urged Bass to shoot him on the spot. Another, Frank Jackson, defended him. When Bass drew his gun, Jackson swore he would have to kill him too. Murphy stayed.

In July, with the Rangers closing in, the gang left Denton and drifted south. Armed guards had been posted on the trains, so they began looking for a bank, four of them now. They studied one in Waco and another in Belton, where Murphy managed to mail a letter to the Rangers saying they were heading to Round Rock, north of Austin. Once there, Bass stared at the Williamson County Bank. It would do.

The robbery was set for Saturday, July 20, 1878. The day before, leaving Murphy in camp, Bass and his last two men rode into town for a final reconnaissance. Inside a store, a pair of deputies noticed they appeared to be wearing pistols, which was discouraged. One asked Bass if he was armed. Startled, he replied, "Yes."

One of Bass's men drew his gun. The store exploded in gunfire. One deputy stumbled outside and fell dead. The other lurched off, badly wounded. Bass and his pals ran for their horses. As they did, Rangers and townspeople emerged from storefronts all around. This was worse than Northfield, an inflamed town backed by a squad of seasoned lawmen. The three outlaws ran for their horses, snapping off shots at people who seemed to be firing from every angle. Bass was hit more than once. One of his men fell dead. He and Frank Jackson managed to mount up and escape.

They found Sam Bass the next morning in a field outside town, lying against a tree. "Don't shoot; I surrender," he murmured as the Rangers hustled up, guns drawn. There was a lot of blood. They loaded him onto a wagon, drove it into town, and laid him on a cot in a tin shop. One of the Rangers pressed him about his confederates. Bass wouldn't name them. "It is agin my profession to blow on my pals," he rasped. "If a man knows anything he ought to die with it in him."

He passed the next day, good to his word.* Not long after, a song

---

*Frank Jackson vanished. Any number of lawmen, including Wyatt Earp at one point, looked for him over the years. They never found him; his fate is lost to history. The gang's Judas,

began making the rounds. It was a Texas favorite for years. You can probably still find some who know it, especially the opening lines:

Sam Bass was born in Indiana,
It was his native home,
And at the age of seventeen,
Young Sam began to roam.
He first came out to Texas,
A cowboy for to be;
A kinder hearted fellow
You'll hardly ever see.*

REPORTERS DRAWN BY THE HARDIN, LONGLEY, AND BASS SPECTACLES recognized them as symbolic of the changes overtaking Texas. One from St. Louis wrote how the Texan that "kills negroes as a matter of accommodation, and shoots white men as a pastime" was passing from the scene, the "worst-class of its devotees . . . being exterminated with the rope."[7] It was true. Texas was maturing. Violence would go on, of course, but the Rangers' triumphs signaled the end of the anarchy. There would be no more Sam Basses or Bill Longleys; their deaths sent a message. When a judge sentenced Hardin to twenty-five years, that did too.

All of which cast the state's last marquee gunfighter at the time, Ben Thompson, into sharp relief. Since his Kansas adventures, Thompson had emerged as a Texas celebrity and a figure of curiosity to editors

---

Jim Murphy, died in 1879 when he inadvertently swallowed belladonna, a poisonous plant a doctor was using to treat an eye condition.

*If you drive through Round Rock on Interstate 35 today, you may notice the sign at Exit 253: Sam Bass Road. It's funny, though. I've mentioned this to several Round Rock acquaintances. Not one had a clue who Bass was.

back east. There was a moment in the late 1870s, after Hickok's death, when he may have been the best-known gunfighter in America, the rare one who could explain, once over a dish of strawberry ice cream, the acceptable way to kill one's adversary. He liked to emphasize that honor, not to mention a verdict of self-defense, required him to always allow an opponent to fire first. "I know that he is pretty certain in his hurry, to miss," he once said. "I never do." Thompson adored this kind of coverage. When traveling, he took to sending the Austin paper telegrams recapping his days. Journalists returned the love. "Ben Thompson," one wrote, "probably comes nearer the ideal knight of chivairous [sic] desperadoism than any other man in Texas."

As he aged, though, Thompson began to drink more heavily and grew prone to a kind of juvenile hell-raising that undercut his gentlemanly reputation. He enjoyed shooting out streetlights, for one thing. He suffered from insomnia, which kept him out too much and too late, inevitably drunk. "While sober he was polite, affable and as much the gentleman as in all the times past," his lawyer wrote, "but . . . when indulging in drink beyond a certain degree he became dictatorial and dogmatic, making it extremely disagreeable to be in his company."[8]

Dangerous too. On Christmas night in 1876, when one of his pals got into a nasty row at a crowded theater with its owner, a hot-tempered type named Mark Wilson, Thompson threw a punch. Wilson pulled out a shotgun behind the bar and pointed it at Thompson; a policeman knocked the barrel aside as Wilson fired, the buckshot hitting a wall. Thompson drew and shot Wilson at least three times, killing him. When a bartender snatched up a Winchester and shot at Thompson, the bullet creased his hip; Thompson's struck the man in the jaw, badly wounding him. The shooting was front-page news across the state; most thought it self-defense. Thompson was tried for murder and acquitted.

Another night, four drunks from the cattle town of Llano were in a downtown bar boasting about how tough Llano men were. Dressed in his top hat and a diamond stickpin, Thompson stepped close to one, a man named William Hannah, and lightly drew the back of his hand down Hannah's cheek. "I'm Ben Thompson," he purred. "If I should go up there, I would serve the boys just so." Whatever that meant, Hannah punched him, knocking off his hat. Both men drew. Hannah shot and missed, his gun jammed, and he ran outside, hiding behind a light pole.

Thompson called on him to step aside. When he did, Thompson said, "Well, I will mark you anyway," raised his pistol, and fired, his bullet striking Hannah's ear. He ran. Thompson fired again, hitting him in the hip. Hannah survived. Thompson was charged with assault, but the case was dismissed. Bystanders said the Llano men started it.

This kind of thing made Thompson a polarizing figure in Austin; the newspaper eventually turned against him. Despite it all, he remained sufficiently popular, or feared, so that when he decided to run for public office, he was elected Austin's city marshal in late 1881. It seems an odd career move—that is, until you read that a critic disclosed after his death that he had used his post to extort a 30 percent share in every major Austin gambling house. It made him a wealthy man, hence the sailboat, and the home he bought across from the new University of Texas's administration building, where he could often be seen in his yard taking target practice. Austin was peaceful on his watch; his signature arrest was that of a drunken traveler, the Mason County feudist Johnny Ringo, en route to infamy in distant Arizona.

Reporters always said the same thing, that it was only a matter of time before Thompson's luck ran out, and it turned out to be true. The seeds of his demise were planted in 1879 while gambling at the Vaudeville Theatre in San Antonio. The trouble began when Thompson, losing big at monte, handed over a gold watch and several loose diamonds as a promise he would pay his debt. But when he retrieved the items the next night, Thompson refused to pay, pulling a pistol on one of the Vaudeville's owners, Joe Foster. He claimed he had been cheated.

The two made up the next day—"I was drunk," Thompson explained—but Foster's partner, a walking volcano named Jack Harris, remained incensed. In the months to come, Harris's ire curdled into something like obsession. Seemingly every time he met someone from Austin, he swore he would kill Thompson; he told one he would use his shotgun to "make a hole in him that a cat can jump through." It went on like this for two years, until Thompson had enough.

On July 11, 1882, a seething Thompson paced in and out of the Vaudeville a half dozen times looking for Harris. One of its other owners, a gambler named Billy Simms, tried repeatedly to calm him down. "No use talking to me Billy," Thompson told him, "there's going to be hell here tonight." When Harris finally appeared, snatching up a shotgun, Thompson was gone. When he returned around sundown, he stood in the street outside. At one point, he stepped off a curb, beyond a streetlight's glow, and leaned over, peering into the dim front saloon. He spied Harris behind a lattice screen, leaning against a wall, a shotgun pointed at him. "What are you doing with that shotgun you damned son of a bitch?" Thompson shouted.

"You kiss my ass you damned son of a bitch," Harris replied, raising the gun. From the street, Thompson drew and fired, an amazing shot, everyone said later. The bullet hit Harris in the chest, staggering him. A second went wide. He was dead soon after.

Thompson calmly returned to his rooms at the Menger Hotel, sending word he would surrender in the morning, and he did. Indicted for murder, he simmered in a San Antonio cell for four months. He resigned as marshal. His trial was among the more spectacular in the state's short history, every twist and turn reported on the front pages.

When the jury acquitted him, he returned to a hero's welcome in Austin, a brass band and a cheering crowd greeting him at the train station.

He should've turned a page. He had just turned forty. He and his wife had been married for twenty years; they had teenagers. But something wasn't right. His drinking was getting out of control. One night Thompson staggered drunk into a theater and opened fire on the audience and the performers; when the crowd panicked, he laughed uproariously. He was firing blanks. One evening in January 1884, when told a friend was in an argument, he barged into the Stockmen's Convention banquet waving a gun, ending up in a standoff with another old friend as the tuxedoed cattlemen stampeded out the exits.

News reports of the incident enraged him. He kicked one reporter in the street before storming into the Austin paper's offices, interrogating a teenage clerk at gunpoint. A San Antonio paper denounced Thompson's "reign of terror"; papers in Chicago and New York ran stories. "The police are afraid of Thompson and he knows it," the Austin paper snapped, "and therefore does as he pleases."

Could it have been PTSD? Or was this just a man haunted by his ghosts, overwhelmed by drink? Whatever it was, he received a surprising invitation in March 1884. One of the Vaudeville's owners, Joe Foster, asked him to come visit. Thompson scoffed: "If I were to go into that place, it would be my graveyard." But then, on March 11, the one-time border hellion King Fisher arrived in Austin, drained a few with Thompson, and for some reason insisted he accompany him to the Vaudeville. Later, everyone wondered why Thompson went. To see his brother, who was in San Antonio that day? A woman? A show? Was it Fisher's attempt to broker a rapprochement with Foster, who hadn't taken his partner's killing well? Or was something darker afoot?

Whatever happened, the two aging gunfighters found themselves on the 4:00 p.m. train south. Deep into a bender, Thompson was at his worst on the ride down. He swiped a bottle of whiskey from a fellow traveler. When a porter irked him, Thompson bashed the bottle over his head, spraying blood all over his own silk top hat. He ripped off the hat's crown and disembarked in San Antonio wearing only its brim.

As word spread of the pair's arrival, police took up positions outside the Vaudeville. After taking in a show elsewhere, Thompson and Fisher brushed past them into the saloon and ordered drinks, then took seats in an upstairs theater to watch a play. Thompson's friend Billy Simms came over with a bouncer; they ordered cigars and whiskey. Simms called to Foster, who was sitting nearby. A policeman in the hall watched as Foster walked over to them. After a moment, they began arguing. Later, it was said Thompson called Foster a thief.

Suddenly gunshots rang out. Pandemonium erupted. Patrons were running and screaming. No one knew what was happening. Moments later, Thompson and King Fisher were found dead in a pool of blood, Thompson shot three times in the head. The three Vaudeville men were holding pistols; Joe Foster was badly wounded and soon dead. When Thompson's gun was checked, it had fired five times. Fisher's never left its holster.

Both gunfighters had been public figures in Texas; these were among the newsiest killings in Texas history to that point. Yet after a San Antonio coroner ruled it self-defense, there was no serious inquiry, leaving far more questions than answers. Was it just an argument and a shoot-out there in the balcony? Or a staged assassination? Were there, as some speculate, hidden riflemen somewhere in the theater, shooting from its proverbial grassy knoll? A coroner in Austin claimed the bullets that killed Thompson came from Winchesters fired from behind him.

Today Ben Thompson is mostly forgotten. The Vaudeville too is long gone, but the spot where it stood, at Commerce and Soledad streets, was known to Texans for years as the "Fatal Corner."

THE FATES OF HARDIN, LONGLEY, AND BASS, AND LATER THE DEATH OF Thompson, prompted the kind of media surge we know well today, a rush of journalists trying to explain everything. All of it fueled the first sustained criticism of Texas-style violence. To this point, the shoot-outs in Kansas, not to mention the state's own murderous feuds, had gotten at best intermittent play in the national press, and as a question of public policy were ignored.

This began to change once they were noticed by Richard Kyle Fox, the editor of *The National Police Gazette*, a popular tabloid-style magazine that featured lurid coverage of crime, sports, and scantily clad women. In 1878 Fox was struck by how many of his murder stories were coming from Texas. His first item blamed its judiciary, claiming "the people of Texas are disgusted with the evident bribery of their courts, which habitually acquit the most habitual of assassins." By the next issue Fox had decided the problem was not Texas courts but Texans themselves. "The fact is," an editorial noted, "the murderer is a hero with the people, the press and the clergy of Texas."[9]

This was probably a little fair. "Bloody Texas" certainly struck a chord with Fox's readers. In 1879 the magazine's coverage of "Terrible Texans" blossomed into a crusade. Typical headlines included: ANOTHER MURDER HORROR FROM THE HOMICIDAL STATE; BOLD BAD BILL BARB: RECORD OF ANOTHER TYPICAL TEXAS MURDER FIEND; and THE TEXAS MURDER BULLETIN.[10] Fox's anti-Texas zeal gained momentum when the British actor Maurice Barrymore, future patriarch of the Barrymore theater family, was shot in the stomach and a companion killed by a drunk while touring in East Texas. The case became a cause célèbre in the eastern newspapers, which would make Texas violence a staple of their coverage for the next several years.

In short order editors discovered the Texas cowboy. By 1880 a number of papers, including several in Kansas, had begun running stories characterizing the cowboy as a menace. Texans, then as now, can be sensitive to criticism, but in this case, a few took the barbs to heart. In February 1882, the *Texas Live Stock Journal* suddenly called for cattlemen to disarm their cowboys:

> The day of the Winchester rifle, ivory-handled pistol and cartridge belt belongs to the past—it is gone never to return, and with it should go every man who cannot discharge his duties on the ranch without being thus accoutered. . . . The necessities of the past produced a cowboy who is out of place in the civilization of the present; but the remnant of that past still lingers to retard the rapid advancement of the business to its full measure. . . .
>
> Ranchmen should no longer make proficiency in handling firearms the requisite qualifications to employment . . . but honesty, industry and experience should be the test of a man's fitness for a cowboy's duties. . . . This wholesale arming of cowboys is a disgrace to stock raising, injurious to the business, provocative of lawlessness and crime, and should be prohibited by the laws of the State, the rules of the association and by the owners of the ranches.[11]

The call for disarmament was seconded by the *Drovers Journal*, which argued "the time is rapidly approaching, if not already at hand, when the average cowboy need not carry the suggestion of a walking arsenal wherever he goes." A flurry of papers jumped in, including the Caldwell, Kansas, *Post*, which headlined its piece SIX-SHOOTERS MUST GO. The national Stockmen's Convention was held a month later and actually adopted a disarmament resolution. "The six-shooter is not an absolutely necessary adjunct to the outfit of a cowboy," it read, "and further we condemn the habit of carrying of six-shooters by cowboys or others especially while visiting" towns.[12] Not everyone, of course, took this all so seriously. In Wyoming, a humorist named Bill Nye cried foul: "Disarm the cowboy? Take his pop from him and bring him down to the level of a common man? Ye Gods, no! In the name of 10,000,000 eastern readers of fiction—no!"[13]

One might reasonably ask: Did any of this remotely matter? Studying the literature, it's hard to find any cowboys who were actually disarmed. Yet one suspects the thrust of editorialists was less about changing workplace rules than ways of thinking. They wanted cattlemen to reconsider the costs of violence. And in this regard, there's a sense they succeeded. There's no escaping the fact that as the 1870s gave way to the 1880s, the cowboy's rowdiest days were passing. After 1880, there are far fewer tales of cowboys "hurrahing" cow towns. The kind of rough justice Wyatt Earp brought to Dodge City, and the Rangers to Texas, was becoming more the rule than the exception.

Likely as a result, the nature of marquee gunfights begins to change. Until 1880, most that made it into the press could be called random: two cowboys fighting over a girl, a drunk facing off with a sheriff. After 1880, the headline gunfights tend to be less about personal honor than personal interest, which makes sense. The frontier was becoming more civilized, its businesses more professional and thus more valuable. In the century's final twenty years, more gunfights would be about *something*, typically someone taking something from someone else, typically in a dispute over resources on a frontier that had less and less of them to share every year. More wealth, meanwhile, meant more money flowing into banks and railcars, making armed robberies, heretofore rare things, more common.

In Texas, the return of the Rangers meant a return to something approaching normalcy. Gunfights went on, including some famous ones. West Texas, made safe for settlement after the defeat of Native

American tribes, took longer to tame; the hardscrabble town of El Paso, as we'll see, was as wild as any in the West into the 1890s.

But with Democrats in control of state government, returning it to "Southern" hands, many Texans no longer felt the pressing need to challenge authority. By 1880 any number of gunmen who had made their names in Texas feuds, not to mention cattlemen looking for more land, had moved on. More than a few found a new home to the west:

New Mexico.

CHAPTER ELEVEN

The Texas Invasion
of New Mexico

New Mexico, 1872 to 1878

Life was held lightly down there in those days.

—A WITNESS EXPLAINING AN 1879
KILLING IN NEW MEXICO

It's easy to forget that Spanish settlers had been living in New Mexico for almost ten years when the first English colonists sloshed ashore at Jamestown in 1607, not that the two-plus centuries of Spanish and then Mexican rule that followed had done much for those who had to live there. At the end of the Civil War, the U.S. territory of New Mexico was a hot mess, desolate and battle-weary, ninety thousand people, mostly Latino, plus remnants of Native American tribes, sprinkled across an archipelago of villages, farms, and reservations dotting a vast emptiness of desert, mountains, and, in the east, prairies.

After defeating a bizarro Confederate invasion from Texas, the army had spent the war years attacking the Navajo and Apache, driving most onto reservations. When the fighting was over, what passed for a postwar economy was mostly subsistence farming, trading with the Comanche, and praying for rain. The handful of Anglos who tried to run things, many of them soldiers, fanned themselves out in isolated forts and in the capital, Santa Fe, population all of four thousand, roughly that of a Park Avenue skyscraper today. There was no railroad. If you wanted to get in or out, or anywhere at all, you needed a horse. Or else.

The problem with New Mexico was there wasn't much there there, which made it an ideal spot for cattle. Two big Texas ranchers, Charles Goodnight and Oliver Loving, began eyeing it during the war and afterward started driving thousands of longhorns north up the Pecos River valley to sell to the army, herding the rest to Denver. Another Texan, John Chisum, moved his herds into southeast New Mexico and stayed, building a sprawling ranch compound outside present-day Roswell and grazing thousands of cattle on millions of acres of open land. They called Chisum the Cattle King of the Pecos. Smaller ranchers followed in his wake, satellites in Chisum's orbit. By 1875 much of eastern New Mexico was controlled by Texas cattlemen.

It was a rough life. Apache and Comanche raiders remained a threat. The real problem was a matter of math: unlimited, unfenced prairie plus thousands of cows minus functioning law enforcement equaled mind-boggling levels of theft. Rustlers swarmed Chisum's herds like gnats. By the 1870s, the state's third-biggest industry after ranching (and some silver mines) had to be the traffic in stolen cattle. Sheriffs—lazy, corrupt, or just plain scared—did little. Chisum appealed to the governor and the army but no one helped. He and his Texas cowboys stayed more or less at constant war with rustlers for years.

The last Comanche, desperate for income after the bison's obliteration, resorted to raiding ranches in Texas and selling what they stole in New Mexico. Cattlemen howled. A Texas rancher named John Hittson finally did the only thing he could think of: he invaded New Mexico. Seriously. In 1872 Hittson gathered a force of ninety men and raided a series of villages on the eastern slope of the Rockies where mixed-blood Comancheros traded openly in stolen cattle. By the time they were done, having reclaimed thirty thousand head, three New Mexicans were dead, including a town marshal. Cattlemen cheered.*

For the next decade, Texas ranchers made raids into New Mexico a regular feature, a kind of irregular roundup, and raiding only increased once the Texas Panhandle opened for cattle in the 1870s. This further inflamed a Latino populace that already loathed Texans as much as Texans loathed them. The Texans' hatred of all things Mexican dated to their secessionist revolt against Santa Anna; the Latinos were outraged Texans were taking their land. Things could get ugly.

A case in point involved the five feuding Horrell brothers—last seen in chapter 4—who fled Texas for New Mexico in 1873. They settled their families with a thousand head on the Ruidoso River. There were squabbles with Latinos over water rights, and once the brothers killed a man digging a ditch, presumably on their land.

The serious trouble started in the Latino town of Lincoln one evening that December, when a Latino deputy disarmed Ben Horrell and three hard-drinking Texans who had fired pistols in the air. An hour later, when the group returned with new weapons and confronted the deputy—the term "damned greaser" surfaces in one account—shots rang out.[1] The deputy and a Texan fell, mortally wounded. When an angry crowd gathered, Horrell and another Texan ran into the night. Their bodies were found the next day in a creek, riddled with bullets. It was widely believed they had been killed after surrendering.

So began what was called the Horrell War. It's a measure of the Texans' notoriety that Lincoln's justice of the peace appealed to the army at nearby Fort Stanton for protection; he was ignored. Two days later, a pair of Latino men were found murdered near the Horrell

---

*The book to read is *John Hittson: Cattle King on the Texas and Colorado Frontier*, by Vernon R. Maddux. A little dry, but thorough.

ranch. The sheriff and a Latino posse rode out and demanded the brothers surrender. They refused. A few shots were fired before everyone returned to town. Two weeks later a mob surrounded the ranch and tried to burn the Horrells out. The families fought them off.

The Texans' response would make headlines across the country. On the night of December 20, 1873, the Horrells and their ranch hands rode into Lincoln and encircled a house where a Latino wedding dance was taking place, broke down the doors, and opened fire. Four men were killed, two badly wounded. The Latinos in Lincoln appealed to the governor. The governor appealed to Washington. This time the commander at Fort Stanton set up camp outside town. No arrests were ever made.

The sheriff and a posse of sixty Latinos stormed the Horrell ranch a month later, but the family had already packed its wagons in the night and left for Texas. En route to the border they were ambushed; a brother-in-law was killed. When two of the Horrells stole some horses near El Paso, yet another posse responded. In this final gunfight at least seven possemen, including five Latinos, were killed. When the Horrells finally reached Central Texas, one was quoted saying of Latinos, "We fought them all the way [home]."[2]

Welcome to New Mexico.

IF TEXAS CATTLEMEN LIKE THE HORRELLS INTRODUCED UNPRECE-dented levels of civilian violence to the state, outlaw gangs, many populated by Texas gunmen seeking easier lives than the Texas Rangers now allowed, played an equal role in shaping New Mexico into the next great theater of the Gunfighter Era. Their largest concentration rose in the state's southeast quadrant, where they preyed on John Chisum's herds before branching out into robbery, rape, and murder. This single, sprawling gang and its affiliates came to be known as "the Boys."

They were led, or at least overseen, by one of the West's great crime bosses, a canny onetime army sergeant named John Kinney. A squat, ruddy New Englander, Kinney bought a ranch north of Mesilla in 1875 and, posing as a legitimate cattle dealer, emerged as the premier fence for stolen beef. His right-hand man was a hatchet-faced killer named Jesse Evans, a twenty-two-year-old Texan. Any number of the hardened crew they assembled, including Robert E. "Dutch" Martin, Pony Diehl, and "Curly" Bill Brocius, would end up peopling the stories of both Billy the Kid's and Wyatt Earp's years in Tombstone.*

Though its first years are thinly documented, it's clear the gang was both bloodthirsty and audacious. When a soldier punched out Kinney during an 1876 New Year's brawl in a Las Cruces dance hall, he and several of the Boys returned and opened fire on the crowd, Horrell-style, killing two people and seriously injuring three others. When four members of a Mexican gang tried to horn in on their rustling business, Evans and his men trailed them across the border, prevailed on locals to arrest them, and after promising to escort the men back to Lincoln for processing, promptly shot all four dead. There were sundry other killings and holdups, too many to relate here.

John Kinney, Jesse Evans, and the Boys began emerging into wider public view in 1877, when a New Mexico editor launched an angry crusade against their depredations; Evans, in return, threatened to shoot the editor on sight. Then, that October, he and his gang suddenly came into sharp focus, on a riotous ride across New Mexico's southern tier, one that would take them from obscurity into history. It began with a small thing, the theft of three horses near the mining town of Silver City. There, they took on a new man. A boy, really. A kid.

---

*A tip of the hat here to the western historian John Boessenecker. While I had read a good deal about the Boys, I hadn't fully grasped their size and evolution before diving into his outstanding 2020 book *Ride the Devil's Herd: Wyatt Earp's Epic Battle Against the West's Biggest Outlaw Gang*. It's superb.

———

ON OCTOBER 2, 1877, AS JESSE EVANS AND EIGHT RIDERS RODE AWAY from Silver City, they were seen by a man named Carpenter who spied a local teenager among them, an eighteen-year-old nobody, a troubled orphan whose origins are elusive, in part because he went by so many names. He was probably born Henry McCarty, in either New York or Indiana, likely in 1859, though he also went by Henry Antrim, his stepfather's surname. He later took an alias no one can explain, William H. Bonney. History knows him as Billy the Kid.*

Billy, as I'll call him, never knew his late father, and neither do we.† He spent his first ten years in Indianapolis, where his widowed mother, Catherine McCarty, an Irish immigrant, met the man who became his stepfather, a hack driver named Bill Antrim. In 1870, even as Texas cowboys began pouring into Abilene, Billy moved with his family to Wichita, where Catherine ran a laundry. From there they headed west, probably to Denver, then definitely to Santa Fe, then, fatefully, south across the scrub to Silver City.

For a time, life was good in the gritty frontier village. The family lived in a tidy one-room cabin. Antrim took odd jobs and staked a mining claim or two. Described as a warm, loving mother, Catherine did laundry and sold her pies. Billy and his brother, among the first Anglo children in town, were put in school. Friends would remember Billy as an unremarkable child, maybe a bit on the mischievous side. Then, in

---

*There are dozens of Billy the Kid biographies. For a quick read, I recommend Robert M. Utley's 1989 *Billy the Kid: A Short and Violent Life*. For a more robust exploration of his life and times, you can do worse than 2007's *Billy the Kid: The Endless Ride*, by the always entertaining Michael Wallis. I have consulted both liberally.

†In legal papers unearthed in Indianapolis, his mother, Catherine, once said her late husband, presumably Billy's father, had been a man named Michael McCarty. You cannot imagine the number of hours modern researchers have spent attempting to identify this man. So far, they haven't.

September 1874, Catherine died after a long battle with tuberculosis; the climate was one of the reasons they had come.

Billy was fourteen. His stepfather promptly vanished, returning only for the briefest visits, leaving the boys with neighbors. Billy became what passed for a street kid, washing dishes at the hotel, stealing a package of butter, heckling the Chinese laundryman. He got into his first real trouble at fifteen, when he accepted a bundle of stolen laundry, got turned in by his landlady, and ended up arrested for larceny and thrown in jail. Two nights later, left alone in a corridor, he wriggled up a chimney and escaped, hid in a barn, and when the sheriff came for him, fled town, seldom to return.

He made his way west to Arizona, a place as remote as Mars in those days. It's tempting to compare his adolescent wanderings to Wes Hardin's, but Hardin ricocheted between relatives. Billy was utterly alone. He found work on a ranch for a time, no doubt improving his knowledge of arms and horsemanship—things we're told he practiced endlessly—but he wasn't skilled enough to keep the job. Let go, he ended up hanging around the saloons and stores outside the cavalry's Fort Grant, teaming up with an older thief to steal saddles and blankets and the occasional horse. He got arrested again and thrown into a brig but slipped from his shackles and disappeared.

By the time he found work at a remote hay camp, Billy was seventeen and already developing the body, personality, and style that legions of Western writers would describe: slim, sinewy, on the small side, five seven, 135, with wavy brownish hair, two protruding front teeth, and the flashing blue eyes so many would remark upon. He couldn't yet grow facial hair, but sometimes tried a wispy mustache. He typically wore dark pants and a vest, often with a sombrero. Growing up alongside so many Latinos, he spoke fluent Spanish.

People liked him. He was of above-average intelligence, cheerful, with an easy smile and laugh, things that would attract friends. He loved to sing and was said to be a good dancer. But friends knew that if he felt wronged, he could display a fast, fierce temper.

Which is what a blowhard ex-soldier named Francis P. Cahill discovered in a Fort Grant cantina on August 17, 1877. Like Luke Short, Billy's size and age—already everyone called him "Kid"—tended to draw bullies. Cahill had been a dumb one, mussing his hair, slapping him, and pushing him down to entertain his buddies.

That night he went too far. Cahill called Billy a pimp. Billy called Cahill a son of a bitch. The two fell to the ground outside grappling as a well-lubricated crowd spilled out to watch. When Billy rolled onto his back, Cahill straddled him, his knees pinning Billy's arms. It was at this point, it appears, that Billy's temper got the best of him. As Cahill began slapping him, he freed one hand, reached for his .45, and shot Cahill in the belly. When he toppled to one side, Billy ran. The next day, after giving a statement, Cahill died.

Charged with murder, Billy fled back to New Mexico, putting up with a friend at a ranch outside Silver City. Though historians suggest he had little to fear from the law—the killing had obvious extenuating circumstances, and Arizona lawmen at the time rarely pursued fugitives into New Mexico—Billy fretted they were coming for him and left. A month later, he was seen riding with Jesse Evans.

WE'LL NEVER KNOW EXACTLY HOW BILLY JOINED UP WITH THE BOYS, but we have an unusually detailed account of that first ride and its aftermath, which gives you a sense of how Evans and company spent their time. After leaving Silver City, they tried to rob a stagecoach, then let it go when the passengers pleaded poverty; ate and drank at three roadhouses on the road to Mesilla, putting each bill on "tabs" they would never pay; stole horses from ranches at Mule Springs and Santa Barbara; opened fire on a posse seeking the horses, hooting in derision as they rode off; got drunk and shot up the town of Tularosa; then confronted a man who had testified against one of them, shooting his dog.

The ride climaxed with a scene of anarchic joy unlike any I know of in the frontier canon. Jesse Evans stood on a tree stump beside a campfire and gave a speech, recapping their exploits, laying out further plans, and welcoming a pair of visiting merchants who sold their stolen horses and cattle—"honor where honor was due," he noted. Evans then announced "promotions," electing himself "colonel" and two others "captains." They actually adopted formal resolutions, condemning the press and proclaiming "the public is our oyster, and that having the power, we claim the right to appropriate any property we may take a fancy to." They then danced around a roaring fire as a captain played the "Rogues' March" on a fine-tooth comb.[3]

The fun ended on October 17 when a fifteen-man posse surrounded Evans and three of his men in an isolated adobe hut and, after a desultory exchange of gunfire, took them in shackles back to the jail in Lincoln. They did not remain there long. A month later, in the hours before dawn on November 17, a group of thirty Boys, Billy among them, rode up to the jail. The guard chose discretion over valor. Moments later Evans and his henchmen were again free, riding south.

The jailbreak, it turns out, was the last time Billy rode with the Boys. The Evans gang was hardcore, and after all he'd been through in the four months since fleeing Arizona, Billy was, at least initially, drawn to something safer, more settled. This likely had little to do with any aversion to criminality—he never had qualms about breaking the law—but rather the lure of a new set of friends, a group of young Anglo farmers and their Latina wives living along the Ruidoso southwest of Lincoln. At some point that autumn, Billy found work with one, a Missourian named Frank Coe, and ended up making friendships that would largely define the rest of his short life.

They were a varied lot. Easygoing Charlie Bowdre had been a

bookkeeper back in Mississippi, and when not farming his few acres could often be found on a barstool. Josiah "Doc" Scurlock was a book-reading intellectual yet wildly temperamental; the two front teeth he was missing, everyone guessed, were lost in a fight. The most influential would be a cowboy named Dick Brewer, a brawny twenty-six-year-old who ran his own spread while working as a foreman on a bigger ranch nearby.

The weeks Billy spent on the Ruidoso sound idyllic. Some evenings Coe and his cousins brought out their fiddles and played at exuberant bailes, or parties, where Billy shone, dancing—his favorite song, they say, was "Turkey in the Straw"—and flirting with senoritas who flirted right back; he soon had a number of lady friends up and down the river. When he wasn't working or hunting, Billy constantly broke down, cleaned, and practiced with his pistols, shedding a hefty Colt .45 for a pair of smaller Colt .41s, "Thunderers," which he could fire quickly since they didn't need to be manually cocked.[4]

It was a respite he sorely needed. It didn't last.

AS BILLY RESTED, JOHN KINNEY AND THE BOYS LEAPED INTO A FURI-ous little war that erupted just across the Texas border, a kind of palate cleanser for the drama to come. They call it the El Paso Salt War. For years Latinos in El Paso had mined salt flats ninety miles to the east; salt was used in processing ore in Mexican silver mines. In 1877 two Anglo investors, one an El Paso judge named Charles Howard, filed a claim on the area, demanding payment from anyone who dared dig up "their" salt.

That September a Latino mob took Howard hostage and demanded he leave town. He did, then returned and shot the mob's leader dead, kicking off the war. Taking Howard's side, a company of Texas Rangers rode in. Hundreds of angry Latinos surrounded them in the town of San Elizario. After a four-day siege, the Rangers surrendered, the only time that's happened in Ranger history. The mob then assembled a firing squad and executed Judge Howard and two of his supporters.

In Washington, the secretary of war ordered in troops that, hamstrung by vague orders, stood by and watched as El Paso's sheriff called in Kinney, never mind that he was a fugitive from a new murder charge. In late December, he, Jesse Evans, and thirty riders exacted a brutal revenge on San Elizario, raping at least one woman and killing six Latinos. The sheriff announced they died resisting arrest; he actually named Kinney a deputy. As scores of Latinos fled across the Rio Grande, the Boys then shot up El Paso, raiding stores and killing a few more people. Kinney ended up in a strange barroom gunfight with a character named "Buckskin Joe" Haytema, who ran out of bullets after emptying his gun at him, wounding him in a knuckle. For whatever reason, rather than killing him, Kinney stalked off.

AS THIS WAS GOING ON, BILLY'S INTERLUDE ON THE RUIDOSO ENDED when his new pal Dick Brewer hired him to cowboy at the ranch where he worked, a job that would draw both into a conflict that produced some of the more memorable violence of the Old West. Their boss, a twenty-four-year-old Englishman named John Tunstall, was not just a gentleman rancher, as some portray him. He is best viewed as a kind of turbocharged Elon Musk wannabe, a brash upstart businessman determined to destroy the corrupt monopoly that all but controlled Lincoln County.

Tunstall had arrived in Vancouver five years earlier to clerk for his father's friend, hated it, left to investigate sheep ranching in California for a year, hated it, then decided to try New Mexico. In Santa Fe he was buttonholed by a Canadian-born lawyer named Alexander

"Mac" McSween, who judged Tunstall might have the right mix of ambition and naivete his client the cattleman John Chisum was looking for in the front man they sought to take on the monopoly. There is little sense Tunstall understood the profound risks involved, though McSween's wife tried to break it to him gently. As she put it later, "I told Tunstall and Mr. McSween they would be murdered."[5]

There was reason to be wary. The monopoly they planned to attack was J. J. Dolan & Co., known as "The House." Run by a rising young political boss named Jimmy Dolan, it was a kind of evil Sears, its dominant dry goods stores not only strangling farmers with onerous credit terms but—and this drove Chisum to apoplexy—orchestrating the trade in stolen cattle, much of it sold to the army and an Apache reservation. The House's preeminent beef supplier was none other than the Boys, which put Dolan deeply in bed with John Kinney and Jesse Evans, a trio few in Lincoln County could imagine challenging. All of it was quietly underwritten by the great serpent of New Mexico politics, the Santa Fe Ring, run by fat-cat lawyers in the capital.

Tunstall, with McSween as his partner, lawyer, and consigliere, started by buying his ranch, putting together two parcels thirty miles south of Lincoln that Dick Brewer ran for him. Next came a big house in town, complete with Victorian furniture and a piano, then a store next door. By mid-1877 Tunstall was already extending credit to farmers, in essence stealing The House's customers. By the time the store finally opened in November with goods hauled in from St. Louis, Jimmy Dolan was already confronting keen financial pressures. He sent one of his partners to Santa Fe to try to renegotiate his loans.

Dolan was desperate. Given who he did business with, everyone in Lincoln understood what that meant. All that autumn of 1877 rumors of violence mounted. Tunstall did what he could to protect himself, hiring cowboys like Billy who knew more about handling Colts than cattle. He even visited Jesse Evans when he landed in jail, trying to assess whether Evans could be persuaded to switch sides. He couldn't.

For all the ominous rumblings, the trouble actually started in court, with a fiendishly creative gambit in which Dolan sought to not only bankrupt Tunstall and McSween but seize their assets. It turned out that McSween, in an entirely separate matter, had somehow retained or, you know, maybe "lost" some insurance money he was supposed to hold when a client died. Dolan persuaded an heir to press embezzlement charges. When the matter came up in a Mesilla court in February 1878, the judge delayed a criminal trial. A parallel civil case, however, required a surety (a deposit), and the court granted a "writ of attachment" for McSween's assets to be inventoried—meaning, in the short term, seized. Because so much of Tunstall's net worth appeared to be tied up with his lawyer's, his assets could be seized too.

All this happened after McSween and Tunstall had left court. Worse, Jimmy Dolan raced back to Lincoln, arriving two days before them. By the time they returned, Dolan's lackey sheriff, a drunk named William Brady, had occupied the store. Tunstall, with Billy and another cowhand at his side, berated them, but it was no use.

This was on February 9, 1878. As Tunstall retreated to his ranch to regroup, Sheriff Brady began assembling a posse of Dolan men and Boys to seize the cattle there. On February 13 they appeared at Tunstall's spread, legal papers in hand. Arguments ensued, at which point men from both sides rode back to Lincoln for further guidance. Four days later, on February 17, as the size of the Dolan posse swelled to forty-four, Tunstall reluctantly decided to surrender his cattle.

But, as soon became clear, Jimmy Dolan wanted more than cows. The next morning, Tunstall and several of his men, including Billy, left the ranch, driving nine horses to Lincoln. When the posse appeared at the ranch an hour later, several argued for going after the horses—

and the Englishman. "Hurry up boys," one said as a pursuit group gathered, "my knife is sharp and I feel like scalping someone."[6]

They caught up with Tunstall's group in a gorge leading down to the Ruidoso. Outnumbered, Billy and others scrambled up to high ground, hollering for Tunstall to follow. For some reason, he didn't. Jesse Evans and a Dolan man shot him in the head and chest. Later, they claimed he had fired first, while resisting arrest, which became the official explanation. But everyone understood it was murder.

Thus began what is called the Lincoln County War, during which Billy the Kid would begin his rise from foot soldier to folk hero. He and Tunstall must've been close, many have surmised, given the zeal with which Billy pursued vengeance for his killing. "I'll get some of them before I die," he said at a viewing of the body. But Billy was a teenager, an orphan, and one imagines his commitment says as much about a wayward eighteen-year-old's need for purpose, for validation, for a sense of belonging, as any bond with the mannered Englishman. It's the age so many of us are drawn to a cause.

The "war" proved a slapdash affair. It took a while for the Dolan side, consisting of company loyalists and Jesse Evans's shaggy outlaws, to even realize what was in the offing; its members didn't fully mobilize for weeks. The initiative lay instead with the Tunstall side, now under the unsteady command of the attorney Mac McSween, a classic indoor westerner. Its riders anointed themselves the "Regulators," a moniker that vigilantes had taken since Revolutionary War times.*

The Regulators, who most days could field anywhere from ten to

---

*The term's origins can be traced to the 1760s, when a government-resistance movement, a kind of warm-up for the American Revolution, sprang up in the backcountry of North and South Carolina. Its members objected to British taxes, fees, and bureaucracy and sought to "regulate their own affairs." Violence eventually broke out, with acts of lynching and a pitched battle or two. This was the period, mentioned in chapter 1, that scholars consider the birth of American vigilantism.

thirty men, formed around a core of a dozen close-knit young gunmen, almost all of them Tunstall's ranch hands or Billy's pals from the Ruidoso. They swore a loyalty oath they called "the iron clad" and worked for the promise of a paycheck down the line. Led by the foreman Dick Brewer, they seized the moral high ground once McSween prevailed on a constable to issue murder warrants against seventeen of the Dolan men. Other warrants were issued for larceny and horse theft.

On March 6, two-plus weeks after Tunstall's death, Brewer led the Regulators south down the Pecos in search of one of the assassins, a rustler named Billy Morton. They spotted him in a group of five riders. Morton and another man peeled off, and a running gun battle ensued. After five miles the pair's horses gave out and, once Brewer promised not to harm them, the two surrendered; the second man turned out to be another they sought, a Boys "captain" named Frank Baker.

The Regulators debated what to do with the prisoners. If they took them to Lincoln, Dolan's crony, Sheriff Brady, might release them. Over the next several days, during which a suspicious character named McCloskey joined the group, they wandered the area, unsure of what to do. In the end, they returned to Lincoln empty-handed, telling McSween a tidy story of how Billy Morton had grabbed McCloskey's gun, shot him dead, then rode off with Baker, at which point the Regulators rode them down and killed them "trying to escape." About as many people believed this as the explanation of Tunstall's death.

Suddenly everyone involved realized how dirty this war would be. Dolan lit out for Santa Fe. McSween and his wife took refuge at John Chisum's ranch, where they seem to have debated the danger Sheriff Brady posed; McSween was due in court in Lincoln, and he was convinced Brady would arrest him, as in fact he planned to do, and then allow Jesse Evans to kill him, as in fact Dolan wanted. Some historians, including Billy's biographer Robert M. Utley, think it's unlikely

McSween ordered Brady's assassination. But it's indisputable that after lying low for three weeks, the Regulators left a meeting at the Chisum ranch with plans to kill the sheriff.

On the morning of April 1, Brady and five of his men walked out of the Lincoln courthouse. When they passed the Tunstall store, Billy and five Regulators rose from behind a low adobe wall and opened fire with Winchesters. Brady fell dead, struck by twelve bullets, as did a deputy. When the gun smoke cleared, Billy and another Regulator strode to Brady's body and leaned over it, apparently to grab some papers McSween wanted. As they did, a deputy, having taken refuge in a nearby house, fired a single round, which struck both men in their thighs. Both scrambled away. This was likely the first time Billy was shot.

The murders caused a sensation, thrusting what had been a local affair onto New Mexico's front pages, where it would remain for months. As it did, on the morning of April 4, fifteen Regulators, including the gimpy Billy, rode into Blazer's Mill, a creek-side hamlet thirty miles southwest of Lincoln that had formed around a sawmill and was now surrounded by an Apache reservation. Why they roamed so far afield is a mystery.* They weren't seeking trouble, much less one of the Old West's storied gunfights. All they asked for was a hot meal.

As they ate inside the two-story adobe building housing the Indian agency, a lookout spotted a dusty figure approaching on a mule. It was Andrew Roberts, known as "Buckshot" Roberts, so named for a load of buckshot he carried in his right shoulder—the gift of a Texas Ranger, some said—that rendered him unable to lift his arm above his waist. Roberts was a Dolan man, and a cantankerous one at that. He had ridden with the posse that seized Tunstall's cattle but wanted no

---

*A group of judicial officials, including a judge and the county's district attorney and clerk, was traveling in the area on its way to hold court in Lincoln. Dolan partisans would later suggest the Regulators had intended to kill the whole group, which seems unlikely, even after the assassination of a sheriff.

part of further violence. He'd already sold his place on the Ruidoso and had come to town to collect his mail before leaving for good.

While several of the Regulators got along with Roberts, his name was on the list of warrants they carried. As he tied his mule outside the building, easing to the ground clutching a Winchester, Billy's friend George Coe stepped out. The two men shook hands. Coe explained the situation. He urged Roberts to surrender. He refused. Coe promised he wouldn't be harmed. There were fourteen other armed Regulators inside the house, Coe emphasized. Again and again, no doubt with the fate of Billy Morton and company in mind, Buckshot Roberts refused.

Finally, the other Regulators lost patience. Three hustled outside. One, Charlie Bowdre, was holding a pistol.

"Throw up your hands, Roberts!" Bowdre barked.

"No," Roberts replied, bringing his Winchester to his hip.

They fired at the same time. Roberts's first bullet hit Bowdre's cartridge belt, ricocheting into another Regulator's hand. Bowdre's struck Roberts in the stomach. Dust rose from his clothes.

All the Regulators spilled into the road. Badly hurt, Roberts backed into a doorway, pumping and firing the Winchester. One Regulator was hit in the chest, another in the leg. Roberts let loose at Billy as he ducked behind a wagon, the bullet grazing his arm. When Billy thought Roberts had fired his last shot, he rushed him with his own Winchester. Roberts shoved his rifle into Billy's belly just as he fired. The bullet went wild. Billy dashed off.

Roberts ducked into an empty office, found a Springfield rifle and a box of cartridges, and threw a mattress across the doorway. Outside, the Regulators' leader, Dick Brewer, was apoplectic. He ordered one Regulator to go talk to this crazy man. He refused, as did the Indian agent. Brewer was so angry he threatened to burn the building down.

Instead, he stalked across the road and made his way a hundred yards down a path parallel to it, looking for a spot where he might get an open shot. He found one when he reached a pile of logs. Laying his Winchester atop them, he could see into the office where Roberts was hunkered down. Brewer fired a shot through the doorway. It hit a wall inside. Peering out, Roberts saw smoke rise from Brewer's position. He laid his Springfield across the mattress and, when Brewer raised his head, fired. Buckshot Roberts must've been one heckuva shot. The bullet struck Brewer in the left eye, killing him.

Not one of the Regulators had the stomach to fight on after that, not even Billy, whose role in the gunplay that day fed his dawning reputation. They rode off. Buckshot Roberts died the next day, the tale of his defense an overnight legend. Though avenging a murder and legally empowered by the warrants they carried, the Regulators suffered by comparison. In three engagements, they had now killed three prisoners, assassinated a sheriff, killed a deputy, and been humiliated by an ornery coot they outnumbered fifteen to one. Across New Mexico, the winds of public opinion began to blow in their faces.

CHAPTER TWELVE

The Rise of Billy the Kid

New Mexico, 1879 to 1880

Not that the Regulators understood this. From their standpoint, things appeared downright rosy. A grand jury had cleared Mac McSween of the embezzlement charge, allowing him to move back into Lincoln, where, with Dolan and his worst henchmen out of sight, the Regulators emerged as a lively presence in his parlor, Billy and the others singing around the piano. On the downside, the grand jury issued indictments against seemingly everyone involved: Billy and three Regulators for killing Sheriff Brady, two others for the deputy; six Regulators for Buckshot Roberts; Jesse Evans plus three for Tunstall. Even Jimmy Dolan himself was indicted as an accessory.

The good news, at least for the Regulators, was that no one seemed in any hurry to make arrests. The new sheriff was a galoot named John Copeland, who fell under McSween's influence. Rather than arrest Billy and the others, Copeland ended up hoisting beers with them. No one worried too much about Dolan, who had gone bankrupt, closed his store, and been seen hobbling around on a splint. Jesse Evans had gotten himself shot and was sitting in an army brig.

Both men still commanded loyalists, though, including Sheriff Brady's surviving deputies, who quietly assembled a force of thirty gunmen to retake Lincoln. For the Regulators, the first whiff of danger came on April 29, 1878, when their new captain, Frank McNab, and two of his men rode into an ambush nine miles south of Lincoln. Two, including McNab, died of their wounds. The other was captured.

By morning the Dolan men had all but surrounded Lincoln, with a few creeping into the abandoned Dolan store. As Regulators scrambled behind adobe walls and onto rooftops, firefights broke out everywhere. With everyone in defensive positions, only one gunman, a Dolanite, was killed. In a panic, Sheriff Copeland appealed to the army at Fort Stanton. After four hours, twenty cavalrymen rode into Lincoln. The shooting stopped. When an officer asked Copeland who he wanted arrested, he replied, "I want the whole damn business."[1]

The thoroughly anticlimactic Battle of Lincoln ended with the thirty Dolan men glumly marching off in custody. The army, though, had little appetite for holding them and promptly returned the men to Copeland, who had no place to put them in his tiny jail. In the end, he meekly released them all, telling them to go home and behave.

And surprisingly, they did. For the next month, in fact, not much happened. The Regulators launched a raid on a Dolan cow camp, captured one of the men who killed Frank McNab, and shot him "escaping." But that was about it. What triggered the lull, one suspects, was a federal investigation. The British government hadn't been pleased with Tunstall's murder and urged Washington to do something. Acting jointly, the Departments of Justice and the Interior dispatched a man named Frank Warner Angel to Lincoln, where, in a jarring note of civility, he began taking depositions from everyone involved, even Billy. As long as Angel was in town, everyone stayed on their best behavior.

It was quiet—too quiet, as a bad Western might say. Behind the scenes, Jimmy Dolan was busy pulling levers in Santa Fe. This time he had the full attention of his patron, Thomas B. Catron, the U.S. attorney who ran the Santa Fe Ring and who, with Dolan bankrupt, found himself in control of his stores and other assets, including cattle the Regulators had dispersed in their raid. The most powerful man in New Mexico, Catron wanted this over, and quickly. He sent a letter to the governor demanding military intervention.

The governor not only consented but did him one better. On May 28, with the county still calm, he suddenly removed John Copeland as sheriff, citing a technicality in his appointment. He replaced him with a Dolan man, a feeble Frenchman named George Peppin, a deputy who had survived Sheriff Brady's murder. Peppin, it was assumed, would actually try to arrest the indicted Regulators. McSween and the Regulators realized too late that they had been outmaneuvered. Seeing the writing on the adobe, the Regulators lit out for the hills.

Into the vacuum Dolan himself invaded with something like an actual army, maybe eighty men in all, sweeping into Lincoln in mid-June, not just Peppin and his cronies, but a cavalry detachment and a dozen deputized outlaws commanded by the crime boss John Kinney. Just as important, Dolan brought a new federal arrest warrant for Billy and everyone who'd been at Blazer's Mill. When they failed to appear before a judge in Mesilla on June 22, they were all indicted for murder.

This was now the full force of official New Mexico determined to hunt down McSween and the dozen or so remaining "iron clads," dead or alive. In the following days, Dolan riders hounded the Regulators across the rugged hills above the village of San Patricio, the Ruidoso River hamlet that had been Billy's favored retreat. They were cornered in the village itself on July 3, taking to the rooftops to fend off an assault. After slipping away, they were cornered once more on a high ridge to the east. The Regulator fire was so intense the Dolan forces were obliged to withdraw. Through it all, only horses were killed.

On July 4 they rode into John Chisum's ranch, hoping for refuge, but the Dolan forces surrounded its big adobe house, leading to a full day of desultory exchanges. Finally, the Regulators slipped away in the night, but it was clear they couldn't go on like this. The strain was taking its toll on Mac McSween. This kind of life, the endless riding and shooting and camping under the stars, was not one he wanted, or was suited for. It was time to end this, he announced more than once. The lawyer had a fatalistic streak, everyone said later. If his time on earth was nigh, he wanted to die with his family.

The size of the force the Regulators managed to assemble in the next week, though, suggests McSween had plenty of fight left in him. Everyone called in their favors, and by the evening of July 15, when they crept back into Lincoln, there were a stunning sixty of them, seemingly everyone who ever worked alongside Tunstall or Chisum, including a group of thirty Latino villagers. Sheriff Peppin's posses were still out hunting them; Dolan and a handful of those who remained in town holed up in the Wortley Hotel, powerless to stop McSween's men, for the moment at least, from retaking it. Many townspeople, meanwhile, took hasty vacations, leaving Lincoln all but empty.

The Dolan forces, by contrast, were melting away. By the time they returned the next day, everyone could see their numbers had dwindled, the cavalry withdrawn, others presumably tiring of a war they had little skin in. Barely forty fighters remained; they were actually outnumbered. By twilight, the two sides had occupied all of Lincoln's strongest buildings, Billy and the Regulators joining McSween in his sturdy U-shaped adobe home, the Latinos in two of the stores. Many of the Dolan men took up positions at the hotel, their headquarters, barely fifty yards from McSween's house. The two sides exchanged a few ragged fusillades, then settled in for the night.

Amazingly, nothing much changed for three full days. It was, from all appearances, a complete stalemate. There were random shots here and there; one Regulator was killed when a bullet seared into the Mc-Sween house, another fell while feeding a horse. Unable to generate much enthusiasm among his men for frontal assaults on the barricaded McSween buildings, Sheriff Peppin did the only sensible thing: he sent word to Fort Stanton, asking the army for a howitzer.

The fort's commanding officer, a haughty lieutenant colonel named Nathan A. M. Dudley, had received new guidance from Washington ordering him to refuse all requests to intervene. Alas, when he dispatched a rider to Lincoln to decline the howitzer request, a Regulator sharpshooter atop the McSween house shot him. Well, actually, he shot *at* him; the rider fell when his horse threw him. The distinction was lost on Colonel Dudley, who termed it "this infamous outrage." The final straw came the next day when an army medical team, sent to tend to a wounded man, drew fire from one of the McSween-held stores.

That did it: orders be damned. On the morning of July 19, people across Lincoln glanced west and saw a startling spectacle: a blue-coated army column, led by Dudley and four mounted officers, followed by eleven cavalrymen, twenty infantrymen, and, in the rear, a twelve-pound mountain howitzer. Oh, and for good measure, a Gatling gun. They tromped through town and set up a camp. A bit later, Sheriff Peppin was spotted riding alongside three troopers.

McSween jumped to a logical conclusion: the army had come to fight alongside the Dolan forces. He scribbled out a message and sent a child to deliver it to Dudley. It began: "Would you have the kindness to let me know why soldiers surround my house. Before blowing up my property I would like to know the reason." Dudley sent back a condescending note of his own, saying the house was not surrounded, but if McSween wanted to blow it up himself, he was cool with that.

In fact, though his sympathies clearly lay with the Dolan forces, Dudley had decided to remain neutral; he was there, he informed

Peppin, solely to protect civilians. But if anyone on either side shot at his men, he let both sides know, they would pay the price.

His first actions, though, seriously alarmed the McSween men. Dudley first pointed the howitzer at the store where Latino fighters had fired on his medical team. Everyone inside ran to the second store. When Dudley turned the gun there, the store emptied completely, all thirty of the Latinos scrambling out and disappearing into the hills, a few shots from the Dolan men fired over their heads as encouragement. By dusk other Regulators were joining them. The next morning, McSween woke to find his force had dwindled from sixty men to precisely thirteen: the iron clads, Billy and his pals Doc Scurlock and Charlie Bowdre and the rest. They were the only ones left. In a single house, outnumbered, surrounded. There would be no easy retreats this time.

At midmorning a deputy approached the house and hollered that he held warrants for McSween's arrest. McSween yelled back that he held warrants for the posse's arrest. "Our warrants are in our guns, you cock-sucking sons-of-bitches," a Regulator added helpfully.[2]

McSween's wife, Sue, was a strong presence, and that afternoon she marched down the street to talk with Colonel Dudley. On her way, she saw possemen making preparations to burn down her home. She and Dudley ended up in a shouting match. If the Regulators wanted to save themselves, he lectured her, they should surrender. He would not interfere with a sheriff carrying out viable arrest warrants.

The Dolan men kept up a steady fire at the McSween house all that day. By afternoon they had crept into positions directly in back of the house, along an adobe wall that ran behind a set of outbuildings, a stable, a privy, and a chicken coop. From these positions, just steps from the house itself, they were able to toss kindling and coal oil against its rear walls. An initial fire was doused with water. A second attempt, however, managed to ignite a lean-to used as a summer kitchen. Attempts to put it out were driven back by bullets.

Slowly the fire advanced into the house. As smoke billowed into the sky, the last Regulators, along with McSween's family, staff, and in-laws, retreated from room to room. At one point, a keg of gunpowder exploded. The flames then spread rapidly. Sue McSween's account of what happened inside the house, the most complete we have, suggests Billy had emerged as the group's leader. As they edged into the last unburned room, a kitchen at a rear corner of the house, her husband sank into a daze. Billy shook and slapped him, trying to arouse his focus. He insisted they could still escape and retreat to safety.

Granted safe passage, the women and children went first. As night fell, those who remained saw but one escape route: out the kitchen door, across the backyard maybe thirty feet to a side gate, then left through a vacant lot toward the river and the hills beyond. Across the lot stood the Tunstall store, filled with gunmen. The yard, though, lay in shadow. Attackers at the rear wall could barely see into it.

The plan was for Billy and four Regulators to dash out first, drawing fire, at which point McSween and the others, including a half dozen Latinos and hired men, would follow. Billy's group inched to the gate safely—wearing socks to muffle their steps, some tales have it—but there they became visible in the light of the flames. Shots rang out. Suddenly bullets zinged everywhere. McSween's law clerk, a man named Harvey Morris, fell dead. The others raced for the river, firing wildly, one of Billy's bullets tearing off John Kinney's mustache. In moments they reached safety, diving behind trees at the riverbank.

Spooked by the gunfire, McSween and the others paused in the darkened yard, two or three ducking into the chicken house. Each time any of them stepped toward the gate, bullets drove them back. After maybe five minutes, McSween called out, "I shall surrender!"

A Dolan man named Robert Beckwith and three others stepped into the backyard and approached McSween at the kitchen door.

"I shall never surrender," the lawyer said.

At that, the yard exploded in gunfire, a moment that has gone down as "the big killing." Beckwith fell, a bullet through his eye. Mc-Sween was struck by five himself, crumpling to the ground, as did three Latinos beside him; one, badly wounded, was playing dead and lived to tell the tale. Several others escaped into the gloom.

It was over. As Billy's band made it to the hills, the Dolan men celebrated deep into the night, laughing and whooping and swigging from bottles, firing their pistols at the moon and forcing two of Mc-Sween's hired men to fiddle as they danced. They had won the Lincoln County War. Of course, they had little sense that the consequences, and the killing, were far from over. Or that the story everyone would remember, Billy the Kid's, was just beginning.

THE NEXT FEW MONTHS SERVED AS A KIND OF INTERMISSION, DURING which parts of Lincoln County sat through the equivalent of an ultra-violent cartoon. It starred one of those wandering gunfighters who, a bit like Wes Hardin, pop up in unrelated Old West narratives. His name was John Selman. A Confederate deserter raised in North Texas, Selman had been a fast-talking deputy up to his ears in that vicious Shackelford County vigilante campaign against rustlers. When his boss, Sheriff John Larn, resigned, the two became rustlers themselves, attacking homesteaders and stealing their cattle. Suspicious, the new sheriff raided Larn's farm, found six hides that were not his, and arrested him. On June 24, 1878, a dozen masked men marched into the Albany jail and shot him dead. Selman, no dummy, rode for New Mexico.

Three weeks later, he dropped into the thick of the Lincoln County War, leading a gang that raided up the Ruidoso, burning George Coe's home as the Regulators fought at John Chisum's. "Selman's Scouts," as they were called, would go on to a monthslong rampage of burning, killing, and rapine. Their depredations are remembered mostly for the snarling reply one of Selman's men gave when asked who they were: "We are demons come from Hell!" History, though, was far from finished with John Selman.

Your intermission is now concluded.

THE NEXT CHAPTER OF THE LINCOLN COUNTY DRAMA DAWNED THAT autumn, when the federal investigator Frank Warner Angel's report landed on desks in Washington. It had a bad word for almost everyone. In its wake the White House sacked the governor. His replacement, tasked with cleaning up the mess, was Lew Wallace, a decorated Civil War general and budding novelist poised to issue his best-known work, *Ben-Hur.*

Lincoln remained on edge, especially after McSween's widow hired a wild-eyed, one-armed lawyer named Huston Chapman to sue the army's Colonel Dudley for his role in the climactic battle. Indictments still hung over almost everyone involved, though the authorities showed little interest in actually making any arrests. Billy and the dozen or so remaining Regulators, meanwhile, had made themselves scarce. After a wild gunfight with the minders of a horse herd they purloined to raise money, they sold the horses and rode up the Pecos to the tiny Latino village of Fort Sumner, a full 140 miles north, east of Albuquerque. They spent a week there carousing, then rode farther north, stopping at a village named Anton Chico.

There they held a summit. Tired of fighting, the two Coe cousins announced they were leaving for Colorado. Billy, now the group's clear leader, said he had unfinished business in Lincoln. "Who wants to go with me?" he asked. Everyone else indicated they would.

That first return was a brief one. They stayed only long enough to steal some more horses and move Charlie Bowdre and Doc Scurlock off their farms. Both men and their wives resettled in Fort Sumner, a place Billy came to favor, at least in part for the two friendly senoritas who lived on its plaza. It would become what passed for his new home base.

They spent the rest of the autumn relaxing and stealing horses, which they herded across the Texas border and sold at Tascosa, the trading center for the new ranches springing up in the Panhandle. By Thanksgiving, though, the other Regulators were falling away, taking cowboy jobs or leaving the state, anything to avoid the indictments most still faced. Billy chose not to flee the area but to try to resolve his legal problems, chiefly the two murder indictments. In December, when he headed south, only one rider went with him, a strapping teenage Texan named Tom O'Folliard, who idolized him, trailing Billy like a puppy.

Billy had sent feelers to Jimmy Dolan, asking whether he was ready to make peace. Dolan replied that they could talk. They agreed to meet in Lincoln on February 18, 1879, one year to the day since John Tunstall's murder. There were maybe fifteen of them in all that night, facing one another across low adobe walls on either side of the street. Dolan was there, flanked by Jesse Evans and a new man, a hardened Texas killer named Billy Campbell. Across the way, Billy stood alongside Tom O'Folliard and a half dozen pals.

Evans almost ruined things by announcing that Billy needed to be shot on the spot. Billy said he hadn't come to fight, and once the air calmed, everyone gathered in the street. They came to a truce agreement: None of them would kill or testify against the others without withdrawing from the pact. Anyone who violated it would be executed. Then they shook on it.

And then, of all things, they decided to celebrate, ducking into one bar, then another, until several of them—not including Billy, who rarely imbibed—were thoroughly besotted. Around 10:30, as they were weaving past the courthouse, they encountered the widow McSween's attorney, the one-armed Huston Chapman, whose face was swathed in bandages, apparently some kind of treatment for a bad toothache.

Billy Campbell demanded to know his name.

"My name is Chapman," he replied.

At that, Campbell, because this kind of thing actually happened in the Old West, drew his pistol, jammed it into the lawyer's chest, and growled, "Then you dance."

After a further exchange of pleasantries, Dolan drew his own gun and fired in the air. Campbell, whether by accident or malevolence, then fired his—into Chapman's chest. "My God, I am killed," the lawyer gasped as he keeled over dead, his clothing on fire.

It is a measure of the barbarity here not that a man was dispatched so callously, but that upon doing so, his killers strolled to a restaurant and ordered an oyster dinner, leaving the smoldering body in the middle of the street. At some point, Billy and O'Folliard excused themselves, mounted their horses, and rode off. "There was really no malice in this shooting," one bystander later insisted. "Life was held lightly down there in those days."[3]

Something like panic broke out in officialdom, the fear being that the war was rekindling. Colonel Dudley sent a detachment to occupy the town. Governor Wallace, having promised to visit Lincoln for months, finally arrived, promptly fired Dudley, and tasked his replacement, a determined captain named Henry Carroll, with bringing Chapman's killers to justice, as well as everyone else indicted during the war, including Billy. Carroll's troopers descended on the area like locusts. Within days, Dolan, Evans, and several of their men were sitting in the Fort Stanton stockade. The problem, it soon became apparent, was finding anyone brave enough to testify against them.

Hiding down in San Patricio, you could almost see the light bulb appear over Billy's head. On March 13, he sent a messenger to deliver a bold proposal to the governor: dismiss the two murder indictments against him, Billy wrote, and he would identify Chapman's killers.*

Two days later Wallace replied, proposing a meeting, at night, at the justice of the peace's adobe shack by the courthouse. Billy arrived alone, as requested. The two men were waiting inside. "I was to meet the governor here," Billy said. "Is the governor here?"

Wallace rose from a table and extended his hand. They ended up making the classic informant's deal. The authorities would stage a fake arrest, giving Billy cover. Billy would tell everything he knew to a grand jury being convened to consider not only the Chapman murder but the entire Lincoln County War. Wallace would then pardon him.

Things moved fast after that. Four nights later, a sheriff's posse surrounded a house in San Patricio and took Billy and O'Folliard into custody. They were installed in a private house in Lincoln. In a smirking letter, Governor Wallace notified the secretary of the interior, terming Billy "a precious specimen nick-named 'The Kid.'"

Billy the Kid has gone down as many things, a gunfighter, an outlaw, a feudist, a folk hero. He now became something else, a snitch, a rat, an informant who gave the government information to save his hide—and in doing so broke the pact he had sworn with Jimmy Dolan. In mid-April Billy held up his end of the deal, testifying before a grand jury, where he named Campbell, Dolan, and Jesse Evans as Chapman's killers; all three were indicted, Evans as an accessory. Billy spoke at length about rustling and other local crimes.

When it came time for the government to hold up its end of the

---

*The letter is among the first where Billy identifies himself. "I am called Kid Antrim," he wrote, "but Antrim is my stepfather's name."

deal, though, there was a hitch. The governor had returned to Santa Fe, and the district attorney, a Dolan man, saw no need to accede to a deal he hadn't been party to. "He is bent on going for the Kid," an aide wrote Wallace. "He is bent on pushing him to the wall."[4]

Wallace did nothing, allowing Billy's prosecution to go ahead despite their deal. In the end, the entire proceeding was a travesty. Two hundred indictments were issued against fifty men. Two came to trial. Neither ended in conviction. Dolan, Evans, and their men went free. Only Billy was bound over for trial, for the murder of Sheriff Brady. The judge granted a change of venue, to Doña Ana County.

By that point, a sympathetic new sheriff, a Wallace man, had given Billy free run of Lincoln. Maybe this was an expression of the governor's guilt, a subtle suggestion that Billy was free to go; Wallace, after all, had broken his word. Or not. Whatever the case, Billy stayed in Lincoln all spring, testifying in open court as part of Sue McSween's lawsuit against Colonel Dudley. (She lost.) He might have stayed longer, but federal prosecutors began making noises about pressing the Buckshot Roberts indictment. Betrayed by the governor, staring at one and perhaps two murder trials, Billy did as you'd expect. On June 17, while the sheriff looked the other way, he and O'Folliard mounted their horses and rode, unopposed, out of town.*

IT'S NOW THAT BILLY BECOMES AN OUTLAW, THOUGH THAT'S A HIGH-falutin term for what he really was: a livestock thief, a bit more ambitious than most, but at base just another of the hundreds of rustlers stealing horses and cattle across New Mexico. Fort Sumner proved an

---

*With him went Doc Scurlock, who had also been arrested. Scurlock then took his family and moved to Texas.

ideal headquarters. A fort had been built there during the Civil War to watch the Navajo, but it had been abandoned. A landowner named Lucien Maxwell acquired it in 1871 and settled the area with two dozen Latino families, many of whose men worked at outlying sheep camps and came to view Billy, with his fluent Spanish and ardor for Latinas, as one of their own. After Maxwell died, his popular son Pete became the de facto jefe. Billy took up with his young sister.*

Fort Sumner lay on the lower tier of San Miguel County, a hundred miles south of the county seat, Las Vegas, too distant for the sheriff to pay it much mind. It had a pair of boisterous saloons—Beaver Smith's and Bob Hargrove's—a growing trade in stolen livestock, and a stream of rough types seeking opportunities Texas no longer afforded. By mid-1879 maybe fifty of them had moved into the area, leading raids that swept strays off the Texas Panhandle ranches and herded them back to sell to fences in New Mexico, often in the boomtowns of White Oaks and especially Tularosa, where an Irishman named Pat Coghlan bought cattle at twelve dollars a head and doubled his money selling them to the army and the Indian reservations.

It's hard to call the men who coalesced around Billy a gang. His only reliable wingmen were Tom O'Folliard and Charlie Bowdre, but others rode with them, most notably the Dodge City Gang's squat Dirty Dave Rudabaugh, he of the questionable hygiene. Rudabaugh was a known killer, and a malodorous one at that.†

---

*Lucien Maxwell was the man whose real estate machinations triggered Clay Allison's Colfax County War.

†From the sheer volume of articles online, Old West hygiene remains a subject of boundless fascination. By today's standards, it was bad. Really bad. Toilet paper wasn't yet in wide use; rolls of it weren't invented until the 1890s. Until then, we're talking torn-up newspapers, grass, and corn cobs. Sanitary pads were in use by 1890; before that, grass, cotton, rabbit furs, and rags were used. Doc Holliday aside, there weren't many dentists outside the cities; cowboys and country folk tended to make do with pliers. Toothbrushes weren't widely available either, though we're told restaurants and stagecoach stations sometimes offered a makeshift community toothbrush of sorts, sometimes horsehair. Bathing was iffy; once a month

No thrilling tales of their cattle raids into Texas survive, but by early 1880, six months after his flight from Lincoln, Billy's reputation as a rustler—and a gunfighter in his own right—was on the rise. Both were highlighted on January 10, 1880, when Billy was in Hargrove's bar negotiating with John Chisum's brother and three of his cowboys, who were diplomatically attempting to dissuade him from raiding their herds.

As they spoke, a drunken Texan named Joe "Texas Red" Grant began to needle Billy, at one point proclaiming, "I'll bet twenty-five dollars that I kill a man today before you do." When Grant stepped toward a Chisum man and lifted his pearl-handled pistol from its holster, Billy asked to see the gun, murmuring, "That's a mighty nice-looking six-shooter you got." When he returned it, Grant didn't notice that Billy had slyly spun the cylinder to an empty chamber.

Turning to the popular frontier pastime of recreational bottle smashing, Grant proceeded to burst an array of glass containers against the bar, going on about how he intended to kill someone. Say this for Grant: though drunk and stupid, he was a man of his word. When Billy turned to leave, he raised the pistol and pulled the trigger.

Click.

Billy whirled, pulled his Colt, and fired three bullets, each striking Grant in the face, killing him. It was only the second man we know for sure he killed. "Joe," Billy muttered over the body, "I've been there too often for you." There would be no repercussions or investigation; it was seen as just another barroom killing. "It was a game of two," Billy shrugged later, "and I got there first."[5]

The odd killing aside, Billy loved it in Fort Sumner, where he was free to romance his senoritas without any serious fear the law would

---

is the rate I've seen often. Shampoo didn't come along till the 1920s. Newspapers helpfully suggested women wash their hair with things like eggs and vinegar.

come for him. He began to put down roots, posing for the one reliable photograph we have of him, even popping up in the 1880 census. When he wasn't stealing cows or selling them in White Oaks and Tularosa, he could often be found in Beaver Smith's playing monte. He darted into Lincoln a time or two, looking in on Sue McSween.

By the fall of 1880, though, Billy was drawing unwanted attention. A range detective hired by angry Texas ranchers rode to White Oaks and identified him as a primary supplier of stolen cattle; the ranchers began assembling an expedition to bring him in. When a rash of counterfeit bank notes appeared, a Secret Service man arrived in Lincoln and tied them to Billy and his Fort Sumner circle.* When he couldn't get anyone in official New Mexico to stir, the operative reached out to area ranchers, including John Chisum, who were more than happy to supply gunmen to finally bring Billy to justice. Before long, both the Texans and the Secret Service were on his trail.

How big a deal was Billy the Kid at this point? Not very. Between his two murder indictments and his role as an informant, his name had appeared intermittently in the New Mexico papers. But as an outlaw, he had mostly flown under the radar. This was poised to change, though, thanks to a bear Billy should never have poked: John Chisum.

The aging cattleman had sold much of his cattle business, but his brothers were still active, and he remained a pillar of the New Mexico ranching community. Somehow Billy got the idea that Chisum owed him money for his service during the Lincoln County War. As Chisum's nephew told it, Billy actually accosted Chisum once as he passed through Fort Sumner. Chisum replied that he didn't owe Billy a thing. "You

---

*No, there is no evidence Billy the Kid was a counterfeiter, but—who knew?—counterfeiting was apparently a persistent problem on the frontier. Several gunfighters were arrested or investigated for passing fake bills, including Mysterious Dave Mather and Butch Cassidy's first partner, Elzy Lay.

can kill me but you won't knock me out of many years," he said. "I'm an old man now."

"Aw," Billy finally said, "you ain't worth killing."[6]

Stories of their "feud" began to circulate, though other than a single raid we're told he launched on Chisum herds, Billy displayed scant evidence of it. John Chisum, though, was not a man to fool with.

CHAPTER THIRTEEN

The Hunts for Billy the Kid

New Mexico, 1880 to 1884

By 1880 John Chisum and his fellow cattlemen had had enough of Billy. Somewhat as the governor of Texas approved hiring a single lawman to track down Bonnie and Clyde fifty-four years later, Chisum and company brought in their own man to get Billy, an unlikely candidate to be sure, a bartender of all things, a towering onetime Texas buffalo hunter named Pat Garrett. Standing six foot four, a head taller than most men of the era, Garrett had arrived in New Mexico two years earlier trailing the requisite air of mystery, an itinerant cowhand who might be a fugitive from Texas justice for a killing or two, or not.* But he was handsome, good with a gun, and having washed up tending

---

*He was not a fugitive, nor a killer. Born in Georgia in 1850, Garrett had grown up wealthy, on a north Louisiana plantation, but the war took its toll, and when his father died, he left behind a mountain of debts. After a furious estate battle with a brother-in-law, Garrett was left penniless. In 1869, at nineteen, he wandered into Texas as fallen men had been doing for decades, working on a Dallas farm before striking out for the frontier, where he hunted buffalo for several years, surviving more than one skirmish with Comanche warriors. In 1877, after a falling-out with a business partner, he headed to New Mexico, hoping for a fresh start he badly needed.

bar at Beaver Smith's in Fort Sumner, eager for income. The ranchers backed him for sheriff and in the fall election he won.

Later, when it was all over, lots of people would bemoan what bosom pals Pat and Billy had been, how Garrett's decision to hunt Billy amounted to this epic betrayal. You can watch an entire movie about it, the unfortunate *Young Guns II*, a dumbed-down sequel to the surprisingly not-awful *Young Guns*, featuring Emilio Estevez as a less than stable Billy. But the idea that Billy and Pat were pals is only lore. Pat probably poured him a drink or two, and they certainly knew many of the same people, notably Billy's lover Celsa Gutierrez, a Fort Sumner woman who happened to be Garrett's sister-in-law. Historians, though, agree that while the two may have been friendly, there is scant evidence they were friends.

Garrett wasted no time pushing possemen into the field. When word came that Billy and his band had stolen a merchant's horses, a posse tracked them to a ranch near White Oaks, northwest of Lincoln. Before dawn on November 27, they surrounded the snowbound main house and sent in a note demanding surrender. Billy sent a written reply: "You can only take me a corpse."[1] When a blacksmith named Jimmy Carlyle was sent inside to reason with him, he ended up drinking with the gang for hours. At one point, a posseman outside fired a shot, and Carlyle, despite a warning to sit tight, panicked and crashed out a window. Billy and two others fired at him as he ran. He fell dead.

The morning erupted in gunfire, none of it lethal. When it finally stopped, the posse, cold and hungry, rode off. Carlyle's killing, though, marked a moment when public opinion began to turn against Billy. A week later the editor of the *Las Vegas Gazette* denounced "Billy the Kid"—the first known appearance of the nickname—as a "desperate cuss" leading "a powerful gang of outlaws . . . terrorizing the people of Fort Sumner." The article soon expanded into a crusade. Billy sent a letter to Governor Wallace denying he had killed Carlyle and blaming his troubles on John Chisum. It was no use. Wallace responded by announcing a reward for his arrest.

By this point Pat Garrett had amassed something like a "super posse," mostly cowboys sent from two mammoth Texas ranches Billy had victimized, the LS and the LIT. Some were already nosing around Fort Sumner. But Garrett turned out to be a canny pursuer. The more he studied things, the clearer he saw the chance to set a trap. He sent the Texans away for the moment. This required discretion.

Rather than chase Billy around the countryside, Garrett eased into a snowbound Fort Sumner in mid-December with a cadre of trusted men. Having tended bar there, he knew the area, and its people. Hearing Billy and his crew were hiding from the Texans at a ranch east of town, Garrett suspected Charlie Bowdre would come in to see his wife. He sent a boy to tell Billy the Texans had left and waited.

Snow lay thick on the ground on the night of December 19 when Garrett's lookouts spied the six shadowy riders trudging into town. His men crept into position. When the riders came in range, Garrett shouted "Halt!" Billy's sidekick Tom O'Folliard got off a shot. As the riders wheeled, Garrett's men opened fire. A minute later, one horse returned, his rider slumped. It was O'Folliard, shot through the chest. Taken into the fort and laid beside a fire, his last words were to Garrett: "Go to hell, you long-legged son-of-a-bitch."[2]

There was no chasing the others in the darkness. Back at the ranch, despondent over O'Folliard's death, Billy decided to send a spy— one of the ranch's owners—into Fort Sumner to try to scope out Garrett's plans. Frightened, the man went straight to Garrett and told all. Garrett sent him back as his own spy; the rancher returned the next day, his beard dripping with icicles, and reported the gang had left, riding east through four inches of snow. Garrett rode out, found their trail, and realized where they must be heading: a remote one-room stone house at a place known as Stinking Springs.

Now joined by the Texans, Garrett and his men, maybe twenty in all, surrounded the house in the hours after midnight on December 23. There were horses outside, their breaths blowing white. The possemen had been told Billy was wearing a sombrero, and at dawn, lying atop their blankets, they spied a figure wearing one in the building's open door, a feed bag in hand. Garrett, who had decided Billy was worth as much dead as alive, drew a bead and fired. Other shots rang out.

The figure crumpled back into the darkened house. From inside a voice yelled they had shot Charlie Bowdre. Drenched in blood, Bowdre lurched back outside, collapsed, and died.

Minutes passed. The outlaws' horses were tethered by ropes that snaked into the house, and as the posse watched, one of the ropes began pulling a horse toward the door. Garrett shot the animal in the chest and it fell, blocking the door. Others shot the remaining ropes. Billy's best chance of escape wandered off into the snow.

Garrett yelled toward the house, asking the gang how it was "fixed in there."

"Pretty well," Billy answered, "but we have no wood to get breakfast."

"Come out and get some," Garrett hollered. "Be a little sociable."

"Can't do it, Pat. Business is too confining."[3]

An hour passed, then two. At one point, realizing they were in a standoff, Garrett took half the posse back to the ranch and ate breakfast. Afterward they returned with a wagon full of food. At midafternoon they built a fire and began grilling beef. The smell of it wafted into the stone house. Billy and his three remaining men—Dave Rudabaugh and two others—hadn't eaten all day. Rudabaugh argued they had to surrender. Their situation was hopeless. They took a vote. Only Billy wanted to hold out. He cursed the others as cowards.

Rudabaugh tied a rag to a Winchester, shoved it through a chimney, and shouted they were ready to give up. Garrett said to come out with their hands up. Only Rudabaugh emerged. He said the others would follow if Garrett promised to protect them, presumably from vengeful cattlemen. Garrett agreed. Rudabaugh returned inside and several minutes later all four men came out, Billy at the rear. It was the first time most of the possemen had seen him in the flesh.

"Kill the son of a bitch," one of them breathed.

But Garrett kept his word. The next morning, Christmas Eve, after an anxious night holding the captives at the ranch, the posse piled them all into a wagon and took them to a blacksmith shop in Fort Sumner, where Billy and Rudabaugh were fitted with shackles and chains. The next day they rode for Las Vegas, where they were met by a crowd of the curious. Billy seemed surprisingly upbeat for a man facing multiple murder charges. "What's the use of looking on the gloomy side of everything?" he told a reporter in a jailhouse interview. "The laugh's on me this time." The reporter was struck by Billy's youth, writing that "he looked and acted like a mere boy."[4]

Billy was taken next to the jail in Santa Fe, where he languished for three months, writing a flurry of letters pleading his case to Governor Wallace, none of which were answered. At the end of March, he was hauled in chains to the southern town of Mesilla and arraigned in federal court for the killing of Buckshot Roberts. After his court-appointed lawyer proved that Roberts hadn't been killed on tribal land, as alleged, the indictment was quashed. In short order Billy was tried instead for the murder of Sheriff Brady. After two days of testimony, he was found guilty. The judge sentenced him to hang.*

Seven armed men, including, oddly, the crime boss John Kinney, loaded Billy in shackles into a wagon and escorted him back to Lincoln, where he was to meet the gallows on May 13. He was locked in a

---

*As one of Billy's biographers, Michael Wallis, notes, of the fifty-odd people indicted for crimes during the Lincoln County War, only Billy was convicted, likely a result of his infamy.

second-story cell in the old Dolan store, which had been converted into a courthouse, the jail, and Garrett's office above. The cell had two windows overlooking town. Garrett assigned two deputies to watch Billy around the clock, his hands still handcuffed, his legs still shackled. One, James W. Bell, was a kindly sort. The other, Bob Olinger, was a bellicose bully.

On the morning of April 28, Olinger made sure Billy watched through the bars as he loaded his shotgun with two shells, each containing eighteen buckshot. "The man that gets one of those loads will feel it," he said. Billy replied, "I expect he will, but be careful, Bob, or you might shoot yourself accidentally."[5]

It was another drowsy day in Lincoln. Garrett was off in White Oaks collecting tax monies or, depending on which story you believe, gathering wood to build the gallows. Around six, Olinger took the other five prisoners across the street to the Wortley Hotel for supper; they typically brought back a meal for Billy afterward. When they left, Billy asked Deputy Bell to take him to the privy, which was behind the courthouse. They were trudging back up the stairs when Billy, still in shackles, suddenly spun and brought his heavy handcuffs down hard on Bell's head, blood gushing from the wound. The two fell to the stairs, furiously grappling for Bell's pistol.

When Billy wrenched the gun away, Bell turned to escape down the stairs. Billy got off a shot or two and one struck home. Bell staggered into the yard and fell dead at the feet of the courthouse caretaker, who turned and hollered for help. At the hotel, Olinger rose from his table and said, "They are having a fight over there."

Billy hop-walked into Garrett's office and snatched up the same shotgun Olinger had loaded that morning. Hopping back into his cell, he threw open a window and peered down at the hotel just as Olinger ran out. The deputy had passed through the courthouse's side gate when Billy, in the window above, said, "Hello, Bob."* When Olinger looked up, Billy let loose with both barrels, the buckshot raking the deputy's head and chest. He fell dead without a sound.

Billy was free for the moment, but in a fix, still in handcuffs and shackles. Taking a seat on a balcony, he called for the caretaker to toss up a pickax, which he used to hack off one of the leg-irons, and managed to slither out of the cuffs. As he worked, he spoke to a crowd nervously gathering below. He insisted that he had no choice but to kill the deputies and would kill any man who tried to stop him from leaving town. After an hour, with one shackle still on his ankle, he hobbled downstairs and mounted a pony the caretaker had brought. The leg-iron spooked the animal, and Billy was thrown.

Remounting, he rode out of town slowly, as if in no hurry. For years, you could find people in Lincoln who swore they heard Billy singing softly to himself as he disappeared into the twilight.

HIS ESCAPE FROM THE LINCOLN JAIL WAS THE MOMENT BILLY VAULTED from obscure regional desperado to national attention, the first American criminal since Jesse James to do so. To that point he had garnered a handful of mentions in *The National Police Gazette*, but now, with a daring escape to his credit, not to mention a catchy new nickname, people everywhere began reading about "Billy the Kid."

These early accounts painted a uniformly dark portrait. The New Mexico papers led the way, *The Daily New Mexican* publishing a special edition, the *Las Vegas Optic* terming Billy a "young demon," "malignant and cruel," and "a murderer from infancy."[6] These accounts were picked up by papers from San Francisco to New York.

---

*Or as some accounts put it: "Hello, old boy."

The seeds of a different take could be seen even then. *The Daily New Mexican*, for one, noted his "coolness and steadiness of nerve in executing his plan." Not that any reporter asked for their opinions, but admiration for Billy among Latinos was mushrooming into something like hero worship. To them, Billy was a "social bandit," a defender of the common people, a plague on cattlemen who stole their land.

By most accounts, in fact, it was Latinos who hid Billy from the possemen who fanned out across the region in search of him. He could easily have fled across the Mexican border. It's a measure of his trust in them that he didn't, and most everyone knew it. And most everyone, at least if they read the papers, knew Billy was probably hiding around Fort Sumner. Beginning in May the Las Vegas papers regularly reported rumors of him there. *The Daily New Mexican* reported that the locals, "half [out] of fear and half [out] of admiration," were giving him shelter. Even the *Denver Tribune*, in a story picked up by papers across the country, reported in early June that Billy was likely at Fort Sumner, adding a twist: he was there for a woman.

AT HIS OFFICE IN ROSWELL, PAT GARRETT INITIALLY APPEARED TO DO little to find Billy. He didn't form a posse; he knew how much time could be wasted racing half-cocked across the hills. He too had expected Billy to head to Mexico. Meanwhile, he was inundated with tips, some barroom gossip, some letters, some imparted in discreet meetings in alleys and offices. Much of this was clearly dreck, but as June wore into July, there was a steady stream of reports that Billy was in fact back at Fort Sumner, maybe living with Latino pals in the outlying sheep camps, maybe slipping in to visit his friend Pete Maxwell's sister Paulita, the only one of his lovers who had written to him in jail. The gossips murmured she was pregnant with his child. Maybe.

This, Garrett sensed, required not just discretion, but stealth. The

Kid's sympathizers, especially among Latinos, served as his de facto intelligence network; an approaching posse would surely set off alarm bells. Garrett called in his two top men, both Texans, John Poe and Thomas C. "Kip" McKinney.* They left on the night of July 11, riding north up the Pecos, staying off the road and out of sight, camping at night. At dawn Poe rode alone into Fort Sumner. Lounging on the plaza, he drew nervous glances. The people seemed on edge.

That night the three lawmen met beyond the northern edge of town, behind a peach orchard fronting the plaza. There were rumors Billy had been seen at Pete Maxwell's place, an adobe house on the west side of the plaza. Another of his lovers, Garrett's sister-in-law Celsa Gutierrez, lived with her husband and son across the way. Garrett knew Maxwell to be trustworthy; he had been one of the first people he met on arriving in New Mexico. He seemed the obvious place to start.

A bright moon was shining around nine as the trio crept into the orchard. When the Maxwell house came into view, they waited, thinking they might actually spy Billy if he was visiting. When they finally began creeping toward the house, Garrett heard voices speaking in Spanish. He froze, motioning for his men to stop. Suddenly, ahead in the shadows, a darkened figure rose from the ground, like a vampire from a grave. He wore a sombrero and a vest. They couldn't see his face. Whoever it was hopped a fence and walked into the plaza.

They waited. Around midnight the trio backed out of the orchard and circled around to approach the far side of the Maxwell house. Ahead, the plaza was quiet. Entering the yard via the gate in a white picket fence, Poe took a seat on the porch steps. McKinney squatted beside the fence. Garrett slid through an open door into Pete Maxwell's corner bedroom. He sat beside him on the bed, nudging him awake.

---

*John Poe was another refugee from Texas feuds. He was the guard who discreetly stepped aside to allow a mob to murder John Larn in Shackelford County in 1878.

As he did, Billy wandered over from Celsa Gutierrez's house, hoping to carve a steak off a freshly killed yearling hanging on the Maxwell porch. He had taken off his boots and sombrero. Poe saw him approaching but had no clue who it was. Billy didn't see the two lawmen until he passed through the gate, when he came face-to-face with Poe. He pulled a .41-caliber Thunderer from his belt. In his free hand was a butcher knife. *"Quién es?"* he asked. Who is it?

He stepped past Poe onto the porch and repeated the question twice. As Poe thought to calm this agitated stranger, Billy backed through the open doorway into Maxwell's bedroom. He didn't see Garrett in the darkness.

"Pedro, quiénes son esos hombres afuera?" he asked toward Maxwell's bed. Pete, who are those men outside?

For a moment, neither Billy the Kid nor Pat Garrett understood what was happening. Garrett guessed this might be Maxwell's son-in-law. But then Billy glimpsed the silhouette leaning on Maxwell's bed.

"Quién es?" he asked. And then, in English: "Who is it?"

"El es," Maxwell whispered to Garrett. It's him.

Garrett drew his Colt .44 and fired twice. From the shadows there was a groan and then low gurgling sounds. Garrett hustled outside, then returned, waving to clear the gun smoke. He found Billy on the floor, a bullet hole in his chest, just above the heart, dead.

SO, YOU MAY BE THINKING: GOOD STORY, SURE, BUT WHY ON EARTH IS Billy the Kid so famous? In the sheer volume of literary portrayals, he towers over everyone but maybe Jesse James. He's been featured in dozens of Hollywood films, nearly fifty in the 1940s alone, everything from *The Left Handed Gun*, starring a young Paul Newman, to *Bill & Ted's Excellent Adventure*, to 1966's *Billy the Kid vs. Dracula*. Plus dozens of songs, including ones from Tom Petty, Bob Dylan, Billy Joel,

Charlie Daniels, and Joe Ely. Aaron Copland composed *Billy the Kid*, a ballet, in 1938. And that's not to mention countless plays and television shows. Or the thousands of comics. Or the poetry. Oof! Don't get me started on the poetry.

Some of this can be explained by the appeal of a stellar nickname and his youth; Hollywood likes its protagonists young, making Billy a better leading man than Hickok or even Earp. What's notable, though, is how books and films from the 1920s uniformly portrayed him as a heroic figure, something he was rarely considered in life. The New Mexico newspapers had greeted his death with relief, one terming him "a vulgar murderer . . . with probably not one redeeming quality."[7]

Billy was, after all, a thief and a murderer. But he also displayed qualities many found admirable: loyalty, daring, and a sense, especially among the Latinos who loved him, that he was fighting on behalf of the downtrodden. His appeal only grew during the 1960s when, in the same way Hollywood reinvented Bonnie and Clyde, he began to be portrayed as a symbol of youthful revolt, something that was almost close to accurate. Like Wyatt Earp, whose filmic rebirth during the 1990s was an antidote to fears of urban crime, his story has morphed to become what each new generation needs.

BILLY THE KID'S DEATH HERALDED THE PASSING OF NEW MEXICO'S MOST notable gunfighter violence, though sundry outlaws and the odd feud plagued the state for years. One other incident is worth mentioning, though, because it may be the single most insane of all Old West shootouts. It was another production staged by Texans.

The frontier had its share of bullet-riddled sieges before this, and some after, but never anything like what was inflicted upon a nineteen-year-old Latino named Elfego Baca in 1884. It happened in a New Mexico hamlet fifteen miles from the Arizona border, Upper San

Francisco Plaza—today's town of Reserve—one of three Latino "plazas," or villages, along the San Francisco River. The Latinos had moved in during the 1870s, Texas ranchers soon after. It hadn't gone well.

The story is not as straightforward as one might imagine. The Hollywood version, and it's been told a time or two, portrays Baca as a new deputy sheriff, a dewy innocent. From all evidence, he was neither. When his father, the marshal in the town of Belen, was jailed for killing two cowboys, Baca bragged of helping him escape. Slender and handsome, he was by his own admission a proud, lippy teenager, fond of guns, and a bit obsessed with sheriffing; by most accounts, the badge he pinned on was a fake he ordered through the mail.

Baca was wearing it that day he rode into the Upper Plaza, either running an errand for the sheriff or, depending on which version you believe, pondering a one-man vigilante campaign to rid the town of the rowdy Texans who periodically shot it up. That evening, when he witnessed a drunken twenty-two-year-old Texan named Charlie McCarty ride around shooting in the air, Baca asked why he wasn't arrested. Because, someone explained, the other Texans would exact revenge. Well, Baca quipped, "there was at least one Mexican in the country who was not afraid of an American cowboy."[8] With that, he pulled his pistol, approached McCarty in the street, and—after, by one account, nestling the gun against his ear—proclaimed he was placing him under arrest.

When the justice of the peace refused to take McCarty into custody—he too was wary of the Texans—Baca took his prisoner to a home in a neighboring village, intent on escorting him to jail in the county seat the next morning. McCarty worked for the Texas rancher John B. Slaughter, and late that night a group of Slaughter's cowboys showed up outside the house and loudly demanded McCarty's release.*

---

*Slaughter is not to be confused with "Texas" John Slaughter, the famed Arizona rancher and lawman.

Baca stepped outside. What happened next is so nuts it sounds like a cartoon, or maybe a dime novel Baca had been reading. But we know from court testimony it happened. Baca announced he was counting to three. If the cowboys weren't gone by then, he would open fire.

One imagines the Texans exchanging glances, maybe even smiles: Seriously?

"One!" Baca said.

More glances. Maybe fewer smiles.

"Two!"

The Texans all sat atop their horses, likely frozen in disbelief. What does this kid think he's—

"Three!"

Baca opened fire. The horses reared. A ranch foreman, a man named Young Parham, was thrown, his horse falling onto him; he would later die.* Another Texan was shot through the knee. The rest rode off.

The next morning, calmer heads prevailed. Area ranchers, having met in the night, sent word that Baca could safely return his prisoner to the Upper Plaza. A different justice of the peace would try him. And he did, fining McCarty all of five dollars. When it was over, though, Baca stepped outside and found a crowd of *eighty* Texas cowboys waiting for him. That's right: eighty. Several began calling Baca unfortunate names. A shot rang out.

Baca lit out down a lane. At its end, in a clearing, sat a one-room mud shack called a jacal, pronounced "hack-all." In town it was known by its owner's name, the Armijo house. Inside was a woman and two boys.

"Vamos!" Baca barked. "Get out before you're killed!"[9]

According to lore, the wild-eyed cowboys rushed the house. In fact, it appears that one of them, William B. "Bert" Hearne, first circulated among the crowd claiming the judge had authorized him to

---

*Young Parham's surname is variously given as Perham, Purham, and Perryman.

arrest Baca for the previous night's shooting.[10] Whatever the legal niceties, Hearne and several cowboys then strode to the jacal and banged on the door. When Baca refused to answer, Hearne kicked it, then yelled, "I'll get this dirty little Mexican out of here."[11]

Two shots rang out from inside. Hearne cursed and fell; dragged away, he too would die.

It was 9:00 a.m. on October 30, 1884. A number of the Texans suddenly remembered errands they needed to run. But those who remained—estimates range from forty to sixty armed men—took up positions along a church and behind houses and sheds. As a wonderfully dry 1928 biography of Baca notes, "It was the practice of the invaders to do their artillery work in volume."[12] They opened fire, and then again, and then over and over, dozens of bullets piercing the mud walls of the tiny jacal.

It was like something out of Peckinpah, a blizzard of lead, except that Baca, miraculously, wasn't hit—not once. He lay pressed against the dirt floor, snapping off a shot whenever the fusillades seemed to pause. Baca had an advantage the cowboys could not see. The floor of the jacal lay twelve to eighteen inches below ground level, meaning their bullets were whizzing harmlessly overhead. And they just kept coming. After the first broadsides, the firing went on intermittently for five minutes, then fifteen, then a full hour.

Baca stayed low. The Texans began hanging blankets between buildings to create better firing positions. Peering through cracks and bullet holes, Baca aimed at any cowboy who exposed a body part. One fell dead; a bit later, another. One of the less brilliant Texans tried approaching the jacal holding some kind of metal sheet as a shield. Baca sent him scurrying off with a shot that grazed his scalp.

It went on like this all afternoon, to little effect. Finally, near dusk, the Texans hit something that mattered, maybe a support beam. Part of the shack collapsed atop Baca, who was pinned beneath the debris.

He snapped off a shot or two to keep the cowboys back, then slithered free. At nightfall the shooting stopped.

Hours ticked by. Near midnight, Baca saw a tiny flame approaching. A moment later, he would recall, there was a deafening explosion—dynamite—that collapsed more of the house. Other witnesses claimed this never happened, that what the Texans threw was either blazing logs or kerosene-soaked rags, neither of which started a decent fire. Whatever it was, the cowboys withdrew for the night.

They returned at dawn to the aroma of coffee and tortillas. Baca was actually making breakfast on a little stove. The Texans opened fire, aiming at the undamaged corner of the jacal where he lay. The shooting continued off and on all day. By late afternoon, word of the siege had spread; everyone wanted it over. A rancher, a deputy sheriff, and one of Baca's friends arrived and called for him to come out, promising he wouldn't be harmed. Covered with dust, Baca emerged in his underwear, a revolver in each hand.* It was over.

In all, four Texans were dead. Baca was tried twice for the killings and, in two of the more famous trials in early New Mexico history, was acquitted both times. The jacal's door alone, introduced as evidence, revealed four hundred bullet holes. Baca went on to a long career as a sheriff, prosecutor, and politician, a hero to many, especially Latinos.†

---

*In old age, Baca gave an interview in which he strongly denied the bit about the underwear. Me, I believe the eyewitness.

†In the late 1950s the Walt Disney Company discovered Baca's story, imagining they could reinvent him as a kind of Latino Davy Crockett. In 1958 it released a ten-part miniseries, *The Nine Lives of Elfego Baca*, starring Robert Loggia, followed in 1962 by a feature film, along with six comic books and assorted merchandise. None of it was wildly popular, though in the process Baca did become one of the first Latino "heroes" in popular culture.

CHAPTER FOURTEEN

Tombstone

Arizona, 1878 to 1881

In 1870 the seven-year-old territory of Arizona was America's idea of hell on earth, its southern reaches dominated by violent Apache tribes, in one historian's words "an utterly barren and worthless waste of sandy deserts and rocky mountains."[1] Barely nine thousand Anglos called it home, many of them Mormon pioneers inching across the northern border from Utah, others clustered around the little capital, Tucson, in the south. Beyond that, Arizona was little but a vast, yawning emptiness—no railroads, few towns, and little governmental authority, just mile after mile of god-awful scrub and, at altitude, pine forests. There were a handful of gold and silver mines, but until the army drove the Apache onto reservations in 1874, there was no real reason to live in Arizona, and every reason to avoid it.

But in the mid-1870s, with (most of) the Apache gone, immigrants rushed in, hungry for land. They were spearheaded by a wave of Texas cattlemen fleeing an onslaught of settlers, drought, and barbed wire fences. Even more than in New Mexico, the Texans transformed the territory. In 1870 Arizona was home to 4,000 cows; by 1891 there would be 1.5 million.[2] "That the frontier of the Anglo-American cattleman in the Southwest was an extension of the Texas experience," a 1967 academic paper notes, "was nowhere more apparent than in Arizona."[3]

From Milam County came the ranching Riggs family, from San Saba the Cavnesses and Pyeatts, from Presidio County John J. Filleman, who complained that Texas was getting "too damned settled."[4] Two big sources of Texas cattle, the Reynolds and Aztec Cattle companies, spread thousands of beeves across the northern ranges east of Flagstaff. One of John Chisum's pals, John H. Slaughter, formed the vast Rancho San Bernardino in the territory's distant southeast.

With these Texas cattlemen came hundreds of Texas cowboys, who essentially created the Arizona ranching system, bringing with them their Texas saddles, Stetson hats, Texas-style chuck wagons, and their Southern-style honor system. A 2010 book emphasizes the importance of honor: "The Texas cowboys who flooded Arizona . . . partook in the honor culture of the Old South. . . . They, like their Southern ancestors, measured success via old rites of manliness, rites of courage, excess and exuberance. . . . They were first and foremost creatures of honor."[5]

"The Texans were undoubtedly difficult to abide," one study of early Arizona ranching concludes. "They were 'proud' and 'provincial'; and they thought Fort Worth was the only city in the country. They tried to out-dance, out-drink and out-fight everyone in the country, and most of the time they succeeded."[6]

And, as in New Mexico, where Texas cattle went, Texas rustlers followed. The most dangerous group by far formed on a string of ranches where Arizona's southeast corner met New Mexico, creating a murderous network whose dimensions have only been appreciated with time; writing in 2020, John Boessenecker termed this band "the largest outlaw gang in the history of the American West."[7] A loose confederation of rustlers easily a hundred strong, it raided into northern Mexico, stealing cattle and horses it sold to shady U.S. ranchers, then stole American livestock and sold it in Mexico. In Arizona the gang came to be known as the "Cowboys," usually spelled "Cow-boys." South of the border, they were named after the state so many came from: "Tejanos." The Texans.

Pressed west by the Texas Rangers and the dwindling frontier, many were refugees from the Southwest's bloodiest conflicts: the Lincoln County War, the El Paso Salt War, the Texas feuds. Two of its prominent members, Joe Olney, aka Joe Hill, and the storied Johnny Ringo, were fleeing Mason County's Hoodoo War. More than a few wandered down from Kansas once Dodge City's light dimmed. The gang's leaders, though, had all ridden with John Kinney and Jesse Evans in New Mexico; the Cowboys were, in essence, a sequel to Kinney's "Boys."

Their formation can be traced to the 1878 flight to Arizona of two of Kinney's nervier gunmen, Robert E. "Dutch" Martin and the uproarious Curly Bill Brocius, né (maybe) Bresnaham. Martin made his name as a stage robber, once holding up John Chisum himself; to history, he is otherwise unknown, a name on court dockets. Not so Curly Bill, who, reanimated by Powers Boothe's indelible portrayal of him as a psychopathic land pirate in the 1993 movie *Tombstone*, has long fascinated those who are, well, fascinated by such types. No one has yet discovered who he really was or where he came from. In his mid-twenties, he is described as a big man, six feet or more, Blackbeard-like, with a heavy beard and dense black curls, often wearing a red tie of some sort. He had been a cowboy in Texas, it's said, and he enters history as one of Kinney's men in the Salt War.

Afterward Curly Bill lingered in El Paso, outside which, on May 21, 1878, he and Martin ambushed an army ambulance bearing a wealthy lieutenant. In a wild gunfight, they wounded two guards, rode off empty-handed, then, with the Rangers in pursuit, crossed to Mexico, where they were detained and plunked back into an El Paso guard-house. That November, sentenced to five years, they dug their way under an adobe wall, escaped, then rode west before putting down stakes along the southern Arizona–New Mexico line. The Cowboys were born.

The two found the outlines of a rustling infrastructure already in place, a half dozen ranchers who didn't ask many questions about the horses and cattle they bought and sold. Among the busiest was New-man H. "Old Man" Clanton, a wily, white-bearded Tennessean who had zigzagged between Missouri, Texas, and California before joining the rush of cattlemen into Arizona. Lousy at the actual business of ranching, Clanton and his rough-hewn sons—Phin, Ike, and Billy—had more success trading stolen livestock; some say they became the western link in a chain selling hot animals to John Kinney's operations in New Mexico and corrupt ranchers in Texas.

In 1878 the Clantons moved to a spot on the San Pedro River ten miles southwest of where Tombstone was soon to be laid out, building a scruffy ranch of adobe houses and corrals. There they befriended a pair of hot-tempered newcomers from Iowa, the twentysomething brothers Tom and Frank McLaury. The McLaury ranch served as a clearinghouse for stolen Mexican cattle driven through the border town of Agua Prieta, near today's Douglas. Both families passed as le-gitimate cattlemen. Arizona's Pima County, the size of Connecticut at the time, was so vast, and so plagued with banditry, that the poor, out-manned sheriff had no time to deal with rumors of small-time rustlers.

From all appearances, the arrival of Curly Bill and Dutch Martin in the winter of 1878 supercharged this nascent cabal. That's when the major raids into Mexico began, and overnight grew to eye-popping proportions; one rancher claimed he had lost thirteen hundred cattle. The Mexican government, citing Martin by name, complained to Wash-ington, which yawned. There was nothing yet like a border patrol, and the army couldn't be bothered. Mexican possemen, soldiers, and the odd *federale* did what they could, but few were eager to take the fight across the border.

By the standards of frontier criminality, this was serious money, a veritable Spindletop of cash. Thirteen hundred beeves, sold into New Mexico at twelve dollars a head—well, you can do the math. By the time the first silver was found and the town of Tombstone laid out seventy miles southeast of Tucson, in March 1879, the entire region was shaping up as a kind of criminal riviera, a South Beach for bad guys. Dozens came, probably hundreds, a number putting down claims on land they turned into scraggly haciendas.

The dozen or so most important lined the isolated San Simon Valley in far southeastern Arizona, which became Cowboy headquarters. The Texas refugees Joe Hill and Johnny Ringo had one, Ike Clanton another, a rancher named George Turner another, where Dutch Martin bunked. This was Villain Central, unlike anything the West had ever seen. The Cowboys centered on this valley were less an organized gang than a way of life, a kind of frontier Mafia sans John Gotti. Though Martin's name dotted the diplomatic cables, they had nothing like a true don; the only sign of anything like an organization, for some at least, was the wearing of a rattlesnake hatband.* Like many a Mafia, they were a classic sack of wolverines, riven with rivalries; more would die by the hand of other Cowboys than the law. They banded together for raids as needed and, when idle, pursued side projects, a stagecoach robbery maybe, stealing horses, or, for entertainment, forcing townspeople to dance at gunpoint.†

Still, while sometimes caricatured as a pack of slobbering wild-eyed goobers—and a high goober quotient can't be denied—the more

---

*Not, as Hollywood would have you believe, a red sash.

†Though it's obviously some primitive form of asserting masculine dominance, I have no idea where this whole "dancing at gunpoint" thing actually came from. It would make a decent academic paper.

prominent Cowboys were also businessmen of a sort and did a decent job at not only posing as upstanding ranchers but getting along with neighbors and townspeople, some of whom saw them as a useful bulwark against the lingering risk of Apache raids. Several in Tombstone would actually describe Curly Bill—you know, murders aside—as an otherwise good egg, courteous and capable. He clearly had his charms. Then again, the gang was soon generating—and spreading around—so much cash it's hardly surprising it made its share of friends.*

For a time, the Cowboys operated with something close to impunity. It wasn't until a few began branching out to rob stagecoaches that official Arizona, jabbed in the ribs by Wells Fargo, began to stir. Now and then an arrest or two got made, but nothing that interrupted the flow of money provided by rustling. By the winter of 1879, in fact, after a year or so of operations, the Cowboys surely understood they had things close to perfect.

Which, as fate would have it, is when Wyatt Earp rode in.

THE DRAMAS THAT UNFOLDED AROUND THE RAMSHACKLE BOOMTOWN of Tombstone in the early 1880s have transfixed generations of armchair historians. The gunfights and intrigues are compelling in their own right, but the story's moral components, one suspects, are also crucial to its appeal. This wasn't two drunk Texans shooting in a Dodge City bar. This was a struggle *about* something. To those who lionize Wyatt Earp, and they've been in the ascendancy these last fifty or so years, it's an inspiring tale of defending one's family against evil, of the power of civilization to ward off the most frightening agents of chaos.

---

*One of my favorite quotes in Casey Tefertiller's wonderful biography of Wyatt Earp comes from an early Tombstone settler named Emma Muir. "Desperadoes, when not working at their business," she observes, "were like anybody else, considerate, honorable, good neighbors."

To those who detest him, and there remain those who view Wyatt's extralegal actions as indefensible, it's an example of violent governmental overreach.*

The climax, a thirty-second gunfight in a vacant lot beside Tombstone's O.K. Corral, remains the most famous in Old West history, probably the only frontier shoot-out many today know anything about. It is easily among the best-known episodes of gun violence in American history. Much of this can be explained by decades of worshipful Wyatt Earp movies, but it was also the best-documented gunfight of the era, thanks to work by two local newspapers and a judicial inquiry that began within days. At a time when shootings perpetuated by Wild Bill Hickok and Wes Hardin remained thinly documented or just rumor, dozens of survivors and eyewitnesses appeared and shared their memories in sworn testimony.

The story begins on December 1, 1879—Billy the Kid was still at large to the east—when wagons carrying Wyatt and his common-law wife, a prostitute named Mattie Blaylock, Wyatt's brother Jim and his family, and Doc Holliday and Big Nose Kate rumbled into Tombstone after the long trip across New Mexico. Thirty miles above the Mexican border, the town was barely eight months old at that point, splayed across a barren slope once known only to Apache, scorpions, and Gila monsters. Thanks to the discovery of silver, it had morphed into a fly-blown camp and then, seemingly overnight, an actual village.†

Prospectors had rushed in first, followed by the usual suspects: gamblers, prostitutes, and merchants. By the time the Earps arrived, there were maybe fifteen hundred people and more tents than buildings.

---

*For a sense of this darker take, the book to read is Andrew C. Isenberg's *Wyatt Earp: A Vigilante Life.*

†The discovery had been made by a prospector named Ed Schieffelin in country still menaced by the Apache, so many a pal told Schieffelin, according to one version, "You'll find your tombstone."

Other than cabins, corrals, and stables, the early structures were almost all saloons and gambling halls, the Can Can and the Bucket of Blood and the Oriental, said to be the most elegant casino between Fort Worth and San Francisco. On Saturday nights they were thronged with grimy miners and cowboys who were prone to the odd fistfight and to howling at the moon. Two hotels were going up, the fifty-room Cosmopolitan, which would attract the well-heeled traveler, and the smaller Grand, which wouldn't. Municipal services were iffy: any puff of wind sent dust and garbage and tumbleweeds blowing down the dirt lanes they called streets.

Wyatt and his people settled into a trio of houses on Fremont and Fifth streets, where they were soon joined by three more Earp brothers: Virgil, who had left his criminal résumé behind in the Midwest and reinvented himself as a lawman in the town of Prescott; Morgan, the cute family favorite; and Warren, who came and went. They were making a long-held dream come true, reuniting their far-flung family in a single place, with a single goal: to get rich.*

And they tried. What money they had they sank into mining claims and vacant lots, but nothing generated much cash. So while the women tended house, the men took jobs, Jim as a bartender, Virgil as a deputy federal marshal. Wyatt had brought along a stagecoach, planning to open a stage line, but when he found two already in operation, he ended up riding for them instead, as a Wells Fargo guard. He and Morgan both found extra work on Virgil's posses. All three moonlighted playing and dealing faro; at one point, Wyatt had a concession at the Oriental. Doc Holliday hovered darkly in their wake, a wheez-

*Like his brothers, Morgan Earp had worked most often as a gambler but had briefly been a policeman in Butte, Montana. He participated in at least one gunfight there, killing an outlaw surnamed Brooks, during which it's said he was badly wounded. Three years younger than Wyatt, he was twenty-nine when he came to Arizona.

ing smudge who seemed to spend every waking moment he wasn't playing cards quarreling with someone, often Big Nose Kate.

Tombstone was a chance for the Earp brothers to redeem themselves after their sundry misadventures, and they were soon on their way. It's pretty clear none of them had any sense of what they were riding into. Still, while they were aware of the Cowboys' depredations, those first six months passed quietly. It would take two years for things to come to a boil. For much of it, the story of Tombstone proceeds on two parallel tracks—Earp and Cowboy—that don't intersect that often. The first time they do came that initial summer, over something picayune in retrospect, yet clearly meaningful to those involved: the theft of six mules from the army's Camp Rucker.

An officer named Joseph H. Hurst tracked them to the McLaury ranch, then called in Virgil, who brought along Wyatt, to ride with soldiers to see. Frank McLaury denied having the animals but promised to find them. He didn't, and actually laughed at Hurst when he saw him two days later. Outraged, the lieutenant took an ad in *The Tombstone Epitaph* offering a reward for the mules and naming McLaury and five Cowboys he thought responsible. McLaury responded with a volcanic letter to the editor, accusing Hurst of stealing the mules himself, adding, in a priceless aside, "Thank God this is the first time in my life that the name of dishonesty was ever attached to me."

The fate of the mules is lost to history, but the spat put the Earps on the Cowboys' radar. Afterward, McLaury demanded to know whether Virgil had a hand in the ad and threatened to kill him if he had. A month later, Wyatt got an earful from both McLaurys, who swore if he came after them again, they would kill him too. The two brothers, it seems clear, didn't share Curly Bill's social skills.

All that first year, 1880, Cowboy raids into Mexico grew in scale and audacity. Mexican ranchers howled even louder; there was gloomy talk of a "diplomatic incident." For the first time American complaints began to surface too, as Arizona ranchers fretted about thefts of cattle and horses. The Southern Pacific was building a railroad across Arizona at the time and plunked down a station in the Cowboys' San Simon Valley; harassing passengers became the gang's fun new pastime. Curly Bill actually tried to joyride one train but couldn't figure out how to drive it.

Things got so bad in the fall that when the president of the United States, Rutherford B. Hayes, left California on the new route, a general boarded in Tucson and warned him that the Cowboys had threatened to stop the train at San Simon. Only after they sent a chunk of the Sixth Cavalry ahead, then piled twenty-five armed volunteers onto the train, was it allowed to proceed, and even then the authorities were so concerned they refused to let the train stop in Cowboy territory.

To Wyatt and the Earps the Cowboys were a volcano smoking on the horizon, too distant to lose sleep over, but a topic of nervous chatter nonetheless. The first serious eruption came that October, when Curly Bill led a late-night pub crawl through Tombstone. To this point, the Cowboys, many of whom lived a good two days' ride east, had remained comparatively well-behaved in town, reserving their worst antics for outlying villages like Charleston. When two of his companions began firing pistols in the air, Curly Bill was actually overheard admonishing them, "This won't do, boys. Don't do that!"

At the sounds of gunshots, Marshal Fred White, a neophyte, rushed into the street, as did Wyatt. White ran up to Curly Bill and demanded his gun. He produced it, muzzle forward. White grabbed the barrel, at which point Wyatt ran up behind Curly Bill and grabbed his arms. Whether having second thoughts or, more likely, alarmed by Wyatt's bear hug, Curly Bill held the gun a moment too long. "You damned son of a bitch," White snapped, pulling it, "give up that gun!"

It went off. White sagged to the ground, a red bloom spreading across his midsection. "I am shot," he blurted, dying.

Billy the Kid: orphan, runaway, murderer, bandit, feudist, ladies' man, escaped fugitive, cattle rustler, folk hero, legend.

Billy the Kid's New Mexico. Counterclockwise from top left: the mob boss John Kinney, standing between two henchmen; Alexander "Mac" McSween, the Scottish-born lawyer Billy fought for during the Lincoln County War; John Selman, in old age, is one of the rare gunfighters who pops up, Zelig-like, in multiple narratives, emerging first as a feudist in postwar Texas, rampaging across Lincoln County during the conflict there, and ending up in El Paso, where he shot and killed John Wesley Hardin; a map of Lincoln during Billy's time there; John Tunstall, the young British heir who bit off far more than he could chew.

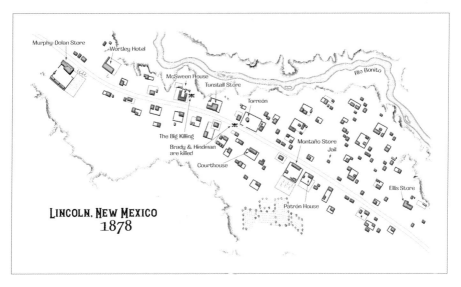

Murphy-Dolan Store
Wortley Hotel
McSween House
Tunstall Store
Río Bonito
Torreón
The Big Killing
Brady & Hindman are killed
Montaño Store
Jail
Courthouse
Ellis Store
Patrón House

LINCOLN, NEW MEXICO
1878

Pat Garrett, on facing page, was a towering Texas bartender who had probably known Billy the Kid but was never the bosom buddy myth suggests. Elected sheriff to subdue him, Garrett proved far more impressive than his résumé. At left, the young Elfego Baca, who faced down a mob of angry Texas cowboys, killed at least three, and following a two-day siege, somehow lived to tell the tale. Above, remains of the adobe house he defended.

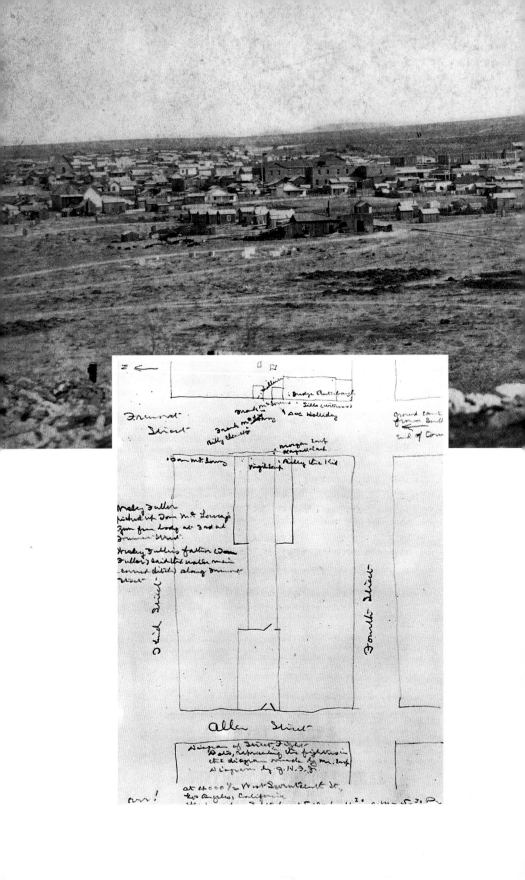

W yatt Earp's Tombstone. Splayed along a parched hillside in southern Arizona, it became the scene of the frontier's most storied melodrama, the struggle between Earp and his brothers and a group of outlaws known below the border as the "Tejanos," i.e., the Texans. Inset, Earp's drawing of the shoot-out beside the O.K. Corral. At left, Earp in a portrait taken during his time in Tombstone.

On facing page, Tombstone's supporting players, alive and dead. Top, left to right, Johnny Ringo, Virgil Earp, and Morgan Earp. Below, the three men who died beside the O.K. Corral: the Cowboys Tom and Frank McLaury, and Billy Clanton. On this page, Tom Horn beside his Wyoming jail cell, circa 1901. The West's most infamous range detective, Horn started out as a legitimate private detective before moving to the dark side, emerging as probably the frontier's best-known paid assassin. He met his fate over the death of a fourteen-year-old boy.

The Pleasant Valley War, which consumed much of central and eastern Arizona during the 1880s, may have been America's deadliest and least-known feud. At bottom of facing page, Commodore Perry Owens, a local sheriff, won its bloodiest shoot-out single-handed, killing three Texans, including the notorious Andy Blevins, above, and wounding another with five shots. John and Ed Tewksbury, top and bottom left, led the Tewksbury forces. At top of facing page, a rider believed to be a feudist.

Swisher Brothers Machine Shop (where Marshal Connelly borrows a rifle)

Lewark & Kloehr Livery Service (original location)

Read Brothers Store

Alley (from which the Dalton Gang enters the plaza)

Oklahoma's Dalton Gang aspired to be the second coming of the James Gang, and failed. At top left on facing page, the brothers Bob, Grat, and Bill Dalton. At left on facing page, incensed by Dalton robberies, railroads begin dispatching armed gunmen on select trains. Across the bottom, a panorama of downtown Coffeyville, Kansas, where the Daltons met their fates. At left, townspeople display two of their dead bodies, believed to be Bob and Grat.

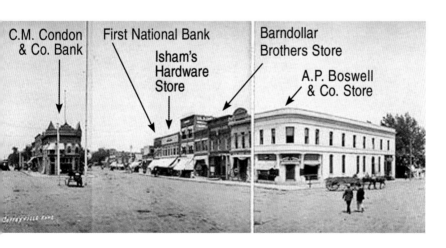

C.M. Condon & Co. Bank

First National Bank

Isham's Hardware Store

Barndollar Brothers Store

A.P. Boswell & Co. Store

Early in his career, Butch Cassidy, on facing page, could've passed for a dreamy college linebacker. His Wild Bunch, top, in one of the Old West's iconic portraits, was probably the canniest outfit of the era after the James Gang. Bottom left, Butch's partner Harry Longabaugh, aka the Sundance Kid, was never the close friend Hollywood suggests. The two may have worked together on as few as two jobs before fleeing for South America. Bottom right, the remote Wyoming cabin where Butch was arrested in 1894.

A weapon wielded by shady Texas and Oklahoma cattleman, the assassin Jim Miller may have been the frontier's deadliest gunman. Miller once claimed to have killed fifty-one men, though if so, his record should come with an asterisk: most were killed from ambush. It didn't end well for Miller. That's him at the far left, swinging from the rafters of an Oklahoma barn.

Wyatt, as he had done so often in Dodge, brought his pistol down atop the Cowboy's head. When he fell, Wyatt brought him to his feet, holding him. "What have I done?" Curly Bill demanded; to him it was an accident. "I have not done anything to be arrested for."

Many in Tombstone, including Wyatt, agreed. There ensued a three-month legal drama during which Wyatt, worried about a lynch mob, first whisked Curly Bill to Tucson, then actually testified on his behalf at a hearing, after which a judge ruled the shooting an accident and ordered him released. In the grand scheme of things, the whole episode ended up being a nonevent, though it did make Curly Bill a public figure, a brand-name outlaw. His name began appearing in the San Francisco papers; he was profiled in *The National Police Gazette*.

It's his behavior afterward, though, one of the more out-there binges in Old West history, that enshrined Curly Bill's legend and established him, for posterity at least, as a villain weighty enough to warrant costar status in the climactic struggle of Wyatt Earp's career. It began twelve days after his release, on a Saturday night, January 8, 1881. Curly Bill and a Cowboy pal—no doubt suitably lubricated—walked into a crowded cantina in Charleston, placed their backs against both doors, and pulled their pistols.

"Strip, every one of you!" Curly Bill announced. "Strike up the music! Now then, dance!" Whether they danced a naked waltz, foxtrot, or Macarena we don't know; we are told only that the startled patrons complied.

After scaring away an armed response outside, Curly Bill and a group of Cowboys staged act two the next morning in a church up the road in Contention. There are several versions of this story. The most likely has the Cowboys drawing their guns, scattering those assembled, leaving the frightened pastor alone. At which point they began shooting, bullets pocking the walls all around the poor man.

If you believe the secondhand accounts, and I'd like to, Curly Bill was a man of many syllables. After a soliloquy or two featuring the word "doxology," he ordered the pastor to "dance a jig." After mild protests, the man shuffled his feet a bit. It was enough.

It went on like this for weeks, Curly Bill Unleashed, galloping through Tombstone, shooting in the air, randomly firing shots at townsfolk in Charleston, once, according to one tale, demanding that patrons in a restaurant stop eating while he ate. When he then fell asleep, the other diners, still frozen, just stared at him, too frightened to move. It got so bad the *Tucson Star* termed Bill "a scab on the body politic." He eventually returned to his raids into Mexico and, for a time, all but faded from view.

IF YOU'RE THINKING SUCH DISPLAYS WOULD LEAD THE CITIZENRY TO clamor for help from the Earps, you would be wrong. That fall, Virgil ran for marshal and lost. Wyatt had briefly been named a deputy sheriff the previous summer; he made a few arrests and solved a murder, then resigned when the Cowboys stuffed ballot boxes during the election for sheriff, leading to the defeat of an Earp ally. A jaunty, feckless fellow named Johnny Behan took his place, promising to make Wyatt his next hire, then didn't, the start of a tense relationship between the Earps and Behan, who was later named sheriff.

If you squint a bit, you can see one reason the Earps weren't wildly popular. Wyatt especially could come across as a tad holier-than-thou; testifying for Curly Bill hadn't made him many friends. This go-it-alone tendency was evident in one of his fabled moments, the rescue of a teenage gambler nicknamed Johnny-Behind-the-Deuce, for his favorite faro bet. His real name was probably Mike Rourke.

Rourke had shot and killed a miner during an argument in Charleston, and a constable whisked him to Tombstone one step ahead of a lynch mob. Virgil and Wyatt took the two into a bowling alley, only to find themselves blockaded by a throng of angry miners. Determined to escort him to safety, Wyatt had Virgil and several pals encircle Rourke. Wyatt, a shotgun in hand, led them out into the crowd.

"Stand back there and make passage," Wyatt announced. "I am going to take this man to jail in Tucson." When the crowd paused, Wyatt turned to one prominent miner, a man named Dick Gird, and indicated that if trouble ensued, he would be the first to die. Gird flinched, the crowd dispersed, and Rourke was taken to Tucson without incident.*

WYATT'S RELATIONS WITH THE COWBOYS, MEANWHILE, BEGAN TO DE-teriorate. He had brought a horse to Arizona and had it stolen—by Old Man Clanton and his sons, he'd heard. In February 1881, a month after saving Johnny-Behind-the-Deuce, he spied the horse in a Charleston corral. Awaiting legal paperwork to seize it, he saw the youngest Clanton, Billy, try to lead it away. Wyatt stopped him, saying the horse was his. Clanton sneered. Once the papers arrived, he "asked me if I had any more horses to lose," Wyatt recalled. "I told him I would keep them in the stable after this, and give him no chance to steal them."

For all the attention that has been paid to Curly Bill and Johnny Ringo, the keenest accelerant thrown onto the simmering Earp–Cowboy fire was provided by four lesser-known Cowboys with outsize ambitions. They were led by an acquaintance of Doc Holliday's, a sickly New York–born jeweler named Billy Leonard, a morphine addict with needle marks up and down his arms and long, greasy hair that fell to his shoulders in ringlets. A consumptive who came west for his health, Leonard knew Holliday from Las Vegas, where he ran a jewelry business. Obliged to flee after killing a man, he had claimed a

---

*From whose jail he promptly escaped. Last seen heading for Texas, he then disappears from history.

plot of government land in the southwest corner of New Mexico, just across the border, and for reasons unknown become an outlaw. He was so violent some thought he had a death wish.

Leonard rose to prominence in November 1880 when, after a heated argument over stolen horses, he and three pals engaged in a fierce if inconclusive gunfight with the Cowboy jefe himself, Dutch Martin. Irked, Leonard and his compadres staged an ambush at Granite Gap, New Mexico, during which Martin was shot in the head and killed. The brazen killing, one imagines, spurred Leonard's criminal ambitions.

Five months later, on March 15, 1881, came the event that set everything in motion. That day, Leonard and his three friends were plotting a robbery at a house outside Tombstone. Holliday, meanwhile, rose at his rooms in town, then rented a horse, rode out, and paid them a visit, probably to play cards. At some point, Holliday headed out to another game. His visit would haunt Holliday, and the Earps, for the rest of their lives.

That same night, a full moon loomed over the desert as a stagecoach containing eight passengers pulled out of the mining town of Contention, twelve miles northwest of Tombstone. Its strongbox held gold bullion valued at $26,000, about $800,000 in today's dollars, a fortune.* Its middle-aged Wells Fargo guard happened to be a friend of the Earps, a onetime California sheriff named Bob Paul, an enormous man for the day, six foot six and 240 pounds, who in a decorated career had brought in or killed numerous malcontents.†

---

*By coincidence, this was the very stagecoach that Wyatt had sold upon moving to Tombstone.

†Paul was probably best known for breaking up California's notorious Tom Bell Gang in 1854. Later, as a stagecoach guard, he had been so successful that Wells Fargo dispatched him to Arizona in 1878 to deal with a series of robberies near the town of Maricopa. Paul was the Earp friend who lost the sheriff's election, after which he filed suit alleging ballot stuffing; his opponent had been loudly supported by the Cowboys, and Paul publicly named Ike Clanton and Curly Bill among those who backed the scheme. He was moonlighting as a

Two miles on, Paul was sitting atop the coach cradling a sawed-off shotgun when he spotted two pairs of gunmen standing on embankments on both sides of the road. One shouted, "Hold!"

"I don't hold for anybody!" Paul shouted back.

Above, Billy Leonard and his men opened fire. So did Paul, whose shotgun blast struck and badly wounded Leonard. At the sound of gunshots, the horses spooked, and as the stage galloped past, the other Cowboys riddled it with bullets, killing the driver, a popular twenty-seven-year-old named Eli "Bud" Philpott, and a passenger. It took Bob Paul a mile or more to bring the horses to a halt. By then Leonard and his men had melted back into the darkness.

The double murder aboard a Wells Fargo–protected stagecoach was major news in Tombstone and, for a day or two, across the West. It's a measure of how far frontier journalism had come—and how impatient with banditry the developing West was becoming—that a pair of killings that might have earned a few paragraphs in 1868 Texas spawned national headlines in 1881 Arizona. "There should be no hesitation in driving this element out of Arizona, and it should be done at once," thundered the San Francisco *Daily Exchange*, one of several papers that monitored goings-on in Tombstone on behalf of California investors doing business there. "Cowboys should be declared outlaws."[8]

Wells Fargo tasked Bob Paul with bringing in the murderers. Within hours he turned to Wyatt, Virgil, and Morgan, accompanied by a visiting Bat Masterson, to fill out his posse. Theirs turned out to be a pursuit for the ages. The five of them, aided by a tracker, pursued Billy Leonard's outfit for sixteen straight days across more than five hundred miles of mountain and desert. At one point, they went sixty hours without food and thirty-six without water. Paul's horse keeled

---

Wells Fargo guard while his lawsuit worked its way through the courts. The book to read is John Boessenecker's *When Law Was in the Holster: The Frontier Life of Bob Paul*.

over dead. Some say it was the most exhaustive pursuit in Old West history.

Finally, at a ranch near the New Mexico line, they surprised and arrested one of Leonard's men, Luther King, who confessed, naming Leonard and two others as his confederates. King was then deposited in Sheriff Johnny Behan's jail in Tombstone, from where, not long after, he inexplicably escaped. A week later, word spread that King had been found lynched. It was assumed to be Leonard's revenge for blabbing.

None of this was good for the Earps. Despite all their efforts, they finally gave up their long chase; three murderers still remained at large. They now feared Sheriff Behan might be in league with the Cowboys. Worse, they had stirred up the Cowboys themselves, who did not forget the intensity of the Earp pursuit. And worst of all, once news of Holliday's "poker game" with the murderers emerged, many in Tombstone came to believe he was complicit, a sentiment that would plague them all in the months to come.

Afterward, angry with both Behan and the Cowboys, Wyatt found himself mulling a run to replace Behan as sheriff. His bona fides seemed sufficient, but he had few accomplishments in Arizona to back them up. It occurred to him that bringing in Billy Leonard's bunch might be enough. Moreover, he heard they had some kind of beef with Old Man Clanton's son Ike, among the most ambitious Cowboys.

On the night of June 2, 1881, Wyatt found Ike Clanton with two other Cowboys, Frank McLaury and Joe Hill, behind the Oriental. He made his pitch: help bring in Leonard's trio, and he would hand over the $3,600 reward. No one would know. Ike was intrigued. He and Leonard had in fact been squabbling over a New Mexico ranch they both claimed; with Leonard gone, it would be his. Ike insisted Leonard and his men would never be taken alive. He asked for Wells Fargo's promise that the reward would be paid dead or alive. Five days later Wyatt had it.

Ike and company agreed to lure the Leonard trio to a ranch on the pretext of planning a mail robbery. It was not to be, for reasons that had nothing to do with Wyatt or Ike Clanton. Tombstone's flamboyantly corrupt justice of the peace, it turns out, a Texas product named Mike Gray, was also tussling over a New Mexico ranch he coveted. It was owned by two former Cowboys, the brothers Ike and Billy Heslet. Rather than fork over the four thousand dollars he'd agreed to give the Heslets for the place, Gray hired Leonard to kill them.

On June 11, just four days after Wyatt cemented his deal with Ike, Leonard and one of the other fugitives, a teenager named Harry "the Kid" Head, lingered in a bar-cum-general-store in the town of Eureka, getting drunk as they waited for their quarry the Heslets to finish work at a mine. (Leonard, still recovering from his gunshot wound, complained about it much of the day.) When they didn't show, the two returned the next day, at which point the Heslet brothers, clearly no fools, rose from behind a fence and shot them to pieces. The third and final fugitive, a budding maniac named Jimmy Crane, avenged them four nights later, finding the Heslets in a saloon and shooting *them* to pieces. Soon after, Crane was ambushed and killed by Mexican soldiers.

So yes, whew, rough neighborhood. The sudden burst of killings, of course, meant the end of Wyatt's secret deal with Ike Clanton. No doubt he was disappointed, though it wasn't something he dwelled on. Yet the deal's existence still carried serious risk for Ike. If the other Cowboys found out what he'd done, he was a dead man.

BY THAT SUMMER CURLY BILL AND THE COWBOYS HAD ALL BUT GONE to war with Mexican ranchers, who had brought in the Mexican army.

A slew of little massacres ensued, four Cowboys killed on a rustling raid, a caravan of eight Mexican traders ambushed and killed in response, then five Cowboys, including Old Man Clanton, killed in a Mexican ambush.*

What alarmed official Arizona was the spread of Cowboy crimes north of the border. Cattle and horse theft was on the rise. As the poster boy for the Cowboys now, Curly Bill got much of the blame; the *Epitaph* even published a song about him, telling of a prospector pushing a donkey up a hill, "for my bronco's gone to San Simon, to carry Curly Bill."[9] Curly ended up shot in the neck during a spat with another Cowboy, recovered, then took a New Mexico vacation till things cooled down, placing him offstage when things erupted that autumn.

What really roused Arizonans, though, were the mysterious stagecoach robberies that continued to plague the area. Various Cowboys got arrested; few were convicted. The California newspapers grew apoplectic, demanding order. The governor appealed to Washington, where the army chief, William Tecumseh Sherman, called for repeal of an act preventing the army from getting involved.[†] In the end Washington, like Sheriff Behan, seemed powerless to stop them.

The Earps stepped into the vacuum. In June, when Tombstone's marshal absconded with a thousand dollars of city money, Virgil was drafted to replace him; he made Wyatt and Morgan special officers. The three Earps spent the next few months chasing and arresting various minor Cowboys for stagecoach and other robberies, including Pete Spence and Frank Stilwell, a pair of Texans they would deal with again. The Earps' was by far the most aggressive campaign anyone had yet mounted against the gang, and it clearly made the brothers public enemy numbers one through three in the eyes of many Cowboys.

---

*This was the same ambush in which Jim Crane, mentioned above, was killed.

†This was the Posse Comitatus Act, passed in 1878, which had whipsawed the army during the Lincoln County War.

In September, when news spread that Tombstone's leading citizens had formed a supposedly secret anti-Cowboy "vigilance committee," the Cowboys blamed the Earps. Frank McLaury confronted Virgil about it in the street. Virgil reminded him that it was the Earps who had spirited Curly Bill to Tucson one step ahead of a lynch mob. McLaury being McLaury, the conversation couldn't end without another dreary death threat.

If McLaury and the more "reputable" Cowboys feared some kind of Earp-led whisper campaign against them, they proved more than capable of returning fire, seizing on the Earps' weakest link: Doc Holliday. Ever since his fateful poker game with Billy Leonard's crew, rumors had flown that Holliday—and by extension, the Earps—was somehow mixed up in the stagecoach robberies. The drumbeat of suspicion reached a crescendo that summer when Big Nose Kate, after yet another knock-down-drag-out with Holliday, went public with accusations it was true. Many believed her. Holliday was beside himself, a Southerner whose honor was besmirched.

Still, violence between the Earps and the Cowboys wasn't seen as imminent. They represented opposite poles of frontier society, it's true, and there was certainly enough ill will to go around. But the spark that lit the bonfire turned out to be something no one saw coming.

BY THIS POINT ANYTHING COULD HAVE TRIGGERED IT, THE MONTHS of back-and-forth threats, the rumors about the stage robberies, the idea that the Earps were behind the vigilante committee. In the end, though, it came down to something deeply personal: Ike Clanton's belief that Wyatt had leaked word of their secret deal to betray Billy Leonard's crew. This was weighing on him when he and Tom McLaury rode into Tombstone that cool Tuesday, October 25, 1881.

Ike's paranoia had been building for weeks, at least since the one outsider in Tombstone who knew of the deal, a Wells Fargo agent named Marshall Williams, had gotten drunk and needled him about it. For some reason Ike suspected Doc Holliday was spreading the word too, and in a drunken tirade had accused him of it. That evening, after a long bout of day drinking, Ike and Tom cornered Wyatt and Virgil at the Alhambra Saloon and accused them of leaking their secret. As Virgil told it, the two Cowboys "said they could not live in this country an hour if Leonard's friends learned" of their betrayal.[10]

What followed was eighteen hours or so of escalating arguments and threats interrupted only by poker games, a court appearance, and naps. Snarling and bellowing, the participants prowled from bar to bar to street corner and back like something out of Eugene O'Neill. Among other things, it becomes a study in gunfighter slang. The word "heeled," you'll notice, is a synonym for "armed." Everyone uses "fight" to mean "gunfight," as if by now there was no other kind. Episodes of HBO's *Deadwood* aside, the most popular curse used in this corner of the frontier would appear to be "son of a bitch."

Before it was over, just about everyone got involved. After Ike laid into Wyatt and Virgil, Holliday wandered in. "You God damned cow thieving son of a bitch," he growled at Ike, "you have been talking about myself and my friends and you must fight me."

Ike insisted that he would if he had his pistol. "Heel yourself," Holliday replied, "or stay that way." Looking on, Wyatt asked Morgan to take Holliday outside, where the sniping continued.

"You son of a bitch," the pallid dentist went on, "if you ain't heeled, go and heel yourself." Morgan chirped in, "Yes, you son of a bitch, you can have all the fight you want now."[11]

It went on like this, everyone repeating "heel" and "fight" and "son of a bitch" until Virgil, no doubt called by the vocabulary police, appeared and broke it up. At which point, bizarrely, Virgil, Ike, Tom

McLaury, and Johnny Behan sat down and enjoyed a peaceful poker game that lasted until dawn—another sign that relations between the two camps remained something short of irreparable.

When Virgil rose to leave, Ike demanded he take a message to Holliday: "The damned son of a bitch has got to fight." Virgil said he wouldn't and warned Ike to stay out of trouble.

"You won't carry the message?" Ike shot back.

"No, of course I won't," Virgil said.

As Virgil turned to leave, Ike sneered, "You may have to fight before you know it." Virgil went home and slept.

This was the moment when something inside Ike Clanton snapped, when the war of words morphed into something deadly. Deeply drunk, he began a dawn patrol of saloons, loudly proclaiming more than once that he and the Cowboys would kill Holliday and the Earps the moment they appeared in the streets that day. A bartender from the Oriental woke Wyatt to warn him. A policeman went to Virgil's and told him Ike was armed and hunting them at that very moment. After dressing, Virgil took Morgan to find and disarm the drunken Cowboy. Wyatt met them on a corner. They split up.

Virgil spotted Ike first, on Fourth Street. He was carrying a Winchester with a six-shooter in his belt. Virgil strode up unseen and snatched the rifle. When Ike went for the pistol, Virgil buffaloed him, knocking him down, and placed him under arrest, during which a bloodied Ike insisted that, had he seen Virgil coming, he would've shot him. Virgil and Morgan then hauled him to police court, a crowd of the curious filing in behind, a simmering Wyatt among them.

As Virgil went to find a judge, Wyatt finally lost it. "You have threatened my life two or three times," he told Ike, "and I have got the best of evidence to prove it, and I want this thing stopped."

"You fellows haven't given me any show at all," Ike replied. "You've treated me like a dog."

Morgan shoved Ike's own pistol toward him. "Here, take this," he jibed. "You can have all the show you want right now."*

At that point, the crowd actually rose as one and scrambled for the exits. Wyatt, Morgan, and Ike continued trading threats as they did, Wyatt declaring Ike a "cattle thieving son of a bitch." More than once he challenged him to a fight. "You've threatened my life enough and you've got to fight!" seem to be his final words.

"Fight is my racket," Ike replied, "and all I want is four feet of ground."

Wyatt stalked out. He ran into Tom McLaury in the street.

"If you want to make a fight," the Cowboy snarled, "I will make a fight with you anywhere."

Wyatt slapped him, then drew his Smith & Wesson.

"All right, make a fight right here!" he said.

McLaury had a pistol on his right hip.

"Jerk your gun and use it!" Wyatt demanded.

When McLaury declined, Wyatt buffaloed him, hard, knocking him to the ground, at least twice. Wyatt then stormed off and was overheard muttering, "I could kill the son of a bitch."

Virgil, meanwhile, found a judge, who fined Ike twenty-five dollars for carrying a gun in town. By this point, at almost two o'clock, the two sides, Cowboy and Earp, each seething, withdrew, like boxers to their corners. One gets a sense that everyone involved felt some kind of line had been crossed, that violence was now inevitable. Several more Cowboys, including Ike's brother Billy, had ridden into town, and a group of them was soon milling around the O.K. Corral, making loud threats.

The weather that Wednesday afternoon has been termed blustery,

---

*Here it appears Ike and Morgan are using the word "show" as a synonym for respect, a usage I hadn't seen elsewhere.

a cold wind blowing dust through town. The Earps gathered outside Hafford's saloon, pondering what to do. At one point, Johnny Behan, having learned of the situation after a nap, strode up and reminded Virgil it was his duty to disarm the Cowboys, not fight them.

"I will not," Virgil snorted. "I will give them their chance to make a fight." After a moment, he calmed down, suggesting to Behan that they disarm the Cowboys together. By this point, though, townspeople were coming up every few minutes, warning of the Cowboys' threats and volunteering to help. After a bit, Behan announced he would try to disarm Ike and company himself. "They won't hurt me," he said.

Moments after Behan disappeared down the street, Doc Holliday walked up, curious. He too was just learning of the situation.

"Where are you going?" he asked.

"We're going to make a fight," Wyatt said.

"Well, you're not going to leave me out, are you?"

"This is none of your affair."

"That is a hell of a thing for you to say to me."

"It's going to be a tough one," Wyatt said.

"Tough ones are the kind I like," Holliday said.[12]

A decision had clearly been made. Virgil handed Holliday a sawed-off shotgun. Holliday gave him his cane. The four men, wearing long dusters against the cold, stepped off the sidewalk and began walking down Fourth Street, shoulder to shoulder.

CHAPTER FIFTEEN

The Fight Is Made

Tombstone, 1881 to 1882

It may be true that violence between the Cowboys and Earps was unavoidable, and it's certainly true that Ike Clanton's paranoia triggered it. But at base, the gunfights that began in Tombstone that day all revolved around the frontier's pervasive codes of honor. By challenging and pistol-whipping Ike and others, the Earps had deeply offended their sense of honor, of self-respect, of manhood. By threatening their lives, the Cowboys had done the same to the Earps. The exchanges between Ike and Wyatt in police court are as telling an expression of this as you'll find.

To shrink from these offenses, in that time and that place, was to risk one's place in society. It was a notion almost as old as America itself, one that found its flower in the antebellum South, was pushed to extremes in postwar Texas, then broadcast—and accepted—so widely across the frontier that few any longer associated it exclusively with Southerners or Texans. It had become a norm.

JOHNNY BEHAN FOUND THE COWBOYS FIRST. HE WAS TOLD THEY HAD gathered down Fremont Street, beside an entrance to the O.K. Corral.

On his way there, he ran into Frank McLaury. He asked for his guns. When McLaury demurred, the two men spotted his brother and the two Clanton brothers in the vacant lot down the street. They found them standing beside two horses in a narrow space between C. S. Fly's photography studio and boardinghouse and the side wall of a home owned by a man named Harwood. The lot was no wider than a good-sized bedroom.

Behan demanded their guns. He patted down Ike, who was un-armed. Tom McLaury opened his coat and insisted he was too. His brother Frank said he would only disarm if the Earps did. "You need not be afraid, Johnny," Ike said. "We are not going to have any trouble."

About then, a voice hollered from back down the street: "Here they come!" Behan glanced back and saw the Earps and Holliday had rounded the corner two blocks back and were striding toward them.

"Wait here," he said. "I see them coming down. I will go up and stop them."

Behan met the Earps up the street, maybe ninety feet away. He later said he simply told them he didn't want trouble. Virgil recalled it differently, saying Behan pleaded with them, "For God's sake, don't go down there or you will get murdered." The Earps, who had little re-spect for Behan, walked right past him, leaving the sheriff to trail them like a panhandler.

"I am going to disarm them," Virgil said.

"I've been down there to disarm them," Behan said. For a moment, Virgil misunderstood, thinking the sheriff had taken their guns. He took his hand off the pistol in his right coat pocket. Not Wyatt, who had his Smith & Wesson ready in his. Someone later claimed they heard one of the four say, "Let them have it." Doubtful.

They kept walking. When they reached the lot, it opened to their left. Wyatt stopped first, at the corner of Fly's boardinghouse. Mor-gan paused a few steps farther, to Wyatt's right. Holliday ranged a pace or two past him. Across the wood-plank sidewalk to their left, arranged in a ragged diagonal, six men and two horses stood: Billy Clanton with the McLaurys at the Earps' far right, beside the Harwood house, just off the sidewalk. Ike Clanton stood on the left, in front of Wyatt. Two other men, a twenty-one-year-old Cowboy named Billy Claiborne and a gambler named Wesley Fuller, lingered.

Virgil immediately saw they had not been disarmed: Billy Clanton and Frank McLaury were carrying holstered pistols. Virgil stepped forward into the lot, now holding Holliday's walking stick in his right hand—his shooting hand—an indication he, at least, hadn't been expecting a gunfight. Virgil didn't have the experience of Wyatt, who had clearly sensed what was coming. "Boys, throw up your hands," Virgil announced. "I want your guns."

Those were the only words he spoke, nine in all, yet enough to set off the most famous gunfight in frontier history. It was as if, after all the buildup and all the threats and all the predictions of violence, Billy Clanton and Frank McLaury didn't hear what Virgil said. All they seemed to process was: Earps. Guns. Both went for their pistols. You could hear the Colts cock, Virgil said later, audible clicks. "Hold on!" he shouted, raising both arms. "I don't want that!"*

It was too late. Wyatt drew. Two guns fired at once, making what most remembered as one sound. Billy Clanton, aiming at Wyatt, fired from the hip and missed. Wyatt, thinking Frank McLaury the most talented gunman, shot at McLaury instead, his bullet hitting him flush in the belly. Virgil switched the cane to his left hand and yanked the pistol from his pocket. As he did, McLaury, though badly wounded, squeezed off a shot that hit his calf. Virgil fell to one knee.

There was a pause, maybe a second or two, in which all ten men calibrated their next move. Three decided not to engage. Wes Fuller

---

*Some accounts say "Hold on," some simply "Hold."

backed away. Unarmed, Ike famously rushed at Wyatt, grabbing his arm, a sloppy attempt at surrender. Wyatt pushed him off, snapping, "The fight has commenced! Go to fighting or get away."* Ike, followed by Billy Claiborne, ducked through a doorway into the boardinghouse.

Only three Cowboys chose to fight, and two were initially distracted. Both McLaury brothers were standing next to horses; the animals were spooked by the shots and began to squirm and buck. For several moments, each man was obliged to focus on controlling a horse, giving the Earps the advantage. As they did, all three brothers proceeded to fire, Virgil from one knee.

The McLaurys, engaged with the horses, survived these initial shots. But Billy Clanton, backing up toward the far wall, stood exposed. A bullet, probably one of three Virgil fired at him, struck Clanton in the midsection; he fell back against the wall before slumping into a sitting position. He kept firing as he dropped, landing on his backside, there balancing his gun on one knee. It was probably one of his shots that struck Morgan in the street. The bullet hit him in one shoulder, tore through his back, and exited the other shoulder. "I am shot!" Morgan yelled, falling to his knees.

The bullets fired that day sounded not like infantry volleys, witnesses would say, but like deep individual reports, several producing faint echoes in the confined space. Everywhere, gun smoke rose, creating a white haze over the little lot. Out in the street, Holliday had drawn the shotgun to his shoulder. Tom McLaury was at the far side of the lot, behind one of the horses. Wyatt fired at the horse, which jumped and ran away. Holliday fired both barrels a moment later. His

---

*The discipline inherent in this remark speaks volumes about Wyatt Earp. He could've punched or even shot Ike Clanton. He didn't, brushing him off in the middle of a gunfight. Plus, you have to love the formality, and the implied sense of duty, in the use of the word "commenced."

twelve buckshot ripped into McLaury's right side. He stumbled across the sidewalk, collapsing in a heap beside a telegraph pole.

Gut-shot, the last Cowboy still standing, Frank McLaury, held his horse by the reins, using it as a shield as it lurched into the street. He fired at Morgan but missed, at which point he too lost control of the horse, which bolted down the street. Defenseless, McLaury found himself facing Holliday, who had thrown down the shotgun and pulled a nickel-plated revolver from his coat. McLaury laid his pistol across his left forearm and shouted, "I've got you now!"

"Blaze away!" Doc replied. "You're a daisy if you have!"

Both men fired. McLaury's shot passed through Holliday's coat, grazing his hip. Holliday's bullet hit the Cowboy in the chest, staggering him. A moment later, Morgan, rising from his knees, fired a shot that struck McLaury in the ear, killing him instantly. Holliday, thinking him still alive, strode up and snarled, "The son of a bitch has shot me, and I mean to kill him." But he was already gone.

Sitting against the far wall, Billy Clanton, struck by three bullets, had managed to reload. But he was too weak, and the one shot he got off went wild. It was the last bullet fired. Moments later, the boarding-house owner, C. S. Fly, rushed over and took his gun.

By most accounts, thirty bullets had been fired in about thirty seconds. The three Cowboys lay dying. In time, Virgil and Morgan would slowly recover from their wounds. Of the seven men who fired guns that gray western Wednesday, only Wyatt remained untouched. As the gun smoke cleared, he studied the fallen bodies around the lot.

"We won't have to disarm that party," he said.

ALMOST FROM THE FIRST MOMENTS AFTERWARD, THE TOWN WAS sharply divided in its judgment of what happened. History views the

Clantons and McLaurys as criminals, and they were, but in October 1881 this was far from clear. They were aligned with the Cowboys, it's true, but as ranch owners they were afforded a respect denied the Billy Leonards of the world. Many considered them legitimate cattlemen, their rustling activities mere rumor. Opinions tended to break down along political lines, Democrats—and the Clantons were vocal Democrats—backing the Cowboys, the "liberal" Republicans backing the Earps. The newspapers, the Republican *Epitaph* and the Democratic *Nugget*, would argue vehemently over the Earps for months.*

It began at the shooting site itself, when Behan walked up and made a half-hearted attempt to arrest Wyatt. "I won't be arrested today," Wyatt said, walking off. But some kind of review was inevitable. The funeral procession the next day, fronted by a brass band, featured twenty-two carriages and wagons and three hundred marchers and stretched two blocks. Afterward Ike filed murder charges. Wyatt and Doc were detained and posted bail. Recuperating from their wounds, Virgil and Morgan weren't, though Virgil was suspended from his job.

Five days after the shoot-out, a justice of the peace named Wells Spicer began a hearing on the murder charges. Everyone hired lawyers, the most vocal being the McLaurys' avenging brother Will, who arrived from Fort Worth and got Wyatt's and Holliday's bail revoked, sending them briefly back to jail. The hearing lasted a full month. Thirty people testified. Spicer ruled the shootings justified.

The Clantons and their supporters were outraged. Everyone understood that this was far from over. In the days after the hearing, the town was awash in rumors the Cowboys had drawn up a death list containing the names of the Earps and their friends they intended to kill.

---

*The shoot-out itself was not especially big news outside Arizona, a few brief accounts on inside pages in the eastern press, a single paragraph on the front page of *The Philadelphia Inquirer*.

It was said to have been sworn out at some kind of midnight ceremony in a distant canyon; Virgil heard they took oaths over blood drawn from Johnny Ringo's arm.

At Christmas, Tombstone remained on edge. Once Virgil and Morgan recovered enough to limp around, rumors of assassination plots flew daily. When someone shot up a stagecoach in which the mayor, an Earp friend, was riding, he loudly blamed the Cowboys. The Earps and their families moved into the Cosmopolitan, judging it safer than their homes, though they otherwise went about their lives as before.

On December 28, Virgil spent the evening with Wyatt and Holliday at the Oriental. Around 11:30, as he headed home, the sounds of shotgun blasts split the night air. Three men were seen racing into the darkness, leaving Virgil writhing in the street. Wyatt and others rushed out and carried him to the hotel, where, as the Earps posted guards outside, two doctors removed buckshot from near his spine and five inches of bone above his elbow. He was lucky to live.

Everyone understood the Cowboys' revenge had begun. Wyatt came to blame Ike and the Cowboy Frank Stilwell for the shooting, claiming to have found Ike's hat at the scene. But nothing was ever proven.

OF ALL THE GUNMEN THE EARPS CONFRONTED IN TOMBSTONE, THE most celebrated is the brooding Johnny Ringo, said to be not only a quicksilver pistoleer but a fallen college man prone to speeches in Latin. One biographer terms Ringo "the apotheosis of the western hero, Byronic, solitary, tortured, and mysterious."[1] Walter Noble Burns called him "a Hamlet among outlaws, an introspective, tragic figure, darkly handsome, splendidly brave, a man born for better things . . . a silent man of mystery." The Western writer Leon Metz judged Ringo "the strangest and most dangerous man to ever strap on a six-shooter." It's quite the legend. As one essayist puts it, with only mild overstatement, "Buffalo Bill, Jesse James and Billy the Kid combined have not had such extravagant claims made for them."[2]

But the truly amazing thing? Not a word of it is true. In fact, if the Gunfighter Era were to hold a contest for counterfeit celebrity, Hickok and Bill Longley would be among the finalists, but the top prize would go to Ringo hands down. The most feared gunfighter? History credits him with one shooting, the wounding of a miner in a drunken barroom argument. He was present at a shoot-out or three during Texas's Hoodoo War. The only other time we're certain Ringo fired a pistol, he shot himself in the foot. College-educated? Latin speeches? Uh, no.

None of this is Ringo's fault. There is no account of him ever making even one such claim. He is in fact purely a writer's contrivance. The actual Johnny Ringo, a cousin of Cole Younger's by marriage, was born John Peters Ringo in Indiana in 1850 and moved to San Jose, California, in 1864. Family members later said he became a teenage drunk—this is a recurring Ringo motif—and at nineteen, he moved to Texas. There, as we've seen, he rode in the Hoodoo War, where he was present—but not responsible—for at least two killings. Later, after his arrest by Ben Thompson in Austin, he briefly shared a jail cell with Wes Hardin. Counting his dealings with Curly Bill, Doc Holliday, and the Earps, Ringo may have come face-to-face with as many top-tier gunfighters as anyone.

There is a difference, though, between meeting famous gunmen and being one. In Arizona Ringo was just another Cowboy, little more significant than his pal Joe Hill, a secondary character at best. Other than riding with several posses and a few arrests, including one for robbing a poker game, he is the focus of precisely two events in the Tombstone saga, which is using the term "event" loosely, and only one of these while he was, you know, alive. It was, however, one of the Old

West's more famous arguments, Ringo and Holliday squabbling in the street outside the Oriental while Wyatt and a crowd looked on.

It happened three weeks after Virgil's shooting, on January 17, 1882. The Earps still suspected Ringo was involved. There are myriad versions of what occurred. The most imaginative—Walter Burns, naturally—has Ringo dangling a handkerchief toward Holliday, challenging him to take hold for a close-quarters "handkerchief fight." In fact, newspaper accounts at the time confirm that, while both had hands near their guns, the only thing exchanged were words.

"Wyatt, let's end this row," Ringo told Earp. "Let Holliday and me get out here in the middle of the street and shoot it out."

To which Holliday rasped, according to one eyewitness: "All I want of you is ten paces out in the street."

It's a classic frontier method of challenging a man to a duel, a contest with which the Georgia-born, Texas-seasoned Holliday was no doubt familiar. It was not to be. A policeman named James Flynn intervened, seizing Holliday's arm and hauling both men to police court. There, in a deflating anticlimax, the would-be duelists were fined thirty-two dollars each for carrying concealed weapons.

And that's it, the sum total of Johnny Ringo's confirmed involvement in the dramas of 1880s-era Tombstone. No gunfights, no killings of any kind, nothing that would even prompt one to term him a gunfighter. Just one super-awkward argument.

The only significant killing in Ringo's entire narrative was his own. His movements in the months after the Holliday argument—the period leading to his death—are mostly unknown; he pops up a time or two in others' recollections, and there is a persistent account he left the area to visit his sisters in San Jose. Whatever he did, he was back by July 4, when he was seen roaring drunk at Tombstone's celebration.

A week or so later, a deputy named Billy Breakenridge ran into Ringo in a pass east of town, still drunk, swilling from a bottle of bourbon with a second bottle in his saddle. According to Breaken-ridge, Ringo was morose, certain he would soon be murdered, presum-ably by friends of the Earps, who had long since left the area. A day or so later, on July 13, a ranch worker heard a gunshot. The next day Ringo was found dead lying against a massive oak, a bullet hole in his tem-ple, a pistol in his hand. The heat, it's said, had turned his body black.

There are many theories of Ringo's death, most declaring it mur-der. Late in life, Wyatt more than once claimed he did it, but no one seriously believed him; he had already left the area, and none of his half-remembered details matched the death scene. The authorities ruled it a suicide. Historians tend to agree.

Forgotten for the next forty years, Ringo, like so many western figures, was rediscovered during the 1920s when writers began churn-ing out bestselling books about the frontier. His unlikely champion was the elderly Deputy Breakenridge, who'd been on friendly terms with the Cowboys. In his 1928 memoir *Helldorado*, Breakenridge por-trayed Ringo as a fearless outlaw, a deadly marksman, and an all-around good sort; it was Breakenridge who floated the notion of Ringo as a college man, apparently because he was able to speak in complete sen-tences.

Walter Burns, who debriefed Breakenridge, then imagined the florid version of Ringo, complete with the Latin hokum, that would transfix a generation of Western writers. One modern debunker sug-gests the Breakenridge-inspired sketch that made it into Eugene Cun-ningham's landmark 1934 *Triggernometry* was the turning point. Cunningham, the dean of the fast-draw school, anointed Ringo "the fastest gunfighter and the deadliest" in Tombstone. "Breakenridge convinced Cunningham," one biographer wrote in a 1980 article, "and Cunningham, in turn, convinced a later generation of writers."[3]

Ringo's legend was kept alive through the 1930s and '40s by a series of lurid articles in pulp magazines such as *Western Story* and *Argosy*. Then, after the title character of 1950's *The Gunfighter* was given the surname Ringo, something like Ringo mania erupted. Every TV Western of the next two decades seemed to feature a character named Ringo at some point. The year 1966 alone brought two Westerns with Ringo in the title. Johnny Ringo even got a series of his own. The high point came in December 1964 when the actor Lorne Greene of *Bonanza* fame scored a number-one pop hit with the Western ballad "Ringo."

None of these efforts even remotely attempted to shine light on the Johnny Ringo of history, or even the fake Ringo imagined by Walter Burns and Eugene Cunningham. Ringo mania seemed propelled mostly by the ring of the name itself, the ease with which it rolls off an American tongue, the way it had come to effortlessly evoke the Old West. As, despite all the debunking articles that cropped up in obscure Western journals, it still echoes today.

ALL THAT WINTER THE *TOMBSTONE NUGGET* KEPT UP A RELENTLESS crusade against Wyatt and the Earps, attacks that peaked in the lead-up to city elections on January 3, 1882, when it charged them not only with being stagecoach robbers but with plotting a "monopoly of gambling, stage robbing" activities to "control the politics and business of Tombstone." When pro-Cowboy candidates all but swept the election, the *Nugget* headline read: EXUENT EARPS!

It wasn't headlines or politics that initially stopped Wyatt from going after Virgil's attackers. It was money. After Virgil's shooting, the U.S. marshal granted his request to be named a deputy. His boss, though, had to go to San Francisco to raise the cash from Wells Fargo needed to pay possemen. Once he had it, they secured warrants for

Ike Clanton and two others. On January 23, six days after the Ringo spat, Wyatt rode out of Tombstone with an eight-man posse to find them. He was soon reinforced by a second posse of twenty-five riders.

After Wyatt's force encircled and searched the town of Charleston, Ike and his remaining brother turned themselves in. When Wyatt couldn't produce any more evidence against them than a hat, the judge set them free. Ike responded by swearing out a new set of warrants against the Earps in Contention. They turned themselves in, posted bail, then watched a judge throw the case out. During this period, Wyatt resigned his position as a deputy marshal. Once these tit-for-tat legal maneuvers concluded, Wyatt and Morgan left town—Virgil was still recuperating—spending three weeks "on patrol" along the border, looking for either Apache raiders, Cowboys, or both. Tombstone stayed quiet in their absence.

On their return, Wyatt remained on keen alert. On Friday night, March 17, he sensed something awry, as if there were people in the shadows studying him. The next evening, with rumors flying of some kind of imminent Cowboy attack, he asked an attorney friend who represented several Cowboys whether he was in danger. He was told the Earps were "likely to get it in the neck at any time."

Wyatt was back at the Cosmopolitan, about to turn in, when he thought better of it, pulled his boots back on, and found Morgan as he came out of the Schieffelin Hall theater. He urged him to call it a night. Morgan insisted on one last game of pool. Wyatt went with him, probably for protection. At Bob Hatch's poolroom, he sat and watched as Morgan played one game, then racked up and began another.

Just before eleven, as Morgan stood before a window watching his opponent line up a shot, two gunshots echoed from the alley outside. One hit the wall above Wyatt's head. The second struck Morgan in the back and tore through his midsection. As he sagged to the floor, Wyatt leaped to his side. It was a mortal wound, blood everywhere.

Wyatt and two friends dragged Morgan to a sofa. When they tried to make him comfortable, he murmured, "Don't, I can't stand it."

"Morgan, do you know me?" one friend asked.

"This is a hard way to die," Morgan said.

Three doctors were at his side within minutes. Morgan lingered for nearly an hour. His last words, by one account, were to Wyatt.

"Do you know who did it?" he asked.

"Yes," Wyatt said, "and I'll get them."

"That's all I ask. But Wyatt, be careful."

In the moments after the shots, several men rushed out into the alley but saw nothing. A witness later said he saw three men running away. Wyatt wasn't sure who they were, but swore he would know soon and, one way or another, avenge his brother's death.

EVER SINCE TAKING HIS FIRST LAWMAN'S JOB IN WICHITA EIGHT YEARS earlier, Wyatt had been an officer who operated within the law, which was saying something in a time and place where so many didn't. He had done it after the fight by the O.K. Corral and after Virgil's shooting. But Morgan's death reset his internal calculus. Maybe it was because Morgan was the family favorite. Maybe it was because Morgan had died in his arms, or because Wyatt had tried to protect his little brother but couldn't. Whatever it was, something inside Wyatt gave way.

Was it a conscious choice as Morgan lay dying? Or would it happen instinctively, in a moment of rage? Wyatt never really said, but the evidence suggests that it was in fact a choice, one that altered the lives of almost everyone involved. What we know for sure is that, by the time Morgan's body was shipped to their parents in California the next day, a Sunday, a coroner's inquest had begun in which a surprise witness produced a list of likely assassins. She was the battered wife of a third-tier Cowboy named Pete Spence, a onetime Texas Ranger who had fled to Arizona after robbing a bank. The angry Mrs. Spence told how her husband and four others, including Frank Stilwell—whom Wyatt already suspected in the attack on Virgil—and a "half-breed" she called Indian Charlie, had left the Spence home with guns, whispering among themselves, then returned after the shooting exultant.*

By the next day, Monday, Wyatt was on a war footing, anticipating further attacks. Virgil, still recuperating at the Cosmopolitan, was an obvious target. After Wyatt persuaded him to head west too, a group escorted Virgil and his wife to the train station at Contention. There someone warned them that Ike Clanton and a group of Cowboys were at the station in Tucson, watching every train. Wyatt and three others decided to go with them, shotguns under their coats.

They arrived in the capital after nightfall and, upon disembarking, thought they glimpsed several Cowboys, including Ike and Frank Stilwell, melting into the welcoming crowd. Wyatt and his men fanned out, studying the depot and an adjacent hotel, but initially saw no more of them. Later, as the train prepared to leave, everyone returned to the cars one by one, Virgil limping with a cane, his arm in a sling. Only Wyatt remained outside, as ever on guard.

It was then, by most accounts, he thought he glimpsed Ike and Stilwell lying atop a flatcar, armed with shotguns. He returned to the platform, where, in the dim light, he peered toward them and saw a pair of gun barrels aimed at the train windows where Virgil and his wife sat

---

*Born in Iowa and raised in Kansas, Stilwell came to Arizona at twenty-one in 1877 and quickly established a reputation for volatility. By the time he came to Wyatt's attention, he had already killed at least two men, a prospector he beat to death with a rock after an argument and a ranch cook he killed, it's said, after the poor man brought him tea instead of coffee. He was acquitted of one killing and had charges dismissed in the other. When Wyatt's investigation led to charges on one of the stagecoach robberies, a judge dismissed them for lack of evidence.

in clear view. At this point, it seems, the two would-be assassins saw him and ran, lighting out down the tracks behind the hotel.

Wyatt raced after them, gravel crunching beneath his boots. After maybe a hundred yards, one stopped and turned. It was Stilwell. "What a coward he was," Wyatt said years later. "He couldn't shoot when I came near him. He stood there helpless and trembling for his life. As I rushed upon him he put out his hands and clutched at my shotgun. I let go both barrels, and he tumbled dead and mangled at my feet."[4]

It's a bracing admission, one at odds with the career of a man who, in the name of upholding the law, had faced down vigilante mobs as varied as those led by Mannen Clements in Wichita and those who sought to lynch Johnny-Behind-the-Deuce. Now, Wyatt admits, he was no better—and proud of it. As the train left the station, he managed to make eye contact with Virgil. "One for Morg!" he mouthed.

The Stilwell killing—an "innocent" man murdered in the heart of the capital—had profound repercussions. For the first time it made Wyatt a public figure, especially in the West, where newspapers that all but ignored Morgan's murder and the shoot-out the previous October now filed daily reports on what came to be known as the Earp "Vendetta," usually written with a capital *V*. The coverage ignited a public debate across the West about the merits of law versus order. It split along political lines: the Cowboy supporters were inevitably conservative Democrats, the Earp supporters liberal Republicans.

Wyatt woke up the next day a wanted man. By Tuesday afternoon, when he and his men returned to Tombstone, a Tucson inquest had issued arrest warrants for all of them. That night the paperwork reached Johnny Behan. Behan took two deputies to the Cosmopolitan, where he found Wyatt, Holliday, and five others outside, about to leave.

In the most plausible version of their conversation, Behan said,

"Wyatt, I want to see you." To which Wyatt, in a storied brush-off, replied, "You can't see me. I've seen you once too often."*[5]

Flicking Behan away like a tick, the Earp posse rode out of town, kicking off what's known as the Vendetta Ride.[†] The next morning, seeking to reclaim what remained of his honor, Behan assembled his own posse and rode after them, only to return while his men continued the hunt. That same day, around noon, Wyatt and his group rode up to a lumber camp thirteen miles northeast of Tombstone. It was run by the lead suspect, Pete Spence. Spence was a criminal, but not a stupid one. The minute he learned of Stilwell's killing, he had turned himself in and was now sitting in the Tombstone jail. Behan had actually let him keep his pistol in case the Earps came for him.

There were three men in camp that day, two more in the brush. Wyatt fired questions at one about Spence, which is when he learned of his seat in jail. As the posse turned to leave, they noticed a mestizo worker on a hillside. Suddenly, the man broke into a run. The posse charged up and over the hill in pursuit, everyone disappearing from view. A few moments later, the men in camp heard gunshots.

The fleeing man turned out to be Florentino Cruz, known as Indian Charlie, who was shortly dead. To this day, no one is sure what happened. Wyatt's biographer Casey Tefertiller notes that he long avoided questions about Cruz's death, suggesting something happened he wasn't proud of. Of the three times he did discuss it with writers

---

*Behan, and the pro-Cowboy *Tombstone Nugget*, later claimed that Wyatt's men had leveled guns at him. I don't believe that, and neither do most other writers and historians.

†There were six in this famous posse, including Wyatt, his brother Warren, Doc Holliday, and Sherman McMaster, a onetime Texas Ranger who had ridden with the Cowboys. Late in life, Wyatt acknowledged what many suspected, that McMaster had served as his informant. So did the fifth member, a onetime rustler named "Turkey Creek" Jack Johnson, a Missourian who appears to have survived gunfights in Newton, Kansas, and Deadwood. The sixth member was a man none of them knew well, who joined at the last minute: "Texas Jack" Vermillion, a former carpenter who actually wasn't from Texas; he too was a Missourian who, like so many, had arrived in Arizona via Dodge City. Asked once why he was called Texas Jack, he is said to have replied, "Because I'm from Virginia."

late in his life, each version was different. Most accounts suggest that Cruz was wounded while being chased, at which point he confessed to being a lookout for Morgan's killing, named his confederates, then received a final bullet, a de facto execution that probably explains Wyatt's reticence. Whatever happened, Wyatt came away with what he believed was a list of the five assassins, led by the late Frank Stilwell and Curly Bill himself.

On Thursday, the Earps rested, making camp north of Tombstone. Behan had launched yet another posse to find and arrest them and, amazingly, had deputized the entire Cowboy leadership to do the same. The next morning, Friday, March 24, a force of twenty-one Cowboys, including Curly Bill and Johnny Ringo, rode out of Charleston in search of the Earps. At some point that day, they split up.

That same morning, Wyatt finished breakfast and sent a man into Tombstone to fetch money he needed to pay his men. (The going rate was five dollars a day, not bad for the time.) They arranged a rendezvous that afternoon at Cottonwood Spring, a watering hole at the southern end of the Whetstone Mountains, thirty miles west of Tombstone.

The spring was sunk into a depression at one end of a broad canyon, visible only upon cresting a rise a hundred yards to the south. After a long, dry ride, Wyatt was the first of the posse to reach the rise. Below, he saw a group of eight or nine armed men. As Holliday and the others rode up, the men began firing at them.

Wyatt's group was caught by complete surprise. Their horses bucked and reared. A bullet felled one animal. Other shots zipped through their clothing. Wyatt leaped from his horse, holding a sawed-off shotgun and his reins. Glancing back, he was startled to see Holliday and the others riding away. With bullets striking all around, he attempted to remount his panicked horse but couldn't.

At this point, Wyatt said years later, he assumed these were his last moments. Turning toward his attackers, he recognized several of them, one above all: Curly Bill. "If I was to die," he would say, "I proposed that Curly Bill at least should die with me."[6]

The man who more than anyone embodied the Cowboy ethic, who had shot up churches and had forced people to dance naked at gunpoint, whom Wyatt came to view as the mastermind behind the attacks on his brothers, was standing upright, firing a shotgun. Wyatt raised his own and fired both barrels. The buckshot tore into Curly Bill's chest. He "yelled like a demon" as he fell, dead.

The other Cowboys kept firing. Bullets tore through the long duster Wyatt wore. He grabbed his horse's saddle, trying in vain to take the Winchester from its scabbard as the animal squirmed; a bullet struck the saddle horn, inches from his nose. In desperation he reached for his six-shooter, but in the tumult his cartridge belt had twisted so completely the gun was in the small of his back. He reached back and got a hand on it, turned, and squeezed off several shots.

Somehow, he got a foot into a stirrup, but by this point his belt had fallen around his thighs, all but immobilizing his legs. For the longest moment he hung there, silhouetted against the afternoon sky, furiously yanking at his belt, bullets flying all the while. When he finally managed to lift it, he gained control of the horse, rode toward the posseman whose horse had fallen, Texas Jack Vermillion, and swept him up, the two riding together over the rise to safety.*

When he reached the others, Holliday looked at Wyatt's shredded duster, gingerly took his arm, and said, "You must be shot all to pieces."[7] Wyatt's left foot had gone numb. He assumed he'd been shot. But

---

*The exact site of the shoot-out long remained a mystery. In his 1927 memoir, Wyatt identified it as "Iron Springs," though the actual Iron Springs does not match his descriptions. A modern researcher named Bill Evans has persuasively identified the actual shooting site as another nearby watering hole, Cottonwood Spring.

when he removed his boot, there was no wound. Somehow, he had made it through unscathed. The others clamored to regroup and take the attack to the Cowboys. Wyatt had had enough. "If you fellows are hungry for a fight you can go on and get your fill," he said.

Wyatt Earp was done with the chase, with the Cowboys, with Tombstone, with Arizona, with all of it. In the end, his vaunted Vendetta Ride lasted barely seventy-two hours and, not counting Frank Stilwell, resulted in the deaths of all of two men. As news of the killings spread, there was the explosion of interest you'd expect, half condemnatory, half salutary. Wyatt and his men passed the media tempest dodging Behan and Cowboy posses at a friendly rancher's, at one point digging in on a remote hillside for a climactic attack that never came.

It was over. On April 14, three weeks after Curly Bill's killing, Wyatt, Doc Holliday, and five pals rode into Billy the Kid's hometown, Silver City, New Mexico, never to return. They headed next to Albuquerque, where they gave an interview, then rode into Colorado to the town of Trinidad, where Bat Masterson was marshal.

They left behind myriad demands and rewards for their arrests, ethical and political debates that lingered for years, and a legend. Only Holliday was ever detained, by a would-be bounty hunter in Denver that spring. Masterson made it go away. The newspaper coverage predictably split along partisan lines. The denouement came a month later, in Washington, when the new president of the United States, the Republican Chester A. Arthur, issued an order concerning "disturbances in Arizona" that authorized the army to disperse the Cowboys. And while the army never really did, the message was received and things quieted down considerably.

One by one, the Cowboys slunk off to their fates. Many died of gunshot wounds. Ike Clanton lived a while longer. Pete Spence went on to murder four men, serve his time, and marry Ike's onetime sister-in-law, running her goat ranch until dying in 1914.* Doc Holliday parted ways with the Earps in Colorado. His last years weren't pretty. His illness progressed, his hair turned gray, and his skills deteriorated. Unable to pay his gambling losses, he shot a debt collector in 1885; the jury acquitted him. He ended up in a hotel in Glenwood Springs, where he died two years later. He was thirty-six years old. The Earps didn't learn of his passing for another two months.

Wyatt would outlive them all.

---

*Ringo's partner, the Texan Joe Hill, né Olney, died after being thrown from a galloping horse in 1884. His brother George, a minor Cowboy, became a successful Arizona businessman and politician, running for governor in 1916. Dirty Dave Rudabaugh, who after riding with Billy the Kid never truly found his footing as a henchman in Arizona, decamped for Mexico, where in 1886 he killed two men in a saloon gunfight over cards. Fearing angry villagers, he ran for his horse, couldn't find it in a crowded parking lot, and returned to the saloon, where he was promptly shot and killed. Someone then decapitated him with a machete and mounted his severed head on a pole. Not, as they say, my next vacation destination.

CHAPTER SIXTEEN

The Deadliest Feud

Arizona, 1883 to 1892

The year 1881, featuring Billy the Kid's death in July, followed three months later by the gunfight in Tombstone, is the climax of the Gunfighter Era. Afterward, marquee gunfights, the kind that made headlines, appear to have declined. Much of this was the march of civilization. The frontier was shrinking. Railroads were bringing central authority within reach of even the remotest areas. Towns like Dodge City were enforcing gun laws. Cattle associations were calling to disarm cowboys. The Rangers were cleaning up Texas. Newspapers, it's fair to say, suffered from gunfighter fatigue.

Outlaws still rode, men still sought revenge for insults, and drunks still shot each other. But the bloodiest episodes of the century's final fifteen years would be ugly demi-wars over land; Texans remained among the central players and the most sought-after gunmen. Most of those conflicts are forgotten today. The last famed gunfighters would come instead from the dwindling pool of outlaws wedged into the remaining corners of lawlessness, desperate men seeking ever-larger scores to buy safety from lawmen who, slowly but surely, would hunt them to extinction.

The worst violence during this period, though, wasn't directed against people. It was directed against an animal. The one thing Texans probably hated most.

HONOR CODES, PERSONAL VIOLENCE, RACISM, AND CATTLE HANDLING weren't the only behaviors Texans inherited from the Old South. In the century's final years, they would draw on a more obscure aspect of their heritage to open an entirely new theater of mayhem. It was an old grudge, likely born in Virginia, carried to Texas by its early settlers, and then spread throughout the West, brought to bear against something cattlemen and cowboys hated more than just about anything—more than Mexicans, more than rustlers, more than Comanche: sheep.

It's hard to overstate the cattleman's hatred of Mary's Little Lamb. It wasn't simply that they competed for land. Texans believed sheep fouled water holes and destroyed grassland. Anywhere one had been, they swore, a cow would not go. Some said cattle objected to their stench, others to the odor of their droppings. A few believed drinking from water used by sheep did something to a cow's nervous system that made it likely to stampede. One pro-cattle writer termed sheep "woolly, maggot-like creatures" calling them "a plague of locusts, greedily devouring the grass, tearing it out by the roots."[1]

These beliefs can be traced to the antebellum South. In 1813 a contemporary of Thomas Jefferson's, John Taylor, published an agricultural paper that included a rant against sheep, claiming they possessed an "insatiable appetite" that "depopulates the country he inhabits." One writer in the 1860s blamed the South's paucity of sheep on Taylor's influence, another on the fact that wool was cotton's natural competitor.

On the floor of Congress, a Virginia legislator declared that he would go out of his way "to kick a sheep."[2]

In Texas, and later in New Mexico, the loathing of sheep was amplified by deep-seated racism toward the people who often made their living herding them: Mexican Americans. "Certainly the prejudice against sheep among cattlemen in the early days was very strong," a New Mexico rancher recalled in 1940. "It came to us from the Texans, from which we derived our range practice and much of our tradition. The Texan associated sheep with Mexicans, and from the day of the Alamo for many years nothing Mexican looked good to Texans."[3]

The first minor "sheep wars" were fought in Texas beginning in the mid-1870s, but the great ones, those that lasted years, raged in Colorado, Wyoming, Montana, and Oregon for four decades afterward. The worst featured armed gunmen and plenty of gunplay, but in truth far fewer men died in these conflicts than sheep. The violence perpetuated against these animals was head-shakingly barbaric. Across the West, cowboys were known to use their idle time to find a herd of sheep and shoot them one at a time until they ran out of bullets. If a sheepherder intervened, he might be beaten or shot as well.

When cattlemen got organized, things could get far worse. In Oregon they formed "sheep shooters associations," raiding herds at night, tying up shepherds, and shooting animals by the dozens. In time, perhaps to save bullets, cowboys came up with creative ways to massacre sheep. In 1905 ten masked men raided a sheep operation outside Thermopolis, Wyoming, and clubbed four thousand to death in one gruesome night. In 1887 a group of Colorado cowboys managed to kill twenty-six hundred by burning a sheepherder's corrals. Still another Colorado raid, in 1894, succeeded in driving four thousand sheep over a thousand-foot bluff into Parachute Creek.

This was no isolated incident. "All that was necessary to get a band of sheep over a bank was to start a few of the leaders off and then the whole band would go over with a rush and cause a 'pile-up' of the . . . dumb brutes," reads one history, "and they were either killed from the fall or smothered by being piled one on top of the other from ten to twenty deep."*[4]

Into the twentieth century—the last major sheep raid was recorded in Colorado in 1920—prosecutions for this kind of thing were few and far between.† Sheep owners seeking justice, or just peace, tended to take things into their own hands. Though little remembered today, the single bloodiest of these conflicts, sometimes called the deadliest feud in U.S. history, broke out across central and eastern Arizona in the 1880s.

They called it the Pleasant Valley War.

IN TERMS OF SHEER QUANTITY, ARIZONA'S PLEASANT VALLEY WAR SHOULD be America's most infamous feud. Depending on how you count the bodies, somewhere between thirty-five and sixty men were killed in just one of its two theaters. Compare that to the thirteen who died in Hatfield versus McCoy. Its obscurity is in part the result of its complexity, its remote killing fields, and the fact that it seldom drew the attention of major newspapers. If the gunfight beside the O.K. Corral is the West's most-documented gunplay, Pleasant Valley might well be its least.

It had more factions than the Russian Civil War. The best way to view it is as several simultaneous conflicts. Cattleman versus sheepherder was only one. At the personal level, the war pitted the Graham

---

*I've seen at least one account that calls this practice "rimrocking." Rimrock is the vertical face of a plateau (i.e., what the sheep were driven over).

†The enmity between cattlemen and shepherds seems to have died down after the 1920s. Today they're cool.

(cattle) family and its allies against the Tewksbury (sheep) family and its allies. But it was also hell-raising Texas cowboys versus Mormon settlers. And fed-up cattlemen against brazen rustlers. By one count, the war's epicenter around Holbrook, Arizona, population 250, was the scene of twenty-six killings. In a single year.

It all began after the discovery of placer gold in the 1860s brought Anglos into fresh corners of central Arizona, where they clashed with Apache and Yavapai tribesmen. The U.S. cavalry drove the Native peoples out, and in the process opened a vast pine forest lying below the Mogollon Rim, the dramatic two-hundred-mile west-to-east escarpment separating Arizona's northern plateau from the pine-sheathed valleys below, what came to be called the Rim Country. Among the choicest of these hollows, northeast of Phoenix, ran thirty miles north–south along Tonto Creek. The early settlers named it Pleasant Valley.

Among the first to arrive was James Tewksbury, a Maine man who brought his Native American wife and four sons after stints in California and Nevada. It's said one of the sons, Ed, lured his handsome pal Tom Graham and Tom's brother John, an Irishman who spoke with a brogue, to the valley, promising its deep grasses could make them all cattle kings. By 1882 the two families had become neighbors tending small herds. The trouble actually began between the Tewksburys and a neighbor, a rancher named James Stinson, who accused them of stealing his cows. The Tewksburys claimed it was an honest mistake and offered to return them. But when a group of Stinson's men rode up to where the Grahams and Tewksburys were building a cabin on New Year's Day 1883, shooting broke out. Two cowboys were wounded.

Charges of attempted murder were filed against several men, but on the eve of the trial, Stinson cut a deal with the Graham brothers: if they would provide evidence proving the Tewksburys were in fact determined thieves, he would give them fifty cows. The Grahams took the deal, testifying against the Tewksburys in early 1884, but a judge threw out the cases after the secret deal was disclosed. The two families soon fell into something like a simmering cold war.

What transformed this inchoate feud into something spawning historic levels of violence was the injection of three elements: Mormons, Texans, and sheep. All through the 1880s, Mormon homesteaders streamed across the Utah border into lands east of Pleasant Valley, in Apache County along the New Mexico border, which would become the war's eastern front. There was a shooting or two with Latinos and lots of arrests for polygamy, but the Mormons typically avoided violence. They function in this story largely as sympathetic victims.

Their oppressors turned out to be maybe the purest—read: wildest—incarnation of all the Texans who migrated onto the frontier in these years. They were brought in by something new in the West, a giant cattle corporation, the New York–owned Aztec Land and Cattle Company, which purchased thirty-three thousand head from the Continental Land and Cattle Company of Texas and moved them onto a Connecticut-sized parcel it acquired, ninety miles long and fifty miles wide, stretching from east of Pleasant Valley north past Flagstaff. Aztec's land was subject to survey, though, and in the time it took to do all this, much of it was settled by Mormons.

The company's cowboys—dubbed "Hashknifes," after the Continental brand—had been notorious in Texas, known for lynching a group of five rustlers at a spot that came to be known as Rustler Springs. The Hashknifes hit the poor Mormons hard, evicting dozens from their homes at gunpoint and shooting up Mormon dances and towns; when there were no Mormons around to haze, they shot one another and the occasional Latino. It's said that one of their favorite saloons, the Bucket of Blood in Holbrook, got its name from the two Mexicans killed by a Hashknife in a gambling dispute. Another tried to shoot out a train lamp and hit the conductor instead.[5]

It was a culture clash as profound as any you'll find on the old frontier. The Mormons regarded the Hashknifes as demons from a swanky Texas hell, duded up in their Coffeyville boots, silver spurs, and Stetson hats, their hat strings, quirts, reins, and long ropes woven with care. The Mormons lived by scripture, the Texans by their peculiar code of honor; as Daniel Justin Herman, the conflict's preeminent modern historian, notes, the cowboys, "like their Southern ancestors, measured success via old rites of manliness, rites of courage, excess, and exuberance."[6] The Mormons refused to put up a fight.

This was the high-water mark of the cattle boom, and by the time the Hashknifes moved in, the Aztec land was already thronged with thousands of animals. While formally responsible for company cattle, many a Hashknife worked just as hard stealing every cow in sight, Aztec or otherwise. "Hashknife," in fact, soon emerged as a synonym for "outlaw." The Mormons appealed to Utah, asking if it was okay to shoot a few. (No, elders ruled.) Rustling rose to epidemic proportions. Area ranchers began talking about extreme measures.

The most notorious of the Texans was fresh-faced Andy Blevins, who arrived from Llano, north of Austin, with his father, Mart, and five brothers, including sixteen-year-old Hamp, who we're told had already spent a year in prison for horse theft.* Somewhat like his spiritual cousin Curly Bill Brocius, little is known of Andy's criminal background, though the fact that he used an alias, "Andy Cooper," suggests he was running from something. Some said it was a beloved's angry family; others said he escaped the Rangers by leaping from a moving train.

Into this tumult arrived the dreaded sheep. Flagstaff's Daggs family had previously spread its herds across the northern plateau, but Aztec

---

*Company records, we are told, don't mention an Andy Blevins, but Mormons in the area considered him a Hashknife. On a separate note, I have my doubts about Hamp Blevins's reported age. A surviving photo shows him with a flowing mustache, suggesting either a factual error or one seriously hairy teenager.

executives and gunmen now blocked access to its land, a move that held up against multiple legal challenges. Facing disaster, the family cut a deal with the Tewksburys to put sheep on their land in Pleasant Valley. Area cattlemen raged. The Grahams, backed by Hashknife cowboys and the Blevins family, declared war, shooting into flocks, driving herds over cliffs, and burning sheepherders' cabins and corrals. The Tewksburys began receiving death threats. Rumors of assassination plots and massacres raced through the Rim Country.

Violence now began to feel inevitable. The tipping point, many believe, came in February 1887 when a Daggs shepherd was found dead, beheaded, his body riddled with bullets. Around the same time, two more sheepmen were found dead. It was beginning.

THAT SUMMER OF 1887, THE BLEVINS PATERFAMILIAS, MART, WENT looking for some missing horses. He didn't return. Three of his sons went in search, eventually splitting up. One, the teenage Hamp, rode into a Hashknife camp and recruited four cowboys to help. By August 9, after several days in the pines, they had found nothing but picked up three more riders, Graham partisans.*

That day they stopped outside a ranch cabin east of Pleasant Valley, either to ask for food, as they later claimed, or because they knew Ed Tewksbury was the foreman. If Mart Blevins had been killed, everyone understood the Tewksburys were likely responsible. Riding up, the Blevins party called out a request for grub. "No sir," a voice from inside replied, "we do not keep a hotel here."[7] The riders then asked whether a friend of theirs was on the premises. "No," the voice said.

Poor Hamp Blevins had no idea what he had ridden into. Seven

---

*What happened to Mart Blevins remains a mystery. Not long after, a body stripped of its flesh was found in the area; some thought it was him. Seven years later a cowboy found a skull and a rusty rifle. All I got.

Tewksbury partisans, including Ed Tewksbury, had been outside when the riders appeared, then scrambled inside unseen; no doubt they felt threatened. Both sides would accuse the other of firing first, but my money is on the Tewksburys. It was a de facto ambush. A barrage of shots exploded from the cabin. One of the first struck Hamp Blevins between the eyes. Another cowboy fell a moment later. Four riders galloped away, leaving behind two badly wounded men, both of whom later staggered into Hashknife camps after days in the wild. The Grahams showed up in force not long after, found the cabin empty, burned it, buried the two dead men, and, later, filed murder charges.

The Tewksburys did not take any of this well. A week later, John and Tom Graham's teenage brother, Billy, rode out alone in search of some missing horses, a poor decision. The squeamish might want to skip this next bit. Billy was ambushed. Shot in the gut, he somehow managed to make his escape, albeit with a sizable portion of his intestines spilling out onto his saddle. At one point, he dismounted, lay down to die, then thought better of it, nudged his insides back into place, then rode to a Graham home. Before dying, he identified his attackers as Ed and six other Tewksburys.

The Grahams struck back in early September, ambushing and killing John Tewksbury and his pal William Jacobs outside the Tewksbury ranch house. More than a hundred rounds were fired, it's said, before the attackers closed in to finish them off, one using a large stone. They then laid siege to the house, firing hundreds more bullets at it. I'd love to tell you more, but everything about the siege is vague—how long it lasted, who was inside, who was outside. Several accounts say the attackers were led by Tom Graham and Andy Blevins. The incident is probably best known for the debate, and I'm half serious here, over the roles played by wild hogs. Some say a Tewksbury woman emerged and begged to bury the bodies lest they be eaten by the hogs. Others have argued that the hogs ate the bodies as the siege wore on.

Part of me, I confess, is chagrined to pass this on. Yet as extraneous as such detail may seem, it's a vivid brushstroke in a barbaric panorama. The next time I hear someone start in on the romance of the Old West, it's the obscenities of this feud—the beheadings, the intestines, the hogs—that will return to me first.

THE VIOLENCE THAT ERUPTED ACROSS CENTRAL ARIZONA IN 1887 CAN be viewed as two distinct but overlapping conflicts: one centered on Pleasant Valley; the other the kind of rustler-extermination campaign Texas ranchers had all but invented. This second theater, in Apache County to the east, has little to do with the Grahams and Tewksburys and everything to do with unprecedented threats to the cattle industry. The drive against rustlers was a direct result of a sudden downturn in the glutted cattle markets. By 1885 many cattlemen were growing desperate. Losses to rustlers that might once have been written off were now perceived as threats to a rancher's survival. The epidemic of rustling in Apache County, by Hashknifes and others, pushed beleaguered cattlemen to think outside the box.

They ended up hiring a new kind of gunman who proliferated during the 1880s, the stock or "range" detective. Typically employed to investigate thefts, the range detective was supposed to be a private eye working the frontier.* In practice he operated within a gray area of the law. Some critics labeled them hired killers, as a few in fact became. The Pinkerton agency brought on its first range detective in Denver in 1886, the Texas cowboy Charles Siringo, a reputable type

---

*The range detective was typically hired by one of the cattlemen's associations that began cropping up in the 1870s to combat livestock theft. The Wyoming Stock Growers Association, among the most militant of such groups, hired one of the first detectives, a man named W. C. "Billy" Lykens in 1877.

who got his start as one of the riders the giant LX Ranch sent after Billy the Kid.

The detective Aztec and its fellow cattlemen hired was a paunchy character named Jonas V. Brighton, one of the West's great unsung gumshoes. At forty, Brighton had already been a teenage Union soldier, a prisoner of war, a cowboy on the trails from Texas, a thief, and a four-year guest of the Kansas penal system. After taking some kind of correspondence course, he had emerged as a private detective of note, solving a Missouri doctor's murder. In Arizona, though, Brighton would go down as maybe the first corporate gunfighter.

He began by going undercover in the flyblown village of Springerville, posing as a corrupt saloonkeeper nicknamed "Rawhide Jake" to cozy up to the rustling fraternity. The first person he managed to get indicted was, of all people, Ike Clanton. After slithering out of Tombstone, Ike and his brother Phin had relocated north to the wilds of Apache County, where they became marquee troublemakers, getting indicted every six months or so and surviving the odd gunfight.

Phin was quickly caught; he drew ten years. But Ike ran. Brighton and a deputy rode south into the White Mountains to find him. Two weeks into the hunt, on May 31, 1887, they were preparing their morning fire at a rancher's cabin when who should ride up unannounced but Ike himself. Brighton yelled hey. Ike, knowing him as the rustler's pal Rawhide Jake, yelled hey back. Then he spotted the deputy. Ike wheeled, grabbing a Winchester from its scabbard.

"Halt!" Brighton yelled. "Throw up your hands!"

Ike lay the rifle across his left forearm.

"Shoot the son of a bitch!" the deputy yelped.

Brighton's first shot struck Ike in the arm, a second passed through his body. When they hustled up to him a moment later, they found him on the ground, "dead as a mackerel," in the detective's words.[8]

Apache County rejoiced. But Brighton was just getting started. Next in his sights was Ike's partner, a seasoned Texas killer named Lee Renfro. It had been Renfro's murder of a leading cattleman that had spurred Brighton's hiring in the first place. Riding with several cavalrymen, the detective was combing the San Carlos Indian Reservation for stolen cattle six weeks later when they spied a man on foot. When the troopers brought him up, Brighton recognized it was Renfro.

"Lee Renfro, throw up your hands," he called twice.

Renfro went for his gun. Brighton drilled him with a single shot over the heart. Renfro's last words, among the West's more plaintive sign-offs, were "Did you shoot me for money?" Brighton said, "No, I shot you because you resisted arrest."[9]

Brighton's third target, a Texas outlaw and murderer named C. W. Johnson, known as "Kid Swingle," proved tougher to find. After authorities in an adjacent county briefly detained Brighton for Ike's death, he apparently thought better of taking credit for his kills. Soon after, Kid Swingle was found lynched, by parties unknown. I'm guessing Brighton held the rope.

When the newspapers turned on him, Jonas V. Brighton skedaddled, leaving behind a question: Had he been a detective, an assassin, or something in between? I'd say detective, but not all would agree. Whatever he was, Brighton remained active for years, helping bring in the California train robber Chris Evans in 1894. He died in Los Angeles in 1928. He was eighty-one.*

THE WAR CLIMAXED WITH A FABLED GUNFIGHT THAT BRIDGED ITS two theaters. Its focus was the notably unpopular Andy Blevins. The

---

*Kudos to historian John Boessenecker for rediscovering Brighton in his splendid *Ride the Devil's Herd: Wyatt Earp's Epic Battle Against the West's Biggest Outlaw Gang.*

Tewksburys had marked him for death. So, it seems, had Apache County ranchers, who viewed him as a rustler par excellence. The Mormons he had tormented were down for anything.

The man obliged to confront Blevins was Commodore Perry Owens, a thirty-five-year-old Tennessean who appears to have stepped out of Buffalo Bill's Wild West show. His one iconic portrait shows him standing, unsmiling, right hand on a Winchester's barrel, left carefully tucked atop a gun belt lined with enormous cartridges; he's wearing a holstered pistol, a round-rimmed cowboy hat, and chaps, sporting a mustache and a torrent of reddish-blond hair that falls to his elbows. He looks like David Crosby at a dude ranch. Owens always claimed he couldn't find a barber, but the man in the photo clearly adores his look.

Vanity, though, doesn't always signal ineptitude. By all accounts, Owens was a crack shot, so adept he could make a tomato can hop across a field using bullets fired by pistols in both hands. He'd honed his talents as a buffalo hunter, he said, then as a cowboy in Oklahoma and New Mexico, before homesteading in Arizona, where he developed a reputation for murdering Navajo tribesmen. His wife claimed that he'd killed fifty, an early author said twenty-five, but Owens once confided it was only one. In Arizona at the time, this was not viewed as much of a crime.

What mattered was his reputation, which inspired Apache County cattlemen and their Mormon cheerleaders to get him elected sheriff in late 1886, on a platform of eradicating rustlers. Skill with a gun, though, doesn't always signal boldness. Owens didn't exactly rush to arrest bad guys. Jonas Brighton had been assigned to him, and Owens let him work alone. When Brighton left, Owens fell under intense pressure to begin tackling the criminal element himself. When he didn't, suggestions of cowardice began to circulate. They stung.

"People have talked enough about me being afraid to arrest men,"

Owens groused to a deputy on Sunday, September 4, 1887, the day he rode into the hamlet of Holbrook to confront Andy Blevins.

It's not at all clear this had been his intention. The details of his change of heart, in fact, provide a striking glimpse of the frontier's honor code at work. According to court testimony, Owens had actually come to the outskirts of Holbrook to see a Latina friend. A deputy in town, a plainspoken gent named Frank Wattron, sent a messenger to inform him that Blevins—going by his alias, Cooper—was in town too. His delicately worded message, we're told, was to "tell that cowardly son of a bitch sacking up with that Mexican bitch that Cooper's in town. If he don't come over here and take care of the god damned bastard I am going to do so and then I am going to take care of that yellow bellied womanish son-of-a-bitching sheriff."[10]

My thought upon first reading this was probably the same as yours: Deputy Wattron would have been fabulous on Twitter. This was a challenge one couldn't ignore in 1887 Arizona. After riding into town, he told Wattron, and then several citizens, that he didn't want their help. He would arrest Blevins alone. It's pretty clear he had to, or risk public shaming.

A group assembled at the railroad depot to watch. In 1887 Holbrook could barely be called a town, just ten or fifteen shacks and a few saloons plopped down in the dirt around the station house. As the locals looked on, Owens sat while he cleaned and loaded his guns.

What delayed this showdown, it appears, wasn't so much cowardice as the fact that he and Blevins had history. They were friendly. It's been suggested that they had been partners stealing horses from the Navajo, which might explain Owens's reputation for killing so many. There's also the fact that the only legal paper justifying Blevins's arrest was a year-old warrant for stealing said horses, a crime few juries of the era would convict a white man of. Blevins had been heard boasting that Owens would never try to bring him in. Some went so far as to say they had a deal: if Owens rode into an Apache County town, Blevins would leave, reducing the chance he would be criticized for inaction.[11]

By and by, Owens rose and strode toward the bungalow members of the Blevins family rented. One of Andy's brothers had spotted him and brought Andy a horse, which was tied to a scraggly cottonwood tree in the yard, awaiting his escape, when the sheriff walked up.

There were no curtains in the windows. Stepping into the yard, a Winchester cradled in one arm, Owens could see the house was crowded. In fact, there were eleven people inside, all Texans it seems, including Andy, his brother John, their fifteen-year-old brother, their newly widowed mother, and assorted women, children, and henchmen.

Someone was standing in the door. As Owens walked up, it slammed shut. He stepped onto the porch and, still using Blevins's alias, called for "Cooper" to come out. Blevins opened the door, holding a pistol. His brother John Blevins appeared at a second door that also led onto the porch, four feet to Owens's right.*

"I want you, Cooper," Owens said.

"What do you want with me?" Blevins replied.

"I have a warrant for you."

"What warrant?"

Owens explained.

"Give me a few minutes," Blevins said, closing the door.

"Cooper, no, wait," Owens said, jamming his boot in the doorway. Blevins raised his gun and ducked behind the door. Owens fired through it. The bullet hit Blevins in the belly. He dropped.

Owens jacked in another shell and backed into the yard. John

---

*Accounts of what happened that day are fairly consistent, with differences mainly in dialogue. I cobbled this one together from Herman's *Hell on the Range*, an account by Marshall Trimble on the *True West* magazine website, and a 1931 article in the *Arizona Historical Review*.

Blevins swung the second door open and fired from a distance of maybe ten feet. His round not only missed but struck and killed that poor horse in the yard, like something out of *Blazing Saddles*. Owens returned fire, hitting Blevins in the shoulder. He too dropped.

Scanning the porch, the sheriff spied Andy, on his knees inside the house, trying to aim his gun. Owens fired a second bullet at him, striking him in the hip. He continued backing away as he did, into the street, allowing him to see the entire house. A cowboy named Mote Roberts leaped out a side window and turned to run away. Later some said he held a gun, others said he didn't. Adrenalized, Owens was taking no chances. He shot Roberts in the back, a mortal wound.

A few moments later, the front door swung open. Fifteen-year-old Sam Houston Blevins charged out, brandishing a pistol. A step behind came his mother, reaching out to stop him. Owens fired a shot into the boy's chest, killing him. His mother fell to his side, wailing.

Which finished it, leaving a lot to process. Wisecracks aside, I find this to be one of the Old West's saddest gunfights. It could've been avoided so easily. Those who entered the house afterward told of how much blood there was, of children covered with splatter. Perry Owens had fired his rifle five times, killing three men—Andy Blevins died by nightfall—and wounding another. The widow Blevins lost another son, bringing her loss to a husband and three sons—soon four—in a scant sixty days. They say she wandered the town sobbing, ghostlike, for fifteen years.

For his part, Sheriff Owens trudged to a stable, dazed.

"Have you finished the job?" someone asked.

"I think I have," he said.

And he had. The Mormons especially rejoiced, all but sanctifying him. Not that it did Owens much good. He lost the next election; that Sunday afternoon in Holbrook would be his only bow on history's stage. "They refused me a second term because I was a killer," Owens once complained. "But a killer was what they needed then."[12] Perry Owens died in 1919, aged sixty-seven. He is buried in Flagstaff.*

THERE WERE TOO MANY OTHER KILLINGS TO MENTION. THE MOST consequential was an ambush that took the lives of the elder Graham brother, the Irish-born John, and the fourth Blevins son to die, Charley. Many thought the war ended there, but in fact it only descended into shadow. Over the next five years, dozens more men were found murdered or lynched in and around Pleasant Valley—three Graham partisans at once—often accompanied by reports of masked perpetrators. In retrospect it was a classic vigilante campaign against rustlers real and perceived, a team effort by Aztec, area ranchers, and their Mormon neighbors to "clean out" the Rim Country. The vigilantes' leader was Jesse Ellison, a Tennessee-born rancher who had grown up in Texas and had served as a Ranger before coming west.

Tensions between the Grahams and Tewksburys, meanwhile, seemed to ease, probably because only two of their original males remained alive: Tom Graham and Ed Tewksbury. Tom Graham finally thought better of lingering and moved to Tempe, where he started a farm. On August 2, 1892, a full five years after most thought the feud was over, Graham went into town to deliver some wheat. Out of nowhere, Ed Tewksbury and a crony rode up behind, leveled their rifles, and shot him dead.

At the trial, Graham's widow crept up behind Tewksbury's pal, pressed a pistol against his back, and pulled the trigger. It misfired. So, in the end, did justice. Ed Tewksbury was convicted but had it thrown

---

*The shoot-out remains sufficiently famous in Arizona that a future governor and presidential candidate, Bruce Babbitt, chose to be sworn in at the Blevins house when he was elected the state's attorney general in 1975. A peculiar choice at a glance, but hey, who could argue that Perry Owens wasn't tough on crime?

out on a technicality; at a second trial he was found innocent. He later moved to the town of Globe, where he briefly worked as a policeman. He died there, peacefully, in 1904.

Gunfights in Arizona raged into the next century, creating a legacy of violence second only to that of Texas. I've seen it argued that the Pleasant Valley War, coming after all that happened in Tombstone, contributed to an image of Arizona so bloody it delayed statehood until 1912. That may not be true, but it's a telling rumor.

CHAPTER SEVENTEEN

The Assassins

Range Wars, Tom Horn,
and "Deacon" Jim Miller

Any whiff of romance that might have been attached to Old West gunplay fell away during the range wars of the 1880s and '90s, when cattlemen across what remained of the frontier lost patience with the homesteaders, sheepherders, and rustlers who, in their view, destroyed, stole, and infringed upon their property. This was cold, nasty murder, bullet-ridden bodies floating in Colorado creeks, shepherds in Texas executed with a single shot to the forehead, children at play one moment, toppling over dead the next, a bullet fired from a high ridge three football fields away.

Much of the killing was driven by tensions brought about by the shrinking frontier and a terrible blizzard that wiped out entire herds in the winter of 1886–87. With railroads now crisscrossing the West, settlers were pouring onto ranges where cattle had grazed. Under pressure from every angle, ranchers, as we've seen, began lashing out, massacring sheep in Colorado, burning out "nesters" and their barbed wire in Texas, and marking for death anyone they suspected of theft.

Even the northernmost of these conflicts had a Texas flavor. Ninety percent of the cattle in Montana and Wyoming had come up from Texas, as had most of the cowboys. Beset by rustlers, a Montana rancher named Granville Stuart gathered his Texans into a vigilante outfit called "Stuart's Stranglers," which shot or lynched two dozen or so accused rustlers. The campaign climaxed in 1884's Battle of Bates Point, where nine rustlers were killed after a siege in which the Stranglers burned their cabin and shot men as they ran out.

Wyoming had the worst of it. Ranchers there took things to an entirely new level. When theft first became an issue, cattlemen formed a trade group, the Wyoming Stock Growers Association, that met at the posh Cheyenne Club. The association hired range detectives, mostly former lawmen, to investigate suspected rustlers and pushed prosecutors to try them.* Proving cattle theft, though, turned out to be a legal challenge. All those settlers, meanwhile, brought an air of populist resentment, and for all the political influence ranchers wielded, Wyoming juries set more than a few accused rustlers free.

The flash point, when it came, was in sparsely populated Johnson County, in north-central Wyoming, southeast of the Bighorn Mountains. Streams cascaded from the heights to the grasslands below, creating probably the best grazing area in the state. Small ranchers and farmers, known in Wyoming as "grangers," thought so too, and by 1890 were so plentiful they assumed control of the government. The county became known among cattlemen as not only a haven for rustlers but, just as important, a place where no jury would convict a thief.

---

*The association's lead detective for years was a Texan named Frank Canton, a man said to be involved in any number of mysterious killings. Canton, who served as a scout during the 1892 Johnson County War, went on to a long career in law enforcement, much of it in Oklahoma. He died in 1927. Not until the 1970s would researchers discover that his real name was Josiah Horner and that he had been prosecuted for several bank robberies and the murder of a soldier in Texas during the 1870s, eventually escaping from a prison work crew. He fled north, reinventing himself as Frank Canton. The book to read is *Alias Frank Canton*, by Robert DeArment.

The trouble began in 1889, when the association, after announcing rewards to anyone who helped convict a rustler, prevailed on Johnson County prosecutors to bring a host of indictments. There were five trials that June and July, almost all of the men associated with a shady Texas-owned outfit known as the Hat brand. All five trials ended in acquittal. The association was outraged. Across the state, ranchers began murmuring about taking "justice" into their own hands.

Lingering tensions climaxed in March 1892, when the association, in one of the more extraordinary decisions in Old West history, decided to literally invade Johnson County. To raise its army, it dispatched a detective named Tom Smith to—where else—Texas, where he recruited a force of twenty-one paid gunmen. Once the county was conquered, this outfit had a list of thirty suspected rustlers to be killed, along with an irksome newspaper editor. When done, the association's death squads were to fan out across the state and kill another forty or so people. Fearing opposition from state militia units, the cattlemen secured the support of the acting governor, who wired militia commanders to take orders only from him.

In terms of harebrained American invasions, what would go down as the Johnson County War probably ranks with the Bay of Pigs as one of the dumbest. Still, it went ahead. The Texans arrived in Cheyenne on a special train on April 4; augmented by cattlemen, detectives, two reporters, and a surgeon, a force of fifty-two then took a second train to Casper. Horses were waiting, and on April 7, the group rode north into a sloppy spring snowstorm, bound for Johnson County.

The plan was to race to the county seat, Buffalo, and kill the marshal and the city council. But when the invaders stopped at a ranch south of town the next afternoon, a range detective rode in to say a group of rustlers led by the notorious Texan Nate Champion—one of several men newspapers had anointed "King of the Rustlers"—was at the KC Ranch, fourteen miles north. The group's leaders fell to arguing. The Texans insisted on sticking to their plans. In the end, though, the allure of killing Nate Champion was too great.

That night they surrounded the ranch, mortally wounding one rustler and capturing two visitors, leaving Champion in the house alone. He was besieged for several hours, and kept a journal throughout, one of the Old West's more plaintive. When he heard people splitting firewood, he realized they would burn him out. "I think I will make a break when night comes, if alive," he wrote. "Goodbye, boys, if I never see you again." When he burst from the back door, pistol blazing, they shot him to pieces. "Cattle thieves beware," they wrote on the note they pinned to his chest.

Afterward, they were heading into Buffalo when word came of a large force approaching, a massive sheriff's posse that may have included as many as two hundred men. The invading Texans, selecting discretion over valor, holed up at a place called the TA Ranch, where the posse besieged them for three days. One of the Texans managed to escape and got a message to the governor, who telegraphed the White House, trying to reach President Benjamin Harrison. Wyoming's two senators followed up, waking Harrison in bed. He sent in the Sixth Cavalry, which rescued the beleaguered Texans the next day. All were taken into custody, where they sat for months but were eventually freed.

The Johnson County War represents the high point of the violence cattlemen wrought in those years. Afterward, across the frontier, they mostly attempted to deal more discreetly with such things. Whether the war was a legitimate response to rampant criminality or a massive—and illegal—overreaction by cattlemen is still an open question.

THE MOST STORIED ASSASSIN OF THE OLD WEST, A SOLITARY FIGURE who took hazy roles in both the Pleasant Valley and Johnson County wars, was a man named Tom Horn. During the 1890s, despite well-regarded work in the Pinkerton service, the Spanish-American War, and Arizona's war with the Apache, he crossed over to become a roving killer for hire, targeting rustlers, sheepherders, and homesteaders for cattlemen in the Rockies. Once a coveted army scout and detective, he was ultimately done in by the inexplicable murder of a fourteen-year-old boy.

A big man for his day, a rangy six foot two, Horn grew up in a large, troubled Missouri family and, like so many before him, drifted west in his teens. He found work as a laborer, stage driver, and cowboy until settling in Arizona, where he worked for a series of ranchers in the early 1880s. Taking odd jobs with the army as well, he ended up chief of scouts in the final campaign against Geronimo in 1886, serving as interpreter when the renegade chief surrendered.

He used his earnings to buy a small ranch northeast of Tucson. Some say his deep hostility toward thieves resulted from the loss of his herd to rustlers, an incident that seems to have drained his savings. A rancher who knew him said Horn "was more down on thieves, and thievery than any man I have ever known."[1] Some say he was involved in one or more of the Pleasant Valley vigilante killings. Good with a gun, he supplemented his income taking jobs helping Arizona sheriffs and proved useful enough that one of them recommended him to the Pinkertons, who brought him to Denver in 1890.

There, sometimes working with the great range detective Charles Siringo, Horn chased train robbers across the frontier and caught a few. He was quiet, serious, and reliable, and his work drew strong reviews, the only blemish a bizarre 1891 arrest for bank robbery in Reno. It was apparently a case of mistaken identity; a judge found him innocent in a scant ten minutes. But it left Horn embittered. Friends later said his deep skepticism of the justice system was born there.

In 1892 the Pinkertons sent Horn into Wyoming to work for

cattlemen. Some say he was involved in a killing or two, or even the Johnson County invasion itself, but the evidence suggests that, at least initially, his work centered more on recruiting potential killers and on conventional detective work than on killing anyone himself. The pay was poor, and he soon quit. He went to work for the Wyoming Stock Growers Association.

This was the pinnacle of rustler paranoia in Wyoming. For a year or so, Horn kept to mainstream techniques to bring in any number of suspected rustlers. But almost all had charges dismissed or were found innocent after trials. This was the last straw for many ranchers—and for Horn. In 1895, convinced that even the most brazen rustlers would never be convicted in a Wyoming courtroom, Horn attended a meeting of the association at the Cheyenne Club. They didn't use the word "murder" or "killing." They didn't have to. Horn proposed doing "whatever is necessary" to rid the state of rustlers. At one point, he strode to the center of the room, cigar in hand. "Men," he said, "I have a system that never fails, when everything else has. Yours has!"

Some nodded. Others were startled. This was not Gold Rush California or postwar Texas. This was 1895; there were laws in place and, increasingly, a sentiment abroad in a maturing America, even in the West, that they should be enforced. "Collecting evidence is one thing," one cattleman protested, "assassination is another."

Summoned to a secret meeting with Wyoming's governor, Horn made the same proposal. When the governor blanched, Horn rose to leave, saying, "I presume that is about all you wanted to know."

Unable to secure official approval for his methods, Horn fell to making discreet arrangements with individual cattlemen. The first, it appears, was a rancher named John Coble, an erudite Pennsylvanian who managed the Iron Mountain Ranch Company near Laramie. When two men accused of rustling were found shot at their homes during August and September 1895, Horn was suspected. A grand jury looked into both killings but issued no indictments.

Because public outrage was so intense, the cattlemen decided to abandon such tactics for a time. Unwanted, Horn returned to Arizona, where he found work as a ranch foreman. He spent the next three years in a series of far-flung adventures, chasing train robbers on behalf of the Union Pacific and working as an army packer during the Spanish-American War. In Cuba he contracted yellow fever, which laid him up for months.

Rustling remained an issue in Colorado, and upon Horn's recovery, he went to work for a cattle company there. By this point, he was already a legend in the mountains, a Bergman-esque specter of Death; the mere sight of him caused fathers to duck behind barns and mothers to herd their children indoors. By the time he returned in 1900, though, he was showing signs of wear. He was drinking heavily, and when drunk, his reserve melted away. He became chatty, loud, and boastful, claiming he was the best shot in the West; the admissions he made in those years, large and small, all came while he was drinking.

He could also be quarrelsome, which led to trouble. Late one night in Denver, he insulted a boxer named Jack McKenna, who beat him senseless; Horn ended up in the hospital with a broken jaw and, for a time, was obliged to wear a full facial cast. After he started a brawl in Baggs, Wyoming, one Texas cowboy knocked him sprawling on his back. Another drew a knife and slashed him from his chest to his neck. He was still fighting, it's said, when he collapsed from loss of blood.

In Colorado, Horn's first assignment was in Brown's Park, where he was later suspected of killing two rustlers, both shot from a distance. Afterward, John Coble lured him back to Wyoming. His final chapter began there in 1901, when he became involved with two squabbling families near the town of Iron Mountain. Jim Miller and his wife owned cattle and their neighbors the Nickells owned sheep; the Millers constantly complained the sheep grazed on their land.

Horn, who was squiring a young schoolteacher rooming with the Millers, had been visiting the family for a while, taking the boys fishing at one point, when, on July 19, fourteen-year-old Willie Nickell was found shot to death outside his home. Two weeks later his father was shot and sixty to eighty of his sheep were found shot or clubbed to death. Jim Miller and two of his sons were arrested.

Six months later, in January 1902, a Texas-born deputy marshal named Joe LeFors, best known for his pursuit of Butch Cassidy's Wild Bunch, had a talk with Horn, ostensibly about a job. Horn was said to be addled after a long night's drinking; whatever his mental state, LeFors came away with what he termed Horn's confession to having killed Willie Nickell, with a rifle shot from three hundred yards. Why Horn would kill a teenage boy went unmentioned.

He was arrested the next day. His patron, the rancher John Coble, paid for his defense; dozens of other cattlemen chipped in, though it's said none minded the idea of Horn getting the gallows. He knew too much. He went to trial in October 1902, in Cheyenne, among curious crowds, in what the Denver papers termed a carnival atmosphere. It was national news. Other than his confession, which he recanted, the evidence was circumstantial. They found him guilty anyway, mostly, people said, because if he didn't kill Willie Nickell, he killed others. He stayed in jail for a year while his appeals were denied, during which time he wrote his autobiography, focusing on his early life. They hanged him in December 1903. Historians debate his guilt to this day.

TOM HORN REMAINS A FRONTIER LEGEND, WHILE AN EVEN MORE PRO-lific assassin has attracted far less notice. He was a dapper, Bible-reading Texan named "Deacon" Jim Miller. There are those who believe he may have killed more men than any other Old West gunman, more than Wes Hardin, Wyatt Earp, and Ben Thompson—combined. Miller claimed fifty-one, though his "record" might be asterisked, given that he seldom engaged in anything like an actual gunfight. He preferred killing by ambush, usually with a shotgun.

Death trailed Miller from an early age. Born in 1861 and raised by grandparents in Central Texas, it's been claimed he was detained for murdering them when he was all of eight years old, though there is no evidence he had a role in their deaths. Sent to a sister's, Miller clashed with her domineering husband. What happened there is documented. When still a teenager, he shotgunned his brother-in-law as he slept. He was sentenced to life in prison, but the verdict was overturned on a technicality. He went free.

By the mid-1880s Miller was working as a cowboy for Wes Hardin's cousin Mannen Clements, who had survived the Sutton-Taylor feud—and his Kansas confrontation with Wyatt Earp—to become a rancher of note in West Texas. The two became close; Miller eventually married Mannen's daughter Sallie. When Mannen ran for sheriff in 1887, the contest grew heated, and one of his opponents shot and killed him in the Senate Saloon in Ballinger. Not long after, the killer was felled by a shotgun blast as he rode home one night. He survived. Everyone said Jim Miller did it. In any case, he vanished for several years.

Rumors and lore aside, Miller only comes into focus in August 1890, when he rode into the far West Texas cattle town of Pecos. He was almost thirty. In later years, old-timers vividly recalled the day Miller appeared, a mysterious stranger in a black overcoat who turned heads riding a gray mare through the heart of the dusty town.

When he dismounted, took off his black Stetson, and stepped into the saloon, people got a better look. He was lean, with long legs, a bony face, and pale-blue eyes, though few noticed them; they were too busy studying the bulky coat he was wearing at the height of a Texas summer.

As the old-timers recalled it, a grimy range boss named Hearn approached Miller just as he was finishing a glass of water.

"That coat of yours," he quipped, "just naturally makes me sweat."

Miller made a face. "I don't like your smell," he said.

"Take it off," Hearn said.

"Go to hell," Miller said.

Hearn went for the .45 on his hip. By the time he drew it, Miller had an ivory-handled six-shooter pressed against his belly.

"Drop it," Miller said.[2]

He ordered Hearn to leave, and he did, riding away with a half dozen cowboys. A crowd of the curious filed in to take their place, including the young sheriff, a man named Bud Frazer. Frazer gingerly asked about the coat. Miller smiled and explained it was the gift of a late friend, a sheriff, who considered it lucky. Miller did too.

The newcomer came across as deferential and polite, a churchgoing man who didn't drink, smoke, or curse. Frazer was impressed. By day's end, he had pinned a deputy's badge on that big black coat.

From this point, Miller's career proceeds in two very different acts. The first is what might be Texas's greatest personal feud. It happened there in Pecos, a flyblown speck out toward New Mexico that sprang up around a rail depot in the early 1880s. Four hundred people called it home. Almost all were cattlemen or people they needed.

Miller slid easily into life there. He was, as promised, a regular at Sunday services, quiet and abstinent. He sent for Sallie Clements and they married. Despite some murmurs about his past, he and Sheriff Frazer proved a capable team, chasing off any number of rustlers preying on the herds. As the months wore on, in fact, Miller spent more and more time away from town chasing rustlers, which was fine, except that, as more than one rancher noted, he never seemed to catch any. Meanwhile, more and more cattle were disappearing.

At a town meeting, Miller was accused of theft. Politely, he denied it, and kept his job. Not long after, he took a prisoner to Fort Stockton and ended up shooting and killing him—while he was trying to escape, Miller insisted. When Sheriff Frazer heard he had in fact killed the prisoner because the man knew about some mules Miller had stolen, he fired him. The two men ran against each other for sheriff in 1892. Frazer won, but many refused to believe a churchgoing gentleman like Jim Miller could be all bad. He ended up being named city marshal.

Miller established his headquarters at his hotel, where he surrounded himself with a crew of hard cases, including Mannen Clements's son, Mannie. Ill will between the two factions grew, and at one point two of Miller's henchmen were overheard plotting Sheriff Frazer's murder. Soon after, the Texas Rangers arrested Miller and Clements on a charge of conspiracy to murder. The youngster who overheard the plot, Con Gibson, fled town, but word soon came back that one of Miller's men had found and killed him in a New Mexico saloon.

Which brought things to a head. One morning in April 1894, Miller was talking with a rancher outside his hotel when he noticed Frazer walking past—behind him. Miller ignored it. Frazer then walked past a second time, and a third. The rancher asked what was going on.

"Well, I don't know," Miller remarked. He turned around and suddenly Frazer was there, a pistol aimed at his midsection.

"Jim, you're a thief and a murderer!" he yelled. "Here's one for Con Gibson!"

The bullet struck Miller square in the chest—and then it fell to the ground, spent, as if it had hit an invisible force field.

As Miller reached for his own gun, Frazer's second round hit him in the right shoulder. Unable to draw with his right hand, Miller grabbed the gun with his left, but his shots went wild. Standing his ground, Frazer fired three more bullets into Miller's chest.

Miller, by all accounts, barely flinched.

Not until Frazer's sixth and final bullet struck Miller near the navel did Deacon Jim stumble and fall. When Frazer stalked off, Miller's pals emerged from the hotel and carried him inside. Only when they undressed him did anyone understand what had happened. Feeling around inside the coat Miller habitually wore, they found an iron plate sewn into the lining, covering his chest.

Miller lived, slowly recovered, and swore revenge. In the meantime, Frazer lost a bid for reelection and moved to New Mexico. In December 1894, when he returned to Pecos to settle the last of his affairs, Miller was waiting in front of the blacksmith's shop. If any words were spoken, no one recorded them. Frazer drew his gun and fired, hitting Miller in the leg and arm, but he still didn't know about the armored coat, and when his next shot, to the chest, had no effect, he was so disconcerted he turned and ran. Miller was left bleeding in the street. Frazer surrendered, and two years later, after a series of legal delays, was acquitted in a jury trial.

It all ended three months after that, in September 1896, when Miller, upon learning Frazer was returning to the area for a poker game, rented a room across from the saloon where he was to play. When Frazer arrived, Miller crossed the street, found an open doorway, and spying Frazer at the table with cards in his left hand, unloaded two barrels of a shotgun into his neck, nearly taking off his head.

Miller's trial, in a town west of Fort Worth, was front-page news across Texas. The jury hung. A second trial was held in January 1899. This time Miller was found not guilty, the jury finding that, given the extent of the feud, "he had done no worse than Frazer."[3]

Which made him a minor celebrity, one of the last notable killers in the state, a man whose skills some still found useful, which led to the second act of his career. It began in 1900, when he moved his family to Fort Worth. He began working as a gun for hire, an assassin available to kill just about anyone for a price, which reportedly began at a hundred and fifty dollars and went as high as two thousand.

Miller's clients appear to have been mostly Texas cattlemen battling rustlers and squabbling over range rights with farmers and the owners of sheep. His biographer puts the number of sheepherders Miller murdered at more than a dozen. Records indicate he shot and killed two men in Midland in 1902, two more in far West Texas, and two Mexicans he found butchering a stolen steer out near the New Mexico border.[4] He was said to have admitted to the assassination of a Lubbock farmer's attorney. Witnesses described seeing a man in a heavy black coat riding nearby at the time, probably the same shadowy figure who shot the attorney in the chest as he rode home one evening in a buggy. Afterward the figure rose from his hiding place in high weeds, strode over, and administered a coup de grâce.

Contract killing afforded Miller a plush life. In Fort Worth, he passed himself off as a businessman, sporting tailored suits, a diamond ring, and a diamond stud in his shirtfront. Most nights he could be found in an armchair among the cattlemen holding court at the elegant Delaware Hotel. On the side, he dabbled in livestock and real estate fraud. At one point, in late 1904, he sold several vacant lots to a friend named Frank Fore, who, sight unseen, resold them to buyers. When the lots' coordinates turned out to place them somewhere in the Gulf of Mexico, Fore threatened to go before a grand jury.

Miller prevented this by trailing Fore into a washroom off the Delaware's lobby, producing a handgun, and killing him with a single bullet. When people rushed in, they found Miller crouched over the dead man's body in tears, blubbering how inexplicable it was that his friend drew a gun on him. Miller turned himself in, and at the trial in 1905 two of his cattlemen friends claimed they witnessed the killing, which was, they insisted, self-defense. A jury acquitted him.

There were other killings in these years, including the shotgun murder of a deputy federal marshal that got Miller arrested in Oklahoma in 1906; the case never went to trial. For many, Miller's place in western history will always revolve around his role in the 1908 murder of Billy the Kid's killer, Pat Garrett. Since Billy's death, Garrett had served as a Texas Ranger, a New Mexico sheriff, and head of the customs office in El Paso. None of it made him much money. Though still a public figure—and an occasional friend of President Teddy Roosevelt—he was deeply in debt. In 1906, now in his mid-fifties, he was forced to sell his possessions to settle debts and lease out the small ranch he owned twenty miles outside Las Cruces. He washed up, penniless, in El Paso, living with a prostitute.

Garrett's ranch was on land coveted by cattlemen, some of whom despised him for his role in an 1890s-era murder probe in which two ranchers were put on trial and acquitted. All of which fueled the conspiracy theories that spread after Garrett was shot and killed while riding in a wagon outside Las Cruces on February 29, 1908. The man who ran to the sheriff and confessed, Wayne Brazel, was leasing Garrett's spread; they'd argued over the sale of some goats.

Some say Brazel actually did it; some say he falsely confessed, for cattlemen's cash, to cover up the involvement of the real killer, Jim Miller. Miller had been seen around Las Cruces on the morning of the killing and through an intermediary had reached out to Garrett about grazing cattle on his land. An investigation discovered a spot overlooking the crime scene with horse droppings and two spent Winchester shells, suggesting Garrett had been killed in an ambush. Whatever happened, Wayne Brazel was inexplicably acquitted at his trial. No evidence of Miller's involvement was introduced, but many believe it was his hand on the trigger that morning.

Miller's final job brought him to a rough Oklahoma town, Ada, population four thousand or so, where two factions of cattlemen had been feuding for years. He was hired to kill a leading citizen named Angus A. Bobbitt by two rivals Bobbitt had chased out of town. As his target rode home in a buggy one cold February evening, Miller hid among trees alongside his route, then on Bobbitt's approach, laid a shotgun through the crotch of an elm and fired twice. Both blasts struck home. "Oh God," Bobbitt cried, toppling from the wagon.

A neighbor who witnessed the killing saw the assassin gallop away. The next morning, a posse followed the shadowy figure's trail twenty miles to a lonely farm, whose young owner denied knowing anything until someone punched him in the face, at which point he confessed the horse had been ridden by his uncle, Jim Miller. A month later, a pair of Texas deputies arrested Miller in another farmhouse, north of Fort Worth. He went peaceably, surrendering his two revolvers, his Winchester, and a shotgun in an oilcloth case.

He was returned to Ada and placed in jail. By the time he was indicted two weeks later, the cattlemen who had paid him two thousand dollars for the killing sat slumped in cells beside him. The cowardly ambush killing had stirred the townspeople, but as a trial date approached, Miller seemed without a care. He dressed in his finest white shirts, shaved twice daily, ordered porterhouse steaks from a restaurant, and gave the jailer five-dollar tips.

They came for Miller and the others after midnight on April 19, 1909, forty or so masked men who overpowered a pair of jailers, secured the prisoners, and dragged them down an alley to a barn. They looped ropes over the low rafters and hanged the cattlemen one by one as Miller watched. When his time came, they urged him to confess. He wouldn't. He had seen more death than anyone there and was determined to meet his with grace. He removed his ring and asked for it to be sent to his wife. The diamond pin he set aside for a kindly jailer.

"Just let the record show that I've killed fifty-one men," Miller announced. Then he asked for his hat. When it was jammed onto his head, he actually laughed. His last words were "Let 'er rip!"

A minute later Jim Miller's quivering body was hanging alongside the others; a photo of four corpses dangling inside the darkened barn remains an evocative image of late frontier life. At one point, a man stepped forward and placed the trademark black coat back onto Miller's shoulders. "It won't help him now," he said.[5]

CHAPTER EIGHTEEN

Death Alley

Oklahoma, 1891 to 1896

As a theater of gunfighter violence, Oklahoma rarely gets much respect. Part of it is geography. By the time noted outlaws emerged there in the 1890s, the frontier had moved on. Oklahoma was poor, and its tired gullies and caves weren't much to look at, not when compared with the dramatic vistas of Wyoming or New Mexico. And as Indian Territory for a half century, it had long been seen as a down-market haven for mangy fugitives, bootleggers, and thieves; its violence didn't strike outsiders as all that new or noteworthy. It had the scent of a backwater, and most of its gunmen were known only to other Oklahomans.

Its marquee outlaws appeared only after settlers were admitted in the great Land Rush of 1889, which gave us modern Oklahoma City and split the territory in half, with the remaining tribal lands to the east. But the "boomers" at least generated more money than Native Americans had, prompting banks and trains to store and move it. Many of the men who tried to steal that money were long regarded within the state—with its deep well of populism and admiration of "social outlaws"—as good-hearted cowboys driven to crime by lean times in the cattle industry.

The late Glenn Shirley, the dean of Oklahoma western writers, always guffawed at this kind of nonsense. One of my favorite quotes in his books comes from an old-timer remembering the state's badmen in 1939: "They were lousy loafers . . . who refused to do their share of the back-breaking labor of pioneering, scum of the civilization that came to the far outposts to tame the wilderness. They lived by stealing from those who did the real work, murdering them if they resisted."[1]

Any discussion of Oklahoma gunfighters begins and pretty much ends with the four Dalton brothers. Their exploits have spawned any number of novels and biographies, three different Westerns starring Randolph Scott, and a song by the Eagles.* The only Oklahoma gunfighters to compare were the lawmen who helped end their reigns and those of many others—Chris Madsen, Bill Tilghman, and Heck Thomas, the vaunted "Three Guardsmen."

The Daltons weren't an especially likable bunch. They hailed from western Missouri, Jesse James country, moved to Kansas, then to Oklahoma during the rush, before finally settling in Coffeyville, in southeast Kansas. The father, Lewis, described as lazy and mean, tried farming, ran a bar, and was known for little else when he dropped dead in 1890. His wife happened to be Cole Younger's aunt, making her sixteen children cousins to the Youngers. Thirteen made it to adulthood. One lived to 1964. Four became outlaws.

Two led the way. Blue-eyed and blond, barely twenty at his father's death, the eighth child, Bob, would emerge as the gang's restless leader,

---

*An undistinguished ballad sung by Don Henley, "Doolin-Dalton" actually references a successor gang also known as the Wild Bunch. It appears on the band's second album, during its mercifully brief "gunfighter" period, the result of a photo book of western gunmen the singer Jackson Browne showed them. The worst line of the song may be "Watch 'em duelin', Doolin-Dalton."

its planner, a dreamer, and, sad to say, probably not the sharpest knife in the drawer. He was easily the best gunman in the family, though, renowned for his skill at firing a Winchester from the hip. Eight years older, the fifth child, brawny, jug-eared Grat, comes off as a nasty brute; Glenn Shirley tells a heartbreaking story of him stopping a Black boy on the street in Tulsa, placing an apple on his head, and as the poor child shivered in fright, shooting it off.

Their story begins when an older brother, Frank, a deputy U.S. marshal, was shot and killed trying to arrest bootleggers in Oklahoma in 1887. Grat replaced him, hiring Bob as a posseman; a year later, both took marshal jobs in Wichita, Bob moonlighting in the Osage Nation police force. It didn't end well. Bob quit in a dispute over pay. Grat was canned after the incident in Tulsa. Both, it's clear, were left with a deep, lasting grudge against the authorities.

After rumors spread that they were stealing horses—Grat was briefly arrested—the two grabbed their adoring kid brother Emmett, a cowboy, and headed to California, where they looked in on yet another brother, Bill, a farmer outside San Luis Obispo. It's here the Daltons attempted their first robbery. On February 6, 1891, two masked men—almost certainly Grat and Emmett—stopped and tried to rob a train north of Bakersfield; when the clerk ran off with keys to the safe, they killed the brakeman in frustration. Lawmen picked up their trail and arrested Grat, who drew a twenty-year sentence at Folsom.

Warrants went out for his brothers too. Bob and Emmett fled east, reaching their mother's new home northwest of Oklahoma City in late April 1891. The law was tipped within hours. The two brothers lit out for the rough borderlands of the Indian Territory sometimes called Hell's Fringe. On their way, they stole some horses; when the owners formed a posse and pursued them, Bob and Emmett ambushed them, killing a man. Overnight, they became two of Oklahoma's most wanted killers.

Thus was the Dalton Gang born. Within days, they added their first new members, two of Emmett's cowboy pals, George "Bitter Creek" Newcomb, nicknamed after a lyric he habitually sang, and "Black-Faced Charley" Bryant, a thin Texas killer named for a powder burn on his left cheek and, thanks to a perpetual fever that left him Doc Holliday pale, a cheerful death wish. "Me," he once quipped, "I want to get killed—in one hell-firin' minute of smoking action!"[2]

A through line of the Dalton story is the maturation of frontier law enforcement. The kind of corrupt or bumbling types who pursued Billy the Kid and Jesse James were being replaced by upright, reliable men, including hardworking federal marshals. In those first days, in fact, the fledgling gang attracted one of the most dogged, a lawman who would become its Javert, a forty-one-year-old former Texas Ranger named Henry Andrew "Heck" Thomas.

His first encounter with the gang conjures up one of those scenes you see so often in movies that rarely happened in life. On May 7, 1891, Thomas and two trackers followed a trail of four horses to the Arkansas River. He raised his field glasses, gazing across the water. He felt they were close. And they were, apparently. Years later, Emmett Dalton told how the outlaws lay in wait across the river, so near they could see the possemen's lips move. But the other side of the river was beyond his jurisdiction, and Thomas, a stickler, would go no farther. The Daltons hooted when he and his men rode off.

This kind of intrepid pursuit incensed Bob Dalton. Already he was dreaming big, imagining the huge score they could use to fund a flight to South America, a fantasy that crowded the mind of more than one late-century outlaw. But the job they pulled just two nights after the Thomas encounter was pure spite, a way of lashing out at their pursuers. Bandannas across their faces, they boarded a Santa Fe train when it stopped at the lonely station at Wharton, today's Perry, in north-central Oklahoma. Corralling the conductor and brakeman, they stepped to the express car and knocked on its door. The clerk, Emmett said later, opened it, asking, "What's up?" Bob pushed into the car and forced him—with a gunshot at his feet—to open the two safes. The gang rode off with maybe $1,750, barely $400 a man, a pittance.*

Heck Thomas was in the area within hours, and for the next forty days combed the state in a search spurred by rewards posted by the Santa Fe Railroad, Wells Fargo, and the state of California; some called it the most intensive in territorial history. The Daltons hid out at a pal's ranch in remote northwest Oklahoma. There, on a high bluff obscured by timber, they excavated an eighteen-foot dugout—a man-made cave—camouflaged the entrance with brush, and brought in bunks and a stove. They spent the entire summer there, cowboying on the ranch to pay their way.

By August they had begun venturing out, which is when Charley Bryant was felled by one of his fevers; in the absence of anything like a hospital, a doctor in Hennessey installed him at the Rock Island Hotel, a Winchester and pistol at his side. Tipped off, a squat, blond marshal named Ed Short surprised and arrested him. The jail was too flimsy to hold off the Daltons, so Short chose to take his prisoner via train the next day, August 23, to Wichita, 150 miles north.

All went well until they neared the town of Waukomis, when Short spied riders in the distance. Handing his pistol to a young clerk to cover the prisoner, Short took his Winchester and stepped outside onto a platform to study the approaching riders. The clerk, not the

---

*One of the Dalton Gang's enduring mysteries centers on a supposed female informant, Bob Dalton's girlfriend, a woman his brother Emmett, in a late-life memoir, named "Eugenia Moore." According to Emmett, Moore supplied the gang with information about train shipments. If such an informant existed, her name was not Eugenia Moore; no such person has ever been found. It's been speculated she was actually a telegraph operator or an express agent. Some say she was actually Charley Bryant's onetime girlfriend, Daisy Bryant. Others have floated the idea she was Flora Quick, aka Tom King, a cross-dressing madam who may have dabbled in horse thievery. Glenn Shirley argued it's all nonsense, that Emmett made up the story to obscure the names of actual informants who were still alive, in all likelihood one or two of the gang's relatives. This makes sense to me.

brightest bulb, slid the gun into one of those pigeonholes used for storing letters.

In a flash, Bryant, though manacled, leaped from his seat and grabbed it. Ordering the clerk and a conductor to freeze, he opened the door onto the platform where Short stood. When the marshal, perched maybe five feet away, turned, Bryant shot him over the heart. Though dying, Short raised his rifle to his hip and fired into Bryant. Bryant fired. Short fired. Bryant Short Bryant Short Bryant.

It was like something out of Sergio Leone or *Red Dead Redemption*. Finally, riddled with bullets, both men fell. "The damn bastard got me" were Short's last words. "But I got him first." As the train coasted to a stop, the two men lay side by side, very dead. Bryant had finally gotten his "one hell-firin' minute of smoking action."

From his distant man cave, Bob pressed on. He replaced Bryant with four new men, all Emmett's cowboy pals, including one whose fame would in time rival his own, a quiet Arkansan named Bill Doolin. Thus reinforced, the gang fell upon a train at a water stop outside Wagoner, in eastern Oklahoma, on September 15. Two shots into the express car persuaded a clerk to hand over its contents, maybe twenty-five hundred dollars, less than four hundred dollars a man.

Afterward, Bob stunned the others by announcing he was quitting; he took Emmett and withdrew to their cave, all but breaking up the gang. It's not entirely clear why. There's been suggestions over the years that the others had disagreed on how to divide the loot, and that Bob ruled them undependable. Maybe. Maybe Bob decided he had enough to make it to South America. More likely, the toll of life as a hunted fugitive was wearing on him, and before making a momentous decision about South America, he wanted to talk to his brother Grat, who, as it happened, had suddenly become available to chat. On September 18, Grat and two prisoners in a California jail loosened bolts on their cell doors, ducked out a window, and vanished.

Bob spent the winter awaiting his return. It took eight months, but in April 1892, after a marathon ride across mountain, desert, and plains, Grat finally made it home. He was seething with anger. Screw South America, Grat snarled. They needed revenge.

So was born the Dalton Gang 2.0, what a music critic might call its classic lineup: the three Daltons, along with Doolin, Newcomb, and two others. Hearing rumors of a seventy-thousand-dollar cash shipment, it made its debut on June 1, at Red Rock, in north-central Oklahoma. The train pulled to a stop at ten thirty, right on time. As the story goes, they were ready to move in when Bob stopped them. One of the passenger cars was strangely dark. There were rumors the railroads had begun carrying carloads of armed marshals. Wary, Bob let the train go. "We just stood here like a bunch of old women and let all that money get away!" Grat blurted.[3]

Moments later a second train could be seen approaching. "I thought so," Bob supposedly said. "It's the one we want." When it stopped, they emerged, took the conductor and brakeman hostage, and marched them to the express car. A clerk and a guard refused them entrance. The gang opened fire, getting off more than sixty shots; after a few more, they relented. The safe ended up holding two thousand dollars. The big money they expected had apparently been aboard the first train.

Train robberies were still comparatively rare, at least in Oklahoma, and another massive manhunt ensued. At least five posses rode, one led by Heck Thomas; another hit the ranch in northwest Oklahoma where Bob and Emmett had built their man cave. The Daltons, though, had moved to the far end of the state. On the night of July 14, they hit a train stopped at Adair, near the Arkansas border.

Everything went smoothly until they stood outside the express car, the conductor and brakeman beside them. Suddenly, from down the train, shots rang out. The Daltons realized that this train actually did contain a carload of armed lawmen and guards, either eight or thirteen, depending on the account. Only three guards proved brave enough to engage, jumping from the train and firing from behind a coal shed. An energetic gunfight broke out as gang members, ducking behind their two hostages, fired back.

Some two hundred shots were exchanged. The lawmen were at a disadvantage, unable to fire for long without endangering the men the Daltons used as human shields. All three were wounded. A local doctor, watching from outside a drugstore, was struck by a stray bullet and killed. The gang made off with something like seventeen thousand dollars, its first strong take, but what goodwill it enjoyed among Oklahomans all but evaporated with the death of a bystander.

Adair thrust the Daltons onto front pages around the country for the first time, one or two accounts comparing them to the James Gang. Murder warrants were issued. The railroads declared war, offering a gobsmacking five-thousand-dollar reward for each man. Heck Thomas was summoned to Kansas City, where eight railroads and three express companies banded together to fund not a posse, but something like a modern task force, based outside Tulsa, complete with new weapons, detectives, and scouts who wouldn't go home until the Daltons were put down for good.

It's often suggested all this attention went to Bob Dalton's head. The audacious plan he now devised as the gang darted between hideouts suggested it had; Bob said more than once it was something even Jesse James had never done. But his second motivation, as Emmett explained later, was to finally make that huge final score, the one that could get them to South America. Heck Thomas was closing in; Emmett called him their "nemesis." Time was running out.

Two banks. They would rob two banks at once. And they would do it in their hometown, Coffeyville. The others thought he was nuts and said so. But Bob insisted. Worse, only five of them would go; Doolin and the others he deemed unreliable. When his brothers said they would be recognized, Bob said not to worry. As always, he had a plan. At some point, probably on one of those final cool mornings in October 1892, the three Daltons sat down and shaved. It was a decision that would seal their doom.

THE DALTONS WERE DONE IN BY, OF ALL THINGS, FAKE BEARDS. THEY were wearing them that morning when they rode into Coffeyville, trotting down the dirt road that became Eighth Street, a cloud of dust behind them, before slipping down an alley that led to the plaza beside the two banks. They hitched their horses to a fence.

Bob and Emmett, we're told, wore jet-black fake beards, Grat a fake mustache and sideburns.

A grocer named Alex McKenna, standing outside his store at the mouth of the alley, noticed the disguises the moment the men emerged onto the plaza. Puzzled, McKenna watched, then followed, as the five, Winchesters at their sides, broke into a trot. Three of them—Grat and two of the gang's regulars, the cowboys Bill Powers and Dick "Texas Jack" Broadwell—ducked into the C. M. Condon Bank on the plaza's north side. Bob and Emmett headed on across a side street to the First National Bank.

Peering inside the Condon Bank, McKenna saw Grat pointing his rifle at a teller. Suddenly he put it all together. "The Daltons are robbing the bank!" he yelled. Within seconds, shouts echoed through the busy streets: "They're robbing the bank!"

Did Grat hear the shouts? When a cashier told him the vault was on a time lock that wouldn't release until 9:45, he glanced at a wall clock. "That's only three minutes," he murmured. "We can wait." It was yet another bad decision. Had he bothered to try the vault door, he would've realized it was already unlocked—the same mistake Jesse James had made at Northfield. The bankers were buying time.

All across town men were snatching up guns and running into the streets. A minute or two later, as Grat's group waited, there was the sound of a gunshot from outside and the tinkling of glass. As everyone inside the bank ducked, two more shots followed. One struck Broadwell in the arm. "I'm hit," he said coolly, before turning to the cashiers. "You'd better get under the counter, or you might get killed by some of those people."[4]

Once the safe was opened, they gathered sacks of money. Outside, the firing was intensifying. Grat asked if there was a back door. Carrying the bags in one hand and rifles in the other, the three robbers hustled out, turned left, and ran for the alley.

As they did, Bob and Emmett were finishing up at First National.* It had gone easily, but as they went to leave, pushing two cashiers in front of them, they were driven back by gunfire. "Let us out the back way!" Bob shouted. When a cashier opened it, they too scrambled out the rear, where they came face-to-face with a teenager named Lucius Baldwin running up. He was holding a revolver.

"Stop!" Bob hollered.

The boy froze. Bob shot him through the chest.

Now forced to circle around a half dozen or more buildings, the two Daltons had a much longer path to the horses than Grat's trio, four or five full blocks. But they had something the others didn't: Bob Dalton's Winchester. Emmett was carrying sacks containing eleven thousand dollars in cash, Bob his rifle, when they returned to Union Street, down from the bank's front door. There, a shoemaker named George Cubine spotted them and fired a shot, missing. Bob shot back. Cubine fell dead.

An elderly man named Charles Brown picked up his gun. Bob shot

---

*As it happened, Bob knew one of the bankers. He addressed him by name. So much for his disguise.

and killed him too. The brothers crossed the street, their eyes still on the bank. Bob saw a cashier raise a rifle. It was a long shot, seventy-five yards. Firing from the hip, Bob put a bullet through the man's cheek. He lived. Bob had killed three men in ninety seconds.

The two brothers ran safely down Eighth Street, Bob firing a shot or two every few steps, then turned left down a narrow alley that dead-ended into the one where the horses waited. At the intersection, they ran into Grat's group stumbling forward, Powers and Broadwell already bleeding from mortal wounds. On the far side of the plaza, men outside a hardware store were firing directly down the alley. Others fired from windows. Another group burst into the alley farther down.

It was a slaughter. They call it "Death Alley" to this day. Grat and Powers died making a stand in a shed. Broadwell crawled to a horse but was hit atop it; after it rode off, his body would be found outside town. Bob backed down the alley, covering Emmett, but when a bullet hit him in the belly, he lurched, landing atop a pile of stones. Rising, he took several more steps, getting off a shot or two, before being struck in the chest. He fell, rolling onto his back.

Only Emmett was able to mount and manage a horse, but, shot through the arm and hip, he noticed Bob was down and rode to him, extending an arm his brother could no longer see. As he did, a barber stepped up and shot him flush in the back with both barrels of a shotgun. He fell.

It was the bloodiest robbery in Old West history: eight men dead in all. Of the gang, only Emmett survived, if barely. Afterward people stood Grat and Bob's dead bodies upright and took photographs alongside them, a morbid joke; Grat is still wearing his mustache.

At its end, the Dalton Gang had operated for all of seventeen months, mounting five disappointing robberies and a single lucrative one, killing a half dozen men in the process, then met their fates in an impressive display of hubris. So how to explain its fame? Part of it was the intensity of the news coverage, those comparisons to the James Gang. Part of it was they were siblings: from the Jameses and the Earps to *The Godfather*, Americans have long prized crime stories that center on family. It makes the story more accessible, their fates a little sadder.

But the real reason, I suspect, is the same one that ensured Wyatt Earp's fame: longevity. Emmett Dalton drew a life sentence, proved a model prisoner, and was pardoned after fourteen years. He went on the lecture circuit, sometimes appearing alongside "Devil Anse" Hatfield, the West Virginia feudist, and wrote and appeared in a silent movie or two. His key contribution, arriving amid the public's new fascination with Old West figures, was a 1931 book, *When the Daltons Rode*, clear-eyed and neo-factual, a cut above much of the claptrap that emerged during the 1920s. It made the Daltons a thing all over again. Hollywood did the rest. Emmett died in 1937, three years before the first Randolph Scott movie.

WAITING IN A FIELD OUTSIDE COFFEYVILLE THAT MORNING WITH FRESH horses stood Bill Doolin and a fourth Dalton brother, Bill, back from California. Grief-stricken, Bill made a ruckus afterward, threatening to sue over a horse and cash supposedly stolen from his brothers. When everyone laughed, Bill accepted Doolin's invitation to form a successor gang. Some call it the Doolin–Dalton Gang, others the Wild Bunch. Thirty-four-year-old Bill Doolin was its leader.

A veteran cowboy in Kansas and Oklahoma, Doolin was tall and thin, with a bushy mustache and a thoughtful manner that drew people to him; he didn't suffer fools. His decision to join the Daltons, it's said, had come after he was blamed for a gunfight at a party in Coffeyville. Some say Doolin and Dalton first rode with the outlaw Henry Starr. Doubtful. They were probably among the four bandits who robbed a cash-free Missouri Pacific train west of Coffeyville a week after the shoot-out; they made off with less than a hundred dollars. Three weeks later, Doolin was positively identified as one of three men who robbed the bank at Spearville, east of Dodge City. A cautious, professional trio, they were in and out in three minutes, making off with $1,700, leaving far more in a vault.*

And then they went quiet for a full eight months. Doolin used the time to recruit a series of men with outstanding nicknames, including Bill Blake, aka Tulsa Jack, and Dan Clifton, aka Dynamite Dick. He also courted and married a woman named Edith Ellsworth, who hailed from the hamlet of Ingalls, northeast of the territorial capital, Guthrie, in northern Oklahoma. Ingalls became the gang's headquarters, small enough, maybe two hundred people, that the gang easily cowed its citizenry. Doolin lived in a nearby cave, it's said, until marrying, when his wife, I'm guessing, insisted on an upgrade.

The revamped gang's first robbery was a train they stopped outside Cimarron, Kansas, north of Dodge City, late one night in June 1893; five of them made off with either thirteen thousand dollars or one thousand dollars, depending on who you believe. As the outlaws rode south, at least two posses raced to cut them off. When one stumbled on their camp, a running long-range gunfight ensued. Someone— either the marshal Chris Madsen or, more likely, a sheriff—fired a bullet that struck Doolin in the left heel, tearing through his foot. The outlaws escaped. Doolin recuperated at the ranch that had housed the Daltons' man cave.

All of this served as prelude to the centerpiece of the Doolin–Dalton saga, an event second only to Coffeyville as a defining moment of Oklahoma outlawry: the Battle of Ingalls. After the territory's new U.S. marshal, Evett Nix, caught wind of the gang's presence in

---

*One of the robbers believed to be at Spearville, an Oklahoma kid named Ol Yantis, was cornered and killed by a sheriff not long after.

the town, he sent in men undercover to assess the situation. One, Orrington "Red" Lucas, set up shop as a fishmonger, scribbling descriptions of Doolin, Dalton, and their men after selling them catfish. By late summer, they were ready to move in. On August 31, two covered wagons containing thirteen federal marshals and deputies left for Ingalls, one from Guthrie, one from Stillwater. The gang was living at the town's unfinished three-story hotel. The plan was to surround the hotel at midnight, but one of the wagons was delayed, forcing everyone to convene and devise a plan B the next morning.

Red Lucas went into town at nine, returning to say that six of the gang, including Doolin and Dalton, had begun day drinking at Ransom's Saloon. The marshal in charge, John Hixon, was growing nervous. He sent for more men. A posse of eleven gathered at Stillwater, promising to arrive later that day. In the meantime, Hixon decided to surround the town, cutting off escape routes. Bad move.

Rather than take up positions outside town, a deputy named Dick Speed rode into it, inexplicably striding into a feed barn and announcing he was a federal officer. At this point, one gang member, Bitter Creek Newcomb, rode up, curious. Speed asked a teenager who he was. When the boy pointed, Newcomb, no fool, raised his rifle. Speed fired first, his bullet hitting Newcomb's gun and ricocheting into his leg. Newcomb whirled and rode away, disappearing into the brush south of town.

Within moments, gunfire erupted across Ingalls, the marshals shooting as they rushed in, Doolin and company firing from the saloon. The gang, though, had a secret weapon, a Missouri kid named Roy Daugherty, known of course as "Arkansas Tom," who was sleeping on an upper floor of the hotel. At the sound of shots, he grabbed a Winchester, rolled to a window, and fired at Deputy Speed, killing him. From his high perch, Arkansas Tom was a sniper commanding the whole town.

Intermittent fire continued as the remaining marshals crept into position around the saloon. When John Hixon called for the gang to surrender, Doolin shouted, "Go to hell!" The marshals opened fire, dozens of bullets ripping through the rickety bar. Though unhit, Doolin saw they couldn't take much more. They were surrounded.

The horses were in a stable across the street. Dalton ran first, followed by the rest; none were hit. As they saddled up, the lawmen took up new positions to target the stable. When they emerged from cover, Arkansas Tom took aim. A deputy fell, a bullet in his bowels.

Suddenly the stable doors opened. All six outlaws emerged, whipping their mounts. Bill Dalton's horse was hit in the jaw. As the others raced away, Dalton struggled to control it, making it seventy-five yards down a lane before it fell. When he rolled over a grass embankment, a deputy named Lafe Shadley ran up, thinking he had killed him. One of Arkansas Tom's shots hit him in the hip. Shadley staggered into a private home, where a panicky woman ordered him out. He had taken only a few steps into the yard when another bullet struck and killed him, fired by either Bill Dalton or Arkansas Tom.

By this point, the other outlaws had stopped, firing back into town to cover Dalton's escape. Bat Masterson's brother Jim was among the lawmen that day. He was the last to have a shot at the fleeing outlaws. When Dalton reached the others, jumping up behind Tulsa Jack, Jim took aim, only to realize he was out of ammunition.

The gang rode off, their injuries minor. The weary marshals, three of their number dead or dying, mounted no pursuit. They coaxed Arkansas Tom down and took him to Guthrie. When rumors swept town that Doolin and Dalton were planning to attack and rescue him, Heck Thomas helmed a battalion of forty lawmen who stood guard for three days. The gang never appeared. The territory was left in an uproar. Arkansas Tom drew a fifty-year sentence.

The rest of the story bears an air of anticlimax. The gang managed to pull off several more robberies, a bank in Woodward, Oklahoma, another in Pawnee, but at some point, they stopped functioning as a group. Dalton dipped into East Texas to rob a bank on his own. Slowly, buoyed by huge rewards, the Three Guardsmen—Heck Thomas, Bill Tilghman, and Chris Madsen—closed in. In June 1894 Dalton was tracked to a farmhouse outside Ardmore. He jumped out a window and ran. The posse opened fire. They say Bill died with the hint of a smile on his face.

Bounty hunters shot and killed Newcomb and another gang member in May 1895, Tulsa Jack around the same time. Chris Madsen shot and killed Dynamite Dick a year later. Doolin was the last of the gang at large.* He spent much of 1895 hiding on a ranch in New Mexico. By then, he was tired of running. Three times, we are told, he reached out to authorities with offers to surrender in return for an abbreviated prison sentence. These offers were rejected.

Late in 1895 he returned and took his wife and their infant son into Kansas, apparently to visit relatives. Bill Tilghman had been watching the wife off and on and, realizing she had disappeared, tracked her to the town of Burden. Doolin was nowhere to be seen, but Tilghman found a letter she had posted to Eureka Springs, Arkansas.

It was his foot, the one where he took a bullet. The pain never went away. He limped. Doolin went to Eureka Springs to take the waters. Sad-eyed and earnest, Tilghman was a veteran officer who had run the Dodge City police for years after Wyatt Earp left. He stumbled on Doolin the day he arrived, January 15, 1896, spotting him across the crowded waiting room in a bathhouse, reading a newspaper. Tilghman introduced himself. Doolin tried to brush him off, then went for his gun. Tilghman grabbed his hand. In the end, he went quietly.†

---

*The last to fall was technically a minor member named "Little Dick" West, killed by marshals working under Chris Madsen in 1898.

†Tilghman was a longtime lawman who began his career as one of Bat Masterson's deputies

Two thousand people turned out to view their return to Guthrie. Doolin proved an easy and amiable interview subject, telling reporters with a smile how it was all a mix-up. Five months later, in June 1896, he and a group of prisoners overpowered a guard, grabbed his pistol, and with a dozen others snatched up clothes and dashed from the jail.

Heck Thomas was soon on his trail. In the end, unable to resist visits to his wife and son, Doolin wasn't that hard to find. Late one night in August, they spied him outside his father-in-law's in Lawton, a wagon already packed for the family's departure. Doolin was out for a walk holding a Winchester, apparently trying to shoo off some unruly children, when Thomas and a half dozen others sprang from cover and ordered him to throw up his hands. Doolin raised his rifle and fired. Thomas's shotgun was among the guns that brought him down.

It was the end of an era, but the beginning of one as well. Oklahoma outlaws would remain active into the 1930s. Several were among the few to bridge the horseback and modern ages of crime. Henry Starr is said to be the first American to rob a bank using an automobile, in 1921. During the Depression, criminals such as Tulsa's Barker Gang, Alvin Karpis, Wilber Underhill ("the Tri-State Terror"), and Pretty Boy Floyd would make national headlines, reviving the state's troubled legacy. But that's a story for another book.

---

in Dodge City. Like Emmett Dalton, he joined the line of Oklahoma gunmen who hit the lecture circuit and made silent movies during the 1910s. Returning to the law at the age of seventy, he was shot and killed by a corrupt prohibition agent in 1924. His body lay in state in the Oklahoma capitol rotunda; two governors served among his pallbearers.

CHAPTER NINETEEN

The Outlaw Trail

Butch Cassidy in the Gloaming

The Texas longhorns that flooded into Colorado, Wyoming, Montana, and parts of Utah and Idaho from the 1870s turned the Mountain West into the final province of the Cattle Kingdom, albeit one where any Texas influence was less pronounced.* Plenty of Lone Star ranchers and cowboys found new northern homes in these years, but by and large, after the initial shock of a "Texas invasion," the livestock they brought along proved more influential than their violent customs.

Cattle, though, introduced a broad swath of changes. From southern Utah to the Canadian border—and actually into Alberta—ranches supervised and sometimes owned by Texans sprang up on land whose only occupants had been Native American tribes and the odd prospector and trapper. But as Texas cattlemen learned in Arizona and New Mexico, moving all those cows into the wilderness, especially one

---

*Texas cattle and cattlemen actually began moving in numbers into Colorado in the 1860s. Among the important early arrivals was John Hittson, the rancher who had "invaded" New Mexico.

lined by remote mountain trails and valleys, was an invitation to thieves. Rustling proved not only a plague but a kind of gateway crime for any number of errant cowboys who graduated from branding unmarked "mavericks" and livestock theft to transform the region into a hot spot for the most lucrative frontier crime of all: train robbery.

By the 1890s several had formed loosely knit gangs whose most desperate—i.e., wanted—members found refuge in the most challenging, hard-to-reach terrain left on the frontier, a series of isolated, easily defensible hideouts astride the spine of the Rockies. It came to be known as the Outlaw Trail. Three are most notable. The northernmost, the Hole-in-the-Wall valley in north-central Wyoming, hid behind an immense wall of red sandstone, its entrance wide enough for maybe a wagon, with a second, narrower aperture barely wide enough for a man on a horse. It's often said one gunman with enough bullets could hold off a battalion there.

The second was Brown's Hole, a thirty-mile valley at the intersection of Wyoming, Colorado, and Utah; bisected by the Green River, it could be entered only by a single steep trail. The third and southernmost, Robbers' Roost, was a sunblasted desert plateau in southeastern Utah reachable only by trails that wound across fifty miles of waterless desolation. According to Charles Kelly's classic 1938 history *The Outlaw Trail*, the Roost was so remote that outlaws only began using it around 1883.[1] By the 1890s, of the handful who dared live there, almost all were Texas-born rustlers, fugitives, or both. They lived in caves and a topple-down cabin or three.

The man who made these strongholds famous, who probably trailed only Jesse James as the era's savviest criminal, was the prince of Mountain West outlaws, a charming Utah cowboy with close-set eyes and a prominent jaw. He could've passed for a dreamy college linebacker. Born Robert LeRoy Parker, history knows him as Butch Cassidy.

BUTCH, AS I'LL CALL HIM, HAS ALWAYS REMINDED ME OF JOHN DIL-
linger, the 1930s bank robber.* Both were genial sorts the public warmed
to. Like Dillinger, Butch was a criminal nobody until almost thirty,
when he emerged from prison to become a somebody. Dillinger learned
his trade from a crew of older inmates whom he later freed. Butch's tu-
telage came before prison, but like Dillinger, his first holdup raised
money for a jailed mentor. The two even used similar tactics. Both realized any mook could rob something. The challenge was getting away.
Dillinger did it with detailed getaway maps taped to his dashboards.
Thirty-five years earlier, Butch did it by stashing fresh horses on his
escape route. Neither enjoyed long careers, Dillinger barely a year,
Butch four. Like Bob Dalton, both dreamed of escaping to South
America after one last score. Butch actually did it.

Born in 1866 to British Mormon immigrants, the oldest of thirteen children, Butch grew up on a sad farm in southwest Utah, a play-
ful kid, a popular sort, it's said, the kind of boy who fed wine to
chickens and had his pals in stitches when the birds wobbled around
drunk. The Parkers were poor. Butch's father jumped from job to job,
but there was money for books; almost every account of Butch's boyhood indicates he was well-read. At seventeen he accompanied his father to work on a ranch, and later joined his mother on another. He
became a skilled horseman and, by several accounts, an excellent shot.
One anecdote has him racing a horse around a tree and firing six shots
into its trunk without a miss. You can read the exact same story about
Billy the Kid. Maybe it was a popular exercise.

---

*The book to read, if you'll allow, is my own *Public Enemies: America's Greatest Crime Wave
and the Birth of the FBI, 1933–34.*

In 1884, when he turned eighteen, Butch left his parents, working as a cowboy in Colorado, Montana, and Wyoming. Three years later he met a shady character named Matt Warner in a Telluride bar. They raced horses together for a time—Butch was briefly arrested in a squabble over one's ownership—until Warner and a tough guy named Tom Mc-Carty got bored and decided to rob a bank, which they did to great success, in Denver in 1889. It went so well they decided to hit another, in Telluride. This time Butch went along. In his criminal debut, Butch effortlessly vaulted the teller cages, the maneuver John Dillinger made famous years later. They got away cleanly, though posses dogged them for weeks on their way to hide in Robbers' Roost.

For the next five years Butch is mostly lost to history. Aficionados call this gap in his résumé "the Wyoming years," because that's where he apparently spent them, cowboying, drinking, and cutting up in Rock Springs and Lander, maybe working as a butcher—one of several ex-planations of his nickname—maybe wandering down to Texas or Ne-braska. Over time, though, as Wyoming ranchers looked for stolen horses and cattle—this was at the height of the paranoia that led to the Johnson County War—Butch's name started coming up.

What we know for sure is that, on a cool morning in 1894, a posse hunting for rustlers crept up on a small ranch in the mountains outside the town of Auburn. After arresting several men outside, they pushed into a cabin. Butch was stepping out a back door. Told he was under arrest, he pulled a pistol and said, "Let's get to shooting!"

Two possemen tackled him instead, and in the struggle a gun went off, the bullet searing Butch's forehead, at which point he fell to the ground with a groan and gave up. In a corral they found eight stolen horses. After two trials, he ended up being sentenced to two years in the Wyoming state penitentiary. He was a model prisoner. In January 1896, after his sentencing judge admitted a series of procedural errors, Butch was freed. He had served eighteen months.

On his release, he rode for Brown's Hole, where Matt Warner had a cabin. Soon after he arrived, though, Warner was involved in a spat over a mining claim in Utah, and ended up in a shoot-out in which two prospectors were killed. Jailed for murder, Warner sent word to Butch that, without money for a top-notch lawyer, he was doomed. Raising funds for Warner's defense was the reason Butch turned to bank robbery; Warner, who lived to old age, always said it. Would Butch have done it anyway? We'll never know.

He found a partner at Brown's Hole. Ellsworth "Elzy" Lay was a handsome Ohio kid who had worked odd jobs across the Mountain West, baling hay, cowboying, and running a Utah saloon before crossing into crime, initially passing counterfeit money. It's said he was educated and actually carried books in his saddlebags, but that sounds a tad Ringo-esque. The two grew inseparable. Butch fans were thus astounded when a later partner, the Sundance Kid, a surly yegg named Harry Longabaugh, shared top billing in the 1969 film rather than Elzy. One biographer tells of Elzy's grandson's puzzled reaction. "I guess they figured who would want to go see a movie called Butch Cassidy and Elzy Lay?" he quipped.

Their first robbery, assisted by a horse-holding schlub with the classic henchman's name of "Bub" Meeks, came in the Idaho town of Montpelier in August 1896. In the first sign of the planning Butch became known for, the trio arrived in the area early, took jobs baling hay, and spent their spare time studying the Bank of Montpelier and the routes out of town. Butch had a sharp eye for targets; the village was so small it didn't have a marshal to lead any pursuit. His innate aversion to violence—pulling that gun at his arrest was a pure panic move—was also on display. During the robbery, a simple in-and-out affair, a tall robber, clearly Elzy, struck a teller. Guarding the door, the other, clearly Butch, said, "Leave that man alone."

Afterward they rode east, easily outdistancing a timid posse. Their take was excellent, $16,500, worth $618,000 today, most of which they passed to Matt Warner's attorney.* Unfortunately, Warner's estranged and very angry wife then told all; suddenly Butch and Elzy's names were splashed across the newspapers. The story proved catnip for reporters. The notion of a robbery staged to help a friend, even an accused murderer—not to mention Butch's protection of the teller—marked the pair as a tad unusual, earning them a burst of notoriety not typically afforded rookie stickup men.

They hid out in a pal's cabin in northeastern Utah. Once a sheriff started nosing around, they moved to Brown's Hole; a rancher's daughter named Ann Bassett later told of the Thanksgiving party she shared with the courteous young outlaws. It was in the remote valley that Butch, who knew the area well and would return regularly, probably first met the men who later joined him in the Wild Bunch.

They remained on the move, riding south into Utah. Once their photographs began circulating, the pair endured a frigid winter camping at Robbers' Roost. By spring, running low on money—Butch's zeal for faro is said to have been matched only by his ineptitude at it—his little starter gang was scouting its next target, a coal company's payroll in the Utah town of Castle Gate. There are stories of Butch and Elzy cowboying in the area before the job. They discovered that because the miners walked to work, horses were rare in town. In an effort to deflect suspicion, Butch decided they would pretend to be racing trainers, donning sporty clothes and strapping English riding saddles to their mounts.

On Wednesday, April 21, 1897, when the payroll train arrived, Butch was waiting in the street in front of the company store as the paymaster and his clerk trudged up from the station holding heavy bags of cash. Suddenly he pulled a gun and told them to drop the sacks.

---

*The lawyer did his job well. Warner got only five years.

The paymaster complied. The clerk dashed into the store, prompting a miner to step out. "Get back in there, you son of a bitch," Elzy barked from atop his horse. "Or I'll fill your belly full of hot lead."*

Butch snatched up the sacks and ran for his horse. But when he tossed them to Elzy, Elzy dropped the reins to Butch's mount, which bolted. "Don't anybody make a mistake, everything's going to be all right," Butch announced as miners began to appear. Elzy cantered over to the horse, slowing it enough for Butch to run and jump atop it.

On their escape, Butch's preparations were evident. They stopped at least once to cut telegraph wires, hoping to delay pursuers. Fresh horses were again waiting at intervals. The haul was once again good, maybe nine thousand dollars. They were back at Robbers' Roost in a day or two. Even after the paymaster identified Butch's photo and the papers guessed where they were, there was no one in official Utah who seemed eager to brave the remote desert canyons to bring them in.

Afterward, Butch and Elzy did something odd. They stopped. For a full two years they laid low, passing as workaday cowboys, first in Arizona, then for a much longer stretch at a ranch near the southwest New Mexico town of Alma, a scant twenty-five miles from the village where Elfego Baca had fought. The ranch foreman, who wrote of the pair years later, insisted they were his top men, smart, hardworking, and seemingly educated, equally adept at breaking horses and herding cattle long distances. When other cowboys quit, the two always seemed to know a replacement to hire. The new arrivals, the foreman noticed, seemed deferential to the one with the prominent jaw.

Then, probably in the spring of 1899, Butch and Elzy decided to split up. Later, Butch told the foreman Elzy was looking for wilder horses to tame, a weak fib. Was it a quarrel of some kind? A disagreement over

---

*Yes, it appears outlaws sometimes did actually talk like this. It's tempting to speculate that Elzy was acting out a scene from a bad dime-novel Western. This was 1897, after all. They had been around for years.

what—and maybe with whom—to rob next? No one knows. Odder still is what happened afterward: during a six-week window around the time they split, and after two-plus years of idleness, both Butch and Elzy teamed up with new gangs to strike what for both was an entirely new kind of target: a train.

RAILROADS BEGAN BEING BUILT IN EARNEST DURING THE 1830S, COV-ered much of the Northeast by the 1860s, and reached across the continent to California in 1869. After the first train robbery, in 1866, the James Gang popularized tactics that should have led to a rush of them, especially on the frontier, whose wide-open vistas provided the space needed to stop, control, and loot a train, not to mention ease the crucial getaway.

For twenty years, though, train robberies were few and far between. The biggest, by far, was Sam Bass's Nebraska raid in 1877. The fact was, robbing a train required the kind of organization and precision that was still rare on the frontier, whose miscreants were seldom geniuses. It typically took at least three men, and six was considered ideal, allowing for what was termed the "2-2-2" approach: two men to seize the locomotive crew, two to guard the passengers, and two to rob the express car, where money was typically secured in safes. (Robbing passengers, which took time and seldom generated a significant return, was mostly for knuckleheads.)

For years, most robbers boarded trains at a station or watering stop, as the Daltons had, until the railroads began posting guards. At that point the bad guys began stopping trains in the countryside. Waving a red lantern sometimes worked, until engineers got wise. Erecting some kind of barricade across the tracks stopped trains until new, larger locomotives proved able to crash through them. Derailing a train wasn't unheard of, though few thieves were eager to face murder charges in the event someone died; in the worst such incident, thirty people were killed when robbers loosened a rail, plunging an Alabama train into a river in 1896. Worse, crashing trains could mean digging through mountains of wreckage to reach the express car, all while dealing with the anger of passengers and crew.

Rather than stop a locomotive from the outside, most outlaws chose to work from the inside, creeping onto trains at darkened stations at night, where they typically hid in the "blind baggage," a platform between the coal tender and the express car; here they could be seen by neither the engineer nor the express clerk. For years railroads debated installing a window in the front of the express car, the better to view the blind baggage. The idea never caught on, in part because breaking the window would provide easy entry into the car. Thus ignored, the blind baggage allowed dozens of outlaws to scramble over the coal tender into the cab, typically at a remote spot, where they rudely jabbed pistols into an engineer's ribs.

Once a train was stopped, the challenge became gaining access to the locked express car, which was typically manned by a single clerk. This was no easy feat. Sam Bass told clerks he was setting the car afire, which worked for him. At least twice, creative bandits had themselves shipped as "corpses" inside coffins, hoping to spring out and surprise the clerk; both times the ruse was discovered. Most battered the car's side doors at their weakest spot, a two-foot-square ventilation grate. A sledgehammer usually did the trick. Wriggling inside, though, left one at the mercy of an armed clerk. Sometimes a gang would push the engineer through to plead its case, keeping the brakeman hostage outside. This worked more than once.

As this suggests, the clerk's character became an issue. Few were willing to risk their lives to protect a safe, but some were. In 1883 a veteran Wells Fargo agent named Aaron Ross became a national hero after surviving multiple attempts by an especially motivated outlaw gang to break into his express car in remote eastern Nevada. When Ross wouldn't open the doors, they shot into the car. Struck twice, Ross returned fire. Then, after separating the cars at a siding, the outlaws actually rammed the locomotive into the express car, damaging one end. Miraculously, it held. The gang then tried to hack through the damage; again, it held. Finally, they piled boards beneath the car and tried to burn Ross out. When the fire died, the gang once more riddled the express car with bullets. Finally, they gave up.

The Ross episode, followed soon after by a Kansas express agent who fought off an outlaw gang, seems to have had a chilling effect. In the next two years there were no train robberies reported where an express messenger was confronted; in 1885 not a single train was robbed anywhere in the West.[2] A Texas cowboy named Rube Burrow broke the drought in December 1886, leading a gang that, in a rarity, pulled jobs in the East and West, robbing trains in Texas, Arkansas, Mississippi, and Alabama; after the Pinkertons led one of the largest manhunts in U.S. history, Burrow was killed in Alabama in 1890.

This set the stage for the 1890s, the golden age of train robbery. There would be 261 in the decade, an average of two a month. Why so many? Certainly there were more trains to be robbed, and more newspapers that carried information about them. The railroads and the Pinkertons actually blamed it on the press, complaining that editors too often depicted train robbery as a daring adventure.

A more plausible explanation was the spread of a newish explosive, dynamite, which solved the riddle of how to enter an express car. A few bandits had tried gunpowder and nitroglycerin explosives, but both were dangerous to handle. Even dynamite was hard for an amateur to master. A California gang set off six explosions during an 1892 robbery and still couldn't get into the express car.

Despite the advantages dynamite afforded, train robbers tended to enjoy brief careers. Once the railroads began to crack down in the mid-

1890s, introducing armored express cars, armed guards, and full-time detectives, few pulled off more than one or two jobs.* Butch and Elzy thought it worth the risk.

BUTCH'S LEGEND RESTS ON A SHAKY PEDESTAL. HIS CAREER CONSISTED of only a handful of robberies. Until they split up, it had just been him and Elzy, and as a "gang" they had robbed exactly two things of note, a bank and a payroll. The group that came to be known as the Wild Bunch, sometimes as the Hole-in-the-Wall Gang, only took shape after their divorce obliged Butch to work with a new set of partners. And while he was this new gang's leader, his new partners were already seasoned crooks in their own right.

The most forceful was a menacing killer named Harvey Logan, aka Kid Curry, a taut, wiry little tough with a push-broom mustache and what one writer called "blowtorch eyes."[3] So yeah, scary guy. Logan was the only one of Butch's partners who might be called a gunfighter. Like Jesse James, Butch was really not; he was a robber people shot at who felt obliged to return fire to get them to stop. There is no record he ever hit anyone the time or two he did shoot.

Raised in Iowa, Logan had come west in his teens, apparently working as a cowboy in Texas and Wyoming before ending up, with three of his brothers, on a place of their own in eastern Montana. There they got into a feud with a local bigwig with the fabulous Old West name of Pike Landusky. It apparently began for the most prosaic of reasons: Landusky borrowed a plow and returned it with a broken handle.† In December 1894, after months of back-and-forth threats, Logan stalked

---

*Among the more notable: the Hedgepeth Four, led by a well-dressed Missourian named Marion Hedgepeth, managed three midwestern train robberies before the Pinkertons tracked him down in San Francisco in 1892.

†The book to read is *The Life and Death of Kid Curry: Tiger of the Wild Bunch*, by Gary A. Wilson.

into a saloon and struck Landusky on the back as he sat drinking. The two fell into a spitting, eye-gouging fight that ended only when Landusky grabbed a pistol and fired at Logan point-blank. The gun misfired. Logan's didn't.

Rather than face murder charges, Logan, then twenty-seven, fled into Wyoming and, with his brother Lonie, became a cattle rustler, working around Hole-in-the-Wall under the guidance of the latest "King of the Rustlers," an enigmatic Canadian named "Flat-Nose" George Currie. In 1897 the trio graduated from rustling to robbery, ranging into South Dakota to hold up the bank at Belle Fourche, thirty miles north of Deadwood. It didn't go well. Their advance man did his scouting in a saloon and was drunk when Currie and the Logans walked into the bank, guns drawn. A teller pulled his own gun and fired point-blank at Harvey, but it misfired, making Logan a leading candidate for luckiest gunfighter of the era. When townsmen appeared outside, the gang ran out with maybe a hundred dollars and rode west. Their drunken scout ended up in jail.

At some point, the Logan trio brought in a fourth man, a penniless Pennsylvania kid who, it's sometimes claimed—apparently based on a library card discovered years later—loved reading dime-novel Westerns. His name was Harry Longabaugh, and he had come west in 1882, at the age of fourteen, to work on an uncle's Colorado ranch. After two years he left to wander the Mountain West, working as a cowboy and picking up arrests for petty theft—cash at one point, a horse and a pistol at another. He was arrested more than once and escaped more than once. After one set of charges was filed in Sundance, Wyoming, the local paper termed him "the Sundance Kid."

Photos suggest he was handsome, though not Robert Redford handsome, with a mustache, a rounded chin, and when duded up, slicked-back blond hair and a sharp part on his left. He was said to be an excellent shot, though there is little evidence to prove it. Depending on who you believe, his personality was either warm and generous or taciturn. He was not a leader, that much is clear. He was always a follower, first of Harvey Logan, later of Butch.

After serving eighteen months on the theft charges, Sundance worked for a few years on a Canadian ranch, briefly tried opening a saloon in Calgary, and then gave it up to rob a train in Montana in 1892. He then went back to cowboying until, at some point, pairing up with the Harvey Logan bunch. Maybe he went on the Belle Fourche job. Maybe they robbed a couple of Nevada banks. No one really knows.

What's known is that Sundance and the Logans hung around Brown's Hole, and that's probably where they met Butch. "The Wild Bunch" was a name either bestowed by the press or chosen because Butch admired Bill Doolin. Its roster was fluid. Butch and Sundance may have worked together for only a single job, three at most.

Their first strike, though, near Wilcox, Wyoming, was a doozy. At 2:18 in the morning on June 2, 1899, the engineer of a westbound Union Pacific train chugging across southern Wyoming stopped upon seeing someone, probably Sundance, waving a red lantern ahead. As he did, a man wearing a cloth handkerchief over his face scrambled across the coal tender and appeared behind him, a pistol in hand. "Now, you son of a bitch!" Butch said. "Do what I say, or I will put light through you."

Another train was approaching from behind, so Butch had the engineer ease across a neighboring bridge, at which point he jumped down, dumped a pile of gunpowder onto the bridge, and lit the fuse. The explosion didn't destroy the bridge, as they had hoped, but it did render it impassable. When Butch ordered the engineer to move the train forward once more, he resisted. Harvey Logan brained him with a pistol. He was about to do it again when Butch told him to stop.

Behind schedule, they turned to the express car. When the clerk, Ernest Woodcock, refused to let them in, they used dynamite to blow a hole in the car and, once inside, dynamited both safes. When the dust settled, everything was coated with something red—not blood, as a dazed Woodcock feared, but juice from a crateful of raspberries. They rode off with $55,000 in red-stained money—roughly $2 million today—a massive haul, probably topping Sam Bass's robbery in Nebraska twenty years earlier as the largest in frontier history.*

Once they were identified, the Wilcox robbery made Butch a public figure, the leader of, depending on who you read, something called the Train Robbers' Syndicate, the Hole-in-the-Wall Gang, or, the name that stuck, the Wild Bunch. Around the time he returned to New Mexico, Elzy Lay rode off alone. He would not prove so fortunate.

AS BUTCH AND THE WILD BUNCH WERE EMERGING AS CELEBRITIES ON the northern Outlaw Trail, their counterparts to the south were a pair of star-crossed gangs confusingly led by Texans with the same nickname, "Black Jack." One, the High Fives, named for a card game of the day, was run by the hefty William "Black Jack" Christian, a small-time thief and whiskey peddler who fled west with his brother after breaking out of an Oklahoma jail in 1895, leaving two dead lawmen in his wake.† The gang's five members, all Texans, tore across Arizona and New Mexico during 1896 and 1897, robbing stagecoaches, general stores, and a bank or two before being ambushed in a canyon, where three of them were shot dead.‡ The two survivors vanished.

The second gang, led by the Texas cowboys Thomas E. "Black Jack" Ketchum and his brother Sam, was accused of any number of murders

*A few days later, after the gang split up, Harvey Logan shot and killed a Wyoming sheriff nosing around his campsite.

†Bob Alexander, in *Desert Desperadoes: The Banditti of Southwestern New Mexico*, suggests the press seized on Christian's nickname to anoint him the gang's leader, when in fact no one knows who, if anyone, led it.

‡The site of the shoot-out, today known as Black Jack Canyon, lies deep in the Big Lue Mountains along the Arizona–New Mexico border.

and train robberies in West Texas and New Mexico during the early 1890s; it's said they sometimes hid at Brown's Hole, where they may have met Elzy. The two holdups that can be confirmed, though, were on a rail line in northern New Mexico, one in 1897, the second a month after Butch's first Wild Bunch robbery in Wyoming, when Elzy had the misfortune to go along. A posse found them the next day, and after two shoot-outs in which two lawmen and Sam Ketchum died of their wounds, Elzy was wounded and sent to prison.*

It seems likely that Elzy's capture prompted, or perhaps simply accelerated, a desire on Butch's behalf to rethink his career options. No doubt the Pinkerton agent who appeared at the ranch made an impression as well. By early 1900 Butch had left New Mexico and returned to Utah, where he queried a Salt Lake City lawyer about surrendering; he said he was confident there was no one who could place him at any of the robberies he was accused of. The lawyer set up two meetings with the governor, who said he couldn't help. Feelers went out to the Union Pacific as well. Nothing came of it.

Butch was tired. He told the lawyer as much. This wasn't like the early years after the war, when gunmen and outlaws all but wandered the West at will. Rewards, Pinkertons, and possemen now seemed to be everywhere. One senses Butch knew he couldn't go on much longer. The frontier was closing around him. The outlaw's day was passing. If he couldn't surrender without facing prison, he had only one option:

Run.

But where? The Pinkertons now carpeted the country. So Butch

---

*Black Jack Ketchum did not participate in this robbery. But in a bizarro postscript, perhaps having lost his mind, he tried to rob the very same train at the very same spot a month later, alone. Maybe it was a calendar mix-up; we don't know. What we do know is that the engineer saw him ride up and, with what one imagines was a quizzical glance, snatched up a shotgun and shot him off his horse. Captured and later put on trial, Ketchum is said to be the only American ever sentenced to death for train robbery, a law later found to be unconstitutional. He is most famous, though, for the gruesome way he died. The hangman badly misjudged his weight, and when Ketchum dropped through the trapdoor, he was all but decapitated.

decided to leave the country—for, of all places, Argentina. Why Argentina? Maybe it was an article in *National Geographic*, which had published several. Cattle ranches were spreading across the country's interior. To get there, though, to set up his own cattle operation, Butch realized he needed more money. Thus was born the classic criminal's dream, the same one John Dillinger had: one last big score, then retirement into distant obscurity.

Or, in Butch's case, two. The first came beside a mesa in southern Wyoming on the night of August 29, 1900, on a dark stretch of the Union Pacific. It was almost an exact replay of the Wilcox job. One masked bandit—Butch, most think—having boarded earlier, scrambled across the coal tender into the cab, jammed a gun into the engineer's ribs, and said to stop when he saw a campfire. A mile ahead, he did. Four masked men stepped up. Harvey Logan was one, Sundance likely another.

After dynamiting the express car, the five riders disappeared into the night. To this day, no one knows how much they got away with. The railroad said fifty dollars or so. The newspapers seemed to think the number was closer to fifty thousand.

A scant ten days later and almost six hundred miles west, three men arrived outside Winnemucca, in northern Nevada, and began studying the First National Bank.* On September 19, the trio—Butch, Sundance, and a onetime member of the Ketchum Gang named Will "News" Carver—sauntered into town. Butch noticed a posse assembling; presumably someone had seen them in the area. They went ahead anyway, Butch saying they would be chased regardless. Who cared by how many?

They walked into the bank just before noon, guns drawn.

---

*The distance has led some to believe the two jobs must've been staged by different gangs; that's a long, long way on horseback. But as Butch's biographer Richard Patterson points out, it's easily manageable by train.

"What is going on here?" the cashier asked.

"It grieves me to inform you," Butch was quoted as saying, "that your bank will be losing out."

After gathering bags of cash and gold coins, and with possemen visible in the street outside, they left through a back door, herding the employees as hostages until they reached the horses. As Butch spurred his toward a gallop, he dropped bags of coins. Everyone dismounted to scoop them up, but they left at least $5,000 in the dirt as they rode away, firing shots in the air to ward off pursuers. It had its effect. They got away clean, and with a huge haul, estimated at $32,500, valued today around $1.2 million.*

Afterward, the trio made for Texas, meeting Harvey Logan and his pal, another onetime Ketchum Gang member named Ben "The Tall Texan" Kilpatrick, in Fort Worth. The occasion was Will Carver's wedding. The trip was memorialized in one of the era's iconic portraits, taken by a professional photographer, the five of them—Butch, Sundance, Logan, Kilpatrick, and Carver—posing solemnly in their Sunday best.

It was a last hurrah. According to one biographer, Butch asked Logan to come with him and Sundance to Argentina. He probably asked them all. No one accepted. They should have. Carver was soon killed by a West Texas sheriff. The following summer, Logan, Kilpatrick, and several others robbed a train in Montana. Kilpatrick was arrested with stolen money in a St. Louis hotel that fall and went to prison.

Logan went out with a bang. In December 1901, during a leisurely tour of the South, his girlfriend was arrested in Knoxville passing bills

---

*For years no one had a clue who the Winnemucca robbers were. Not until 1994, when a British researcher named Mike Bell stumbled upon a 1912 article in a Buenos Aires English-language newspaper, did it become clear it was Butch and Sundance. The article amounts to a moment-by-moment retelling of the robbery, likely told by Sundance to someone who then briefed the writer. Today it's widely regarded as credible and largely accurate.

from a robbery. When officers confronted Logan—deep breath now—he shot two of them, got away, robbed another train in Montana, inexplicably returned to Knoxville, got himself arrested and imprisoned, escaped, and vanished.

In June 1904 three men robbed a train in western Colorado. When a posse tracked them down, a shoot-out ensued. One robber was badly wounded; before he could be captured, he raised a pistol to his head and fired, committing suicide. After a swirl of rumors, the body was exhumed. Despite later stories that had him living a long life everywhere from Brazil to Montana, the Pinkerton service confirmed the body was in fact Harvey Logan's.

Butch and Sundance, meanwhile, accompanied by Sundance's paramour Ethel Place, made their way to New York, where they spent a month seeing the sights. On February 20, 1901, the three stepped onto a dock in Brooklyn and boarded a 310-foot freighter named the *Bellarden*, bound for Buenos Aires. Way back west, a place Butch would never see again, high on the mesas in Arizona and New Mexico, in the remote valleys of Wyoming and Colorado, in the whorehouses and saloons of Texas and Oklahoma, the foolhardy were still making plans to rob trains and the occasional bank, still getting offended by drunken insults, still shooting one another with guns. But the unnoticed departure from American shores of the last two great western outlaws represents in a real sense the end of the Gunfighter Era. It was over.

Epilogue

From Headlines to History

Except it wasn't over. It's never really been over. But the frontier was no more, and with it the idea of the Wild West passed from headlines to history. What followed was its propulsive romanticization, beginning with novels such as Owen Wister's *The Virginian* in 1902 and the paintings and sculpture of Frederic Remington, spreading via Hollywood Westerns silent and then spoken, then the rediscovery of figures such as Billy the Kid, Wyatt Earp, and Wild Bill Hickok by popular authors in the 1920s, all of it reaching a crescendo with television's Western craze during the 1950s. Gunfights didn't suddenly end when Butch and Sundance boarded that freighter, but they were fading out, and in the years afterward, Western literature, art, and cinema drew far more attention than western violence.*

---

*Aficionados may cluck over gunfights I've failed to mention. These might include El Paso's "Four Dead in Five Seconds" gunfight in 1881, which alas takes far longer to explain. Or "The Big Fight" in Tascosa, Texas, in 1886, a shoot-out between cowboys and rustlers that left three dead, memorable for its verbiage: a criminal group known as the System; a gunman called the Catfish Kid, suggesting the frontier was running out of good nicknames; and the detail that stays with me, the cowboy who taunted a rival by demanding he call him

The sun had been setting for years by then, of course. By the 1890s, electric streetcars were clanging down the avenues of Fort Worth, Denver, and San Francisco. Automobiles weren't far behind. The best known of the early gunfighters, from Cullen Baker to Ben Thompson, were decades in the ground. Most who survived lived out peaceful lives. After surrendering following Jesse's death and earning an acquittal in a robbery trial, Frank James ended up a shoe salesman. He gave the odd lecture before dying on the family farm in 1915.

After his release from prison in 1901, Cole Younger joined Frank on the lecture circuit for a time; he died in 1916. Virgil Earp died from pneumonia in 1905. Heck Thomas passed in 1912, of Bright's disease. After prison, Elzy Lay died quietly in Southern California in 1934. Joe LeFors, who debriefed Tom Horn, died in obscurity in 1940. Of those chronicled here, the last to pass appears to have been New Mexico's Elfego Baca, who died in bed in 1945, three weeks after an atomic bomb was dropped on Japan. He was eighty years old.

Wyatt Earp never wore a badge again, much less shot anyone. After Tombstone, he roamed the West as far afield as Alaska for the next forty years, prospecting, gambling, bartending, refereeing the odd prizefight, and granting the occasional interview. In the 1910s he and his wife, Josephine—the actress he famously romanced in Tombstone— ended up in Los Angeles, where he was invited onto film sets, acting as a technical adviser on a Western or two and befriending movie stars. By the time the Old West was rediscovered in the 1920s, Wyatt was already being debriefed by biographers. His memory was pretty bad, as was the single biography that resulted. He died in 1929, at eighty.

Not everyone went quietly. Wes Hardin was released from prison in 1894, having served seventeen years. He was forty. Behind bars he

---

Daddy. Maybe the West's deadliest gunfight, Oklahoma's Goingsnake Massacre, broke out inside a Cherokee Nation courtroom during a murder trial in 1872. Eleven people died, including a deputy U.S. marshal and the defendant's attorney.

had read widely and written his autobiography. He became, of all things, a lawyer. He moved to El Paso, serving as one of Deacon Jim Miller's attorneys for a time. A year after his release, a deputy there arrested his girlfriend for carrying a gun. The two men argued; some say Hardin pistol-whipped him. As it happened, the deputy's father was the aging John Selman, the onetime Texas feudist and New Mexico raider who after years hiding out in Mexico became a constable in El Paso.

On August 19, 1895, Selman and Hardin argued in the street. That night, as Hardin was throwing dice in the Acme Saloon, Selman walked in unseen, stepped behind him, and shot him in the head. He fired three more shots into him after he fell. Hardin was buried the next day. Selman's trial ended in a hung jury. Before he could be retried, he was shot and killed by a U.S. marshal during an argument over cards.

For those outlaws who continued their careers into the twentieth century, things seldom ended well. After emerging from prison in 1911, the Wild Bunch's Ben Kilpatrick was killed a year later when a bystander bashed him over the head with an ice mallet as he robbed a train in Texas. Because armed robberies remained so prevalent in Arizona, the territory took a page from Texas and in 1901 created the Arizona Rangers, tasking the force with subduing the bandits who some felt were delaying statehood. These Rangers engaged in a series of storied gunfights with sundry bad guys before being disbanded in 1909.

Butch and Sundance ranched peacefully for several years on a fifteen-thousand-acre spread they bought in the shadow of the Andes. When Pinkertons began sniffing around, they robbed a bank in the town of Villa Mercedes, then split up for nearly a year, Butch moving on to Bolivia while Sundance took Ethel Place to San Francisco. He returned alone. She vanished from history.

In Bolivia they worked as payroll guards for a year or so, until they realized how easy robbing one would be, and when they tried, it was: they made off with roughly twelve thousand dollars in today's money. They fled to the mountain town of San Vicente, where their luck ran out. The mayor recognized a stolen mule and called in the *federales*, who surrounded a house where they were staying. When Butch met them at the door, gunfire erupted. Hollywood famously portrayed them cut down as they charged out into a storm of bullets. In reality, they were found dead inside the house. From the position of their bodies, police theorized that Sundance had been badly wounded, Butch killed him to relieve his misery, and then killed himself with a shot to the temple.*

Their fame was slow in coming. Butch was not notably rediscovered during the 1920s. In an era where even fake gunfighters like Bill Longley and Johnny Ringo were given television shows, he earned only three minor movies during the Western-crazed 1950s. His popularity, in fact, derives almost solely from the 1969 film. Generations of moviegoers who hear the name "Butch Cassidy" think only of Paul Newman. And fair enough.

BY CONVENTIONAL MEANS OF MEASURING HISTORY, THE GUNFIGHTERS of the Old West are of scant importance. They left no political or socio-

---

*Butch and Sundance were not the only American outlaws to migrate to South America in the early years of the twentieth century. According to a 1996 article in the *WOLA Journal*, another pair whose crimes are sometimes confused with theirs, Robert Evans and a Texan named William Wilson, robbed several stores and kidnapped a wealthy rancher in Argentina between 1908 and 1911. Evans, who knew Butch and stayed at his ranch for a time, was said to have ridden with the Ketchum Gang and apparently had known Butch in the States. He and Wilson were killed near the Chilean border by a police patrol in 1911. The best known of their peers was George West Musgrave, a young Texas cowboy who was the last known survivor of the High Fives. He relocated to Paraguay in 1911 or 1912, where he became a rancher, rustler, and—his biographers allege—swindler. He died there in 1947. The book to read is *Last of the Old-Time Outlaws: The George West Musgrave Story*, by Karen Holliday Tanner and John D. Tanner Jr.

economic legacy, little that would justify even inclusion in a history textbook. Their impact is instead cultural, as symbols beloved or reviled, most notably in our entertainments, maybe in our affinity for firearms as well; one is tempted to sense their presence in the way children play with toy guns. The forces that formed their world, that made the late nineteenth-century frontier so very violent, slowly faded. Law enforcement spread and professionalized; expectations of a man's behavior evolved. Honor still mattered in the years afterward, and to a degree still does today; revenge and payback remain part of the human condition. But there is a clear sense it's not the social currency it once was. The notion of killing to defend one's honor, or a family's, isn't unknown today, but I don't sense anyone considers it a serious societal problem, at least not in mainstream America.

Texas calmed down, though Texans never lost their reputation for firearms knowledge and expertise. A notable reminder of this came in 1934, when the FBI's J. Edgar Hoover, supervising squads of inexperienced desk agents, needed hardened gunmen who could shoot it out with public enemy number one, John Dillinger. He specifically asked his right-hand man, Pop Nathan, to find them in Texas, and he did. The two new agents who killed Dillinger in Chicago that summer were veteran officers they recruited, one from Oklahoma, the second from Texas.

You can still find the gunfighters if you know where to look. Wyatt Earp lies with his wife beneath a tasteful black marble headstone in Colma, south of San Francisco; William Randolph Hearst and Joe DiMaggio are nearby. Jesse James is buried with his wife beneath a simple stone marker in Kearney, Missouri; it lists his military affiliations. In Deadwood, Hickok has maybe the flashiest grave, a full bust atop; there's another bust in his Illinois hometown.

Few of these graves give you much in the way of background, though there's a historical marker inside the cage they've erected to protect Wes Hardin in El Paso's scruffy Concordia Cemetery, a dirt-and-gravel expanse a stone's throw from Interstate 10. Someone's hung some art atop the cage with the initials "JWH" and a pair of pistols. It's strange to contemplate it while eighteen-wheelers rumble by.

The most evocative gravesite may be Billy the Kid's. Unlike most, it's very much a presentation for tourists. Buried in an old cemetery outside Fort Sumner, behind a little museum and the chamber of commerce, Billy is in a cage too—a black-iron thing, redolent of jail bars—lying beside his buddies Tom O'Folliard and Charlie Bowdre, each grave covered in concrete onto which visitors have tossed hundreds of coins; the marker above says "Pals," which seems a bit much. Billy's original gravestone is locked in a tiny cage in one corner, retrieved after being stolen twice, in 1951 and 1976. On a recent morning, someone had jammed a half-smoked cigarette into it.

A hundred miles south, the state of New Mexico has kept Lincoln the best-preserved of gunfighter sites. Many of the original buildings still stand, including the Tunstall store and the Dolan store-turned-jail from which Billy escaped that day in 1880. Laid between hills rising quickly on both sides, it's an intimate place. You can sit in the second-story window from which Billy killed Bob Olinger. There are white stones to mark the spots where Olinger and his partner died.

Out on the plains of western Kansas, where towering white windmills have replaced Texas herds on the horizon, little has been preserved in Dodge City. It's a bustling city of thirty thousand or so now, dominated by grain elevators and tanker trucks. The main street is Wyatt Earp Boulevard, but the statue outside the visitor's center turns out to be not Wyatt but the actor James Arness of *Gunsmoke* fame. A statue of Doc Holliday, sitting at a gambling table poised to draw, is down the street. Nearby is the Famous Gunfighters Wax Museum, a sad place. The less said about this, the better. But the Boot Hill Museum, renovated in 2020, is excellent. Wyatt, Masterson, and other gunfighters get only a small room and a few portraits, but there's a nice replica of Front Street, and the cemetery has been preserved.

Would that Tombstone had received such treatment. Today it is a worn tourist town with billboards promising GUNFIGHTS DAILY!, Ike Clanton's Haunted Hotel, and an RV-and-biker vibe. Allen Street, the main drag, is lined with knickknack stores. The site of the gunfight is in private hands, behind a souvenir shop and a musty one-room museum. The space where the bullets flew lies in a courtyard at the rear, a patch of gravel adorned with eight manikins whose gun arms rise and fall like metronomes. Reenactors shoot it out here every day. When I saw a rotund character in a red shirt getting ready—a Curly Bill, he seemed—I had to leave. History deserves better than this.

Monuments to gunfighters are few and far between. There's a seven-foot-high statue of the rustler Nate Champion at a tidy museum in Buffalo, Wyoming. Another lies beside a vacant lot in Reserve, New Mexico, today a lonely mountain crossroads. Elfego Baca squats there amid fallen lumber, firing at the package store across the street. The marker explains he was responding to "atrocities" perpetuated by marauding Texans, which is the version Baca's partisans prefer. On the cool April morning I was there, there was not a soul in sight.

The most telling spots, the ones that nod toward modern society's ambivalence toward all this, are those passing into history. In West Texas, the town of Pecos has reburied Clay Allison in a brick enclosure in a downtown park. Both his original headstone and a new one installed in the 1970s—"He never killed a man that did not need killing"—are there, but there's nothing explaining who the man was. In Holbrook, Arizona, the bungalow Commodore Perry Owens made famous still stands, a sign on the front saying BLEVINS HOUSE. There's a marker in the yard, but it's about another matter entirely. They've built onto the back of the house. It's a medical clinic now.

How you feel upon visiting these places, one imagines, depends on how you feel about gunfighters and their stories. Some still thrill to their exploits; I watched a beaming Australian teenager duded up in a Stetson and a holstered toy gun with his parents at Tombstone. Others, well, not so much. "Be still," I heard a family's mother admonish a fidgety child. "Your grandfather really likes this shit."

Perhaps the lure of the gunfighter legends is dimming. The writers who updated the canon in the last sixty years are passing from the scene. The movies, a Hickok here, a Billy there, have slowed to a trickle; few are worth noting. "Don't think they get many tourists; not many people care about the Old West anymore," a man told me in Lincoln. On the other hand, there were twenty people lined up outside when the gunfight display opened in Tombstone one recent morning.

These places tend to draw mostly enthusiasts, naturally. You don't hear much about those who wish these stories would go away, who feel they glorify the kind of violence many would like to see wither and die. I can understand such sentiments. But what I know is that history doesn't go away. It can't be ignored into disappearing, nor am I sure doing so in this case would accrue any serious benefit, any more than banning stories of serial killers would reduce murder rates. To those who wish it would, I can only say what almost any historian might. The surest way to address history, especially its "unpleasant" aspects, is to engage with it, to learn. The truth, whether about fabulists like Wild Bill Hickok and Bill Longley, murderers like Jesse James and Wes Hardin, or those like Wyatt Earp who tried to limit such men, tends to win in the end.

ACKNOWLEDGMENTS

This is a book I've been writing in my head for twenty years. It's a kind of prequel to my 2004 book on the FBI's drive against Depression-era criminals, *Public Enemies*. I kid my editor at Penguin Press, Scott Moyers, because he doesn't remember snubbing this idea after *Public Enemies*. But once I moved back full-time to Texas, a spiritual home of the gunfighter, he thought it sounded perfect for me. All kidding aside, Scott is among the best in the business.

I began actual research in 2018, took two years off to coauthor another book, 2021's *Forget the Alamo*, then returned to it late in the pandemic. Because it's a survey of the canon, I spent more time immersed in books written by others than in libraries and archives; I am on very good terms with my Amazon delivery people. It was a more solitary endeavor than other books, and probably unsurprisingly, I ended up relying more heavily on friends and family for support.

Maggie Walsh was there at the beginning, listening patiently in her kitchen as I excitedly mansplained the aha moments that started the process. Jason Stanford, Beverly Lowry, Jeff Goodell, and my sons Dane and Griffin Burrough were never too busy to listen to me work through thoughts. Chris Schnoor read early chapters and gave savvy feedback. My parents, Mac and Mary Burrough, remain my bedrock, maybe not grasping my fascination here, but sure I knew what I was doing.

I am especially grateful to a series of Western authors and writers for their guidance, especially their dean, the estimable John Boessenecker, to whom the briefest email prompts long, link-filled replies. Rick Miller sent me my first reading list and was the first professional to read the manuscript; his approval allowed me to sleep much better at night. Thanks to Thomas Bicknell, for his insights on Ben Thompson; Erik Wright, for sending articles from his collection; Charles Leerhsen on Butch Cassidy; and to Bill O'Neal, Kip Stratton, Chuck Parsons, and Robert M. Utley, for their valuable input. Thanks to Randolph Roth, for explaining Old West homicide rates.

At Penguin Press, Mia Council spent months expertly supervising the manuscript's final development. Here in Austin, Jasmine DeFoore hunted up and secured dozens of period photographs. Authors, if you need a good photo researcher, you can't do better than Jasmine.

I am very fortunate to have had the same editor for twenty-five years, and the same agent, Andrew Wylie, for thirty-five. Andrew's colleague Jeff Posternak has been the sturdy shore on which my waves have crashed for years now. And last: I got married while writing this book. The woman who endured this process for the last five years, from morning coffee to walks along the river beside her West Texas pastureland, is my wife, Amy Pfluger. I can't thank her enough for her love, intelligence, and curiosity. It's meant everything.

NOTES

PROLOGUE

1. The description of this fight is derived from two Hickok biographies, Tom Clavin's 2019 *Wild Bill: The True Story of the American Frontier's First Gunfighter* (New York: St. Martin's) and Joseph G. Rosa's 1974 edition of *They Called Him Wild Bill: The Life and Adventures of James Butler Hickok* (Norman: University of Oklahoma Press).
2. Thomas King Whipple, *Study Out the Land* (University of California Press, 1943), p. 59.
3. John Boessenecker, *Ride the Devil's Herd: Wyatt Earp's Epic Battle Against the West's Biggest Outlaw Gang* (Toronto: Hanover Square Press, 2020), p. 320.
4. Eugene Cunningham, *Triggernometry: A Gallery of Gunfighters* (Norman: University of Oklahoma Press, 1996), p. xiii.
5. Joseph G. Rosa, *The Gunfighter: Man or Myth?* (Norman: University of Oklahoma Press, 1969), p. 84.
6. George Ward Nichols, "Wild Bill," *Harper's New Monthly Magazine* 34 (Feb. 1867): 276.

CHAPTER 1: THE THING ABOUT TEXAS

1. Joseph Leach, *The Typical Texan: Biography of an American Myth* (Dallas: Southern Methodist University Press, 1952), p. 1.
2. Bill O'Neal, "Texas, Gunfighter Capital of the West," *Wild West*, Oct. 2011.
3. O'Neal, "Texas."
4. Emerson Hough, *The Story of the Outlaw: A Study of the Western Desperado* (1907; repr., n.p.: Badgley, 2012), pp. 180–81.
5. William Oliver Stevens, *Pistols at Ten Paces: The Story of the Code of Honor in America* (Boston: Houghton Mifflin, 1940), p. 12.
6. Stevens, *Pistols at Ten Paces*, p. 30.

7. Excerpt from "New Orleans City Park: Its First Fifty Years," at duelingoaks.com, accessed Oct. 20, 2020.

8. Grady McWhiney, *Cracker Culture: Celtic Ways in the Old South* (Tuscaloosa: University of Alabama Press, 1988), pp. 148, 156.

9. Dominic Erdozain, *One Nation under Guns: How Gun Culture Distorts Our History and Threatens Our Democracy* (New York: Crown, 2024), p. 50.

10. Daniel Justin Herman, *Hell on the Range: A Story of Honor, Conscience, and the American West* (New Haven, Conn.: Yale University Press, 2010), p. 195.

11. Stevens, *Pistols at Ten Paces*, p. 40.

12. Paul Wellman, *Spawn of Evil* (New York: Modern Literary Editions, 1964), p. 19.

13. Stevens, *Pistols at Ten Paces*, p. 96.

14. Barbara Holland, *Gentlemen's Blood: A History of Dueling from Swords at Dawn to Pistols at Dusk* (New York: Bloomsbury, 2003), p. 184.

15. Stevens, *Pistols at Ten Paces*, p. 96.

16. Dick Steward, *Duels and the Roots of Violence in Missouri* (Columbia: University of Missouri Press, 2000), p. 181.

CHAPTER 2: THE FIRST GUNFIGHTERS

1. Joseph Leach, *The Typical Texan: Biography of an American Myth* (Dallas: Southern Methodist University Press, 1952), p. 45.

2. Leach, *The Typical Texan*, p. 43.

3. Leach, *The Typical Texan*, pp. 28, 32.

4. T. R. Fehrenbach, *Lone Star: A History of Texas and the Texans* (New York: Da Capo, 2000), p. 527.

5. Jim Rasenberger, *Revolver: Sam Colt and the Six-Shooter That Changed America* (New York: Scribner, 2020), pp. 192–93.

6. Rasenberger, *Revolver*, p. 235.

7. Fehrenbach, *Lone Star*, p. 481.

8. John Boessenecker, *Gold Dust & Gunsmoke: Tales of Gold Rush Outlaws, Gunfighters, Lawmen, and Vigilantes* (New York: John Wiley & Sons, 1999), p. 9.

9. Rasenberger, *Revolver*, p. 264.

10. Charles L. Convis, *Outlaw Tales of Nevada* (Guilford, Conn.: TwoDot, 2006), p. 10.

11. Boessenecker, *Gold Dust & Gunsmoke*, p. 86.

12. Mark Twain, *Roughing It* (Digireads.com, 2004), p. 147.

13. Twain, *Roughing It*, p. 67.

CHAPTER 3: THE CAULDRON

1. Drew Gilpin Faust, *This Republic of Suffering: Death and the American Civil War* (New York: Vintage, 2008), p. 267.

2. Brian Matthew Jordan, *Marching Home: Union Veterans and Their Unending Civil War* (New York: Liveright, 2014), p. 43.

3. Jordan, *Marching Home*, p. 48.

4. Chuck Parsons, *Clay Allison: Portrait of a Shootist* (Seagraves, Tex.: Pioneer, 1983), pp. 2–3.

5. T. J. Stiles, *Jesse James: Last Rebel of the Civil War* (New York: Vintage, 2002), p. 41.
6. N. R. Buttrick and J. Mazen, "Historical Prevalence of Slavery Predicts Contemporary American Gun Ownership," PNAS Nexus 1, no. 3 (2022): pgac 117, doi.org/10.1093/pnasnexus/pgac117.
7. James M. Smallwood, Kenneth W. Howell, and Carol C. Taylor, *The Devil's Triangle: Ben Bickerstaff, Northeast Texans, and the War of Reconstruction in Texas* (Denton: University of North Texas Press, 2007), p. 17.
8. Kenneth W. Howell, ed., *Still the Arena of Civil War: Violence and Turmoil in Reconstruction Texas, 1865–1874* (Denton: University of North Texas Press, 2012), loc. 74, Kindle.
9. George C. Rable, *But There Was No Peace: The Role of Violence in the Politics of Reconstruction* (Athens: University of Georgia Press, 2007), p. 86.
10. Barry A. Crouch and Donaly E. Brice, *Cullen Montgomery Baker: Reconstruction Desperado* (Baton Rouge: Louisiana State University Press, 1997), p. 13.
11. Crouch and Brice, *Cullen Montgomery Baker*, p. 67.
12. Crouch and Brice, *Cullen Montgomery Baker*, p. 166.
13. Robert M. Utley, *Billy the Kid: A Short and Violent Life* (Lincoln: University of Nebraska Press, 1989), p. 4.
14. C. L. Sonnichsen, *I'll Die Before I'll Run: The Story of the Great Feuds of Texas* (Lincoln: University of Nebraska Press, 1988), pp. 8–9.
15. "The 15 Deadliest Blood Feuds in United States History," at bestliberalartscolleges.org.
16. C. L. Sonnichsen, *10 Texas Feuds* (Albuquerque: University of New Mexico Press, 2000), p. 82.
17. Randolph Roth, *American Homicide* (Cambridge, Mass.: Belknap Press of Harvard University Press, 2009), p. 340.
18. James M. Smallwood, Barry A. Crouch, and Larry Peacock, *Murder and Mayhem: The War of Reconstruction in Texas* (College Station: Texas A&M University Press, 2003), loc. 147, Kindle.

CHAPTER 4: THE KILLING MACHINE

1. Richard C. Marohn, *The Last Gunfighter: John Wesley Hardin* (College Station, Tex.: Creative, 1995).
2. Benedict Carey, "Scott Lilienfeld, Psychologist Who Questioned Psychology, Dies at 59," *The New York Times*, Oct. 16, 2020, p. 25.
3. Bill O'Neal, *Encyclopedia of Western Gunfighters* (Norman: University of Oklahoma Press, 1979), p. 5.
4. Chuck Parsons and Norman Wayne Brown, *A Lawless Breed: John Wesley Hardin, Texas Reconstruction, and Violence in the Wild West* (Denton: University of North Texas Press, 2013), pp. 18–19.
5. John Wesley Hardin, *The Life of John Wesley Hardin* (Enhanced Media, 2018), pp. 18–19.
6. Leon Metz, *John Wesley Hardin: Dark Angel of Texas* (Norman: University of Oklahoma Press, 1996), p. 16.

7. Parsons and Brown, *A Lawless Breed*, p. 55.
8. Parsons and Brown, *A Lawless Breed*, p. 126.
9. James M. Smallwood, *The Feud That Wasn't: The Taylor Ring, Bill Sutton, John Wesley Hardin, and Violence in Texas* (College Station: Texas A&M University Press, 2008), loc. 914, Kindle.
10. Parsons and Brown, *A Lawless Breed*, p. 162.
11. Parsons and Brown, *A Lawless Breed*, p. 170.
12. Parsons and Brown, *A Lawless Breed*, p. 170.
13. Sonnichsen, *I'll Die Before I'll Run*, p. 155.
14. Terry Anne Scott, *Lynching and Leisure: Race and the Transformation of Mob Violence in Texas* (Fayetteville: University of Arkansas Press, 2022), p. 11.
15. David Johnson, *The Mason County "Hoo Doo" War, 1874–1902* (Denton: University of North Texas Press,2012), loc. 2040, Kindle.
16. Johnson, *The Mason County "Hoo Doo" War*, loc. 2181, Kindle.
17. Walter Prescott Webb, *The Great Plains* (Lincoln: University of Nebraska Press, 1981), p. 206.
18. Richard Maxwell Brown, *Strain of Violence: Historical Studies of American Violence and Vigilantism* (Oxford: Oxford University Press, 1975), p. 238.

CHAPTER 5: GUNFIGHTERS OF THE CATTLE KINGDOM

1. T. R. Fehrenbach, *Lone Star: A History of Texas and the Texans* (New York: Da Capo, 2000), p. 559.
2. Ernest Staples Osgood, *The Day of the Cattleman* (Chicago: University of Chicago Press, 1966), p. 24.
3. Terry G. Jordan, *North American Cattle-Ranching Frontiers* (Albuquerque: University of New Mexico Press, 1993), p. 221.
4. E. C. "Teddy Blue" Abbott and Helena Huntington Smith, *We Pointed Them North: Recollections of a Cowpuncher* (Norman: University of Oklahoma Press, 1955), p. 26.
5. Richard Maxwell Brown, *Strain of Violence: Historical Studies of American Violence and Vigilantism* (Oxford: Oxford University Press, 1975), p. 268.
6. Abbott and Smith, *We Pointed Them North*, p. 23.
7. Joseph G. Rosa, *The Gunfighter: Man or Myth?* (Norman: University of Oklahoma Press, 1969), p. 84.
8. Tom Clavin, *Wild Bill: The True Story of the American Frontier's First Gunfighter* (New York: St. Martin's, 2019), p. 97.
9. Clavin, *Wild Bill*, p. 147.
10. According to the outstanding analysis of Thomas C. Bicknell and Chuck Parsons in *Ben Thompson: Portrait of a Gunfighter* (Denton: University of North Texas Press, 2018), pp. 69–71.
11. Bicknell and Parsons, *Ben Thompson*. They put Thompson's arrival "most likely in early April" (p. 110).
12. Leon Metz, *John Wesley Hardin: Dark Angel of Texas* (Norman: University of Oklahoma Press, 1996), p. 55.
13. Metz, *John Wesley Hardin*, pp. 70–71.

14. Clavin, *Wild Bill*, p. 187; Joseph G. Rosa, *They Called Him Wild Bill: The Life and Adventures of James Butler Hickok* (Norman: University of Oklahoma Press, 1974), pp. 196–97.

15. Rosa, *They Called Him Wild Bill*, p. 194.

16. Rosa, *They Called Him Wild Bill*, p. 196.

17. Rosa, *The Gunfighter*, p. 92.

18. Clavin, *Wild Bill*, p. 237.

CHAPTER 6: "GET YOUR GUNS, YOU TEXAS SONS OF BITCHES, AND FIGHT"

1. Casey Tefertiller, *Wyatt Earp: The Life behind the Legend* (New York: John Wiley & Sons, 1997), p. 11.

2. Tefertiller, *Wyatt Earp*, p. 11.

3. Kristine Schmucker, "No Sunday West of Newton: Newton's Bloody Sunday, Part 1," in *Newton's General Massacre*, an online publication of the Harvey County (Kansas) Historical Museum, hchm.org/newtons-bloody-Sunday/.

4. Tefertiller, *Wyatt Earp*, p. 6. The memoirist was local attorney Ira E. Lloyd.

5. W. B. (Bat) Masterson, *Famous Gunfighters of the Western Frontier: Wyatt Earp, Doc Holliday, Luke Short and Others* (Mineola, N.Y.: Dover, 2009), pp. 29–30.

6. William M. Walton, *Life and Adventures of Ben Thompson: The Famous Texan* (Houston: Frontier Press, 1954), p. 32.

7. Masterson, *Famous Gunfighters of the Western Frontier*, p. 31.

8. Herbert Asbury, *Sucker's Progress: An Informal History of Gambling in America* (n.p.: Hauraki, 2016), p. 362.

9. Thomas C. Bicknell and Chuck Parsons, *Ben Thompson: Portrait of a Gunfighter* (Denton: University of North Texas Press, 2018), loc. 1686, Kindle.

10. Tefertiller, *Wyatt Earp*, p. 14.

CHAPTER 7: LEGENDS IN THE MAKING

1. Tom Clavin, *Dodge City: Wyatt Earp, Bat Masterson, and the Wickedest Town in the American West* (New York: St. Martin's, 2017).

2. Casey Tefertiller, *Wyatt Earp: The Life behind the Legend* (New York: John Wiley & Sons, 1997), p. 16.

3. Robert R. Dykstra and Jo Ann Manfra, "How Dodge City Became a Symbol of Frontier Lawlessness," *Smithsonian Magazine*, Jan. 23, 2018.

4. I found this version in a seemingly well-documented 2006 article on HistoryNet, which describes the 1913 testimony as "the unpublished trial record." It's not mentioned in earlier Masterson biographies.

5. W. B. (Bat) Masterson, *Famous Gunfighters of the Western Frontier: Wyatt Earp, Doc Holliday, Luke Short and Others* (Mineola, N.Y.: Dover, 2009), p. 36.

6. Herbert Asbury, *Sucker's Progress: An Informal History of Gambling in America* (n.p.: Hauraki, 2016), p. 373.

7. Chuck Parsons, *Clay Allison: Portrait of a Shootist* (Seagraves, Tex.: Pioneer, 1983), p. 14.

8. Parsons, *Clay Allison*, p. 21.
9. Parsons, *Clay Allison*, p. 51.
10. Parsons, *Clay Allison*, p. 55.

CHAPTER 8: "YOU HAVE LIVED LONG ENOUGH"

1. Casey Tefertiller, *Wyatt Earp: The Life behind the Legend* (New York: John Wiley & Sons, 1997), p. 28.
2. Tefertiller, *Wyatt Earp*, p. 29.
3. Robert K. DeArment, *Bat Masterson: The Man and the Legend* (Norman: University of Oklahoma Press, 1979), pp. 207–8.
4. For the best version of what happened, see Jack DeMattos and Chuck Parsons, *The Notorious Luke Short: Sporting Man of the Wild West* (Denton: University of North Texas Press, 2015).
5. Gary L. Roberts, *Doc Holliday: The Life and Legend* (New York: John Wiley & Sons, 2006), p. 109.
6. Roberts, *Doc Holliday*.
7. Nyle H. Miller and Joseph W. Snell, *Why the West Was Wild: A Contemporary Look at the Antics of Some Highly Publicized Kansas Cowtown Personalities* (Norman: University of Oklahoma Press, 2003), p. 459.
8. Miller and Snell, *Why the West Was Wild*, p. 464.
9. Miller and Snell, *Why the West Was Wild*, p. 469.

CHAPTER 9: THE TROUBLE WITH JESSE JAMES

1. Lynne Pierson Doti and Larry Schweikart, *Banking in the American West: From the Gold Rush to Deregulation* (Norman: University of Oklahoma Press, 1991).
2. T. J. Stiles, *Jesse James: Last Rebel of the Civil War* (New York: Vintage, 2002), p. 369.

CHAPTER 10: THE TAMING OF TEXAS

1. C. L. Sonnichsen, *I'll Die Before I'll Run: The Story of the Great Feuds of Texas* (Lincoln: University of Nebraska Press, 1988), p. 274.
2. Chuck Parsons and Norman Wayne Brown, *A Lawless Breed: John Wesley Hardin, Texas Reconstruction, and Violence in the Wild West* (Denton: University of North Texas Press, 2013), p. 222.
3. Parsons and Brown, *A Lawless Breed*, p. 223.
4. Rick Miller, *Bloody Bill Longley: The Mythology of a Gunfighter* (Denton: University of North Texas Press, 2011), p. 47.
5. Rick Miller, *Sam Bass & Gang* (Austin, Tex.: State House Press, 1999), p. 61.
6. Miller, *Sam Bass & Gang*, p. 62.
7. *St. Louis Globe-Democrat*, Oct. 7, 1877.
8. William M. Walton, *Life and Adventures of Ben Thompson: The Famous Texan* (Houston: Frontier Press, 1954), p. 197.
9. David Hamilton Murdoch, *The American West: The Invention of a Myth* (Reno: University of Nevada Press, 2001), p. 53.

10. Murdoch, *The American West.*
11. Clifford P. Westermeier, "The Cowboy in His Home State," *Southwestern Historical Quarterly* 58, no. 2 (Oct. 1954): 218–34.
12. Westermeier, "The Cowboy in His Home State."
13. Westermeier, "The Cowboy in His Home State."

CHAPTER 11: THE TEXAS INVASION OF NEW MEXICO

1. David Johnson, *The Horrell Wars: Feuding in Texas and New Mexico* (Denton: University of North Texas Press, 2014), loc. 987, Kindle.
2. Sonnichsen, *I'll Die Before I'll Run,* p. 132.
3. Michael Wallis, *Billy the Kid: The Endless Ride* (New York: W. W. Norton, 2007), pp. 135–36.
4. Robert M. Utley, *Billy the Kid: A Short and Violent Life* (Lincoln: University of Nebraska Press, 1989), p. 33.
5. Utley, *Billy the Kid,* p. 36.
6. Utley, *Billy the Kid,* p. 45.

CHAPTER 12: THE RISE OF BILLY THE KID

1. Robert M. Utley, *Billy the Kid: A Short and Violent Life* (Lincoln: University of Nebraska Press, 1989), p. 80.
2. Utley, *Billy the Kid,* p. 95.
3. Utley, *Billy the Kid,* pp. 114–15.
4. Utley, *Billy the Kid,* pp. 118–21.
5. Utley, *Billy the Kid,* p. 132.
6. Utley, *Billy the Kid,* p. 133.

CHAPTER 13: THE HUNTS FOR BILLY THE KID

1. Mark Lee Gardner, *To Hell on a Fast Horse: The Untold Story of Billy the Kid and Pat Garrett* (New York: HarperCollins, 2011), p. 107.
2. Michael Wallis, *Billy the Kid: The Endless Ride* (New York: W. W. Norton, 2007), p. 238.
3. Gardner, *To Hell on a Fast Horse,* p. 131.
4. Wallis, *Billy the Kid,* p. 240.
5. Gardner, *To Hell on a Fast Horse,* p. 144.
6. Robert M. Utley, *Billy the Kid: A Short and Violent Life* (Lincoln: University of Nebraska Press, 1989), pp. 183–84.
7. Kent Ladd Steckmesser, *The Western Hero in History and Legend* (Norman: University of Oklahoma Press,1997), p. 70.
8. Kyle S. Crichton, *Law and Order, Ltd.: The Rousing Life of Elfego Baca of New Mexico* (Greenville, Ohio: Coachwhip, 2014), p. 33.
9. Crichton, *Law and Order, Ltd.,* p. 35.
10. Howard Bryan, *Incredible Elfego Baca: Good Man, Bad Man of the Old West* (Santa Fe: Clear Light, 1993), p. 33.

11. Crichton, *Law and Order, Ltd.*, p. 35.
12. Crichton, *Law and Order, Ltd.*, p. 36.

CHAPTER 14: TOMBSTONE

1. Hubert Howe Bancroft, *History of Arizona and New Mexico* (n.p.: First Rate Publishers, 2020), p. 594.
2. Nathan Sayre, "The Cattle Boom in Southern Arizona: Towards a Critical Political Ecology," *Journal of the Southwest* 41, no. 2 (1999): 239–71.
3. James A. Wilson, "West Texas Influence on the Early Cattle Industry of Arizona," *Southwestern History Quarterly* 71, no. 1 (July 1967): 26–36.
4. Wilson, "West Texas Influence on the Early Cattle Industry of Arizona."
5. Daniel Justin Herman, *Hell on the Range: A Story of Honor, Conscience, and the American West* (New Haven, Conn.: Yale University Press, 2010), pp. 98–99.
6. Wilson, "West Texas Influence on the Early Cattle Industry of Arizona," p. 35.
7. John Boessenecker, *Ride the Devil's Herd: Wyatt Earp's Epic Battle Against the West's Biggest Outlaw Gang* (Toronto: Hanover Square Press, 2020), inside cover.
8. Boessenecker, *Ride the Devil's Herd*, p. 163.
9. Boessenecker, *Ride the Devil's Herd*, p. 199.
10. Casey Tefertiller, *Wyatt Earp: The Life behind the Legend* (New York: John Wiley & Sons, 1997), p. 113.
11. Boessenecker, *Ride the Devil's Herd*, p. 247.
12. Boessenecker, *Ride the Devil's Herd*, p. 258.

CHAPTER 15: THE FIGHT IS MADE

1. Jack Burrows, *John Ringo: The Gunfighter Who Never Was* (Tucson: University of Arizona Press, 2016), p. 8.
2. Jack Burrows, "John Ringo: The Story of a Western Myth," *Montana: The Magazine of Western History* 30, no. 4 (Autumn 1980): 2–15.
3. Burrows, "John Ringo."
4. *Denver Republican*, May 14, 1893.
5. Casey Tefertiller, *Wyatt Earp: The Life behind the Legend* (New York: John Wiley & Sons, 1997), p. 231. The wording varies, but this exchange appears in some form in every major account of the Vendetta Ride.
6. Tefertiller, *Wyatt Earp*, p. 238.
7. Tefertiller, *Wyatt Earp*, p. 239.

CHAPTER 16: THE DEADLIEST FEUD

1. John Perkins, "Up the Trail from Dixie: Animosity toward Sheep in the Culture of the U.S. West," *Australasian Journal of American Studies* 11, no. 2 (December 1992): 1–18.
2. Perkins, "Up the Trail from Dixie."
3. Perkins, "Up the Trail from Dixie."

4. Harry Sinclair Drago, *The Great Range Wars: Violence on the Grasslands* (New York: Dodd, Mead, 1970), p. 256.
5. Daniel Justin Herman, *Hell on the Range: A Story of Honor, Conscience, and the American West* (New Haven, Conn.: Yale University Press, 2010), p. 97.
6. Herman, *Hell on the Range*, p. 99.
7. Herman, *Hell on the Range*, p. 122.
8. John Boessenecker, *Ride the Devil's Herd: Wyatt Earp's Epic Battle Against the West's Biggest Outlaw Gang* (Toronto: Hanover Square Press, 2020), p. 392.
9. Boessenecker, *Ride the Devil's Herd*, p. 393.
10. Herman, *Hell on the Range*, p. 161.
11. Herman, *Hell on the Range*, p. 138.
12. Herman, *Hell on the Range*, p. 163.

CHAPTER 17: THE ASSASSINS

1. Larry D. Ball, *Tom Horn in Life and Legend* (Norman: University of Oklahoma Press, 2014), p. 118.
2. Glenn Shirley, *Shotgun for Hire: The Story of "Deacon" Jim Miller, Killer of Pat Garrett* (Norman: University of Oklahoma Press, 1970), pp. 4–5.
3. Shirley, *Shotgun for Hire*, p. 49.
4. Shirley, *Shotgun for Hire*, pp. 56–57.
5. Shirley, *Shotgun for Hire*, pp. 114–15.

CHAPTER 18: DEATH ALLEY

1. Glenn Shirley, *West of Hell's Fringe: Crime, Criminals, and the Federal Peace Officer in Oklahoma Territory, 1889–1907* (Norman: University of Oklahoma Press, 1990), p. 38.
2. Shirley, *West of Hell's Fringe*, p. 42.
3. Shirley, *West of Hell's Fringe*, p. 78.
4. Paul Wellman, *A Dynasty of Western Outlaws* (Lincoln: University of Nebraska Press, 1986), p. 178.

CHAPTER 19: THE OUTLAW TRAIL

1. Charles Kelly, *The Outlaw Trail: A History of Butch Cassidy and His Wild Bunch* (Lincoln: University of Nebraska Press, 1996).
2. Richard Patterson, *Train Robbery: The Birth, Flowering, and Decline of a Notorious Western Enterprise* (Boulder, Colo.: Johnson, 1981), p. 49.
3. Charles Leerhsen, *Butch Cassidy: The True Story of an American Outlaw* (New York: Simon & Schuster, 2020), p. 13.

BIBLIOGRAPHY

Abbott, E. C. "Teddy Blue," and Helena Huntington Smith. *We Pointed Them North: Recollections of a Cowpuncher.* Norman: University of Oklahoma Press, 1955.

Adams, Ramon F. *Six-Guns and Saddle Leather: A Bibliography of Books and Pamphlets on Western Outlaws and Gunmen.* Norman: University of Oklahoma Press, 1969.

Alexander, Bob. *Bad Company and Burnt Powder: Justice and Injustice in the Old Southwest.* Denton: University of North Texas Press, 2014.

———. *Desert Desperadoes: The Banditti of Southwestern New Mexico.* Silver City, N.Mex.: Gila, 2006.

Anderson, Dan, and Laurence Yadon. *100 Oklahoma Outlaws, Gangsters and Lawmen, 1839–1939.* Gretna, La.: Pelican, 2007.

Anderson, Gary Clayton. *The Conquest of Texas: Ethnic Cleansing in the Promised Land, 1820–1875.* Norman: University of Oklahoma Press, 2005.

Anderson, John Q., ed. *Tales of Frontier Texas 1830–1860.* Dallas: Southern Methodist University Press, 1966.

Arenson, Adam, and Andrew R. Graybill, eds. *Civil War Wests: Testing the Limits of the United States.* Oakland: University of California Press, 2015.

Arthur, George Clinton. *Bushwhacker: A Story of Missouri's Most Famous Desperado.* N.p.: CMP, 2019.

Asbury, Herbert. *Sucker's Progress: An Informal History of Gambling in America.* N.p.: Hauraki, 2016.

Askins, Col. Charles. *Texas, Guns & History.* New York: Winchester, 1970.

Atherton, Lewis. *The Cattle Kings.* Bloomington: Indiana University Press, 2019.

Ayers, Edward L. *Vengeance & Justice: Crime and Punishment in the 19th-Century American South.* New York: Oxford University Press, 1984.

Baldick, Robert. *The Duel: A History.* New York: Barnes & Noble, 1996.

Ball, Larry D. *Desert Lawmen: The High Sheriffs of New Mexico and Arizona, 1846–1912.* Albuquerque: University of New Mexico Press, 1992.

———. *Tom Horn in Life and Legend.* Norman: University of Oklahoma Press, 2014.

———. *The United States Marshals of New Mexico & Arizona Territories, 1846–1912.* Albuquerque: University of New Mexico Press, 1978.

Bancroft, Hubert Howe. *History of Arizona and New Mexico.* N.p.: First Rate Publishers, 2020.

Barra, Allen. *Inventing Wyatt Earp: His Life and Many Legends.* Edison, N.J.: Castle, 2005.

Batson, James L., Jr. *James Bowie and the Sandbar Fight: Birth of the James Bowie Legend and the Bowie Knife.* Huntsville, Ala.: Batson, 2018.

Bazin, André. *What Is Cinema? Essays Selected and Translated by Hugh Gray.* Berkeley: University of California Press, 2005.

Bell, Bob Boze. *Bad Men: Outlaws & Gunfighters of the Old West.* Phoenix: Tri Star–Boze, 1999.

———. *Classic Gunfights.* 2 vols. Phoenix: Tri Star–Boze, 2003–5.

Bellesiles, Michael. *Arming America: The Origins of a National Gun Culture.* Brooklyn, N.Y.: Soft Skull, 2000.

Bicknell, Thomas C., and Chuck Parsons. *Ben Thompson: Portrait of a Gunfighter.* Denton: University of North Texas Press, 2018.

Billington, Ray Allen. *Land of Savagery, Land of Promise: The European Image of the American Frontier in the Nineteenth Century.* Norman: University of Oklahoma Press, 1981.

Bird, Harrison. *War for the West, 1790–1813.* New York: Oxford University Press, 1971.

Block, Eugene B. *Great Train Robberies of the West.* New York: Coward-McCann, 1959.

Boatright, Mody C., and Donald Days, eds. *From Hell to Breakfast.* Denton: University of North Texas Press, 2000.

Bodenhorn, Howard. *A History of Banking in Antebellum America: Financial Markets and Economic Development in an Era of Nation-Building.* Cambridge: Cambridge University Press, 2000.

Boessenecker, John. *Badge and Buckshot: Lawlessness in Early California.* Norman: University of Oklahoma Press, 1988.

———. *Gold Dust & Gunsmoke: Tales of Gold Rush Outlaws, Gunfighters, Lawmen, and Vigilantes.* New York: John Wiley & Sons, 1999.

———. *Ride the Devil's Herd: Wyatt Earp's Epic Battle Against the West's Biggest Outlaw Gang.* Toronto: Hanover Square, 2020.

———. *Texas Ranger: The Epic Life of Frank Hamer, the Man Who Killed Bonnie and Clyde.* New York: St. Martin's, 2016.

Bold, Christine. *The Frontier Club: Popular Westerns and Cultural Power, 1880–1924.* New York: Oxford University Press, 2013.

———. *Selling the Wild West: Popular Western Fiction, 1860–1960.* Bloomington: Indiana University Press, 1987.

Botkin, B. A., ed. *A Treasury of Western Folklore: The Stories, Legends, Tall Tales, Traditions, Ballads and Songs of the People of the Great Plains and Far West.* New York: Bonanza, 1975.

Boyer, Glenn G. *I Married Wyatt Earp: The Recollections of Josephine Sarah Marcus Earp.* Stamford, Conn.: Longmeadow, 1976.

Brodhead, Michael J. *Isaac C. Parker: Federal Justice on the Frontier.* Norman: University of Oklahoma Press, 2003.

Brown, Norman Wayne, and Chuck Parsons. *Bad Blood: The Violent Lives of John Wesley Hardin, His Brothers, and Associates*. Fort Worth: Eakin, 2022.

Brown, Richard Maxwell. *No Duty to Retreat: Violence and Values in American History and Society*. Norman: University of Oklahoma Press, 1991.

———. *Strain of Violence: Historical Studies of American Violence and Vigilantism*. Oxford: Oxford University Press, 1975.

Brown, Ryan. *Honor Bound: How a Cultural Ideal Has Shaped the American Psyche*. New York: Oxford University Press, 2016.

Brownlee, Richard S. *Gray Ghosts of the Confederacy: Guerrilla Warfare in the West, 1861–1865*. Baton Rouge: Louisiana State University Press, 1986.

Bruce, Dickson D., Jr. *Violence and Culture in the Antebellum South*. Denton: University of North Texas Press, 2013.

Bryan, Howard. *Incredible Elfego Baca: Good Man, Bad Man of the Old West*. Santa Fe: Clear Light, 1993.

———. *Robbers, Rogues and Ruffians: True Tales of the Wild West*. Santa Fe: Clear Light, 1991.

Burrows, Jack. *John Ringo: The Gunfighter Who Never Was*. Tucson: University of Arizona Press, 2016.

Burton, Arthur T. *Black, Red and Deadly: Black and Indian Gunfighters of the Indian Territory, 1870–1907*. Fort Worth: Eakin, 1991.

Burton, Jeffrey. *The Deadliest Outlaws: The Ketchum Gang and the Wild Bunch*. Denton: University of North Texas Press, 2009.

Butler, Ken. *Oklahoma Renegades: Their Deeds and Misdeeds*. Gretna, La.: Pelican, 2000.

Cain, Del. *Lawmen of the Old West: The Good Guys*. Dallas: Republic of Texas, 2000.

Caldwell, Clifford R. *John Simpson Chisum: The Cattle King of the Pecos Revisited*. Santa Fe: Sunstone Press, 2010.

Carrigan, William D. *The Making of a Lynching Culture: Violence and Vigilantism in Central Texas, 1836–1916*. Urbana: University of Illinois Press, 2006.

Cash, W. J. *The Mind of the South*. New York: Vintage, 1991.

Cawelti, John G. *The Six-Gun Mystique Sequel*. Bowling Green, Ohio: Bowling Green State University Popular Press, 1999.

Chapel, Charles Edward. *Guns of the Old West: An Illustrated Reference Guide to Antique Firearms*. New York: Skyhorse, 2013.

Charles, Patrick J. *Armed in America: A History of Gun Rights from Colonial Militias to Concealed Carry*. Amherst, N.Y.: Prometheus, 2019.

Chrisman, Harry E. *The Ladder of Rivers: The Story of I.P. (Print) Olive*. Kearney, Neb.: Dawson County Historical Society, 1995.

Cimino, Al. *Gunfighters: A Chronicle of Dangerous Men & Violent Death*. New York: Chartwell, 2016.

Clavin, Tom. *Dodge City: Wyatt Earp, Bat Masterson, and the Wickedest Town in the American West*. New York: St. Martin's, 2017.

———. *The Last Outlaws: The Desperate Final Days of the Dalton Gang*. New York: St. Martin's, 2023.

———. *Tombstone: The Earp Brothers, Doc Holliday, and the Vendetta Ride from Hell*. New York: St. Martin's, 2000.

———. *Wild Bill: The True Story of the American Frontier's First Gunfighter.* New York: St. Martin's, 2019.

Cleere, Jan. *Outlaw Tales of Arizona: True Stories of the Grand Canyon State's Most Infamous Crooks, Culprits, and Cutthroats.* Guilford, Conn.: TwoDot, 2012.

Collins, Michael L. *A Crooked River: Rustlers, Rangers, and Regulars on the Lower Rio Grande, 1861–1877.* Norman: University of Oklahoma Press, 2018.

Convis, Charles L. *Outlaw Tales of Nevada: True Stories of the Silver State's Most Infamous Crooks, Culprits, and Cutthroats.* Guilford, Conn.: TwoDot, 2012.

———. *Outlaw Tales of Texas: True Stories of the Lone Star State's Most Infamous Crooks, Culprits, and Cutthroats.* Guilford, Conn.: TwoDot, 2012.

Cool, Paul. *Salt Warriors: Insurgency on the Rio Grande.* College Station: Texas A&M University Press, 2008.

Coppedge, Walter. *Henry King's America.* Metuchen, N.J.: Scarecrow, 1986.

Courtwright, David T. *Violent Land: Single Men and Social Disorder from the Frontier to the Inner City.* Cambridge, Mass.: Harvard University Press, 1996.

Cox, William R. *Luke Short and His Era: A Biography of One of the Old West's Most Famous Gamblers.* Garden City, N.Y.: Doubleday, 1961.

Crabb, Richard. *Empire on the Platte.* Cleveland: World, 1967.

Cramer, Clayton E. *Armed America: The Story of How and Why Guns Became as American as Apple Pie.* Nashville: Nelson Current, 2006.

Crichton, Kyle S. *Law and Order, Ltd.: The Rousing Life of Elfego Baca of New Mexico.* Greenville, Ohio: Coachwhip, 2014.

Crouch, Barry A., and Donaly E. Brice. *Cullen Montgomery Baker: Reconstruction Desperado.* Baton Rouge: Louisiana State University Press, 1997.

———. *The Governor's Hounds: The Texas State Police, 1870–1873.* Denton: University of North Texas Press, 2011.

Crouch, Gregory. *The Bonanza King: John Mackay and the Battle over the Greatest Riches in the American West.* New York: Scribner, 2018.

Culley, John H. (Jack). *Cattle, Horses & Men.* Tucson: University of Arizona Press, 1984.

Cunningham, Eugene. *Triggernometry: A Gallery of Gunfighters.* Norman: University of Oklahoma Press, 1996.

Dale, Edward Everett. *The Range Cattle Industry.* Norman: University of Oklahoma Press, 1930.

Dary, David. *Cowboy Culture: A Sage of Five Centuries.* Lawrence: University Press of Kansas, 1989.

———. *Seeking Pleasure in the Old West.* Lawrence: University Press of Kansas, 1995.

Davis, John W. *Wyoming Range War: The Infamous Invasion of Johnson County.* Norman: University of Oklahoma Press, 2010.

Dean, Eric T., Jr. *Shook over Hell: Post-Traumatic Stress, Vietnam, and the Civil War.* Cambridge, Mass.: Harvard University Press, 1997.

Dearen, Patrick. *Saddling Up Anyway: The Dangerous Lives of Old-Time Cowboys.* Guilford, Conn.: TwoDot, 2006.

DeArment, Robert K. *Alias Frank Canton.* Norman: University of Oklahoma Press, 1996.

———. *Bat Masterson: The Man and the Legend.* Norman: University of Oklahoma Press, 1979.

———. *Bravo of the Brazos: John Larn of Fort Griffin, Texas.* Norman: University of Oklahoma Press, 2002.

———. *Deadly Dozen: Forgotten Gunfighters of the Old West.* Vol. 1. Norman: University of Oklahoma Press, 2015.

———. *Deadly Dozen: Forgotten Gunfighters of the Old West.* Vol. 2. Norman: University of Oklahoma Press, 2012.

———. *Jim Courtright of Fort Worth: His Life and Legend.* Fort Worth: TCU Press, 2004.

———. *Knights of the Green Cloth: The Saga of Frontier Gamblers.* Norman: University of Oklahoma Press, 1982.

DeArment, Robert K., and Jack DeMattos. *A Rough Ride to Redemption: The Ben Daniels Story.* Norman: University of Oklahoma Press, 2010.

Del Mar, David Peterson. *Beaten Down: A History of Interpersonal Violence in the West.* Seattle: University of Washington Press, 2002.

DeMattos, Jack. *Mysterious Gunfighter: The Story of Dave Mather.* College Station, Tex.: Creative, 1992.

DeMattos, Jack, and Chuck Parsons. *The Notorious Luke Short: Sporting Man of the Wild West.* Denton: University of North Texas Press, 2015.

Derrig, John. *Dirty Dave Rudabaugh, Outlaw Feared by Billy the Kid.* 2014.

Dick, Everett. *The Dixie Frontier: A Social History.* Norman: University of Oklahoma Press, 1993.

Dimsdale, Thomas. *The Vigilantes of Montana: Violence and Justice on the Frontier.* London: Lume, 2016.

Dobie, J. Frank. *Cow People.* Austin: University of Texas Press, 1964.

———. *The Longhorns.* Austin: University of Texas Press, 1980.

———. *Stories of Christmas and the Bowie Knife.* Austin: Steck, 1953.

———. *Tales of Old-Time Texas.* Austin: University of Texas Press, 1992.

———. *Tone the Bell Easy: Slave Songs, Mexican Tales, Treasure Lore.* Austin: Texas Folklore Society, 1965.

Dolan, Samuel K. *Hell Paso: Life and Death in the Old West's Most Dangerous Town.* Guilford, Conn.: TwoDot, 2021.

Doti, Lynne Pierson, and Larry Schweikart. *Banking in the American West: From the Gold Rush to Deregulation.* Norman: University of Oklahoma Press, 1991.

Drago, Harry Sinclair. *The Great Range Wars: Violence on the Grasslands.* New York: Dodd, Mead, 1970.

———. *The Legend Makers: Tales of the Old-Time Peace Officers and Desperadoes of the Frontier.* New York: Dodd, Mead, 1975.

———. *Outlaws on Horseback.* Lincoln: University of Nebraska Press, 1998.

Dworkin, Mark. *American Mythmaker: Walter Noble Burns and the Legends of Billy the Kid, Wyatt Earp and Joaquín Murrieta.* Norman: University of Oklahoma Press, 2015.

Dykstra, Robert R. *The Cattle Towns.* Lincoln: University of Nebraska Press, 1983.

Eason, Al. *Cullen Baker: Purveyor of Death and Other Stories.* Kilgore, Tex.: Ford Printing, 1981.

Eckhardt, C. F. *Tales of Bad Men, Bad Women, and Bad Places: Four Centuries of Texas Outlawry.* Lubbock: Texas Tech University Press, 1999.

Editors of *Guns & Ammo. Guns and the Gunfighters.* New York: Bonanza Books, 1982.

Editors of Time-Life Books. *The Gamblers.* Alexandria, Va.: Time-Life, 1978.

Egerton, Douglas R. *The Wars of Reconstruction: The Brief, Violent History of America's Most Progressive Era.* New York: Bloomsbury, 2014.

Emmett, Chris. *Shanghai Pierce: A Fair Likeness.* Norman: University of Oklahoma Press, 1974.

Enss, Chris. *Outlaw Tales of California: True Stories of the Golden State's Most Infamous Crooks, Culprits, and Cutthroats.* Guilford, Conn.: TwoDot, 2013.

Ernst, Donna B. *The Sundance Kid: The Life of Harry Alonzo Longabaugh.* Norman: University of Oklahoma Press, 2009.

Erwin, Allen A. *The Southwest of John Horton Slaughter 1841–1922.* Spokane, Wash.: Arthur H. Clark, 1997.

Etulain, Richard W., and Glenda Riley, eds. *With Badges & Bullets: Lawmen & Outlaws in the Old West.* Golden, Colo.: Fulcrum, 1999.

Farber, James. *Texans with Guns.* San Antonio: Naylor, 1950.

Faust, Drew Gilpin. *This Republic of Suffering: Death and the American Civil War.* New York: Vintage, 2008.

Fehrenbach, T. R. *Lone Star: A History of Texas and the Texans.* New York: Da Capo, 2000.

Fellman, Michael. *Inside War: The Guerrilla Conflict in Missouri during the American Civil War.* Oxford: Oxford University Press, 1989.

Findlay, John M. *People of Chance: Gambling in American Society from Jamestown to Las Vegas.* New York: Oxford University Press, 1986.

Fischer, David Hackett. *Albion's Seed: Four British Folkways in America.* Oxford: Oxford University Press, 1989.

Fisher, O. C., and J. C. Dykes. *King Fisher: His Life and Times.* Norman: University of Oklahoma Press, 1966.

Foner, Eric. *Reconstruction: America's Unfinished Revolution, 1863–1877.* New York: HarperCollins, 2014.

Ford, Lacy K., Jr. *Origins of Southern Radicalism: The South Carolina Upcountry, 1800–1860.* New York: Oxford University Press, 1988.

Forrest, Earle R. *Arizona's Dark and Bloody Ground.* Tucson: University of Arizona Press, 1979.

Franklin, John Hope. *The Militant South 1800–1861.* Urbana: University of Illinois Press, 1984.

Franscell, Ron. *The Crime Buff's Guide to Outlaw Southwest.* Denver: WildBlue Press, 2017.

———. *The Crime Buff's Guide to Outlaw Texas.* Guilford, Conn.: GPP, 2011.

Frantz, Joe B., and Julian Ernest Choate Jr. *The American Cowboy: The Myth and the Reality.* Norman: University of Oklahoma Press, 1955.

Frazier, Donald S. *Blood & Treasure: Confederate Empire in the Southwest.* College Station: Texas A&M University Press, 1995.

Freeman, Joanne B. *The Field of Blood: Violence in Congress and the Road to the Civil War.* New York: Picador, 2019.

French, Peter A. *Cowboy Metaphysics: Ethics and Death in Westerns.* Lanham, Md.: Rowman & Littlefield, 1997.

Gannett, Lewis, ed. *Glory, God and Gold.* Garden City, N.Y.: Doubleday, 1954.

Gard, Wayne. *The Chisholm Trail.* Norman: University of Oklahoma Press, 1976.

———. *Frontier Justice.* Norman: University of Oklahoma Press, 1981.

Gardner, Mark Lee. *To Hell on a Fast Horse: The Untold Story of Billy the Kid and Pat Garrett.* New York: HarperCollins, 2011.

Garrett, Pat. *The Authentic Life of Billy the Kid.* Norman: University of Oklahoma Press, 1965.

Gatto, Steve. *Curly Bill: Tombstone's Most Famous Outlaw.* Lansing, Mich.: Protar House, 2003.

Goodrich, Thomas. *War to the Knife: Bleeding Kansas, 1854–1861.* Mechanicsburg, Pa.: Stackpole, 1988.

Goodstone, Tony, ed. *The Pulps: Fifty Years of American Pop Culture.* New York: Chelsea House, 1970.

Gorn, Elliott J. *The Manly Art: Bare-Knuckle Prize Fighting in America.* Ithaca, N.Y.: Cornell University Press, 1986.

Graham, Don. *Kings of Texas: The 150-Year Saga of an American Ranching Empire.* New York: John Wiley & Sons, 2003.

Graham, Hugh Davis. *The History of Violence in America: A Report to the National Commission on the Causes and Prevention of Violence.* New York: Bantam, 1969.

Greenberg, Amy S. *Manifest Manhood and the Antebellum American Empire.* New York: Cambridge University Press, 2005.

Greer, James Kimmins. *Texas Ranger: Jack Hays in the Frontier Southwest.* College Station: Texas A&M University Press, 1993.

Griffith, T. D. *Outlaw Tales of South Dakota: True Stories of the Mount Rushmore State's Most Infamous Crooks, Culprits, and Cutthroats.* Guilford, Conn.: TwoDot, 2015.

Guinn, Jeff. *The Last Gunfight: The Real Story of the Shootout at the O.K. Corral—and How It Changed the American West.* New York: Simon & Schuster, 2011.

Hahn, Steven, and Jonathan Prude. *The Countryside in the Age of Capitalist Transformation: Essays in the Social History of Rural America.* Chapel Hill: University of North Carolina Press, 1985.

Halaas, David Fridtjof. *Boom Town Newspapers: Journalism on the Rocky Mountain and Mining Frontier, 1859–1881.* Albuquerque: University of New Mexico Press, 1981.

Hale, Will. *Twenty-Four Years a Cowboy & Ranchman.* Norman: University of Oklahoma Press, 1959.

Hanchett, Leland, Jr. *Arizona's Graham-Tewksbury Feud.* Phoenix: Pine Rim, 1994.

Hardin, John Wesley. *The Life of John Wesley Hardin.* N.p.: Enhanced Media, 2018.

Hartz, Louis. *The Founding of New Societies: Studies in the History of the United States, Latin America, South Africa, Canada and Australia.* New York: Harcourt, Brace & World, 1964.

Henn, Nora True. *Lincoln County and Its Wars.* Lincoln: Henn-Johnson Library, 2017.

Herman, Daniel Justin. *Hell on the Range: A Story of Honor, Conscience, and the American West.* New Haven, Conn.: Yale University Press, 2010.

Hogge, Kevin. *The Troubled Life and Mysterious Death of Johnny Ringo.* Barto, Pa.: Cold West, 2018.

Holland, Barbara. *Gentlemen's Blood: A History of Dueling from Swords at Dawn to Pistols at Dusk.* New York: Bloomsbury, 2003.

Hollon, W. Eugene. *Frontier Justice: Another Look*. New York: Oxford University Press, 1974.

Hoock, Holger. *Scars of Independence: America's Violent Birth*. New York: Crown, 2017.

Horan, James D. *The Gunfighters: Accounts by Eyewitnesses and the Gunfighters Themselves*. New York: Gramercy, 1994.

———. *The Outlaws: Accounts by Eyewitnesses and the Outlaws Themselves*. New York: Gramercy, 1994.

Horn, Calvin. *New Mexico's Troubled Years: The Story of the Early Territorial Governors*. Albuquerque: Horn & Wallace, 1963.

Hough, Emerson. *The Story of the Outlaw: A Study of the Western Desperado*. N.p.: Badgley, 2012.

Howell, Kenneth W., ed. *The Seventh Star of the Confederacy: Texas during the Civil War*. Denton: University of North Texas Press, 2012.

———. *Still the Arena of Civil War: Violence and Turmoil in Reconstruction Texas, 1865–1874*. Denton: University of North Texas Press, 2012.

Hulbert, Matthew Christopher. *The Ghosts of Guerrilla Memory: How Civil War Bushwhackers Became Gunslingers in the American West*. Athens: University of Georgia Press, 2016.

Hunter, J. Marvin. *The Trail Drivers of Texas*. Mount Pleasant, S.C.: Arcadia, 2016.

Hunter, J. Marvin, and Warren Hunter. *The Album of Gunfighters*. Helotes, Tex.: Warren Hunter, 1973.

Inciardi, James A., and Anne E. Pottieger, eds. *Violent Crime: Historical and Contemporary Issues*. Beverly Hills: Sage, 1978.

Isenberg, Andrew C. *Wyatt Earp: A Vigilante Life*. New York: Hill & Wang, 2013.

James, Bill C. *Jim Miller: The Untold Story of a Texas Badman*. Wolfe City, Tex.: Henington, 2001.

Jameson, W. C. *Rocky Mountain Train Robberies: True Stories of Notorious Bandits and Infamous Escapades*. Guilford, Conn.: TwoDot, 2019.

———. *Texas Train Robberies: True Stories of Notorious Bandits and Infamous Escapades*. Guilford, Conn.: Lone Star Books, 2017.

Jessen, Kenneth. *Frontier Colorado Gunfights: True Stories of Outlaws & Lawmen in the American West*. Loveland, Colo.: J.V. Publications, 2017.

Johnson, David. *The Cornett-Whitley Gang: Violence Unleashed in Texas*. Denton: University of North Texas Press, 2019.

———. *The Horrell Wars: Feuding in Texas and New Mexico*. Denton: University of North Texas Press, 2014.

———. *John Ringo: King of the Cowboys*. Denton: University of North Texas Press, 2012.

———. *The Mason County "Hoo Doo" War, 1874–1902*. Denton: University of North Texas Press, 2012.

Jones, Daryl. *The Dime Novel Western*. Bowling Green, Ohio: The Popular Press, 1978.

Jordan, Brian Matthew. *Marching Home: Union Veterans and Their Unending Civil War*. New York: Liveright, 2014.

Jordan, Philip D. *Frontier Law and Order: Ten Essays*. Lincoln: University of Nebraska Press, 1970.

Jordan, Terry G. *North American Cattle-Ranching Frontiers*. Albuquerque: University of New Mexico Press, 1993.

———. *Trails to Texas: Southern Roots of Western Cattle Ranching*. Lincoln: University of Nebraska Press, 1981.

Kelly, Charles. *The Outlaw Trail: A History of Butch Cassidy and His Wild Bunch*. Lincoln: University of Nebraska Press, 1996.

Kimmel, Michael. *Manhood in America: A Cultural History*. New York: Oxford University Press, 2012.

Kirchner, L. R. *Robbing Banks: An American History, 1831–1999*. Rockville Centre, N.Y.: Sarpedon, 2000.

Kirchner, Paul. *Bowie Knife Fights, Fighters, and Fighting Techniques*. Boulder, Colo.: Paladin Press, 2010.

Kirschner, Ana. *Lady at the O.K. Corral: The True Story of Josephine Marcus Earp*. New York: Harper Perennial, 2013.

Kitses, James, and Gregg Rickman, eds. *The Western Reader*. New York: Limelight, 1998.

Klasner, Lily. *My Girlhood among Outlaws*. Tucson: University of Arizona Press, 1972.

Knowlton, Christopher. *Cattle Kingdom: The Hidden History of the Cowboy West*. Boston: Mariner, 2017.

Lamar, Howard R. *The Far Southwest, 1846–1912: A Territorial History*. Albuquerque: University of New Mexico Press, 2000.

———. *Texas Crossings: The Lone Star State and the American Far West, 1836–1986*. Austin: University of Texas Press, 1991.

Lanning, Jim, and Judy Lanning, eds. *Texas Cowboys: Memories of the Early Days*. College Station: Texas A&M University Press, 1984.

Laycock, George. *The Mountain Men: The Dramatic History and Lore of the First Frontiersmen*. Guilford, Conn.: Lyons, 2016.

Leach, Joseph. *The Typical Texan: Biography of an American Myth*. Dallas: Southern Methodist University Press, 1952.

Leakey, John, as told to Nellie Snyder Yost. *The West That Was: From Texas to Montana*. Lincoln: University of Nebraska Press, 1967.

Leerhsen, Charles. *Butch Cassidy: The True Story of an American Outlaw*. New York: Simon & Schuster, 2020.

Leyburn, James G. *Frontier Folkways*. New Haven, Conn.: Yale University Press, 1935.

Limerick, Patricia Nelson. *The Legacy of Conquest: The Unbroken Past of the American West*. New York: W. W. Norton, 1987.

Lindsey, Ellis, and Gene Riggs. *Barney K. Riggs: The Yuma and Pecos Avenger*. N.p.: Xlibris, 2002.

Lyman, George D. *The Saga of the Comstock Lode: Boom Days in Virginia City*. New York: Charles Scribner's Sons, 1934.

Lyon, Peter. *The Wild, Wild West*. New York: Funk & Wagnalls, 1969.

Mackay, James. *Allan Pinkerton: The First Private Eye*. Edison, N.J.: Castle, 2007.

Maddux, Vernon R. *John Hittson: Cattle King on the Texas and Colorado Frontier*. Niwot: University Press of Colorado, 1994.

Malsch, Brownson. *"Lone Wolf" Gonzaullas, Texas Ranger*. Norman: University of Oklahoma Press, 1998.

Markley, Bill. *Billy the Kid & Jesse James: Outlaws of the Legendary West.* Guilford, Conn.: TwoDot, 2019.

Marks, Paula Mitchell. *And Die in the West: The Story of the O.K. Corral Gunfight.* Norman: University of Oklahoma Press, 1989.

Marohn, Richard C. *The Last Gunfighter: John Wesley Hardin.* College Station, Tex.: Creative, 1995.

Marriott, Barbara. *Outlaw Tales of New Mexico: True Stories of the Land of Enchantment's Most Infamous Crooks, Culprits, and Cutthroats.* Guilford, Conn.: TwoDot, 2012.

Marten, James. *Texas Divided: Loyalty and Dissent in the Lone Star State, 1856–1874.* Lexington: University Press of Kentucky, 1990.

Masterson, W. B. (Bat). *Famous Gunfighters of the Western Frontier: Wyatt Earp, Doc Holliday, Luke Short and Others.* Mineola: Dover, 2009.

McCord, Monty. *Calling the Brands: Stock Detective in the Wild West.* Guilford, Conn.: TwoDot, 2018.

McCormack, Kara L. *Imagining Tombstone: The Town Too Tough to Die.* Lawrence: University Press of Kansas, 2016.

McCoy, Joseph G. *Historic Sketches of the Cattle Trade of the West and Southwest.* N.p.: Pantianos Classics, 2020.

McCright, Grady E., and James H. Powell. *Jessie Evans: Lincoln County Badman.* College Station, Tex.: Creative, 1983.

McGrath, Roger D. *Gunfighters, Highwaymen and Vigilantes: Violence on the Frontier.* Berkeley: University of California Press, 1984.

McKanna, Clare V., Jr. *Court-Martial of Apache Kid: Renegade of Renegades.* Lubbock: Texas Tech University Press, 2009.

McLachlan, Sean. *Outlaw Tales of Missouri: True Stories of the Show Me State's Most Infamous Crooks, Culprits, and Cutthroats.* Guilford, Conn.: TwoDot, 2014.

McNeal, Thomas Allen. *When Kansas Was Young.* New York: Macmillan, 1922.

McWhiney, Grady. *Cracker Culture: Celtic Ways in the Old South.* Tuscaloosa: University of Alabama Press, 1988.

Meinig, D. W. *Imperial Texas: An Interpretive Essay in Cultural Geography.* Austin: University of Texas Press, 1969.

Metz, Leon. *The Encyclopedia of Lawmen, Outlaws, and Gunfighters.* New York: Checkmark, 2003.

———. *John Selman, Gunfighter.* Norman: University of Oklahoma Press, 1992.

———. *John Wesley Hardin: Dark Angel of Texas.* Norman: University of Oklahoma Press, 1996.

———. *Pat Garrett: The Story of a Western Lawman.* Norman: University of Oklahoma Press, 1974.

———. *The Shooters: A Gallery of Notorious Gunmen from the American West.* New York: Berkley, 1996.

Miller, Nyle H., and Joseph W. Snell. *Why the West Was Wild: A Contemporary Look at the Antics of Some Highly Publicized Kansas Cowtown Personalities.* Norman: University of Oklahoma Press, 2003.

Miller, Rick. *Bloody Bell County: Vignettes of Violence and Mayhem in Central Texas.* Belton, Tex.: Bell County Museum, 2011.

———. *Bloody Bill Longley: The Mythology of a Gunfighter.* Denton: University of North Texas Press, 2011.

———. *Sam Bass & Gang.* Austin, Tex.: State House Press, 1999.

———. *The Train Robbing Bunch.* College Station, Tex.: Creative, 1983.

Milner, Clyde A., II, Carol A. O'Connor, and Martha A. Sandweiss. *The Oxford History of the American West.* New York: Oxford University Press, 1994.

Moneyhon, Carl H. *Texas after the Civil War: The Struggle of Reconstruction.* College Station: Texas A&M University Press, 2004.

Moore, Jacqueline M. *Cow Boys and Cattle Men: Class and Masculinities on the Texas Frontier, 1865–1900.* New York: New York University Press, 2010.

Murdoch, David Hamilton. *The American West: The Invention of a Myth.* Reno: University of Nevada Press, 2001.

Myers, Larry E. *Trailing the Herd: The Cattle Trade in the American West.* Dallas: De-Golyer Library, Southern Methodist University, 2000.

Nash, Jay Robert. *Encyclopedia of Western Lawmen & Outlaws.* New York: Da Capo, 1994.

Neal, Bill. *From Guns to Gavels: How Justice Grew Up in the Outlaw West.* Lubbock: Texas Tech University Press, 2008.

———. *Getting Away with Murder on the Texas Frontier: Notorious Killings and Celebrated Trials.* Lubbock: Texas Tech University Press, 2006.

Nisbett, Richard E., and Dov Cohen. *Culture of Honor: The Psychology of Violence in the South.* Boulder, Colo.: Westview, 1996.

Nix, Evett Dumas, as told to Gordon Hines. *Oklahombres: Particularly the Wilder Ones.* Lincoln: University of Nebraska Press, 1993.

Nolan, Frederick, ed. *The Billy the Kid Reader.* Norman: University of Oklahoma Press, 2007.

———. *The West of Billy the Kid.* Norman: University of Oklahoma Press, 1998.

Nonte, George C., Jr. *Firearms Encyclopedia.* New York: Harper & Row, 1973.

O'Neal, Bill. *The Arizona Rangers.* Fort Worth: Eakin, 1987.

———. *The Bloody Legacy of Pink Higgins: A Half Century of Violence in Texas.* Fort Worth: Eakin, 1999.

———. *Cattlemen vs. Sheepherders: Five Decades of Violence in the West.* Austin: Eakin, 1989.

———. *Encyclopedia of Western Gunfighters.* Norman: University of Oklahoma Press, 1979.

———. *Images of America: Texas Gunslingers.* Mount Pleasant, S.C.: Arcadia, 2014.

———. *John Chisum: Frontier Cattle King.* Fort Worth: Eakin, 2018.

———. *The Johnson County War.* Austin: Eakin, 2004.

———. *War in East Texas: Regulators vs. Moderators.* Denton: University of North Texas Press, 2006.

Osgood, Ernest Staples. *The Day of the Cattleman.* Chicago: University of Chicago Press, 1966.

Owens, Ron. *Oklahoma Justice: The Oklahoma City Police, a Century of Gunfighters, Gangsters and Terrorists.* Paducah, Ky.: Turner, 1995.

Parsons, Chuck. *Captain Jack Helm: A Victim of Texas Reconstruction.* Denton: University of North Texas Press, 2018.

———. *Clay Allison: Portrait of a Shootist*. Seagraves, Tex.: Pioneer, 1983.

Parsons, Chuck, and Norman Wayne Brown. *A Lawless Breed: John Wesley Hardin, Texas Reconstruction, and Violence in the Wild West*. Denton: University of North Texas Press, 2013.

Patterson, Richard. *Butch Cassidy: A Biography*. Lincoln: University of Nebraska Press, 1998.

———. *Train Robbery: The Birth, Flowering, and Decline of a Notorious Western Enterprise*. Boulder, Colo.: Johnson, 1981.

———. *The Train Robbery Era: An Encyclopedic History*. Boulder, Colo.: Pruett, 1991.

Pearce, John Ed. *Days of Darkness: The Feuds of Eastern Kentucky*. Lexington: University Press of Kentucky, 2010.

Perkins, Doug, and Nancy Ward. *Brave Men and Cold Steel: A History of Range Detectives and Their Peacemakers*. Fort Worth: Texas and Southwestern Cattle Raisers Foundation, 1984.

Pfeifer, Michael J. *Rough Justice: Lynching and American Society 1871–1947*. Urbana: University of Illinois Press, 2004.

Pickering, David, and Judy Falls. *Brush Men and Vigilantes: Civil War Dissent in Texas*. College Station: Texas A&M University Press, 2000.

Pinkerton, Allan. *Thirty Years a Detective*. Warwick, N.Y.: 1500 Books, 2007.

Pointer, Larry. *In Search of Butch Cassidy*. Norman: University of Oklahoma Press, 1977.

Potter, David M. *The Impending Crisis 1848–1861*. New York: Harper & Row, 1976.

Prassel, Frank Richard. *The Great American Outlaw: A Legacy of Fact and Fiction*. Norman: University of Oklahoma Press, 1993.

Preece, Harold. *The Dalton Gang: End of an Outlaw Era*. New York: Hastings House, 1963.

Pyle, Jinx. *Pleasant Valley War*. Payson, Ariz.: Git A Rope!, 2013.

Rable, George C. *But There Was No Peace: The Role of Violence in the Politics of Reconstruction*. Athens: University of Georgia Press, 2007.

Rascoe, Burton. *Belle Star: "The Bandit Queen."* Lincoln: University of Nebraska Press, 2004.

Rasenberger, Jim. *Revolver: Sam Colt and the Six-Shooter That Changed America*. New York: Scribner, 2020.

Rathmell, William. *Life of the Marlows: A True Story of Frontier Life of Early Days*. Denton: University of North Texas Press, 2004.

Reasoner, James. *Draw: The Greatest Gunfights of the American West*. Berkeley: Berkeley Trade, 2003.

Redford, Robert. *The Outlaw Trail: A Journey through Time*. New York: Grosset & Dunlap, 1976.

Reno, John. *The Autobiography of John Reno: World's First Train Robber*. 2015.

Reynolds, Donald E. *Texas Terror: The Slave Insurrection Panic of 1860 and the Secession of the Lower South*. Baton Rouge: Louisiana State University Press, 2007.

Richardson, Heather Cox. *How the South Won the Civil War: Oligarchy, Democracy, and the Continuing Fight for the Soul of America*. New York: Oxford University Press, 2020.

Ridings, Sam P. *The Chisholm Trail: A History of the World's Greatest Cattle Trail*. New York: Skyhorse, 2015.

Ripley, Thomas. *They Died with Their Boots On: True Tales of Gun-Slinging Desperadoes and Hard-Riding Law Men.* New York: Pocket, 1949.

Roberts, Gary L. *Doc Holliday: The Life and Legend.* New York: John Wiley & Sons, 2006.

Robertson, James. *After the Civil War: The Heroes, Villains, Soldiers, and Civilians Who Changed America.* N.p.: National Geographic, 2015.

Roland, Charles P. *Albert Sidney Johnston: Soldier of Three Republics.* Lexington: University Press of Kentucky, 2001.

Rollins, Philip Ashton. *The Cowboy: An Unconventional History of Civilization on the Old-Time Cattle Range.* Norman: University of Oklahoma Press, 1997.

Rosa, Joseph G. *Age of the Gunfighter: Men and Weapons on the Frontier 1840–1900.* Norman: University of Oklahoma Press, 1995.

———. *The Gunfighter: Man or Myth?* Norman: University of Oklahoma Press, 1969.

———. *They Called Him Wild Bill: The Life and Adventures of James Butler Hickok.* Norman: University of Oklahoma Press, 1974.

Rose, Peter R. *The Reckoning: The Triumph of Order on the Texas Outlaw Frontier.* Lubbock: Texas Tech University Press, 2012.

Rosenberg, Bruce A. *The Code of the West.* Bloomington: Indiana University Press, 1982.

Roth, Randolph. *American Homicide.* Cambridge, Mass.: Belknap Press of Harvard University Press, 2009.

Rottenberg, Dan. *Death of a Gunfighter: The Quest for Jack Slade, the West's Most Elusive Legend.* Yardley, Pa.: Westholme, 2008.

Rutter, Michael. *Outlaw Tales of Utah: True Stories of the Beehive State's Most Infamous Crooks, Culprits, and Cutthroats.* Guilford, Conn.: TwoDot, 2011.

Sanchez, Joseph P., Robert L. Spude, and Arthur R. Gomez. *New Mexico: A History.* Norman: University of Oklahoma Press, 2013.

Sandoz, Mari. *The Cattlemen: From the Rio Grande across the Far Marias.* Lincoln: University of Nebraska Press, 1958.

Schatz, August Herman. *Longhorns Bring Culture.* Boston: Christopher Publishing, 1961.

Schwartz, David G. *Roll the Bones: The History of Gambling.* New York: Gotham, 2006.

Seal, Graham. *The Outlaw Legend: A Cultural Tradition in Britain, America and Australia.* Cambridge: Cambridge University Press, 1996.

Secrest, William B. *California Desperadoes: Stories of Early California Outlaws in Their Own Words.* Clovis, Calif.: Word Dancer, 2000.

———. *Lawmen & Desperadoes: A Compendium of Noted, Early California Peace Officers, Badmen and Outlaws 1850–1900.* Spokane, Wash.: Arthur H. Clark, 1994.

Seitz, Don C. *Famous American Duels: With Some Account of the Causes That Led to Them.* N.p.: Papamoa, 2017.

Shaw, Ian W. *Into the Sunset: Emmett Dalton and the End of the Dalton Gang.* Lawrence: University of Kansas Press, 2023.

Shenkman, Richard. *Legends, Lies & Cherished Myths of American History.* New York: William Morrow, 1988.

Shillingberg, William B. *Dodge City: The Early Years, 1872–1886.* Norman: University of Oklahoma Press, 2009.

Shirley, Glenn. *Belle Starr and Her Times: The Literature, the Facts and the Legends.* Norman: University of Oklahoma Press, 1990.

———. *Law West of Fort Smith: A History of Frontier Justice in the Indian Territory, 1834–1896.* Lincoln: University of Nebraska Press, 1968.

———. *Shotgun for Hire: The Story of "Deacon" Jim Miller, Killer of Pat Garrett.* Norman: University of Oklahoma Press, 1970.

———. *West of Hell's Fringe: Crime, Criminals, and the Federal Peace Officer in Oklahoma Territory, 1889–1907.* Norman: University of Oklahoma Press, 1990.

Siringo, Charles A. *A Texas Cowboy, or, Fifteen Years on the Hurricane Deck of a Spanish Pony.* 2015.

Skaggs, Jimmy M. *The Cattle-Trailing Industry: Between Supply and Demand, 1866–1890.* Norman: University of Oklahoma Press, 1991.

Sloan, Irving J. *Our Violent Past: An American Chronicle.* New York: Random House, 1970.

Slotkin, Richard. *The Fatal Environment: The Myth of the Frontier in the Age of Industrialization, 1800–1890.* Norman: University of Oklahoma Press, 1998.

———. *Gunfighter Nation: The Myth of the Frontier in Twentieth-Century America.* Norman: University of Oklahoma Press, 1998.

———. *Regeneration through Violence: The Mythology of the American Frontier, 1600–1860.* Norman: University of Oklahoma Press, 2000.

Smallwood, James M. *The Feud That Wasn't: The Taylor Ring, Bill Sutton, John Wesley Hardin, and Violence in Texas.* College Station: Texas A&M University Press, 2008.

Smallwood, James M., Barry A. Crouch, and Larry Peacock. *Murder and Mayhem: The War of Reconstruction in Texas.* College Station: Texas A&M University Press, 2003.

Smallwood, James M., Kenneth W. Howell, and Carol C. Taylor. *The Devil's Triangle: Ben Bickerstaff, Northeast Texans, and the War of Reconstruction in Texas.* Denton: University of North Texas Press, 2007.

Smith, Duane. *Rocky Mountain West: Colorado, Wyoming, and Montana, 1859–1915.* Albuquerque: University of New Mexico Press, 1992.

Smith, Robert Barr. *Bad Blood: The Families Who Made the West Wild.* Guilford, Conn.: TwoDot, 2014.

———. *Outlaw Tales of Oklahoma: True Stories of the Sooner State's Most Infamous Crooks, Culprits, and Cutthroats.* Guilford, Conn.: TwoDot, 2013.

Smithwick, Noah. *The Evolution of a State, or Recollections of Old Texas Days.* Austin: University of Texas Press, 1983.

Sonnichsen, C. L. *From Hopalong to Hud: Thoughts on Western Fiction.* College Station: Texas A&M University Press, 1978.

———. *I'll Die Before I'll Run: The Story of the Great Feuds of Texas.* Lincoln: University of Nebraska Press, 1988.

———. *10 Texas Feuds.* Albuquerque: University of New Mexico Press, 2000.

———. *Tularosa: Last of the Frontier West.* Albuquerque: University of New Mexico Press, 1980.

Southworth, Dave. *Feuds on the Western Frontier.* N.p.: Wild Horse, 2010.

Stamps, Roy, and Joann Stamps, eds. *The Letters of John Wesley Hardin.* Fort Worth: Eakin, 2001.

Steckmesser, Kent Ladd. *The Western Hero in History and Legend.* Norman: University of Oklahoma Press, 1997.

Stevens, William Oliver. *Pistols at Ten Paces: The Story of the Code of Honor in America.* Boston: Houghton Mifflin, 1940.

Steward, Dick. *Duels and the Roots of Violence in Missouri.* Columbia: University of Missouri Press, 2000.

Stiles, T. J. *Jesse James: Last Rebel of the Civil War.* New York: Vintage, 2002.

Stuart, Granville. *Forty Years on the Frontier.* Lincoln: University of Nebraska Press, 1977.

Sutherland, Daniel E. *A Savage Conflict: The Decisive Role of Guerrillas in the American Civil War.* Chapel Hill: University of North Carolina Press, 2009.

Swierczynski, Duane. *This Here's a Stick-Up: The Big Bad Book of American Bank Robbery.* Indianapolis: Alpha, 2002.

Tanner, Karen Holliday, and John D. Tanner Jr. *Last of the Old-Time Outlaws: The George West Musgrave Story.* Norman: University of Oklahoma Press, 2002.

Tatum, Stephen. *Inventing Billy the Kid: Visions of the Outlaw in America, 1881–1981.* Tucson: University of Arizona Press, 1997.

Taylor, Don. *Tombstone: The First Fifty Years 1879–1929.* N.p.: Old West, 2020.

Taylor, Lonn, and Ingrid Maar. *The American Cowboy.* Washington, D.C.: American Folklife Center, 1983.

Tefertiller, Casey. *Wyatt Earp: The Life behind the Legend.* New York: John Wiley & Sons, 1997.

Thompson, Jerry D., ed. *Juan Cortina and the Texas-Mexico Frontier, 1859–1877.* El Paso: Texas Western Press, 1994.

Trachtman, Paul, with editors of Time-Life Books. *The Gunfighters.* Alexandria, Va.: Time-Life, 1974.

Trimble, Marshall. *Arizona Outlaws and Lawmen.* Mount Pleasant, S.C.: History, 2015.

Twain, Mark. *Roughing It.* Digireads.com, 2004.

Utley, Robert M. *Billy the Kid: A Short and Violent Life.* Lincoln: University of Nebraska Press, 1989.

———. *High Noon in Lincoln: Violence on the Western Frontier.* Albuquerque: University of New Mexico Press, 1987.

———. *Lone Star Justice: The First Century of the Texas Rangers.* Oxford: Oxford University Press, 1992.

Vestal, Stanley. *Queen of Cowtowns: Dodge City, "The Wickedest Little City in America," 1872–1886.* Lincoln: University of Nebraska Press, 1972.

Vulich, Nick. *Shot All to Hell: Bad Ass Outlaws, Gunfighters, and Lawmen of the Old West.* Self-published, 2016.

Waite, Kevin. *West of Slavery: The Southern Dream of a Transcontinental Empire.* Chapel Hill: University of North Carolina Press, 2021.

Waller, Brown. *Last of the Great Western Train Robbers.* Cranbury, N.J.: A. S. Barnes, 1968.

Wallis, Michael. *Billy the Kid: The Endless Ride*. New York: W. W. Norton, 2007.

Walton, William M. *Life and Adventures of Ben Thompson: The Famous Texan*. Houston: Frontier Press, 1954.

Warren, Mark. *The Long Road to Legend: Wyatt Earp, an American Odyssey*. Guilford, Conn.: TwoDot, 2021.

Webb, Walter Prescott. *The Great Plains*. Lincoln: University of Nebraska Press, 1981.

———. *The Texas Rangers: A Century of Frontier Defense*. Austin: University of Texas Press, 1991.

Weidensaul, Scott. *The First Frontier: The Forgotten History of Struggle, Savagery & Endurance in Early America*. Boston: Houghton Mifflin, 2012.

Wellman, Paul. *A Dynasty of Western Outlaws*. Lincoln: University of Nebraska Press, 1986.

———. *Spawn of Evil*. New York: Modern Literary Editions, 1964.

———. *The Trampling Herd: The Story of the Cattle Range in America*. Lincoln: University of Nebraska Press, 1988.

Wexler, Bruce. *The Gunfighters: How the West Was Won*. New York: Skyhorse, 2011.

White, Richard. *"It's Your Misfortune and None of My Own": A New History of the American West*. Norman: University of Oklahoma Press, 1991.

Wilkins, Frederick. *The Law Comes to Texas: The Texas Rangers, 1870–1901*. Austin: State House Press, 1999.

Williams, Jack K. *Dueling in the Old South: Vignettes of Social History*. College Station: Texas A&M University Press, 1980.

Williamson, G. R. *Frontier Gambling: The Games, the Gamblers and the Great Gambling Halls of the Old West*. N.p.: Indian Head Publishing, 2011.

———. *Texas Pistoleers: The True Story of Ben Thompson and King Fisher*. Mount Pleasant, S.C.: History, 2010.

Wilson, Charles Reagan, and William Ferris, eds. *Encyclopedia of Southern Culture*. Chapel Hill: University of North Carolina Press, 1989.

Wilson, Gary A. *The Life and Death of Kid Curry: Tiger of the Wild Bunch*. Guilford, Conn.: TwoDot, 2016.

———. *Outlaw Tales of Montana: True Stories of the Treasure State's Most Infamous Crooks, Culprits, and Cutthroats*. Guilford, Conn.: TwoDot, 2012.

Wilson, R. Michael. *Great Train Robberies of the Old West*. Guilford, Conn.: TwoDot, 2007.

———. *Outlaw Tales of Wyoming: True Stories of the Cowboy State's Most Infamous Crooks, Culprits, and Cutthroats*. Guilford, Conn.: TwoDot, 2013.

Winkler, Adam. *Gunfight: The Battle over the Right to Bear Arms in America*. New York: W. W. Norton, 2011.

Worcester, Don. *The Texas Longhorn: Relic of the Past, Asset for the Future*. College Station: Texas A&M University Press, 1987.

Wyatt-Brown, Bertram. *The Shaping of Southern Culture: Honor, Grace, and War, 1760s–1880s*. Chapel Hill: University of North Carolina Press, 2001.

———. *Southern Honor: Ethics and Behavior in the Old South*. New York: Oxford University Press, 2007.

Yadon, Laurence J., and Dan Anderson. *200 Texas Outlaws and Lawmen, 1835–1935*. Gretna, La.: Pelican, 2008.

Yeatman, Ted P. *Frank and Jesse James: The Story behind the Legend*. Nashville: Cumberland, 2000.

Young, Richard, and Judy Dockrey Young, eds. *Outlaw Tales: Legends, Myths, and Folklore from America's Middle Border*. Little Rock, Ark.: August House, 1992.

Young, Roy B., Gary L. Roberts, and Casey Tefertiller. *A Wyatt Earp Anthology: Long May His Story Be Told*. Denton: University of North Texas Press, 2019.

ILLUSTRATION CREDITS

Insert One

Page 1. Top: Everett Collection Historical/Alamy Stock Photo; bottom: Chronicle/Alamy Stock Photo

Page 2. Top right: Courtesy of True West Archives; bottom left: Everett Collection Inc./Alamy Stock Photo

Page 3. Courtesy of True West Archives

Pages 4 and 5. Spread: Courtesy of the Church History Library, The Church of Jesus Christ of Latter-day Saints

Page 5. Inset: Courtesy of Fort Worth Star-Telegram Collection, Special Collections, The University of Texas at Arlington Libraries

Page 6. Everett Collection Historical/Alamy Stock Photo

Page 7. Bottom left: Bettmann via Getty; top left: Science History Images/Alamy Stock Photo

Page 8. Top left: Bettmann via Getty Images; top right: Pictorial Press Ltd/Alamy Stock Photo; bottom: BLM Collection/Alamy Stock Photo

Page 9. GL Archive/Alamy Stock Photo

Page 10. Top: Everett Collection Historical/Alamy Stock Photo; right: Archivah/Alamy Stock Photo

Page 11. Historic Images/Alamy Stock Photo

Page 12. Top left: nsf/Alamy Stock Photo; bottom left: C. S. Fly via Everett Collection/Shutterstock

Page 13. Top right: MSM Archive/Alamy Stock Photo

Page 14. Top left: American Photo Archive/Alamy Stock Photo; top right: American Stock Archive via Getty Images; bottom left: GL Archive/Alamy Stock Photo; bottom right: Courtesy of True West Archives

Page 15. Private Collection/AF Eisenbahn Archiv/Alamy Stock Photo

Page 16. Courtesy of Texas State Library and Archives Commission

ILLUSTRATION CREDITS

Insert Two

Page 1. GL Archive/Alamy Stock Photo

Page 2. Top: Bennett & Burrall. New Mexico Rustlers. Courtesy of the Palace of the Governors Photo Archives (NMHM/DCA), 014264

Page 3. Top: Historic Images/Alamy Stock Photo; bottom: Bad Hoss Maps

Page 4. IanDagnall Computing/Alamy Stock Photo

Pages 5 and 6. Courtesy of True West Archives

Page 7. Bottom: GL Archive/Alamy Stock Photo

Page 8. Top left: Zuri Swimmer/Alamy Stock Photo; top center: FLHC 1C/Alamy Stock Photo; right center and bottom: FLHC MADB1/Alamy Stock Photo

Page 9. University of Wyoming, American Heritage Center

Page 10. Top left: Courtesy Arizona Historical Society, PC 1000, Portraits-Tewksbury, John #2018; top right and bottom left: Courtesy of True West Archives

Page 11. Bottom: Danvis Collection/Alamy Stock Photo

Page 12. Top left and top center: Rapp Halour/Alamy Stock Photo; center: Underwood Archives via Getty

Pages 12 and 13. Bottom: Historic Images/Alamy Stock Photo

Page 13. Top right: Oklahoma Historical Society Photograph Collection

Page 14. Top: World History Archive/Alamy Stock Photo; bottom left: Science History Images/Alamy Stock Photo; bottom right: Courtesy of True West Archives

Page 15. Gibson Green/Alamy Stock Photo

INDEX

Abbott, Teddy, 91, 93
Abilene, Kans., 1, 14, 17, 93–95, 100–107,
    112, 123, 133, 147, 214
alcohol, 17, 40, 52, 72, 91, 132, 156, 165,
    339, 341
Algerio, Alberto, 121
Allen, J. S., 178–79
Allison, Clay, 4, 6, 52, 91, 133–34, 142–49,
    240, 381
American individualism, 3–4, 7, 24
Ames, Adelbert, 177, 179
Anderson, "Bloody Bill," 171–73
Anderson, Hugh, 112–13
Angel, Frank Warner, 228, 235
Antrim, Bill, 214–15
Apache County, Ariz., 310, 314–19
Argentina, 372–74, 377–78
Argosy, 295
Arizona Rangers, 377
Arizona Territory, 200
    Billy the Kid in, 215–17
    Butch Cassidy in, 363
    cattle ranching in, 261–66, 314, 317, 321,
        327, 329
    description of, 261
    gunfighters in, 164, 271–72, 374
    gunfights in, 14, 274, 277, 300–301, 309,
        313, 316, 319–22, 377
    lawmen in, 216
    outlaw gangs in, 262–66, 278, 370
    railroads arrive in, 270
    robberies in, 171, 377

statehood of, 322, 377
Texas cattle rustlers in, 261–66
and Texas cattle trade, 15, 89, 357–58
transformed by Texans, 15, 261–62
war with Apache, 327
See also Tombstone, Ariz.
Arkansas, 23, 26, 53, 57–59, 64, 84, 128,
    175, 354, 366
Armstrong, John, 189–91
Arthur, Chester A., 303
Austin, Tex., 55, 77–78, 119–23, 140, 191,
    199–202, 292
Aztec Land and Cattle Company, 310–12,
    315, 321

Baca, Elfego, 255–59, 363, 376, 381
Bailey, Billy, 112
Baker, Cullen, 9, 56–61, 69, 101, 170,
    191–93, 376
Baker, Frank, 223
bank robberies, 197, 206, 298, 327, 355
    by Butch Cassidy, 360–62, 367,
        372–73, 377
    by Jesse James, 3, 56, 169–80, 347
    in Minnesota, 177–80
    in Missouri, 3, 56, 173
    in Oklahoma, 339–40, 346–49, 354
    by outlaw gangs, 351, 354, 368, 370
    by Sundance Kid, 372–73, 377
Barnes, David, 166
Barrymore, Maurice, 204
Bass, Sam, 4, 193–98, 204, 364–65, 370

Battle of Bates Point, 324
Battle of Ingalls, 351–53
Battle of Walker's Creek, 36–37
Bean, Joshua, 42
Beckwith, Robert, 233–34
Behan, Johnny, 272, 276, 278, 281–86, 290, 299–303
Bell, James W., 250
Bell, Tom, 42, 274
Beni, Jules, 48
Bickerstaff, Ben, 60–61, 64
Bideno, Juan, 104–5
"Big Nose Kate," 139, 267, 269, 279
Billy the Kid, 9, 213, 292, 303, 342, 359
    in Arizona, 215–17
    in books/films, 246, 254–55, 375, 381
    as cattle ranch hand, 215, 219–21
    as cattle/horse rustler, 235–36, 239–43, 246–47
    childhood/family of, 214–15
    death of, 254–55, 305, 336
    descriptions of, 215–16, 249, 251–52, 255
    escapes convictions/prison, 249–51, 380
    fame of, 3, 5, 14, 70, 95, 109, 161, 167, 169, 241
    first crimes/killings of, 215–17
    as folk hero, 222, 251–55
    Garrett's hunt for, 245–50, 252–54
    gravesite of, 380
    gunfights of, 14, 63, 224–26, 233–35, 241, 246
    his "gang," 240–41, 246, 304
    indictments against, 227–29, 236–39, 242, 249
    as informant, 238–39, 242
    joins "the Boys," 216–17
    and Lincoln County War, 221–39, 242–43
    newspaper reports on, 242, 246, 249, 251–52, 255
    an outlaw, 239–42, 267, 315
    photograph of, 242
    retreats in Ruidoso, 217–19, 223, 229
    Rudabaugh rides with, 164
    skills with a gun, 215, 218, 220, 241
Billy the Kid (ballet), 255
Blacks, 54, 64, 189
    enslaved, 22, 53, 55
    freed, 53, 55, 57
    killed by gunfighters, 70–72, 75–77, 138, 191–92
    lynching of, 23, 55, 60, 188
    in Texas State Police, 73, 75
    violence against, 53–61, 66–67, 173
    See also slavery
Blake, Bill. See Tulsa Jack
Blaylock, Mattie, 267
Blazer's Mill (N.Mex.), 224, 229
Blevins, Andy, 311–13, 316–20
Blevins, Charley, 321
Blevins, Hamp, 311–13
Blevins, John, 319–20
Blevins, Mart, 311–12
Blevins, Sam Houston, 320
Blevins family, 319, 381
Bodie, Calif., 15, 17, 45
Boessenecker, John, 5, 38–39, 44, 262
Boles, Charles E., 45
Bolivia, 27, 377–78
Bolton, Martha, 183–84
Bonney, William H. See Billy the Kid
books
    dime novels, 5, 99, 109, 169, 171, 368
    on gambling, 117
    by gunfighters, 9, 71, 330, 377
    gunfighters in, 4–6, 44, 134, 191, 255, 340
    reintroduce gunfighters, 5–7, 45, 109, 294, 350
    sort fact from fiction, 8–10
    on Wyatt Earp, 126–27
    See also Western literature
Boone, Daniel, 19
Boot Hill (Dodge City), 131
Boot Hill Museum (Dodge City), 380–81
Boot Hill (Tombstone), 131
bounty hunters, 74, 137, 188, 192, 195, 303, 354
Bowdre, Charlie, 217–18, 225, 232, 235–36, 240, 247–48, 380
Bowen, Brown, 78, 189–91
Bowen, Jane. See Hardin, Jane Bowen
Bowie, Jim, 27–28
bowie knife, 27–28, 33, 40–41, 44, 71, 79
boxing, 154–55, 159, 161, 329, 376
"Boys, the," 212–13, 216–20, 223, 263
Brady, William, 221, 223–24, 227–29, 239, 249
Brazel, Wayne, 336
Breakenridge, Billy, 293–94
Brennan, Mollie, 135–36

Brennan's Saloon (Ellsworth, Kans.), 123–25
Brewer, Dick, 218–20, 223, 225–26
Brighton, Jonas V., 315–17
Broadwell, Dick "Texas Jack," 347–49
Brocius, "Curly" Bill, 213, 263–66, 269–74, 277–79, 292, 301–3, 311
"Brocky Jack," 113–14
brothels, 49, 111, 129–30, 132, 374
Brown, "Longhair Sam," 41
Brown, Richard Maxwell, 8, 88, 92–93
Brown's Hole, 358, 361–62, 369, 371
Bryant, "Black-Faced Charley," 342–44
Buffalo Bill. *See* Cody, Buffalo Bill
buffalo hunters, 13, 210, 245, 317
Bull's Head Saloon (Abilene), 102–3
Burns, Walter Noble, 6, 291, 293–95
Burr, Aaron, 20, 25
Burrow, Rudb, 366
bushwhackers, 171–74, 182

Cahill, Francis P., 216
California, 13–14, 92, 278, 343–44, 364
  gambling in, 117
  gunfighters' graves in, 379
  gunfighters in, 38–45, 101, 376–77
  outlaw gangs in, 39, 274
  train robberies in, 341, 366
  violence in, 45
  Wyatt Earp in, 128, 376
  See also Gold Rush
Camp Rucker, Ariz., 269
Campbell, Billy, 236–38
Carlyle, Jimmy, 246–47
carpetbaggers, 56, 60, 69, 72–74, 175
Carroll, Henry, 237
Carson City, Nev., 41, 46
Carver, Will "News," 372–73
Cassidy, Butch
  description of, 358–59
  fame of, 9, 367, 378
  flees to Argentina, 3, 372–75
  late life/death of, 377–78
  newspaper reports on, 362, 372
  robberies by, 170, 359–64, 367, 369–71
  on the run, 330, 371–72
Catron, Thomas B., 229
cattle trails, 92–93, 141, 153, 315
cattle ranching
  American system of, 262
  and armed cowboys, 205–6

corruption in, 219–20, 264
  and longhorns, 82, 90, 92, 140, 210, 357
  newspaper reports on, 212
  Spanish traditions of, 82
  Texas traditions of, 82–84, 89–94
  See also specific states
cattle rustlers, 42, 217
  in Arizona, 261–66, 269–70, 278, 290, 309–11, 314–17, 321
  and frontier violence, 13, 82–88, 90
  in Mexico, 263–66, 269–70, 272, 277–78
  in New Mexico, 210–13, 219–23, 228–29, 234, 238–43, 264–65, 377
  in Texas, 54, 83–88, 194, 234, 240–42, 247, 306, 332–35, 358
  in Wyoming, 360, 368
cattlemen, 13, 24, 337
  associations for, 305, 314, 324–26
  and code of conduct, 87–88
  in Dodge City, 133, 151–53
  and gambling, 114, 124–25
  as gunfighters, 4, 14, 74–75, 80
  the press on, 205–6
  versus sheepherders, 306–14, 330, 335
  and violence, 13–14, 83–88, 323–26
  See also Stockmen's Convention
Central Overland stations, 47
Champion, Nate, 325–26, 381
Chapman, Huston, 235, 237–38
Charleston, Ariz., 270–73, 296, 301
Charleston, S.C., 24, 26, 82
Cheery, Noah, 36
Cherokee Bob, 41, 45
Cheyenne, Wyo., 108, 148
Chicago, 92, 101, 125, 161, 175, 202, 379
Chinese immigrants, 14, 39, 43, 215
Chipley, William, 189–90
Chisum, John, 210, 212, 220, 223–24, 230, 234, 241–47, 262, 263
Christian, William "Black Jack," 370
Cimarron, N.Mex., 143, 145
Civil War, 82, 187
  firearms of, 52–53
  gunfighters in, 52, 119–21, 142–43
  and Jesse James, 171–73
  outlaw violence in, 54–56, 64–65
  and postwar violence, 51–67, 88

Civil War (*cont.*)
  and Texas cattle trade, 91–93
  veterans of, 1, 51–55, 60, 64–65, 83, 98,
    119–21, 142–43, 177, 185
Claiborne, Billy, 288
Clanton, Billy, 264, 273, 282, 286–90
Clanton, Ike, 274, 298, 303
  arrest warrant for, 295–96
  cattle rustling by, 264–65
  death of, 315–16
  secret deal with Earp, 276–77, 279–82
  in Tombstone gunfight, 285–88, 290
  and Tombstone today, 381
  and Virgil Earp's death, 291
Clanton, Newman "Old Man," 264,
    273, 278
Clanton, Phin, 315
Clark, Dick, 117–18, 133
Clement, Archie, 172–73
Clements, Jim, 102
Clements, Mannen, 74, 111–12, 299,
    331, 333
Clements, Mannie, 333
Clements, Sallie. *See* Miller, Sallie
    Clements
Clements brothers, 74–75, 78, 101–2
Clifton, Dan. *See* Dynamite Dick
Coble, John, 328–30
Code of the West, 61–67, 81–82, 87–88
Cody, Buffalo Bill, 90, 108, 292, 317
Coe, Frank, 217–18, 235
Coe, George, 225, 234–35
Coe, Phil, 102, 106–7, 121, 123
Coffeyville, Kans., 15, 311, 340, 346–51
Cohron, Billy, 104
Colbert, "Chunk," 143–44, 146
Colfax County War, 144–45, 240
Collier, Elisha, 33
Collins, Joel, 194–95
Colorado, 162
  Brown's Hole hideout in, 358
  Butch Cassidy in, 360
  cattle ranching/rustlers in, 329, 368
  gunfighters in, 156–57, 165, 374
  robberies in, 360, 374
  sheep raids/wars in, 307–8, 323
  and Texas cattle trade, 357
  Wyatt Earp in, 158, 303–4
Colt, Samuel, 34–38, 40
Colt Walker revolver, 37–40

Comanche, 16, 32–36, 86, 108, 134, 209–11,
    245, 306
Comanche, Tex., 80–81
Comique Theater (Dodge City),
    141–42, 152
Confederates, 1, 56, 175, 209
  and bushwhackers, 171–73
  gunmen/outlaws as, 9, 52, 69, 72,
    119–20, 177
  postwar feuds and, 64
  terrorize Union sympathizers, 54,
    172–73
  and Texas cattle trade, 83, 92
Contention, Ariz., 271, 274, 296, 298
Cooley, Scott, 86–87
Coombs, John, 120–21
Copeland, John, 227–29
Cortina, Juan, 187
Corydon, Iowa, 174
Cosmopolitan Hotel (Tombstone), 168,
    291, 296, 298–99
Couger, Charles, 105
counterfeit money, 242, 361
Courtright, Jim, 52, 159–60
cowboys, 114
  and Cowboy Code, 62
  disarming of, 205–6, 305
  favored weapons of, 91
  and gunfighting, 14, 89, 194, 340
  newspaper reports on, 204–6
  and Southern customs, 311
  the "Texas cowboy," 89–91
  in Western literature, 5–6
  See also Hashknifes; Hollywood films:
    cowboys in
Cowboys gang, 292, 294
  cattle rustling by, 264–66, 269–72,
    277–78
  and Earp brothers, 269–83, 296–303
  and elections, 272, 274, 295
  founding of, 262–64
  gunfights of, 263, 270–71, 274, 277
  last days of, 303–4
  newspaper reports on, 275, 278
  rob stagecoaches, 265–66, 274–75,
    278–79
  in Tombstone gunfight, 285–91
Crawford, Edward, 125
Crittenden, Thomas, 182–84
Crockett, Davy, 19, 32

Cruz, Florentino, 300–301
Cunningham, Eugene, 6–7, 294–95
Curly Bill. *See* Brocius, "Curly" Bill
Currie, "Flat Nose" George, 368

Daggs family, 311–12
Daily New Mexican, The, 251–52
Dallas, Tex., 54, 88, 117, 138, 166, 195
Dalton, Bill, 341, 350–54. *See also*
    Doolin-Dalton Gang
Dalton, Bob, 340–49, 359
Dalton, Emmett, 341–50
Dalton, Frank, 341
Dalton, Grat, 341, 344–45, 347–49
Dalton Gang, 15, 342–50
Daugherty, Roy "Arkansas Tom," 352–53
Davis, Jonathan R., 44
de Mouche, Louis, 161–62
De Toth, André, 7
Deadwood, S.Dak., 108–9, 194, 379
DeArment, Robert, 8, 147
Democrats, 207, 290, 299
Denton, Tex., 54, 194–96
Denver, Col., 171, 303, 329–30
    bank robberies in, 360
    Bat Masterson in, 154, 158, 160
    cattle herds in, 92, 210
    gambling in, 117–18, 138, 154
    Pinkerton detectives in, 314–15, 327
Denver Tribune, 251
Department of Justice, 228
detectives, 5–6, 105, 160, 164, 175, 195, 346,
    367. *See also* Pinkerton; range
    detectives
DeWitt County, Tex., 77–78
Dillinger, John, 359–60, 372, 379
Dobie, J. Frank, 63
Dodge City Gang, 162–64, 240
Dodge City, Kans., 123, 163, 263
    Clay Allison in, 142, 146–47, 149
    description of, 131–34, 139
    gambling in, 131–33, 140–41, 158, 166
    and gunfighter Luke Short, 157–59
    gunfighter Mather in, 164–66
    gunfighter sites in, 380–81
    gunfights in, 14, 136, 140–42, 153–54,
      165–66
    Kenedy-Kelley incident in, 151–53
    lawmen in, 6, 136–37, 139–42,
      165–66, 354

laws/ordinances of, 103, 157–58, 305
murder rate of, 17
myths/notoriety of, 131–33
and Texas cattle/cowboys, 112, 130–36,
    139–42, 146–47, 151–53, 157, 166
Wyatt Earp and, 133–34, 153, 158–59,
    206, 271
Dodge City War, 158–59
Dolan, Jimmy, 220–24, 227–30, 236–39, 380
Dolan forces, 227–34, 239
Doolin, Bill, 9, 344–47, 350–55, 369
Doolin, Edith Ellsworth, 351, 354
Doolin-Dalton Gang, 350–55
Driskill, Tobe, 140–42
Dudley, Nathan A. M., 231–32, 235,
    237, 239
duelists, 19–21, 27–28
duels, 40, 119, 143, 183
    causes of, 25, 28–29, 116
    and codes of honor, 10–11, 20–24, 27–29
    history of, 19–29
    methods/rules for, 24–26, 28, 293
    morph into gunfights, 24, 26–28
    in Texas, 54, 57, 63
    weapons for, 25, 28, 33
Duncan, Jack, 189–90
Dykstra, Robert R., 17
Dynamite Dick, 351, 354

Earp, James, 127–30, 267–68
Earp, Josephine, 376, 379
Earp, Morgan, 126–29, 268, 275, 278–82,
    286–91, 296–98, 301
Earp, Virgil, 272–73
    brothers seek revenge for, 295–99
    in Civil War, 52, 128
    and Cowboys gang, 280–83
    criminal career of, 127–29
    death of, 376
    pursues Leonard gang, 275
    in Tombstone gunfight, 286–91
    as Tombstone marshal, 268–69,
      278–83, 290
    wounded, 126, 287–91, 298
Earp, Warren, 127, 268, 300
Earp, Wyatt, 170, 206, 266, 354
    arrest warrants for, 296, 299–303
    arrests Ben Thompson, 126, 129
    childhood/family of, 127–28
    and Clay Allison incident, 146–47

Earp, Wyatt (*cont.*)
  in Colorado, 158, 303–4
  and Cowboys gang, 269–70, 273–82
  and Curly Bill incident, 270–71
  as deputy, 111–12, 295–96
  in Dodge City, 131–34, 136–37, 140–42
  and Dodge City sites, 380–81
  on Driskill incident, 140–41
  an escaped prisoner, 8, 126–29
  fame of, 3–6, 9, 14, 91, 95, 109, 126–27,
    131, 155, 161, 167, 169, 350
  in famous gunfight, 285–91, 297
  on the fast draw, 7, 100
  first lawman job of, 129–30, 297
  gambling of, 115, 126, 268, 376
  and gunfighter Luke Short, 158–59
  in gunfights, 44, 141–42
  interviews of, 303, 376
  and Johnny Ringo, 292–94, 296
  and Kenedy-Kelley incident, 151–53
  late life/death of, 376, 379
  as lawman, 8, 126–30, 133–37, 140–41,
    146, 151–53, 272, 278–83, 299, 381
  men killed by, 127, 299, 331
  in New Mexico, 162, 164, 303
  newspaper reports on, 141, 295, 299, 303
  origin story of, 139–42
  portrayals of, 5, 126–27, 255, 267, 375
  pursues Leonard and gang, 275–77
  seeks revenge for brothers, 295–99
  on Sweetwater gunfight, 135–36
  in Tombstone, 153, 213, 267–69, 376
  as Wells Fargo guard, 268
Earp "Vendetta"/"Vendetta Ride," 298–303
East Las Vegas, N.Mex., 162–67
Edwards, John Newman, 175, 177, 181
El Paso Salt War, 218–19, 263
El Paso, Tex., 207, 212, 218–19, 263–64,
  336, 375, 377, 380
Ellsworth, Kans., 112–14, 123–26, 128, 133,
  140, 151
Evans, Jesse, 213–17, 219–23, 227–28,
  236–39, 263

Fehrenbach, T. R., 38, 62–63, 89
feudists, 4, 6, 90, 187–88, 200, 238, 350, 377
feuds, 13, 45, 57
  in Arizona, 308–14, 321–22
  of cattle ranchers, 13, 81–91, 207,
    211–13, 337

  causes of, 23, 367
  and codes of honor, 21–22
  deadly ones, 23, 53–54, 204, 310, 314
  Early–Hasley, 64
  Graham–Tewksbury, 308–14
  Hatfield–McCoy, 23, 64, 308
  Lee–Peacock, 64–67
  in New Mexico, 255
  post–Civil War, 63–67
  Sutton–Taylor, 77–80, 188, 331
  in Texas, 24, 54, 63–67, 71, 188, 207, 263,
    331–34
  See also Pleasant Valley War
First Fast Draw, The (L'Amour), 57
Fisher, King, 9, 187–89, 202–3
Florida, 21, 34, 69, 188–89
Fly, C. S., 286, 289
Folsom prison, 341
Ford, Charley and Bob, 184–85
Fort Grant, N.Mex., 215–16
Fort Griffin, Tex., 137–39
Fort Stanton, N.Mex., 228, 231, 237
Fort Sumner, N.Mex., 235–36, 239–43,
  246–54, 380
Fort Worth, Tex., 83, 118, 156, 159–62, 165,
  262, 334–35, 373
Foster, Joe, 201–3
Fox, Richard Kyle, 204
Frazer, Bud, 332–34
Fredericksburg, Tex., 54–55, 87
Freedmen's Bureau, 57, 72
frontier
  becomes civilized, 206–7, 305
  and last of the outlaws, 371, 375–76
  romanticization of, 375–76
  shrinking of, 323
frontier violence
  extrajudicial, 23–24, 29, 88, 267
  fades out, 375–76, 379
  introduction to, 13–18
  personal, 13, 18, 22, 32–33, 306
  Texas-style, 91–93, 198, 204–6, 323–24
  various types of, 26, 32
frontiersmen, 19, 26, 31–32, 61
Fuller, Wesley, 287–88

Gallatin, Mo., 173–74, 185
gambling, 76, 101–2, 107, 292, 376
  in boomtowns, 94, 108, 112
  cheating in, 115, 117, 139, 151, 189

and drinking, 138
on the frontier, 6, 40–41, 72–73, 114–18
by gunfighters, 155–57, 362
and lawmen, 140
laws for, 115–16
leads to gunfights, 2, 4, 73, 120, 123–26, 138, 145, 151, 161–62, 166, 189, 201
professionals in, 115–18, 121–22, 157–59
in the South, 22, 41
Garrett, Pat, 4, 19, 245–50, 252–54, 336
Gentlemen's Blood (Holland), 25
Georgia, 26, 53, 137–38
Geronimo, 327
Gold Rush, 15, 28, 38–45, 88, 117
Gonzales County, Tex., 74–78, 189
Goodnight, Charles, 92, 210
Gordon, James, 96
Gordon, Mike, 163
Graham, Billy, 313
Graham, John, 309, 313, 321
Graham, Tom, 309, 313, 321–22
Graham–Tewksbury feud, 308–14, 321–22
Grant, Joe "Texas Red," 241
Grant, Ulysses S., 122
Great Plains, The (Webb), 88
Green, Jonathan H., 117
Grey, Zane, 62
Griego, Francisco "Pancho," 145–46
Gunfighter, The (film), 7, 295
Gunfighter Era, 3, 14–16, 38–39, 91, 103, 130, 169, 212, 292, 305–6, 374
Gunfighter: Man or Myth?, The, 8
gunfighters
    as celebrities, 95, 109, 169, 198, 349–50, 354
    concept/term of, 4–9, 98
    the last, 305–6, 375–76, 379
    legacy of, 4, 378–82
    monuments to, 379–82
    mystique of, 46–47
    myths/tropes of, 3–6, 9, 14, 94–98, 142
    origins of, 18–29
    post–Civil War, 53, 56–67
    See also specific names; specific states
gunfights
    causes of, 3, 73, 91, 115, 206, 374, 379
    commonalities in, 10–11, 18
    duels morph into, 24–29
    first Wild West–style, 3, 38–39
    notable ones, 4–5, 13–14

post–Civil War, 3, 51–55, 60, 65–66
    synopsis of, 145
    See also gambling: by gunfighters
guns
    Americans' views of, 5, 53, 379
    for "buffaloing," 133, 136, 281–82
    fast draw and, 7–8, 57, 160–61, 294
    fines for carrying, 114, 282, 293
    from Civil War, 52–53
    and frontier violence, 10–11, 13–17, 267
    gunfighters' skill with, 341, 379
    gunmanship and, 36–38
    history of/advances in, 33–36
    laws for, 103, 305, 377
    pistols, 25, 33, 35–36, 40–41, 99
    and road agent's spin, 75, 103
    and Texans, 32–38, 379
    turned in to sheriffs, 103
    wearing of, 26, 40, 52–53, 99, 115, 139
    See also revolvers; rifles
guns for hire, 4, 327, 334–35
Gunsmoke (radio show), 131
Gunsmoke (TV show), 8, 131, 380
Gutierrez, Celsa, 246, 253–54

Hamilton, Alexander, 20–21, 25
"handkerchief fight," 143, 293
Hannah, William, 200
Hardin, Jane Bowen, 75–76, 79
Hardin, Joe, 79–80
Hardin, John Wesley "Wes," 111, 128, 138, 234, 267
    aliases of, 188, 190
    arrests of, 73–77, 80–81, 292
    capture/arrest of, 188–91, 193, 198
    chief rival of, 191–93
    childhood/family of, 71, 95, 215
    as cowboy/cattleman, 72, 74–76, 80, 101
    criminal career of, 170, 191
    face off with Hickok, 102–6, 147
    fame of, 9, 69–70, 91, 95, 101, 105, 126
    gambling of, 72–73, 76, 80, 115, 189, 190
    gravesite of, 380
    killing sprees of, 67, 70, 72–73, 75–77
    late life/death of, 376–77
    men killed by, 331, 381
    newspaper reports on, 75–77, 101–2, 104–5, 204
    and Sutton–Taylor feud, 77–80
Hargrove's Saloon (Fort Sumner), 240–41

Harper's Weekly, 44, 97–99
Harris, Jack, 201
Hartman, Louis C., 158
Hashknifes, 310–14
Hatfield–McCoy feud, 23, 64, 308
Hayes, Rutherford B., 270
Hays, John "Jack," 35–36, 40
Hays, Kans., 99–100, 131
Hearne, William B. "Bert," 257–58
Helldorado (Breakenridge), 294
Helm, Jack, 4, 78–79
Heslet, Billy, 277
Heywood, Joseph L., 178–80, 185
Hickok, James "Wild Bill," 45, 113, 121,
    126–27, 159, 193, 267, 292, 381
  childhood/youth of, 95
  in Civil War, 52
  death of, 108–9, 194, 199, 379
  face off with Hardin, 102–6, 147
  face off with Tutt, 1–3, 7, 10, 22, 28,
    63, 97
  fame of, 4–9, 14, 94–95, 101, 144, 192
  gambling of, 2, 108, 115
  as a gunfighter, 95–97, 99–100, 106–7
  Harper's article on, 97–99
  later life, 107–9
  as marshal, 1, 94–95, 99–107
  in Missouri, 170
  portrayals of, 5, 255, 375, 381
  skills with a gun, 7, 95, 99–100, 109, 176
  wardrobe of, 99, 108–9
  in Wild West shows, 5, 107–8
hideouts, 43, 358, 368, 371
Higgins, John Pinckney "Pink," 9, 85–86
High Fives gang, 370, 378
High Noon (film), 7, 142
Hill, Joe, 263, 265, 276, 292, 304
Hite, Wood, 181, 183–84
Hittson, John, 210–11, 357
Hixon, John, 352–53
Holbrook, Ariz., 309–10, 318–20, 381
Hole-in-the-Wall Gang, 367–70
Hole-in-the-Wall hideout, 358, 368
Holland, Barbara, 25
Holliday, Doc, 17, 45, 153, 240, 292
  argument with Ringo, 293
  bond with Driskill outfit, 141
  and Cowboys gang, 273–76, 279–81, 283
  description of, 137–39
  in Dodge City, 132–34, 139, 141
  fame of, 169, 380
  gambling of, 115, 141, 269, 304
  last days of, 304
  moves to Tombstone, 267–69
  in New Mexico, 162–64
  in Tombstone gunfight, 286–91
  on "Vendetta Ride," 299–303
Hollywood films, 16, 46, 144, 381
  on Baca shootout, 256, 259
  and Billy the Kid, 246, 254–55
  cowboys in, 62, 90
  gunfighters in, 4–9, 69, 109, 142, 155,
    340, 361
  lawmen in, 126–27, 142
  outlaws in, 169, 263, 350, 378
  rediscover Old West, 5–9, 375–76
  romanticize the Wild West, 375–76
  and Wyatt Earp, 126–27, 267, 376
Holshousen, Maje, 71–72
honor, 318, 379
  codes of, 20–29, 285
  and gambling, 115, 117
  and gunfights, 10–11, 63, 199, 206, 285
  South's tradition of, 21–29, 61–63, 93,
    262, 306
  Texas cowboys and, 262, 306, 311
  See also Code of the West; duels; feuds
"Hoodoo Brown," 163–64
Hoodoo War, 86–87, 263, 292
Hoover, J. Edgar, 379
Horn, Tom, 4, 327–30, 376
Horony, Mary Katherine. *See* "Big
    Nose Kate"
Horrell brothers, 84–86, 188, 211–13
horse racing, 80, 159, 181, 194, 360
Hough, Emerson, 15
Houston, Sam, 20, 32
Howard, Charles, 218–19
Hoy, George, 142, 146
Hudson, Rock, 69, 90
Hurst, Joseph H., 269
Hutchinson, William H., 190
hygiene, 240

Idaho, 41, 117, 357, 361–62
I'll Die Before I'll Run (Sonnichsen), 63
Illinois, 20, 51, 93, 95, 127–28, 159, 379
immigrants, 14, 19, 39, 261, 359
Indian Charlie, 298, 300–301
Indian Territory, 101, 128, 339, 341

Indianola, Tex., 79–80
Ingalls, Okla., 351–53

J. J. Dolan & Co., 220
Jackson, Andrew, 20, 34, 37, 116
Jackson, Frank, 196–97
James, Frank, 171–82, 184, 376
James, Jesse, 10, 292, 342, 346, 358, 381
    aliases of, 176, 183
    childhood/family of, 171–72
    in Civil War, 52, 171–73, 185
    crime spree of, 181–83
    criminal career of, 176–77, 367
    death of, 185, 376, 379
    description of, 172
    in East Las Vegas, 167
    fame of, 167, 169, 175, 251
    lives on Tennessee farms, 180–82
    politics and, 8–9, 170, 177
    portrayals of, 169, 254
    and the press, 9, 174–76, 181–82
    reward for, 182–84
    robberies of, 3, 15, 56, 169–81, 184–85,
        195, 347
James, Zee, 172, 176, 185, 379
James Gang, 170–71, 174–84, 195,
    346, 350
Johnny-Behind-the-Deuce, 272–73, 299
Johnson, Dick, 66–67
Johnson County War, 324–27, 360
Jones, James, 25

Kansas, 8, 74, 147, 155, 171, 205, 315, 331
    Ben Thompson in, 198
    feuds in, 204
    gambling in, 117, 123–26
    gun laws in, 103
    gunfighter sites in, 380
    gunfighters in, 69, 77, 118, 123–25, 162,
        191, 340, 354
    gunfights in, 14, 91, 101–7, 111–14,
        151, 192
    Hardin in, 102–6
    Hickok in, 1, 94–107, 144
    Jesse James in, 183
    murders in, 17, 94, 105, 113
    robberies in, 351
    and Texas cattle trade, 15, 88–94,
        111–14, 125, 130, 153
    Texas cowboys in, 91, 94, 123, 132, 155

Texas-style violence in, 91–93
    Wyatt Earp in, 129, 137, 331
Kansas City, Mo., 158, 182–84, 346
Kansas City Times, 175, 182
Kelley, Jim "Dog," 151–52
Kelly, Charles, 358
Kenedy, James "Spike," 151–53
Kentucky, 26–27, 31, 59, 170, 174–77,
    179–83, 185
Ketchum, Sam, 371
Ketchum, Thomas "Black Jack," 370–71
Ketchum Gang, 372–73, 378
Kilpatrick, Ben "The Tall Texan," 373, 377
King, Luther, 276
King, Melvin A., 135–36
Kinney, John, 213, 218–20, 229, 233, 249,
    263–64
Kirkman, William G., 58–59
knives, 28, 40, 91, 143. See also bowie knife
Ku Klux Klan, 23, 53, 55, 57–60, 66, 88

Lackey, John, 75
Lady Gay Saloon (Dodge City),
    135–36, 153
Lambert, Henry, 145
L'Amour, Louis, 57
Lampasas, Tex., 84–85, 188
Landusky, Pike, 367–68
Larn, John, 234, 253
Las Cruces, N.Mex., 213, 336
Las Vegas Gazette, 163, 246
Las Vegas, N.Mex., 249, 251, 273
Las Vegas Optic, 251
Latinos, 310
    admire Billy the Kid, 251–52, 255
    Anglo oppression of, 44
    El Paso Salt War and, 218–19
    gunfighters, 42–45
    Horrell War and, 84, 211–12
    Lincoln County War and, 230, 232–34
    massacres of, 14, 54, 219
    in New Mexico, 209–13, 240
    in New Mexico shootout, 255–59
    See also Baca, Elfego
law enforcement, 113, 165
    in California, 45
    corrupt, 136, 210, 277, 342
    federal marshals, 342, 351–53, 377
    improvement in, 206
    increase in, 371

law enforcement (*cont.*)
  lack of, 17, 23, 27, 210
  maturation of, 342, 379
  rudimentary, 39–40, 72
  See also Arizona Rangers; lawmen; Texas
    Rangers; *specific names*
Lawless Breed, The (film), 69
lawmen, 4, 6, 8, 13–14, 19, 103, 111, 216.
  See also specific names
laws/legal system, 4, 22, 26, 39–40, 87–88,
  204, 206, 324. *See also* guns: laws for;
  law enforcement
Lay, Ellsworth "Elzy," 242, 361–64, 367,
  370–71, 376
Leach, Joseph, 32
lecture circuit, 117, 185, 350, 355, 376
Lee, Bob, 65–67, 71, 73, 101
Lee–Peacock feud, 64–67
LeFors, Joe, 330, 376
Leonard, Billy, 273–77, 279–80, 290
Liddil, Dick, 181–85
Lincoln, Abraham, 20
Lincoln, N.Mex., 211–12, 217–24, 227–42,
  249–51, 380–81
Lincoln County War, 221–39, 242–43,
  249, 263
Livingston, Brockholst, 25
Llano, Tex., 199–200
Logan, Harvey, 19, 367–70, 372–74
Long Branch Saloon (Dodge City), 140,
  152, 157–58
Longabaugh, Harry. *See* Sundance Kid
Longley, "Wild Bill," 9, 191–93, 198, 204,
  292, 378, 381
Louisiana, 26, 64, 175
Love, Harry, 43–44
Loving, Oliver, 92, 210
Lowe, Rowdy Joe, 133
Lowry Gang, 56
lynching, 143, 164, 188, 271, 276, 299
  in California, 40, 42
  of cattle rustlers, 83, 86, 310, 324
  common in South/Old West, 23–24, 40
  newspaper reports on, 83
  and postwar feuds, 64, 78
  in Texas, 54–55, 60, 64, 78, 83, 86, 111

Madsen, Chris, 340, 351, 354
Mann, James, 190–91
Martin, Robert E. "Dutch," 213, 263–65, 274

Mason County, Tex., 86–87, 263
Masterson, Bat, 6, 115, 126–27, 163–64, 354
  and Ben Thompson, 118, 123
  childhood/youth of, 134–35
  and Clay Allison incident, 146–47
  in Denver, 158, 160
  on Doc Holliday, 137–39
  in Dodge City, 132–36, 139–42, 146–47,
    152–54, 166
  fame of, 8–9, 134, 154–55
  friendship with Earp, 136–39
  gambling of, 138–39, 141, 154, 156
  and gunfighter Luke Short, 155–60
  and gunfights, 135–36, 138, 142, 153–54
  and Kenedy-Kelley incident, 152–53
  late life/death of, 154–55
  as lawman, 134–37, 155, 275, 303
  magazine articles by, 155
  museum tribute to, 380–81
  in Tombstone, 153, 156–57, 275
Masterson, Ed, 139–40
Masterson, Jim, 136, 141–42, 151–53, 353
Mather, Josiah, 166–67
Mather, Mysterious Dave, 9, 133,
  164–67, 242
Maxwell, Lucien, 240
Maxwell, Pete, 240, 252–54
McCall, Jack, 109
McCanles, David, 96
McCarty, Catherine, 214–15
McCarty, Charlie, 256–57
McCarty, Tom, 360
McClung, Alexander Keith, 27
McCluskie, Mike, 112–13
McCoy, Joseph G., 93, 112
McCulloch, Ben, 40
McGrath, Roger, 8, 17
McKenna, Alex, 347
McKinney, Thomas "Kip," 253–54
McLaury, Frank, 264, 269, 276, 279,
  286–91
McLaury, Tom, 264, 269, 279–82,
  286–91
McLaury, Will, 290
McMaster, Sherman, 300
McNab, Frank, 228
McSween, Alexander "Mac," 219–24, 227,
  229–35
McSween, Sue, 232–33, 235, 239, 242
Metz, Leon, 105, 291–92

Mexican Americans, 120, 306–7. *See also* Latinos
Mexican War, 27, 36–38, 127
Mexico, 28, 54, 175, 209
    Ben Thompson in, 121
    border of, 5, 13–14, 16, 24, 32, 187, 264–65, 296
    cattle raids in, 262–65, 272, 277–78
    cattle ranching in, 82, 269–70, 277–78
    Cowboys gang raids into, 269–70
    gunfighters/outlaws flee to, 74, 263–64, 304, 377
    outlaw of, 42–45
    and raids into Texas, 32, 61, 187–88
    Texans' rebellion against, 31–32, 35, 55, 211
    vaqueros of, 101–2, 104, 213
Miller, Clell, 174, 178–79, 181
Miller, "Deacon" Jim, 4, 9, 330–38, 377
Miller, Ed, 181–82
Miller, Jim, 329–30
Miller, Rick, 192–93
Miller, Sallie Clements, 331–32
Miner, Bill, 45
Minnesota, 24, 170, 177–80
Mississippi River, 19–20, 27, 116
Missouri, 23, 64
    and Civil War atrocities, 170–73
    duels in, 26, 28
    Earp brothers in, 128, 170
    Jesse James in, 169–77, 180–84, 340
    Jesse James's grave in, 379
    robberies in, 3, 56, 173, 182–83
    and Texas cattle trade, 3, 92–93
    and Wild Bill Hickok, 97–99, 170
Mitchell, Bob and Frank, 85
mob violence, 23, 86, 111, 120–21, 129, 337. *See also* lynching; vigilantism
Montana, 13, 24, 307
    feuds in, 367–68
    gunfighters in, 45–46, 191, 360
    gunfights in, 268, 368, 374
    mining in, 45–46
    robberies in, 171, 369, 373–74
    and Texas cattle trade, 89–90, 324, 357
Moore, James, 122
Morco, "Happy Jack," 113–14, 123–25
Mormons, 261, 309–11, 317, 320–21, 359
Morton, Billy, 223–25
Mulvey, Bill, 100

murder rates, 17, 53
Murphy, Henderson, 196
Murphy, Jim, 196–98
Murrieta, Joaquin, 4, 15, 42–45, 101

Nashville, Tenn., 161, 176, 181–82
Nathan, Pop, 379
National Police Gazette, The, 129, 159, 204, 251, 271
Native Americans, 4, 41, 82, 240, 316, 339, 341, 357
    alcohol sold to, 156
    battles with, 13, 16, 19, 28, 32, 35–36, 54, 99, 209–10
    defeat of, 206–7
    forced from homelands, 90, 209, 261, 309
    killed by gunfighters, 86, 101
    in New Mexico, 209–10
    raids by, 35–36, 61, 147, 210, 266
    See also specific tribes
Navajo, 209, 240, 317–18
Navarro County, Tex., 72–73
Nebraska, 13, 47, 99, 156
    feuds in, 90–91
    Hickok's shootout in, 95–97
    Jesse James in, 183
    and Texas cattle trade, 153
    train robberies in, 195, 364–65, 370
Neill, Hyman G. *See* "Hoodoo Brown"
Nevada, 41, 45–47, 118, 171, 309, 366, 369, 372
New Mexico Territory, 153, 185, 261, 307, 317, 339
    Anglo settlers in, 209–10, 214
    Baca shootout in, 255–59
    Billy the Kid in, 167, 217–26, 380
    Butch Cassidy in, 363, 370
    cattle ranching in, 142–48, 207, 219–21, 230, 245–46, 251, 256–57, 276–77, 336, 363
    cattle/horse rustlers in, 210–11, 239–43, 262–65, 377
    Colfax County War in, 144–45
    description of, 209–10
    gunfighter sites in, 380–81
    gunfighters hide out in, 354
    gunfighters in, 6, 52, 90, 142–48, 160–67, 207, 212–13, 374, 376
    gunfights in, 14, 63, 223–28, 233–37, 241, 246–48

New Mexico Territory (*cont.*)
Horrell War in, 84–86, 211–12
lawmen in, 210, 245–46, 336
Mexican land grants in, 145
outlaws in, 212–13, 222, 255, 273–74, 370
robberies in, 171, 371
Spanish/Mexican rule of, 209
and Texas cattle trade, 88–90, 210–13, 357–58
Wild Bill Hickok in, 95
See also East Las Vegas, N.Mex.; Lincoln County War
New Mexico *Daily Optic*, 148–49
New Orleans, La., 20, 24, 26, 37, 92, 116, 119, 159
New York newspapers, 15, 32, 70, 98, 113, 118, 145, 154, 202, 251
Newcomb, George "Bitter Creek," 342, 345, 352, 354
Newman, Paul, 9, 378
newspapers/the press, 6, 217
on Clay Allison, 144, 147–48
eastern, 31–32, 98, 132, 204, 251, 290
on gunfighters, 6, 39, 59, 75–77, 118, 158–59, 271–72
on gunfights, 5, 77, 101–2, 105–6, 143–45, 162, 199–203, 305
on guns/gun violence, 15, 37–38
interview gunfighters, 9, 97–99, 191–93, 249, 303, 355
on murders, 74, 204, 224
on Texas-style violence, 198, 204–6
See also New York newspapers; *specific names*
Newton, Kans., 112–13, 132, 300
"Newton's General Massacre," 112–13
Nichols, George Ward, 97–99
Nickell, Willie, 330
Nix, Evett, 351–52
Nixon, Tom, 165–66
Northfield, Minn., 15, 177–80, 185, 197, 347
Norton, John. *See* "Brocky Jack"

O'Folliard, Tom, 236–40, 247, 380
O.K. Corral, 126, 169, 267, 282, 285, 290, 297, 308
Oklahoma, 379
Battle of Ingalls in, 351–53
cattle ranching in, 340, 343
cattlemen feuds in, 336–37

cowboys in, 317, 350
gunfights in, 344–54
gunmen/outlaws in, 339–55, 374
Land Rush in, 339–40
lawmen in, 152, 340, 343–46, 351–54
robberies in, 339–49, 354
Olinger, Bob, 250–51, 380
Olive, Isom Prentice "Print," 4, 83–85, 90–91, 151
Olive, Jay, 84, 90
Olney, Joe. *See* Hill, Joe
O'Neal, Bill, 14
Orr, Thomas, 57–59
Orrington, "Red" Lucas, 352
outlaw gangs, 41–48, 262–66, 370–71. *See also specific names*
Outlaw Trail, 358, 370
Outlaw Trail, The (Kelly), 358
Owens, Perry, 317–21, 381

Paramore, Green, 75–76
Parker, Robert LeRoy. *See* Cassidy, Butch
Parsons, Chuck, 52, 72, 148, 188
Paul, Bob, 274–76
payroll thefts, 182, 362–63, 367, 377–78
Peacock, A. J., 153–54
Peacock, Lewis, 65–67. *See also* Lee–Peacock feud
Pecos, Tex., 148–49, 331–34, 381
Peoria, Ill., 128–29
Peppin, George, 229–32
Perdue, A. J., 190
photographs, 91, 159, 165, 242, 317, 338, 349, 362–63, 368, 373
pimps, 8, 73, 126–29
Pinkerton, 175–76, 188, 195, 314, 327, 366–67, 371–74, 377
Pinkerton, Allan, 176
Pitts, Charlie, 178–80
Place, Ethel, 374, 377
Pleasant Valley War, 308–14, 316–22, 326–27
Poe, John, 253–54
police forces, 113–14, 123, 125
politics, 157, 303, 317, 324
corruption in, 145, 200, 272, 274
elections and, 23, 130, 295–96
and feuds, 13, 23
in New Mexico, 145–46, 220

and outlaws, 9, 170, 172–77, 290, 295, 299
and Southern customs, 18
Pollard, Ala., 189–90
popular culture, 4, 131, 169, 259. *See also* books; Hollywood films; television shows; Western literature
Powers, Bill, 347, 349
prostitutes, 8, 73, 94, 106, 111, 114, 128, 131–32, 135, 139, 157, 159, 267, 336, 374

race riots, 39, 53
racism, 39, 69, 73, 191, 211, 306–7
railroads, 92, 305, 323–24
    armed guards on, 364, 367
    armed marshals on, 345–46
    building of, 116, 153, 270, 364
    crack down on robberies, 366–67
    detectives of, 195, 367
    and gunfighters/outlaws, 101, 270
    offer rewards, 343, 346, 371
    See also train robberies
range detectives, 147, 242, 314–16, 324–28
range wars, 13–14, 323–38
Rapp, John, 120
Reconstruction, 9, 53, 56, 60–61, 65
Regulator-Moderator War, 54
Regulators, the, 222–36
Remington, Frederic, 375
Renfro, Lee, 316
Reno Gang, 3, 56
Republicans, 73, 177, 290, 299, 303
Revolutionary War, 19–20, 222
revolvers, 16, 47, 91
    Colts, 2, 34–40, 99, 137, 218
    "cross draw" and, 99–100
    invention of, 32–38
    six-shooters, 29, 37–39, 54, 205–6, 241, 292
    skill with, 6–7, 39, 95, 155–57
    Smith & Wesson, 282, 286
    Thunderers, 218, 254
    wearing of, 53, 99, 103
Rhodes, Eugene Manlove, 6, 64
Ringo, Johnny, 8, 17, 87, 200, 263, 265, 273, 291–96, 301, 378
Robbers' Roose hideout, 358, 360, 362–63
Roberts, Andrew "Buckshot," 224–27, 239, 249

Roosevelt, Theodore, 154–55, 336
Ross, Aaron, 365–66
Roth, Randolph, 17
Roughing It (Twain), 46–47
Rourke, Mike, 272–73
Rudabaugh, "Dirty Dave," 164, 240, 248–49, 304
Ruidoso, N.Mex., 217–19, 222–23, 225, 229, 234

Samuel, Reuben, 171, 176
Samuel farm, 171–73, 176
San Antonio Cart War, 54
San Antonio, Tex., 64, 194, 200–203
San Elizario, Tex., 219
San Francisco, 39–40, 117, 146, 171, 251, 271
San Francisco *Daily Exchange*, 275
San Patricio, N.Mex., 229, 238
San Quentin prison, 41, 45
San Simon Valley (Ariz.), 265, 270, 278
Sandbar Fight, 27–28
Santa Fe *Daily New Mexican*, 143–45
Santa Fe, N.Mex., 210, 214–15, 219–20, 223, 229, 239, 249
Santa Fe Railroad, 162, 342–43
Santa Fe Ring, 145–46, 220, 229
Scott, Randolph, 340, 350
scouts, 2, 5, 35, 43, 97, 99, 135, 156, 163, 327, 346
Scurlock, Josiah "Doc," 218, 232, 235–36, 239
Secrest, William B., 38–39, 44
self-defense rulings, 40, 71, 145, 157, 160, 199, 203, 335
Selman, John, 90, 234–35, 377
Shackelford County, Tex., 83, 90, 234, 253
sheepherding
    and deadly feuds, 308–14
    and gunmen, 90, 307, 327, 335
    by Mexican Americans, 307
    and range wars, 13, 323
    and violence, 306–8, 312, 323, 330, 335
Sheets, John W., 173, 175, 185
sheriffs, 6, 8, 17, 39–40, 103, 131, 142, 195, 206, 210. *See also specific names*
Sherman, William Tecumseh, 97, 137, 278
Shirley, Glenn, 340–41
"shootist," 6, 144. *See also* gunfighters
Short, Ed, 343–44
Short, Luke, 4, 91, 115, 133–34, 155–62, 216

Silver City, N.Mex., 213–16, 303
Simms, Billy, 201, 203
Siringo, Charles, 147, 314–15, 327
Slade, Jack, 47–49, 101
Slaughter, Gabriel, 80
Slaughter, John B., 256
Slaughter, John H., 262
slavery, 18, 21–22, 27, 53–55, 64, 116
Smith, Tom, 94, 100
Smith's Saloon (Fort Sumner), 242, 246
songs, 7, 69, 197–98, 218, 254–55, 278,
    295, 340
Sonnichsen, C. L., 63
South, the
    code of honor in, 20–29, 61–63, 93,
      262, 285
    customs/mores of, 18–24, 311
    dueling in, 20–29, 40, 63, 143
    as frontier, 24, 26–29, 40
    gambling in, 22, 41, 116–17
    post–Civil War, 53, 56, 92, 175, 177
    and ranching customs, 82
    ruling class of, 22, 24
South America, 3, 117, 342, 344, 346, 359,
    378. *See also* Argentina
South Carolina, 23, 25, 82
South Dakota, 108–9, 141, 193–94, 368
Spanish ranches/cattle, 82
Spanish-American War, 327, 329
Speed, Dick, 352
Speights, Sonny, 76
Spence, Pete, 278, 298, 300, 303–4
Spicer, Wells, 290
Springfield, Mo., 1–3, 10, 97–98
St. Joseph, Mo., 183
St. Louis, Mo., 20, 23, 101, 116, 144,
    175–76, 198, 220
stagecoach robberies, 13, 45, 295
    in Arizona, 265–66, 274–79, 298
    by Jesse James, 181–82
    newspaper reports on, 275
    by outlaw gangs, 42, 164, 174–75, 194,
      216, 265–66, 274–75, 370
stagecoaches, 47–48, 95–96, 268
Stanley, Henry M., 98
Starr, Henry, 350, 355
Sterling, John, 124
Stevens, William Oliver, 20, 27
Stilwell, Frank, 278, 291, 298–301, 303
Stinston, James, 309

Stockmen's Convention, 202, 205–6
Storms, Charlie, 156–57
Stuart, Granville, 324
Sublett, Philip, 76
Sundance Kid, 3, 361, 368–69, 372–75,
    377–78
Sutton, Bill, 77–80
Sutton–Taylor feud, 77–80, 188, 331
Sweetwater, Tex., 135–36

Talbot, Henry J. *See* Cherokee Bob
Taylor, Buck, 78
Taylor, Creed, 77. *See also*
    Sutton–Taylor feud
Taylor, Jim, 78–80
Taylor, John, 306
Taylor, Pitkin, 78–79
Taylor, Zachary, 37
Teagarden, William, 71
television shows, 7–9, 16, 109, 131, 155, 169,
    191, 255, 280, 295, 375, 378
Tennessee, 18, 26, 32, 56, 167, 180–82
Tewksbury, Ed, 9, 309, 312–14, 321–22. *See*
    also Graham–Tewksbury feud
Tewksbury, James, 309
Tewksbury, John, 313
Tewksbury family, 312–14, 317
Texas
    cattle ranching in, 15, 82–88, 264, 331–34
    chauvinism of, 61–63
    during Civil War, 54–56
    gunfighter sites in, 381
    gunfighters in, 11, 14–15, 70, 101, 165,
      191–93, 305, 374
    gunfights in, 101, 135–36, 196–97,
      263–64
    history of, 16, 18, 32
    myths/tropes about, 31–32
    and penchant for violence, 32–33, 89–91
    post–Civil War, 53, 56–67, 69
    as a Southern State, 18–24, 63, 207, 306
    "Texas cowboy" of, 89–91
    train robberies in, 366, 371, 377
    transforms western states, 15, 82, 261–62
    violence in, 53–56, 60–67, 70–71, 88, 91,
      187, 198, 204–6, 322
Texas Life Stock Journal, 205
Texas Rangers, 32, 40, 87, 224, 298, 321, 342
    arrest cattle rustlers, 333
    clean up Texas, 305

and El Paso Salt War, 218–19
history/role of, 35–38, 81
Horrell War and, 85–86, 188
Pat Garrett as, 336
pursue train robbers, 195–98
return of, 187, 206–7
stamp out feuds, 80, 86, 187–88
target outlaws, 188–91, 212, 263
Texas State Police, 73–81, 84
Texas Troubles, 54
Thomas, Henry Andrew "Heck," 4, 340, 342–43, 345–46, 353–55, 376
Thomason, John, 173–74
Thompson, Ben, 19, 101–3, 133, 176
arrested by Earp, 126, 128
as Austin marshal, 200–201, 292
description of, 119–21, 200
in Ellsworth gunfight, 123–26
fame of, 118, 198–99, 202
gambling of, 4, 101, 114–15, 120–22, 138, 200–201
gunfights of, 136, 199–203
imprisoned in Huntsville, 122–23
killings/violence of, 119–22, 331
late life/death of, 199–203, 376
origin story of, 117–23
and the press, 118, 198–203
Thompson, Billy, 120, 123–25, 133, 135–36
Three Guardsmen, 340, 354
Tilghman, Bill, 152, 340, 354–55
Tolby, Frank J., 145
Tom Bell Gang, 42, 274
Tombstone (film), 263
Tombstone, Ariz., 87, 103, 134, 213, 275–76
Curly Bill incidents in, 270–72
description/history of, 264–69
Dirty Dave Rudabaugh in, 164
Earp brothers move to, 153, 267–69
Earps as lawmen in, 268–69, 272–73, 278–83
elections in, 295–96
famous gunfight in, 267, 285–91, 297, 305, 322, 381
gambling in, 156–57, 267–68, 272, 280–81
gunfights in, 14, 126, 157, 266, 296
today, 381–82
and warrants for Earps, 299–300
Tombstone Epitaph, The, 269, 278, 290
Tombstone Nugget, 290, 295, 300

train robberies, 13, 137, 165, 316, 327, 358, 373–74
Arizona Rangers and, 377
armed marshals and, 345–46
by Butch Cassidy, 367, 369–72
by Dalton brothers, 341–46, 364
dynamite used for, 366–67, 369, 372
increase in, 206
by Jesse James, 56, 170–71, 174–77, 181–83, 195
newspaper reports on, 195, 346, 366, 372
in Oklahoma, 339–46, 350–51
by outlaw gangs, 3, 56, 164, 350–51, 364
pursuit of perpetrators, 195–97, 329
by Sam Bass, 194–97, 364–65, 370
by Sundance Kid, 369–70, 372
tactics for, 364–67, 369
Train Robbers' Syndicate, 370
Triggernometry: A Gallery of Gunfighters (Cunningham), 6–8, 294
Trinidad, Col., 303–4
True West, 62
Tucson, Ariz., 261, 270–71, 273, 279, 298–99
Tucson Star, 272
Tularosa, N.Mex., 217, 240, 242
Tulsa Jack, 351, 353–54
Tunstall, John, 219–24, 227–28, 230, 233, 236, 380
Turk–Jones feud, 23
Tutt, Davis, 1–3, 7, 10, 22, 28, 63, 97
Tutt–Everett feud, 23
Twain, Mark, 46–49, 70
Typical Texan: Biography of an American Myth, The (Leach), 32

Union/Unionists, 2, 54–55, 59–61, 64–66, 97, 121, 128, 172–73, 176–78, 182
Union League, 64
Union Pacific, 194, 329, 369, 371–72
Updegraff, Al, 153–54
Upper San Francisco Plaza (Reserve), N.Mex., 255–59
U.S. Army, 34, 187, 209–12, 220, 230–32, 240, 261, 278, 303
U.S. Cavalry, 13, 57, 128, 156, 192, 215, 228–31, 270, 309, 326
Utah, 90, 261, 310–11, 357–59, 361–63, 371
Utley, Robert M., 8, 62, 223

Van Sickle, Henry, 41
Vance, Billy, 119–20
Vásquez, Tiburcio, 41–42
Vaudeville Theatre (San Antonio), 200–203
Vega, Cruz, 145
Venard, Steve, 44–45
Vermillion, "Texas Jack," 300, 302
Vicksburg, Miss., 27, 116
vigilance committees, 42, 54, 125, 158, 164, 279
vigilantism, 22, 158, 256, 299
  against cattle rustlers, 86, 234, 321, 324, 327
  born in the South, 23, 82, 222
  committees for, 39–40, 279
  and gunfighter ethos, 23–24
Virginia City, Nev., 15, 41, 46–47
Virginian, The (Wister), 375

Waco, Tex., 60, 73, 101, 126, 197
Walker, Samuel H., 36–38
Wallace, Lew, 235, 237–39, 246–47, 249
Wallace, William "Big-Foot," 32
Warner, Matt, 360–62
Wattron, Frank, 318
Webb, Charles, 80–81, 188
Webb, Walter Prescott, 87–88
Wellman, Horace, 96
Wells Fargo, 164, 266, 268, 274–77, 280, 295, 343, 365–66
Western art, 375
Western literature, 5–6, 97
  and codes of honor, 10, 61
  on gunfighters, 15, 49, 142, 191, 291–95
  on gunfighters' origins, 18–19
  passes folklore as fact, 193
  romanticizes Wild West, 375
  See also books
Western Story, 295
When the Daltons Rose (Dalton, Emmett), 350
Whipple, Thomas K., 4

White, Fred, 270–71
White Oaks, N.Mex., 240, 242, 246, 250
Whitney, Chauncey, 124–25
Wichita, Kans., 111–12, 129–30, 133, 163, 214, 297, 299, 341, 343
Wichita Tribune, The, 101–2
Wild Bunch, 330, 362, 367–71, 377
Wild West shows, 5, 107–8, 317
Williams, Mike, 106–7
Williams, Thomas, 84
Williamson, Tim, 86–87
Williamson County, Tex., 83–84
Willoughby, Bill, 41
Wilson, Mark, 199
Wister, Owen, 375
Wohrle, John, 87
Wood, James, 96
Wortley Hotel (Lincoln, N.Mex.), 230, 250
Wren, Bill, 85
Wright, Bob, 141–42, 147
Wright, Charles, 161–62
Wyoming, 192, 206, 307, 339
  Butch Cassidy in, 360, 372
  cattle ranches/rustlers in, 360, 367–68
  gunfighters in, 108, 374, 381
  gunfights in, 14, 371
  outlaw hideouts in, 358
  range wars in, 14, 324–30
  and Texas cattle trade, 15, 89–90, 324, 357
  train robberies in, 369–72
Wyoming State Penitentiary, 360
Wyoming Stock Growers Association, 324–27

Younger, Bob, 177–78, 180
Younger, Cole, 174–75, 177–80, 292, 340, 376
Younger, Jim, 175–80
Younger, John, 175–76